WORKBOOK IN LATIN TWO YEARS

By CHARLES I. FREUNDLICH

Author of
Latin for the Grades, Books I, II, III
Latin First Year
Latin Three and Four Years

When ordering this book, please specify:

either **N 335 W** *or*

WORKBOOK IN LATIN TWO YEARS

AMSCO SCHOOL PUBLICATIONS, INC.

315 Hudson Street   New York, N. Y. 10013

ISBN 0-87720-556-6

Please visit our Web site at:

www.amscopub.com

PREFACE

In foreign language study, the second year is generally considered the crucial year. It is then that the student discovers whether or not he has sufficient understanding of the language to proceed to the third year. This *Workbook in Latin Two Years* was written to help the student in his second-year work and give him confidence to continue the study of Latin.

Patterned after the author's *Workbook in Latin First Year*, this Workbook gives the student ample opportunity to learn by doing. The book contains sixteen units, each one an entity in itself. Starting with a section devoted to verbs, conveniently classified as to active and passive, indicative and subjunctive, the book takes up in succession nouns, adjectives, adverbs, pronouns, and prepositions.

The problem of idioms is adequately dealt with in a separate unit, and grammatical structures receive thorough treatment in a number of lessons. A unit on passages for translation and comprehension affords the student an opportunity to test his skill in these important areas.

In line with the audio-lingual approach so popular today in the teaching of modern languages, the author has included a unit on oral Latin in the classroom. One section consists of passages in Latin to be read aloud at a slow pace by the teacher. After the reading, questions in Latin based on the particular passage are also read aloud by the teacher to test student comprehension. Students and teachers alike will welcome this attempt to breathe life into a language that was the principal means of communication for well over a thousand years.

Following the unit on oral Latin come units on derivation and Roman civilization exhaustively detailed. Vocabulary lists and examinations comprise the final sections of the Workbook.

An innovation is the use of subscripts in connection with explanatory material. This device helps visually to clarify a point in illustrating a rule.

The exercises at the end of each unit are many, varied, and graded in difficulty. In each exercise the questions also proceed from the simple to the more complex. The student of Latin will find plenty of work to do in this Workbook. Space is provided for writing the answers to questions directly in the book if the student so desires. He need not follow the sequence of units, but may work, at any particular time, on any unit in which he needs practice.

Teachers of Latin, eager to have their students become more proficient in the language, will not hesitate to recommend this Workbook as a supplement to the regular textbook in Latin.

—C. I. F.

CONTENTS

Unit I—Verbs, Indicative Active

Unit V—Subjunctive Mood

Unit VI—Nouns

Unit VII—Adjectives, Numerals, and Adverbs

Unit VIII—Pronouns

Unit IX—Prepositions

Unit X—Idioms

Unit XI—Grammatical Structures

Unit XII—Passages for Translation and Comprehension

Unit XIII—Oral Latin for the Classroom

Unit XIV—Derivation and Word Study

Unit XV—Roman Civilization and Culture

Unit XVI—Vocabularies

Examinations

Unit I—Verbs, Indicative Active

Lesson 1—PRESENT INDICATIVE ACTIVE OF FIRST AND SECOND CONJUGATION VERBS

<table>
<tr><td colspan="2" align="center">FIRST CONJUGATION</td><td colspan="2" align="center">SECOND CONJUGATION</td></tr>
<tr><td colspan="2" align="center">(Present infinitive ends in -āre.)</td><td colspan="2" align="center">(Present infinitive ends in -ēre.)</td></tr>
<tr><td colspan="2" align="center">servāre, to save; present stem, servā-</td><td colspan="2" align="center">monēre, to warn; present stem, monē-</td></tr>
<tr><td>SINGULAR</td><td>PLURAL</td><td>SINGULAR</td><td>PLURAL</td></tr>
<tr><td>servō I save</td><td>servāmus we save</td><td>moneō I warn</td><td>monēmus we warn</td></tr>
<tr><td>servās you save</td><td>servātis you save</td><td>monēs you warn</td><td>monētis you warn</td></tr>
<tr><td>servat he or she saves</td><td>servant they save</td><td>monet he or she warns</td><td>monent they warn</td></tr>
</table>

Note

1. The present stem of a verb is found by dropping the ending **-re** of the infinitive.

2. The present tense is formed by adding to the stem the personal endings **-ō, -s, -t, -mus, -tis, -nt.** (Observe that in the form **servō** the final **ā** of the stem is omitted.)

3. The present tense may be translated in several ways:

> **servat**   he saves, he is saving, he does save
>
> **monēmus** we warn, we are warning, we do warn

4. Latin personal pronouns (**ego, tū,** etc.), used for emphasis or contrast, are generally not needed as subject, since the personal endings indicate the person. These endings are:

> **-ō** = I   **-mus** = we
>
> **-s** = you (sing.)   **-tis** = you (pl.)
>
> **-t** = he, she, it   **-nt** = they

Amīcum servā*mus.*	*We* are saving our friend.
Fēmina properat. Līberōs mone*t.*	The woman is hurrying. *She* warns the children.

5. The Latin verb generally comes at the end of a sentence. For emphasis, however, it may appear earlier.

Terram vāstant.	They are destroying the land.
Vāstant terram.	*They are destroying* the land.

NEGATIVE FORM OF VERBS

A verb may be made negative by placing **nōn** in front of it.

Perīculum **nōn** videt.	He does not see the danger.
Pugnāre **nōn** possunt.	They are not able to fight.

INTERROGATIVE FORM OF VERBS

There are three ways of asking a question in Latin when there is no interrogative word:

1. When the answer expected is either *yes* or *no*, attach the enclitic **-ne** to the verb and place the verb at the beginning of the sentence.

Vidēs*ne* puerum?	Do you see the boy?

1

2. When the answer expected is *yes*, start the sentence with **nōnne**.

Nōnne puerum vidēs?   Don't you see the boy? (You see the boy, don't you?)

3. When the answer expected is *no*, start the sentence with **num**.

Num puerum vidēs?   You don't see the boy, do you?

Note

A sentence with an interrogative word does not need the enclitic **-ne** to show it is a question.

Quid scrībit puella?   What is the girl writing?
Cūr discēdunt?   Why are they leaving?

COMMON VERBS OF THE FIRST CONJUGATION

accūsāre, to accuse, blame
aedificāre, to build
amāre, to love
ambulāre, to walk
appellāre, to name, call
appropinquāre, to approach
armāre, to arm, equip
cēnāre, to dine
citāre, to urge on
  incitāre, to urge on, arouse
clāmāre, to cry out, shout
cōnfīrmāre, to strengthen, confirm
cūrāre, to care for, look after
dare, to give
  circumdare, to put around, surround
dōnāre, to give, present
dubitāre, to hesitate, doubt
exīstimāre, to think, consider
explōrāre, to search out, explore
habitāre, to inhabit, live
hiemāre, to spend the winter
imperāre, to command
iūdicāre, to judge, decide
iūrāre, to swear, take an oath
labōrāre, to work
laudāre, to praise
līberāre, to free, set free
locāre, to place, put
  collocāre, to place, set up
mandāre, to entrust, command
mōnstrāre, to show, point out
  dēmōnstrāre, to show, point out
nārrāre, to tell, relate
nāvigāre, to sail
nūntiāre, to report, announce
  ēnūntiāre, to proclaim

renūntiāre, to bring back word, report
occupāre, to seize, occupy
ōrāre, to beg
pācāre, to subdue, pacify
parāre, to prepare
  comparāre, to prepare, make ready
portāre, to carry, bring
  comportāre, to bring together
  importāre, to bring in
  trānsportāre, to carry across, transport
postulāre, to demand
properāre, to hurry, hasten
pugnāre, to fight
  expugnāre, to take by storm, capture
  oppugnāre, to attack
putāre, to think
rogāre, to ask
  interrogāre, to ask, question
servāre, to save, keep, guard
  cōnservāre, to keep, preserve
spectāre, to look at, watch
  exspectāre, to wait for, expect
spērāre, to hope
  dēspērāre, to give up hope, despair of
stāre, to stand
  praestāre, to stand out, excel
superāre, to defeat, surpass
tardāre, to slow up, delay
temptāre, to try
turbāre, to disturb
  perturbāre, to disturb greatly, confuse
vāstāre, to destroy
vigilāre, to be watchful, keep awake
vocāre, to call
  convocāre, to call together
vulnerāre, to wound

COMMON VERBS OF THE SECOND CONJUGATION

audēre, to dare, be bold (semi-deponent; see page 94)

augēre, to increase

cavēre, to beware of

complēre, to fill, complete

dēbēre, to owe, ought

docēre, to teach, show

exercēre, to train, exercise

habēre, to have

　prohibēre, to prevent, keep from
　a changes to i

iubēre, to order

manēre, to stay, remain

　remanēre, to stay, remain

monēre, to advise, warn

movēre, to move

　commovēre, to alarm, arouse

　permovēre, to alarm, arouse

　removēre, to move back, withdraw

nocēre, to injure, harm

pārēre, to obey

patēre, to lie open, extend

respondēre, to reply

sedēre, to sit

　obsidēre, to sit down, besiege
　e changes to i

studēre, to be eager

suādēre, to advise

　persuādēre, to persuade

tenēre, to hold

　continēre, to hold together or back
　e changes to i in all the compounds

　obtinēre, to hold, obtain

　pertinēre, to extend, pertain to

　retinēre, to hold back

　sustinēre, to uphold, withstand

terrēre, to frighten

　perterrēre, to frighten (thoroughly)

timēre, to fear

valēre, to be strong or well

vidēre, to see

EXERCISES

A. Complete the English translation.

1. Obsidēs dant. _____ hostages.

2. Nāvēs nāvigāre iubet. _____ the ships to sail.

3. Vulnerantne nostrōs? _____ our men?

4. Num timētis, mīlitēs? _____, soldiers?

5. Agrōs vāstāmus. _____ the fields.

6. Lēgātīs nōn respondēs. _____ to the ambassadors.

7. Nōnne eum rēgem appellant? _____ him king?

8. Diū manēre dēbeō. _____ to stay a long time.

9. Exercitum castrīs continet. _____ the army in camp.

10. Hostēs ācriter pugnant. The enemy _____ fiercely.

11. Pācatne Caesar Gallōs? _____ the Gauls?

12. Impetum sustinēmus. _____ the attack.

13. Nōnne perīculum vidētis? _____ the danger?

14. Victōriam ēnūntiō. _____ the victory.

15. Animōs virōrum cōnfīrmās. _____ the minds of the men.

B. Make each sentence negative.

1. Ad montēs pertinet. _____

2. Frātrem amātis. _____

3. In agrīs labōrāmus. _____

4. Hostēs oppugnāre temptant. _____

5. Cūr sedēs? _____

C. Make each sentence interrogative.

1. Fīnēs occupat. _____

2. Germānī bellum comparant. _____

3. Castra movētis. _____

4. Studēmus properāre. _____

5. Equōs retinēs. _____

D. Write the correct form of the verb in the present indicative active.

1. _laudāre:_   Nōs Caesarem _____.

2. _incitāre:_   Gallī bellum _____.

3. _persuādēre:_ Cōnsul omnibus _____.

4. _cōnservāre:_ _____ vōs pācem?

5. _obtinēre:_   Tū imperium _____.

6. _exercēre:_   Cūr dux suōs _____?

7. _nāvigāre:_   Ego ad Graeciam _____.

8. _permovēre:_   Nōnne imperātor cīvēs _____?

9. _rogāre:_   Servī lībertātem _____.

10. _docēre:_   Vōs līberōs _____.

E. Translate the following verbs into English in three different ways:

1. convocant _____

2. monēmus _____

3. appropinquat _____

4. putātis _____

5. teneō _____

F. Write all the specified forms in the present indicative active.

1. _audēre_ and _locāre:_ third person singular _____

2. _spērāre_ and _augēre:_ first person plural _____

3. _cūrāre_ and _valēre:_ second person singular _____

4. _manēre_ and _putāre:_ third person plural _____

5. _imperāre_ and _iubēre:_ first person singular _____

G. Translate into Latin.

1. she replies   --
2. we are preparing   --
3. they do not think   --
4. it extends   --
5. do you (sing.) advise?   --
6. don't they surpass?   --
7. you (pl.) are preventing   --
8. he doesn't expect, does he?   --
9. I am showing   --
10. the Romans are shouting   --
11. Lucius holds back   --
12. you (sing.) are not hesitating   --
13. are we giving?   --
14. the girls do not have   --
15. you (pl.) are destroying   --

Julius Caesar

Lesson 2—PRESENT INDICATIVE ACTIVE OF THIRD CONJUGATION VERBS

(Present infinitive ends in **-ere**.)

vin**cere**, to conquer; present stem, **vince-**

vinc**ō**	I conquer	vinc**imus**	we conquer
vinc**is**	you conquer	vinc**itis**	you conquer
vinc**it**	he or she conquers	vinc**unt**	they conquer

Note

In forming the present tense of third conjugation verbs, the final **e** of the stem is dropped in the first person singular, changed to **u** in the third person plural, and to **i** in all the other persons.

COMMON VERBS OF THE THIRD CONJUGATION

agere, to drive, do
   cōgere, to collect, compel
   a is dropped
cadere, to fall
   accidere, to fall down, happen
   a changes to i
caedere, to cut, kill
   occīdere, to cut down, kill
   ae changes to i
cēdere, to go, move, yield
   accēdere, to go toward, approach
   concēdere, to yield, withdraw
   discēdere, to go away, leave
   excēdere, to go out, leave
   prōcēdere, to go forth, advance
claudere, to close
cognōscere, to learn, find out
cōnsīdere, to sit down, encamp
cōnsistere, to stand still, halt
contendere, to strive, hasten, fight
crēdere, to believe, trust
currere, to run
   prōcurrere, to run forward
dēdere, to give up, surrender
dēfendere, to defend, ward off
dīcere, to say, tell
dīvidere, to separate, divide
dūcere, to lead
   addūcere, to lead toward, influence

dēdūcere, to lead down or away
ēdūcere, to lead out
prōdūcere, to lead forth
redūcere, to lead back
trādūcere, to lead across
gerere, to carry on, wage
incendere, to set on fire, burn
īnstruere, to draw up, arrange
iungere, to join
   coniungere, to fasten together, join
legere, to choose, read
   dēligere, to choose
   e changes to i
   intellegere, to understand, realize
lūdere, to play
mittere, to send
   āmittere, to send away, lose
   committere, to join, entrust
   dīmittere, to send away
   intermittere, to interrupt, stop
   permittere, to allow, entrust
   praemittere, to send ahead
   remittere, to send back
ostendere, to show
pellere, to drive, rout
   expellere, to drive out
   impellere, to drive on, urge
   repellere, to drive back

petere, to seek, attack

pōnere, to put, place

   expōnere, to set out or forth, explain

   prōpōnere, to set forth, propose

premere, to press, oppress

   opprimere, to press against, crush
    e changes to i

quaerere, to seek, inquire

reddere, to give back, return

regere, to rule, guide

relinquere, to abandon, leave behind

resistere, to resist

scrībere, to write

   cōnscrībere, to enlist, enroll

solvere, to loosen, set sail

statuere, to set up, decide

   cōnstituere, to decide, station
    a changes to i

   īnstituere, to establish, decide
    a changes to i

sūmere, to take, assume

   cōnsūmere, to use up, spend

tollere, to raise

trādere, to surrender

trahere, to drag, draw

vertere, to turn, change

   animadvertere, to turn the mind to, notice

   revertere, to return

vincere, to conquer

EXERCISES

A. Rewrite the following sentences, changing the singular verbs to the plural, and the plural verbs to the singular:

1. Equōs agit. _____

2. Rem cognōscimus. _____

3. Īnstruunt aciem. _____

4. Reddisne librōs? _____

5. Omnia prōpōnō. _____

6. Nōnne cēditis? _____

7. Bellum nōn gerunt. _____

8. Cōnstituimus discēdere. _____

9. Petitne pācem? _____

10. Num oppidum relinquis? _____

B. Translate the *rewritten* sentences in Exercise A into English.

1. _____

2. _____

3. _____

4. _____

5. _____

6. _____

7. _____

8. _____

9. _____

10. _____

C. Write all the specified forms in the present indicative active.

1. *ostendere:*   third person singular   ---
2. *cōnscrībere:* first person plural   ---
3. *intellegere:* second person singular   ---
4. *regere:*   third person plural   ---
5. *occīdere:*   second person plural   ---

D. Add the correct ending of the present indicative active.

1. Caesar mīlitēs addūc ------------------.   6. Virī proelium intermitt ------------------.
2. Cōg ------------------ tū cōpiās?   7. Dīc ------------------ vōs vēra?
3. Quis contend ------------------?   8. Nōnne trād ------------------ Rōmānī?
4. Nōs Gallōs prem ------------------.   9. Cōnsul sē nōn dēfend ------------------.
5. Ego pecūniam remitt ------------------.   10. Pater fīliusque leg ------------------.

E. Translate the English words into Latin.

1. Suōs in castra *he leads.*   ---
2. Caesar Labiēnō *is writing.*   ---
3. Hostēs proelium *are joining.*   ---
4. Cūr *do you (sing.) choose* eum?   ---
5. *We are sending ahead* explōrātōrēs.   ---
6. *Do you (pl.) understand* ratiōnem?   ---
7. *I decide* contendere.   ---
8. In agrīs *they are playing.*   ---
9. Labor omnia *conquers.*   ---
10. *Aren't we losing* spem?   ---

The Olive

Because of the many uses of its oil, the olive was the most valuable fruit in ancient Rome. Olive oil took the place of butter in the diet and soap in the bath. It was also used for preparing food, for fuel in lamps, for cleaning purposes, for anointing the body, and for producing perfumes and cosmetics of every kind.

Lesson 3—PRESENT INDICATIVE ACTIVE OF -*IŌ* THIRD AND FOURTH CONJUGATION VERBS

-IŌ THIRD CONJUGATION

(Present infinitive ends in **-ere**.)

cap*ere*, to take; present stem, **cape-**

FOURTH CONJUGATION

(Present infinitive ends in **-īre**.)

imped*īre*, to hinder; present stem, **impedī-**

cap*iō*	I take	cap*imus*	we take
cap*is*	you take	cap*itis*	you take
cap*it*	he or she takes	cap*iunt*	they take

imped*iō*	I hinder	imped*īmus*	we hinder
imped*īs*	you hinder	imped*ītis*	you hinder
imped*it*	he or she hinders	imped*iunt*	they hinder

Note

1. The present tense endings of **-iō** third and fourth conjugation verbs look very much alike.

2. In **-iō** third conjugation verbs, the final **e** of the stem is changed to **i** before the personal endings are attached. In the third person plural, the ending is **-unt** instead of **-nt**.

3. In fourth conjugation verbs, the ending of the third person plural is also **-unt** instead of **-nt**.

COMMON VERBS OF THE -IŌ THIRD CONJUGATION

SIMPLE VERBS

capere, to take, capture, seize
cupere, to wish, want
facere, to make, do

fugere, to flee
iacere, to throw
specere, to see, behold

COMPOUND VERBS

capere (the **a** of the stem is weakened to **i**)
  accipere, to receive
  excipere, to take out, receive
  incipere, to begin
  recipere, to take back, receive
  suscipere, to undertake
facere (the **a** of the stem is weakened to **i**)
  cōnficere, to finish
  dēficere, to fail, revolt
  efficere, to bring about, accomplish

  interficere, to kill
  perficere, to accomplish
  praeficere, to put in charge
iacere (the **a** of the stem is dropped)
  conicere, to throw (together)
  dēicere, to throw down, dislodge
  ēicere, to throw out, expel
specere (the **e** of the stem is weakened to **i**)
  cōnspicere, to observe, see
  perspicere, to perceive, examine

COMMON VERBS OF THE FOURTH CONJUGATION

audīre, to hear
dormīre, to sleep
fīnīre, to limit, bound
impedīre, to hinder
mūnīre, to fortify
scīre, to know
  nescīre, not to know, to be ignorant

sentīre, to feel, perceive
venīre, to come
  circumvenīre, to surround
  convenīre, to come together
  invenīre, to come upon, find
  pervenīre, to arrive

9

EXERCISES

A. Complete the English translation.

1. Mārcum domī invenit. _____ Marcus _____ at home.
2. Cum sociīs fugiunt. _____ with their allies.
3. Aquilam recipimus. _____ the eagle.
4. Audītisne tubam? _____ the trumpet?
5. Cibum nōn cupiō. _____ food.
6. Nōnne iter scīs? _____ the route?
7. Difficultātem sentiunt. _____ the difficulty.
8. Num dormit? _____?
9. Oppidum mūnīmus. _____ the town.
10. Cūr tēla iacitis?   Why_____ weapons?

B. Write all the specified forms in the present indicative active.

1. *facere* and *scīre:* third person singular _____
2. *convenīre* and *fugere:* first person plural _____
3. *audīre* and *excipere:* second person plural _____
4. *dēficere* and *fīnīre:* third person plural _____
5. *incipere:* first and second person singular _____

C. Complete the Latin translation.

1. We arrive quickly.   Celeriter _____.
2. The consul finishes the speech.   Cōnsul ōrātiōnem _____.
3. Are you (pl.) surrounding the camp? _____ castra?
4. I am not taking the arms.   Arma _____.
5. You (sing.) are making a sword, aren't you? _____ gladium?
6. The soldiers begin to flee.   Mīlitēs _____.
7. Why are the tribes revolting?   Cūr nātiōnēs _____?
8. The conqueror receives the reward.   Victor praemium _____.
9. We hear the good report.   Fāmam bonam _____.
10. Today you (pl.) are coming together.   Hodiē _____.

D. Change each verb to the plural.

1. Causam bellī scit.   Causam bellī _____.
2. Fīnem perīculī faciō.   Fīnem perīculī _____.
3. Perficisne labōrem? _____ labōrem?
4. Mīles captīvum interficit.   Mīlitēs captīvum _____.
5. Sentiō causam eius reī. _____ causam eius reī.

E. Write the present indicative active of each verb for the subjects indicated.

1. *suscipere:* quis _____ tū _____
2. *invenīre:* puerī _____ nōs _____
3. *mūnīre:* rēx _____ vōs _____
4. *accipere:* māter paterque_____ ego _____
5. *cupere:* Caesar _____ obsidēs _____

Roman Mosaics

The Romans made much use of marble tiles as a floor covering, in patterns similar to those used in modern public buildings. Mosaics were also popular, one of the most common being the mosaic of a dog with the warning **"cave canem."**

Lesson 4—REVIEW OF THE PRESENT INDICATIVE ACTIVE

A. Complete the English translation.

1. Mīlitēs dūcit. --- the soldiers.

2. Temptant hoc posterō diē. ------------------------------------ this the following day.

3. Geritisne bellum? -- war?

4. Cūr mūrōs facitis? Why --- walls?

5. Equitātum ex castrīs mittimus. ------------------------------ the cavalry out of camp.

6. Circiter mīlia VI conveniunt. About 6000 -------------------------------------.

7. Salūtem petere dēbēs. --- safety.

8. Domī maneō. -- at home.

9. Quis eōs discēdere iubet? Who ---------------- them ----------------?

10. In cōnspectum hostium veniunt. ------------------------ in sight of the enemy.

11. Nōnne ad exercitum contendit? ------------------------------ to the army?

12. Num timēs, Iūlia? --, Julia?

13. Eōs premunt. --- them.

14. Nostrōs spē cōnfīrmat. -------------------------------- our men with hope.

15. Omnia intellegimus. -- everything.

16. Eum ducem appellātis. --- him leader.

17. Prīma lūce fugiō. -- at dawn.

18. Habēsne duōs frātrēs? ------------------------------------- two brothers?

19. Cōpiās cōgunt. --- their troops.

20. Barbarum interficit. -- the native.

B. Underline the correct verb form.

1. Rēx obsidēs (dant, dat, datis).

2. Nōs amīcōs (vidēmus, vident, vidētis).

3. (Prohibētisne, Prohibetne, Prohibēsne) tū caedem?

4. Gallī eum (circumveniunt, circumvenit, circumvenīs).

5. Ego lēgātum (dīmittit, dīmittō, dīmittimus).

6. Vōs gladiōs (capiunt, capis, capitis).

7. Quid (facit, facis, faciunt) Caesar?

8. Omnēs tēla (conicitis, coniciunt, conicimus).

9. (Persuādentne, Persuādēsne, Persuādetne) captīvīs dux?

10. Nōs cōnsilia (cognōscō, cognōscimus, cognōscitis).

C. Translate into Latin.

1. she thinks
2. we are calling
3. do you (sing.) hope?
4. I do not receive
5. you (pl.) are warning
6. they find
7. who is conquering?
8. Marcus decides
9. isn't he yielding?
10. Sextus and Quintus are writing
11. you (sing.) are not trying, are you?
12. we do play
13. I uphold
14. they are teaching
15. he enlists
16. do they hinder?
17. you (pl.) join
18. they are shouting
19. it resists
20. Caesar puts in charge

D. Write the English meaning and the Latin infinitive of each of the following verb forms:

	ENGLISH MEANING	INFINITIVE
1. accēdunt		
2. hiemat		
3. redūcimus		
4. crēdisne?		
5. nōn postulātis		
6. cōnspiciō		
7. nōnne aedificant?		
8. pārēmus		
9. cadit		
10. trahis		
11. num dēditis?		
12. nōn animadvertit		
13. iūdicāmus		

14. repellunt -------------------------------------- --------------------------------------

15. perspicitisne? -------------------------------------- --------------------------------------

16. nōn vigilō -------------------------------------- --------------------------------------

17. nōnne concēdit? -------------------------------------- --------------------------------------

18. ambulāmus -------------------------------------- --------------------------------------

19. efficiunt -------------------------------------- --------------------------------------

20. prōcurris -------------------------------------- --------------------------------------

E. Write all the specified forms in the present indicative active.

1. *complēre* and *incendere:* third person plural --------------------------------------

2. *dēicere* and *iūrāre:* first person plural --------------------------------------

3. *claudere* and *impedīre:* second person singular --------------------------------------

4. *patēre* and *stāre:* third person singular --------------------------------------

5. *comportāre* and *sūmere:* second person plural --------------------------------------

6. *expellere* and *fīnīre:* first person singular --------------------------------------

7. *cōnsūmere:* third person singular and plural --------------------------------------

8. *dōnāre:* first person singular and plural --------------------------------------

9. *nescīre:* second person singular and plural --------------------------------------

10. *remanēre:* third person singular and plural --------------------------------------

F. Change the singular verbs to the plural, and the plural verbs to the singular.

1. expugnant --------------------------------------

2. ēiciō --------------------------------------

3. patet --------------------------------------

4. prōcēdis --------------------------------------

5. trādūcimus --------------------------------------

6. habitātis --------------------------------------

7. cōnsīditne? --------------------------------------

8. nōn solvunt --------------------------------------

9. dēspērō --------------------------------------

10. curris --------------------------------------

G. Supply the missing vowel or vowels in the following verb forms, all in the present indicative active.

1. mand _____ t

2. aug _____ mus

3. accid _____ nt

4. suscip _____ ō

5. dorm _____ nt

6. pār _____ ō

7. cōnsist _____ tis

8. perturb _____ s

9. coniung _____ t

10. praefic _____ nt

Lesson 5—IMPERFECT INDICATIVE ACTIVE OF ALL CONJUGATIONS

FIRST CONJUGATION

servāre, to save;
present stem, **servā-**

I was saving, I saved,
I used to save, I did save

servā*bam*	servā*bāmus*
servā*bās*	servā*bātis*
servā*bat*	servā*bant*

SECOND CONJUGATION

monēre, to warn;
present stem, **monē-**

I was warning, I warned,
I used to warn, I did warn

monē*bam*	monē*bāmus*
monē*bās*	monē*bātis*
monē*bat*	monē*bant*

THIRD CONJUGATION

vincere, to conquer;
present stem, **vince-**

I was conquering, I conquered,
I used to conquer, I did conquer

vincē*bam*	vincē*bāmus*
vincē*bās*	vincē*bātis*
vincē*bat*	vincē*bant*

-IŌ THIRD CONJUGATION

capere, to take; present stem, **cape-**

I was taking, I took,
I used to take, I did take

capiē*bam*	capiē*bāmus*
capiē*bās*	capiē*bātis*
capiē*bat*	capiē*bant*

FOURTH CONJUGATION

impedīre, to hinder; present stem, **impedī-**

I was hindering, I hindered,
I used to hinder, I did hinder

impediē*bam*	impediē*bāmus*
impediē*bās*	impediē*bātis*
impediē*bat*	impediē*bant*

Note

1. The endings of the imperfect, which are the same for all conjugations, are:

-bam	-bāmus
-bās	-bātis
-bat	-bant

These endings are attached to the present stem. However, in **-iō** third conjugation verbs an **i** is inserted before the final **e** of the stem, and in fourth conjugation verbs an **ē** is added to the stem, before the endings of the imperfect are attached.

2. The personal endings of the imperfect differ from those of the present only in the first person singular, where the ending is **-m** instead of **-ō**.

USES OF THE IMPERFECT

The imperfect tense is used:

1. To express continuous or progressive action in past time.

Nostrōs **exspectābat.**   He was (*or* kept) waiting for our men.

2. To express repeated action in past time.

Saepe cum servīs **labōrābat.**   He often worked with his slaves.

3. To express customary or habitual action in past time.

Ad merīdiem **dormiēbat.**   He used to sleep until noon.

EXERCISES

A. Underline the correct English translation.

1. narrābās   (he was telling, you were telling, I was telling)

2. vertēbat   (it turned, they turned, you turned)

3. cūrābant   (he cared for, we cared for, they cared for)

4. crēdēbāmus   (we believed, we are believing, you believed)

5. audiēbam   (we used to hear, she used to hear, I used to hear)

B. Change each verb from the present to the imperfect.

1. Rōmānī clāmant. ---------------------------------------

2. Hostibus resistimus. ---------------------------------------

3. Ōrō eōs auxilium. ---------------------------------------

4. Claudisne portam? ---------------------------------------

5. Negōtium suscipit. ---------------------------------------

6. Ubi quaeritis cōnsilium? ---------------------------------------

7. Quis dēspērat? ---------------------------------------

8. Cōpiās redūcunt. ---------------------------------------

9. Frūmentum cōnsūmimus. ---------------------------------------

10. Viam impedīs. ---------------------------------------

C. Complete the English translation.

1. Perīculum populō vidēbat.   ---------------- the danger to the people.

2. Calamitātem intellegēbant.   ------------------------------ the misfortune.

3. Cūr bellum gerēbātis?   Why ------------------------------ war?

4. Lēgātōs mittere nōn audēbam.   ------------------------------ to send envoys.

5. Mittēbāsne litterās ad amīcum?   ------------------------------ a letter to your friend?

6. Oppidum occupābāmus.   ------------------------------ the town.

7. Num auxilium portābat?   ------------------------------ aid, -------------?

8. In Galliā hiemābant.   ------------------------------ in Gaul.

9. Cum frātre cēnābam.   ------------------------------ with my brother.

10. Nōnne lūdōs spectābās?   ------------------------------ the games?

D. Using the subjects given, fill in the proper form of the imperfect active and translate the verb into English.

	IMPERFECT ACTIVE	MEANING
1. *importāre:* mercātōrēs	-------------------------	-------------------------
2. *impellere:* vōs	-------------------------	-------------------------
3. *fīnīre:* flūmen	-------------------------	-------------------------
4. *augēre:* nōs	-------------------------	-------------------------
5. *ēicere:* Caesar	-------------------------	-------------------------

6. *coniungere:* omnēs -------------------------- --------------------------

7. *valēre:* tū -------------------------- --------------------------

8. *cadere:* ego -------------------------- --------------------------

9. *explōrāre:* Quīntus et frāter -------------------------- --------------------------

10. *dēdūcere:* Belgae -------------------------- --------------------------

E. Write all the specified forms in the imperfect indicative active.

1. *praeficere:* first person singular and plural --------------------------

2. *collōcare:* third person singular and plural --------------------------

3. *pārēre:* second person singular and plural --------------------------

4. *dēdere* and *dormīre:* third person plural --------------------------

5. *patēre* and *dēicere:* third person singular --------------------------

F. Translate the English words into Latin.

1. *He was running* ad flūmen. --------------------------

2. *They were standing* in mūrō. --------------------------

3. *Were you (sing.) eager* auxilium dare? --------------------------

4. *We were fortifying* castra. --------------------------

5. *I was observing* summum montem. --------------------------

6. *You (pl.) used to set sail* mediā nocte. --------------------------

7. *They kept delaying* hostēs. --------------------------

8. Quis *was sitting* diū? --------------------------

9. Germānī *were demanding* concilium. --------------------------

10. Imperātor *was driving out* Gallōs. --------------------------

Aquila

The **aquila** (eagle) was a favorite figure on Roman military standards. It was made of silver or bronze, with outstretched wings, and was perched on top of the standard. The eagle, still a popular bird, appears on the official seal of the United States of America.

Lesson 6—FUTURE INDICATIVE ACTIVE OF FIRST AND SECOND CONJUGATION VERBS

<table>
<tr><td align="center">FIRST CONJUGATION</td><td align="center">SECOND CONJUGATION</td></tr>
<tr><td align="center">servāre, to save; present stem, servā-</td><td align="center">monēre, to warn; present stem, monē-</td></tr>
<tr><td align="center">I shall (will) save</td><td align="center">I shall (will) warn</td></tr>
</table>

servā*bō*	servā*bimus*	monē*bō*	monē*bimus*
servā*bis*	servā*bitis*	monē*bis*	monē*bitis*
servā*bit*	servā*bunt*	monē*bit*	monē*bunt*

Note

1. The endings of the future active of first and second conjugation verbs are:

-bō   -bimus
-bis   -bitis
-bit   -bunt

These endings are attached to the present stem.

2. The personal endings are the same as those of the present active.

EXERCISES

A. Change the italicized verbs to the future.

1. Obsidēs *postulat.*   ------------------------------

2. Caesarī *renūntiant.*   ------------------------------

3. *Iubeō* hostēs removērī.   ------------------------------

4. Ad hōram nōnam *exspectābatis.*   ------------------------------

5. Servō *persuādēmus.*   ------------------------------

6. *Armāsne* nāvēs?   ------------------------------

7. Oppidum *expugnant.*   ------------------------------

8. Cūr cōpiās nōn *trānsportās?*   ------------------------------

9. Diū *remanēbat.*   ------------------------------

10. Nōnne praemia *dōnātis?*   ------------------------------

B. Underline the correct Latin translation.

1. he will sit   (sedēbit, sedēbat, sedet)

2. we shall build   (aedificāmus, aedificābāmus, aedificābimus)

3. will they swear?   (iūrābantne?, iūrābuntne?, iūrantne?)

4. I shall fill   (compleō, complēbam, complēbō)

5. you will see   (vidēbis, vidēs, vidēbās)

6. you will walk   (ambulābātis, ambulātis, ambulābitis)

7. will she ask?   (interrogābisne?, interrogābitne?, interrogābitisne?)

8. they will judge   (iūdicābunt, iūdicābuntne, iūdicābant)

9. it will move   (movet, movēbit, movēbat)

10. we shall praise   (laudābimus, laudābitis, laudābō)

C. Complete the English translation.

1. Captīvōs comportābunt.   --- the prisoners.

2. Mūrus longē patēbit.   The wall --- far.

3. Parābisne magnās cōpiās?   --- large forces?

4. Germānōs prohibēbimus.   --- the Germans.

5. Secundā vigiliā nāvigābitis.   At the second watch----------------------------------.

6. Mox appropinquābō.   Soon --.

7. Suōs prōcēdere iubēbit.   --- his men to advance.

8. Num auxilium dabunt?   ------------------------- aid, -------------------------?

9. Impetum sustinēbimus.   --- the attack.

10. Quid dēmōnstrābō?   What --?

D. Write all the specified forms in the future indicative active.

1. *mandāre:* third person singular and plural   --

2. *augēre:* first person singular and plural   --

3. *circumdare:* second person singular and plural   --

4. *sedēre* and *perturbāre:* third person plural   --

5. *praestāre* and *nocēre:* third person singular   --

E. In each group there is one verb in the future tense. Underline it and then write its meaning.

1. valēbat, valēbis, valēbam   --

2. clāmant, clāmābāmus, clāmābit   --

3. pugnābimus, pugnābātis, pugnantne   --

4. vāstābās, temptābō, properātis   --

5. pācābunt, manēbātis, persuādēmus   --

Janus

Janus, the Roman god of beginnings, was represented with two faces. The month of January was named after him.

Lesson 7—FUTURE INDICATIVE ACTIVE OF THIRD, -IŌ THIRD, AND FOURTH CONJUGATION VERBS

THIRD CONJUGATION	-IŌ THIRD CONJUGATION	FOURTH CONJUGATION
vincere, to conquer; present stem, **vince-**	**capere,** to take; present stem, **cape-**	**impedīre,** to hinder; present stem, **impedī-**
I shall (will) conquer	I shall (will) take	I shall (will) hinder

vinc*am*	vinc*ēmus*	cap*iam*	cap*iēmus*	imped*iam*	imped*iēmus*
vinc*ēs*	vinc*ētis*	cap*iēs*	cap*iētis*	imped*iēs*	imped*iētis*
vinc*et*	vinc*ent*	cap*iet*	cap*ient*	imped*iet*	imped*ient*

Note

1. The endings of the future active of third, -iō third, and fourth conjugation verbs are:

-am	-ēmus
-ēs	-ētis
-et	-ent

These endings are attached to the present stem. However, in third conjugation verbs the final **e** of the stem is dropped, and in -iō third conjugation verbs the final **e** of the stem is changed to **i**, before the endings of the future are attached.

2. The personal endings are the same as those of the imperfect.

3. Because of the close resemblance of the future endings of third conjugation verbs and the present endings of second conjugation verbs, confusion often results. Distinguish the following:

THIRD CONJUGATION		SECOND CONJUGATION	
FUTURE		PRESENT	
vinc*ēs*	you will conquer	mon*ēs*	you warn
vinc*et*	he will conquer	mon*et*	he warns
vinc*ēmus*	we shall conquer	mon*ēmus*	we warn
vinc*ētis*	you will conquer	mon*ētis*	you warn
vinc*ent*	they will conquer	mon*ent*	they warn

EXERCISES

A. Complete the English translation.

1. Ad Caesarem cōpiās mittet. _____ forces to Caesar.

2. Cūr nāvēs coniungētis? Why _____ the boats?

3. Rem mox suscipient. _____ the matter soon.

4. Spatium fīniēmus. _____ the distance.

5. Opus efficiam. _____ the work.

6. Solvēsne tertiā vigiliā? _____ at the third watch?

7. Dormiēmus sex hōrās. _____ for six hours.

8. Accidetne rūrsus? _____ again?

9. Epistulam perspicient. _____ the letter.

10. Currum trahet. _____ the chariot.

20

B. Write the correct form of the verb in the future indicative active.

1. *cōnsistere:* Mīlitēs _____.

2. *impedīre:* Impetus nōs _____.

3. *excipere:* Nōs captīvum _____.

4. *sūmere:* _____ tū togam?

5. *trādūcere:* Ego equitātum _____.

6. *pervenīre:* Cūr _____ vōs tardē?

7. *fugere:* Pater fīliusque nōn _____.

8. *scīre:* Quis omnia _____?

9. *caedere:* Dux magnam partem hostium _____.

10. *cupere:* Ego mox ambulāre _____.

C. Write all the specified forms in the future indicative active.

1. *cōnsīdere:* first person singular and plural _____

2. *sentīre:* third person singular and plural _____

3. *facere:* second person singular and plural _____

4. *concēdere* and *audīre:* third person plural _____

5. *incipere* and *venīre:* third person singular _____

D. Translate the English words into Latin.

1. Omnia oppida *they will burn.* _____

2. Nōs hostibus *we shall surrender.* _____

3. Ancorās *you (pl.) will not raise.* _____

4. *I shall throw* tēla. _____

5. *Will you (sing.) come* mēcum? _____

6. Quis *will find* gladium? _____

7. *He will leave behind* sex mīlia hominum. _____

8. *Won't they surround* oppidum? _____

9. *We will join* proelium. _____

10. Imperātor *will choose* locum. _____

E. In each group there is one verb in the future tense. Underline it and then write its meaning.

1. prōcēdet, habet, exercet _____

2. pārēmus, audēmus, cadēmus _____

3. remanēs, dēdēs, continēs _____

4. prohibent, augent, prōcurrent _____

5. repellētis, sustinētis, perterrētis _____

Lesson 8—PRESENT, IMPERFECT, AND FUTURE INDICATIVE OF *SUM* AND *POSSUM*

esse, to be			posse, to be able		
PRESENT	IMPERFECT	FUTURE	PRESENT	IMPERFECT	FUTURE
I am	I was	I shall (will) be	I am able, I can	I was able, I could	I shall (will) be able
su*m*	e*ram*	er*ō*	pos*sum*	pot*eram*	pot*erō*
e*s*	e*rās*	e*ris*	pot*es*	pot*erās*	pot*eris*
es*t*	e*rat*	e*rit*	pot*est*	pot*erat*	pot*erit*
su*mus*	e*rāmus*	e*rimus*	pos*sumus*	pot*erāmus*	pot*erimus*
es*tis*	e*rātis*	e*ritis*	pot*estis*	pot*erātis*	pot*eritis*
su*nt*	e*rant*	e*runt*	pos*sunt*	pot*erant*	pot*erunt*

Note

1. **Posse** is a compound of **esse**. Its base is **pos-** when it is followed by the letter **s,** and **pot-** when followed by a vowel.

Thus, *pos*sum, *pos*sumus, *pos*sunt; but *pot*est, *pot*eram, *pot*erō.

2. The third person of **esse** may sometimes be translated as follows:

est	there is	**sunt**	there are
erat	there was	**erant**	there were
erit	there will be	**erunt**	there will be

3. Other compounds of **esse** are:

> **abesse,** to be away, to be absent
> **adesse,** to be near, to be present
> **deesse,** to be lacking, to be wanting
> **praeesse,** to be in charge

EXERCISES

A. Complete the English translation.

1. Cōpiae erant multae.   The forces _____ many.

2. Trēs discipulī absunt.   Three pupils _____.

3. Lēgātus praeerit.   The lieutenant _____.

4. Estisne parātī?   _____ ready?

5. Frūmentum deerat.   Grain _____.

6. Castra adsunt.   The camp _____.

7. Potesne solvere?   _____ to set sail?

8. Erimus sociī.   _____ allies.

22

9. Est multitūdō hominum. _____ a crowd of men.

10. Dormīre nōn poteram. _____ to sleep.

11. Nōnne poteris audīre? _____ to hear?

12. Erant decem praesidia in castrīs. _____ ten guards in camp.

13. Nāvēs dēsunt. Ships _____

14. Aderisne nocte? _____ at night?

15. Quis praeerat? Who _____?

B. Change each verb to the plural.

1. possum legere _____ legere

2. eris dux _____ ducēs

3. ūnus abest multī _____

4. equus deerat equī _____

5. praeerō castrīs _____ castrīs

6. adestne? _____

7. lēgātus dūcere poterat lēgātī dūcere _____

8. aberās _____

9. erit vigilia _____ vigiliae

10. eram incolumis _____ incolumēs

C. In the space before each verb in column *A*, write the letter of its English equivalent in column *B*.

Column A		*Column B*	
_____	**1.** poterat	*a.*	we are
_____	**2.** erimus	*b.*	there are
_____	**3.** praeerāsne?	*c.*	are you in charge?
_____	**4.** sunt	*d.*	he will be able
_____	**5.** sumus	*e.*	there will be
_____	**6.** poterit	*f.*	we shall be
_____	**7.** adsum	*g.*	were you in charge?
_____	**8.** praeerisne?	*h.*	he could
_____	**9.** erunt	*i.*	I shall be present
_____	**10.** potest	*j.*	we were
_____	**11.** aderō	*k.*	I was present
_____	**12.** praeesne?	*l.*	there were
_____	**13.** erāmus	*m.*	he can
_____	**14.** aderam	*n.*	I am present
_____	**15.** erant	*o.*	will you be in charge?

D. Write all the specified forms in the indicative active.

1. *posse:* future third singular and plural --

2. *esse:* imperfect first singular and plural --

3. *abesse:* present second singular and plural --

4. *esse* and *posse:* present third plural --

5. *adesse* and *praeesse:* future third singular --

E. Translate into Latin.

1. they could --

2. she will be --

3. Caesar is in charge --

4. I am able --

5. we were present --

6. will you (sing.) be absent? --

7. it was lacking --

8. you (pl.) can --

9. were they? --

10. we shall be able --

Neptune

Neptune, called **Poseidon** by the Greeks, was the Roman god of the sea. The trident, or three-pointed spear, was the symbol of his power. The planet Neptune is named after the god.

Lesson 9—REVIEW OF THE PRESENT, IMPERFECT, AND FUTURE INDICATIVE ACTIVE

A. Underline the correct English translation.

1. dōnābunt   (they gave, they will give, they are giving)

2. studeō   (I am eager, I shall be eager, I was eager)

3. quaerēbat   (he will seek, he is seeking, he was seeking)

4. crēdētis   (you believe, you will believe, you believed)

5. scīmus   (we know, we shall know, we used to know)

6. sedēs   (you will sit, you sat, you are sitting)

7. pōnetne?   (will he put?, did he put?, is he putting?)

8. perturbātis   (you were disturbing, you disturb, you will disturb)

9. poteram   (I can, I could, I shall be able)

10. pāret   (she obeys, she obeyed, she will obey)

B. Write a synopsis (three tenses active) of the following verbs in the form indicated:

		PRESENT	IMPERFECT	FUTURE
1. *complēre:*	3rd sing.			
2. *accēdere:*	3rd pl.			
3. *vigilāre:*	1st pl.			
4. *mūnīre:*	2nd pl.			
5. *perficere:*	1st sing.			
6. *cūrāre:*	2nd sing.			
7. *audīre:*	3rd pl.			
8. *abesse:*	3rd sing.			
9. *docēre:*	2nd sing.			
10. *incitāre:*	1st pl.			

C. Change each verb to the plural.

1. repellō

2. valēbās

3. praeficiet

4. clāmābatne?

5. impediam

6. tardābō

7. cōgisne?

8. obtinēbat

25

9. vulnerābit ----------------------------------

10. eris ----------------------------------

D. In the space before each expression in column *A*, write the letter of its Latin translation in column *B*.

	Column A	*Column B*
------	**1.** he will read	*a.* incipiēbam
------	**2.** they were throwing	*b.* venīs
------	**3.** are you coming?	*c.* legit
------	**4.** I shall begin	*d.* habitābimus
------	**5.** they will throw	*e.* iaciēbant
------	**6.** he read	*f.* leget
------	**7.** he comes	*g.* habitābāmus
------	**8.** we live	*h.* iacient
------	**9.** he is reading	*i.* incipiō
------	**10.** you are coming	*j.* legēbat
------	**11.** I am beginning	*k.* iaciunt
------	**12.** we shall live	*l.* venit
------	**13.** I began	*m.* incipiam
------	**14.** we used to live	*n.* habitāmus
------	**15.** they are throwing	*o.* venīsne

E. Complete the English translation.

1. Ad Rhēnum pervenient. -- at the Rhine.

2. Centum obsidēs postulat. ---------------------------------- one hundred hostages.

3. Librum scrībēbam. -- a book.

4. In agrīs erimus. -- in the fields.

5. Quis virōs exercēbit? Who ------------------------------- the men?

6. Expellitisne Gallōs? ---------------------------------- the Gauls?

7. Nātiōnēs dēficiēbant. The tribes --

8. Accipiēsne amīcōs? ---------------------------------- your friends?

9. Līberī dormiunt. The children --

10. Fābulam nārrābit. -- a story.

11. Multitūdinem permovēbāmus. ---------------------------------- the crowd.

12. Cūr virōs retinēs? Why ---------------------------------- the men?

13. Portās claudam. -- the gates.

14. Cōpiās cōgēbat. -- the forces.

15. Īnsulam animadvertunt. ---------------------------------- the island.

F. The following verbs are either in the present or future. Put a check in the proper column o indicate the tense of each verb, and then translate into English.

	PRESENT	FUTURE	TRANSLATION
1. iubet	------	------	------
2. cognōscet	------	------	------
3. cēdent	------	------	------
4. persuādent	------	------	------
5. dūcēmus	------	------	------
6. audēmus	------	------	------
7. timētis			------
8. mittētis	------	------	------
9. gerēs	------	------	------
10. obsidēs	------	------	------

G. Draw a line through the form that does *not* belong with the others in each group.

1. pācās, respondēs, impedītis, contendis
2. locābit, habēbit, curret, iubet
3. pertinent, audīs, damus, pellitis
4. cōnservābant, capiet, mittō, obtinēbis
5. timēbāmus, prohibēmus, agēbāmus, lūdēbāmus
6. docent, statuent, nāvigant, interficiunt
7. vocābō, scrībimus, dormiam, studētis
8. sedetne, valēsne, trahisne, incendisne
9. postulant, quaerit, caditis, adsunt
10. cōnspiciam, importābit, cōnsūment, prōcēdimus

H. The following verbs are either in the present, imperfect, or future. Put a check in the proper column to indicate the tense of each verb, and then supply the other two forms.

	PRESENT	IMPERFECT	FUTURE
1. spectābat	------	------	------
2. faciunt	------	------	------
3. fīniēmus	------	------	------
4. remanēs	------	------	------
5. capiam	------	------	------
6. dīcitis	------	------	------
7. vidēbit	------	------	------
8. sciēbāmus	------	------	------
9. opprimō	------	------	------
10. erant	------	------	------

I. Rewrite the sentences below, making *all* changes required by the directions in parentheses.

1. *Agricolae* in agrīs labōrant. (substitute *Nōs*)

----

2. Cibum *pārābam.* (substitute equivalent form of *removēre*)

----

3. *Legisne* omnēs librōs? (change to the plural)

----

4. *Ego* Rōmānus sum. (substitute *Vir*)

----

5. In castrīs *hiemābunt.* (change to the singular)

----

6. Fīnēs *patent.* (change to the imperfect)

----

7. Dīcere nōn *poterat.* (change to the plural)

----

8. Ducem *monēbit.* (substitute equivalent form of *audīre*)

----

9. Hostēs *expellēbātis.* (change to the present)

----

10. *Mīlitēs* auxilium petent. (substitute *Ego*)

Bridges

The Tiber was crossed by eight bridges, some of which were so expertly built that they are functioning to this very day. The Fabrician Bridge is one of the most famous of these arched bridges. Similar bridges span countless rivers throughout the world.

Lesson 10—PERFECT INDICATIVE ACTIVE OF FIRST AND SECOND CONJUGATION VERBS

FIRST CONJUGATION	SECOND CONJUGATION
servāre, to save; perfect stem, **servāv-**	**monēre,** to warn; perfect stem, **monu-**
I saved, I have saved, I did save	I warned, I have warned, I did warn

servāv*ī*	servāv*imus*	monu*ī*	monu*imus*
servāv*istī*	servāv*istis*	monu*istī*	monu*istis*
servāv*it*	servāv*ērunt*	monu*it*	monu*ērunt*

Note

1. The perfect tense of all verbs is formed by adding to the perfect stem the following endings:

-ī = I	**-imus** = we
-istī = you	**-istis** = you
-it = he, she, it	**-ērunt** = they

2. The perfect stem varies in formation. In the first conjugation, most verbs form their perfect stem by adding the letter **v** to the present stem.

PRESENT INFINITIVE	PRESENT STEM	PERFECT STEM
dōnāre	**dōnā-**	*dōnāv-*
locāre	**locā-**	*locāv-*
nārrāre	**nārrā-**	*nārrāv-*

By exception, the perfect stem of **dare** is **ded-**; of **stāre, stet-**; and of **praestāre, praestit-**.

3. In the second conjugation, many verbs form their perfect stem by changing the final **ē** of the present stem to **u.**

PRESENT INFINITIVE	PRESENT STEM	PERFECT STEM
patēre	**patē-**	*patu-*
studēre	**studē-**	*studu-*
valēre	**valē-**	*valu-*

4. The following second conjugation verbs differ from the pattern given above:

PRESENT INFINITIVE	PRESENT STEM	PERFECT STEM
augēre	**augē-**	*aux-*
cavēre	**cavē-**	*cāv-*
complēre	**complē-**	*complēv-*
iubēre	**iubē-**	*iuss-*
manēre (and its compounds)	**manē-**	*māns-*
movēre (and its compounds)	**movē-**	*mōv-*
respondēre	**respondē-**	*respond-*
sedēre (and its compounds)	**sedē-**	*sēd-*
suādēre (and its compounds)	**suādē-**	*suās-*
vidēre	**vidē-**	*vīd-*

5. The verb **audēre** falls in a special category. Its perfect system will be taken up in a subsequent lesson.

6. Both the imperfect and perfect represent action in past time. The perfect tense is more commonly used, and generally indicates an action that is completed and final. However, in a situation where the action was in progress, repeated, or customary, then the imperfect is preferred.

Nāvem **aedificāvit.**
perfect

He built a ship.
action
completed

Nāvem **aedificābat.**
imperfect

He was building a ship.
action in progress

EXERCISES

A. Put a check in the proper column to indicate whether the verb should be translated in the imperfect or the perfect.

	IMPERFECT	PERFECT
1. He was running home.	-------	-------
2. Has she finished her homework?	-------	-------
3. I lost my book.	-------	-------
4. They used to live here.	-------	-------
5. Did you take my pen?	-------	-------
6. We were carrying bundles.	-------	-------
7. You have seen the worst.	-------	-------
8. The child fell.	-------	-------
9. We kept on traveling.	-------	-------
10. Why did she put it down?	-------	-------

B. Complete the English translation.

1. Ad Britanniam nāvigāvērunt. _____ to Britain.

2. Nostrōs perturbāvit. _____ our men.

3. Magnum spatium patuit. _____ a great distance.

4. Vīdistīne fontem? _____ the fountain?

5. Cūr dēsperāvistis? Why _____?

6. Iter tardāvimus. _____ the journey.

7. Diū nōn remānsī. _____ a long time.

8. Omnēs nāvēs armāvērunt. _____ all the ships.

9. Suōs incitāvit. _____ his men.

10. Pontem rescindī iussimus. _____ the bridge to be cut down.

C. Write all the specified forms in the perfect indicative active.

1. *movēre* and *putāre:* third person plural _____

2. *superāre* and *vidēre:* first person singular _____

3. *nūntiāre* and *sedēre:* second person singular _____

4. *augēre* and *temptāre:* third person singular --

5. *appellāre* and *complēre:* first person plural --

D. Translate into Latin.

1. we have built ---

2. did you (sing.) persuade? ---

3. he did swear ---

4. I tried ---

5. haven't you (pl.) seen? ---

6. they have not subdued ---

7. she obeyed ---

8. he has freed ---

9. we wounded ---

10. it stood ---

E. Underline the correct English translation.

1. postulāvit   (he was demanding, he demanded, he demands)

2. exercuistī   (you trained, he has trained, I trained)

3. ōrāvimus   (we have begged, we used to beg, we do beg)

4. iussērunt   (they were ordering, they are ordering, they ordered)

5. habitāvī   (you lived, I lived, she lived)

6. sēdistis   (you did sit, they sat, we have sat)

7. deditne?   (did you give?, did I give?, did she give?)

8. locāvērunt   (they have put, they were putting, they are putting)

9. rogāvī   (you asked, I did ask, he has asked)

10. auxistis   (you [sing.] increased, you [pl.] increased, he increased)

The Rubicon was a stream separating Caesar's province of Cisalpine Gaul from Italy proper. By crossing it with his legions, Caesar committed an illegal act, tantamount to a declaration of war. Today crossing the Rubicon means making an irrevocable decision.

Caesar Crossing the Rubicon

Lesson 11—PERFECT INDICATIVE ACTIVE OF THIRD CONJUGATION VERBS

vincere, to conquer; perfect stem, **vīc-**

I conquered, I have conquered, I did conquer

vīcī	vīcimus
vīcistī	vīcistis
vīcit	vīcērunt

Note

The perfect stem of third conjugation verbs varies considerably. However, there are some patterns which many verbs follow.

1. The perfect stem of the following verbs ends in **s:**

PRESENT INFINITIVE	PRESENT STEM	PERFECT STEM
claudere	claude-	*claus-*
dīvidere	dīvide-	*dīvīs-*
lūdere	lūde-	*lūs-*
mittere (and its compounds)	mitte-	*mīs-*

2. The perfect stem of the following verbs ends in **ss:**

cēdere (and its compounds)	cēde-	*cess-*
gerere	gere-	*gess-*
premere (and its compounds)	preme-	*press-*

3. The perfect stem of the following verbs ends in **x:** (The **x** often takes the place of **cs** or **gs.**)

dīcere	dīce-	*dīx- (dīcs-)*
dūcere (and its compounds)	dūce-	*dūx- (dūcs-)*
īnstruere	īnstrue-	*īnstrūx-*
intellegere	intellege-	*intellēx- (intellēgs-)*
iungere (and its compounds)	iunge-	*iūnx- (iūngs-)*
regere	rege-	*rēx- (rēgs-)*
trahere	trahe-	*trāx-*

4. *a.* The perfect stem of the following verbs ends in **d:**

accidere	accide-	*accid-*
contendere	contende-	*contend-*
dēfendere	dēfende-	*dēfend-*
incendere	incende-	*incend-*
occīdere	occīde-	*occīd-*
ostendere	ostende-	*ostend-*

b. In two forms the perfect tense of these verbs is spelled exactly the same as the present tense. These forms are the third person singular and the first person plural. Only the context can indicate which form is meant.

<u>contendit</u>
present or perfect

he hastens or he hastened

<u>contendimus</u>
present or perfect

we hasten or we hastened

5. The perfect stem of the following verbs has a reduplicated form. This means the repetition of a syllable, usually the initial syllable, and sometimes a vowel change.

PRESENT INFINITIVE	PRESENT STEM	PERFECT STEM
cadere	cade-	*cecid-*
caedere	caede-	*cecīd-*
cōnsistere	cōnsiste-	*cōnstit-*
crēdere	crēde-	*crēdid-*
currere (and its compounds)	curre-	*cucurr-*
dēdere	dēde-	*dēdid-*
pellere	pelle-	*pepul-*
reddere	redde-	*reddid-*
resistere	resiste-	*restit-*
trādere	trāde-	*trādid-*

6. *a.* The perfect stem of the following verbs must be learned separately:

agere	age-	*ēg-*
cōgere	cōge-	*coēg-*
cognōscere	cognōsce-	*cognōv-*
cōnsīdere	cōnsīde-	*cōnsēd-*
expellere	expelle-	*expul-*
impellere	impelle-	*impul-*
legere (and its compounds)	lege-	*lēg-*
petere	pete-	*petīv-*
pōnere (and its compounds)	pōne-	*posu-*
quaerere	quaere-	*quaesīv-*
relinquere	relinque-	*relīqu-*
repellere	repelle-	*reppul-*
scrībere (and its compounds)	scrībe-	*scrīps-*
solvere	solve-	*solv-*
statuere (and its compounds)	statue-	*statu-*
sūmere (and its compounds)	sūme-	*sūmps-*
tollere	tolle-	*sustul-*
vertere (and its compounds)	verte-	*vert-*
vincere	vince-	*vīc-*

b. Three verbs in the list above have the same spelling for the present and perfect in two of their forms. These forms are the third person singular and the first person plural. Only the context can indicate which form is meant. The verbs are **solvere, statuere,** and **vertere.**

<u>solvit</u>
present or perfect

he sets sail, he set sail

<u>solvimus</u>
present or perfect

we are setting sail, we have set sail

EXERCISES

A. Write the correct form of the verb in the perfect.

1. *claudere:*   Puer portam _____.
2. *scrībere:*   Ego litterās _____.
3. *dēdere:*   Nōs hostibus _____.
4. *redūcere:*   Quis _____ cōpiās?
5. *prōcēdere:*   Mārcus frāterque _____.
6. *solvere:*   Cūr _____ vōs?
7. *cōnsūmere:*   Tū frūmentum _____.
8. *cōgere:*   Cōnsulēs multitūdinem _____.
9. *cadere:*   _____ puella?
10. *petere:*   Omnēs īnsulam _____.

B. Write all the specified forms in the perfect indicative active.

1. *quaerere:* third person singular and plural   _____
2. *crēdere:* second person singular and plural   _____
3. *iungere:* first person singular and plural   _____
4. *incendere* and *regere:* third person singular   _____
5. *sūmere* and *resistere:* third person plural   _____

C. Change each verb to the perfect.

1. In fīnēs Belgārum contendet.   _____
2. Eōrum cōnsilia cognōscunt.   _____
3. Lēgātōs mittēbāmus.   _____
4. Prōcēdisne?   _____
5. Mīlitēs ēdūcam.   _____
6. Terram petitis.   _____
7. Rōmānī hostēs caedunt.   _____
8. Equitēs pellēbat.   _____
9. Duās legiōnēs cōnscrībimus.   _____
10. Quō modō currum trahēs?   _____

D. Translate into English.

1. gessit   _____
2. dēlēgimus   _____
3. trādidērunt   _____
4. nōn dīxistī   _____
5. expulistisne?   _____

6. animadvertī

----

7. oppressit

----

8. vīcimus

----

9. dēfendistī

----

10. sustulērunt

E. Underline the correct Latin translation.

1. they led   (dūxit, dūxērunt, dūxistī)

2. we have put   (posuimus, pōnimus, pōnēmus)

3. you (sing.) did drive   (ēgistis, agis, ēgistī)

4. I left   (discessī, discēdō, discēdam)

5. did it happen?   (acciditne?, accidistīne?, accidetne?)

6. you (pl.) abandoned   (relīquistī, relīquērunt, relīquistis)

7. she has decided   (cōnstituistī, cōnstituit, cōnstituet)

8. we understood   (intellegimus, intellegēmus, intellēximus)

9. he did approach   (accessit, accēdit, accēdet)

10. they ran   (currunt, cucurrērunt, current)

Porta Maggiore

The rounded arch found in aqueducts and gateways is a Roman contribution to architecture. Famous modern constructions employing the Roman arch include the Arch of Triumph in Paris, the Brandenburg Gate in Berlin, and the Washington Arch in New York City.

Lesson 12—PERFECT INDICATIVE ACTIVE OF *-IŌ* THIRD AND FOURTH CONJUGATION VERBS

-IŌ THIRD CONJUGATION

capere, to take; perfect stem, **cēp-**

I took, I have taken, I did take

FOURTH CONJUGATION

impedīre, to hinder; perfect stem, **impedīv-**

I hindered, I have hindered, I did hinder

cēp*ī*	cēp*imus*	impedīv*ī*	impedīv*imus*
cēp*istī*	cēp*istis*	impedīv*istī*	impedīv*istis*
cēp*it*	cēp*ērunt*	impedīv*it*	impedīv*ērunt*

Note

1. Most **-iō** third conjugation verbs form their perfect stem by changing the **a** or **i** of the present stem to **ē.**

PRESENT INFINITIVE	PRESENT STEM	PERFECT STEM
capere (and its compounds)	**cape-**	*cēp-*
facere (and its compounds)	**face-**	*fēc-*
iacere (and its compounds)	**iace-**	*iēc-*

2. The perfect stem of the following verbs must be learned separately:

cupere	**cupe-**	*cupīv-*
fugere	**fuge-**	*fūg-*
specere (and its compounds)	**spece-**	*spex-*

3. In the fourth conjugation, many verbs form their perfect stem by adding the letter **v** to the present stem.

audīre	**audī-**	*audīv-*
dormīre	**dormī-**	*dormīv-*
fīnīre	**fīnī-**	*fīnīv-*
impedīre	**impedī-**	*impedīv-*
mūnīre	**mūnī-**	*mūnīv-*
scīre (and its compounds)	**scī-**	*scīv-*

4. The perfect stem of the following verbs must be learned separately:

sentīre	**sentī-**	*sēns-*
venīre (and its compounds)	**venī-**	*vēn-*

5. Observe the difference between

PRESENT		PERFECT	
fugit	he flees	**fūgit**	he fled
fugimus	we flee	**fūgimus**	we fled
venit	he comes	**vēnit**	he came
venīmus	we come	**vēnimus**	we came

36

EXERCISES

A. Change each verb to the perfect.

1. Sē recipiunt.   ------------------------------------
2. Ad montem perveniēmus.   ------------------------------------
3. Iaciēbāsne tēla?   ------------------------------------
4. Negōtium perficiam.   ------------------------------------
5. Castra mūnit.   ------------------------------------
6. Hostēs nōn impedītis.   ------------------------------------
7. Dōna accipiēbāmus.   ------------------------------------
8. Omnēs nātiōnēs convenient.   ------------------------------------
9. Cūr regiōnem perspicit?   ------------------------------------
10. Ōrātiōnem audiēbam.   ------------------------------------

B. Complete the English translation.

1. Ad exercitum vēnit.   -- to the army.
2. Nostrōs cōnspexērunt.   -- our men.
3. In silvam fūgimus.   -- into the forest.
4. Calamitātem impedīvistī.   -- the disaster.
5. Cupīvī clāmāre.   -- to shout.
6. Nōn dormīvistis bene.   -- well.
7. Incēpērunt oppidum oppugnāre. ------------------------------- to attack the town.
8. Pācem in terrīs effēcit.   -- peace on earth.
9. Idem sēnsimus.   -- the same way.
10. Invēnistīne cibum?   -- the food?

C. Write all the specified forms in the perfect indicative active.

1. *fīnīre:* third person singular and plural   ------------------------------------
2. *perspicere:* first person singular and plural ------------------------------------
3. *venīre:* second person singular and plural   ------------------------------------
4. *suscipere* and *mūnīre:* third person plural   ------------------------------------
5. *nescīre* and *interficere:* third person singular ---------------------------------

D. Translate into Latin.

1. they made   ------------------------------------
2. he has put in charge ------------------------------------
3. we surrounded   ------------------------------------
4. did you (sing.) know? ------------------------------------
5. I have arrived   ------------------------------------
6. you (pl.) did seize ------------------------------------

7. they have undertaken

8. she threw

9. we did not observe

10. I hindered

E. Change each verb to the plural.

1. dēfēcit

2. excēpistī

3. spexī

4. fūgitne?

5. nescīvī

The Torch

The earliest torches were made of pine splinters bound together and saturated with pitch, asphalt, or resin. They were used outdoors to light the way, since there was no street lighting. The torch has always denoted that which enlightens or illuminates, such as the torch of knowledge. A classic example of the burning torch as a symbol of freedom is the one seen on the Statue of Liberty in New York Harbor.

Lesson 13—PERFECT INDICATIVE OF *SUM* AND *POSSUM*

esse, to be; perfect stem, **fu-**

I was, I have been

posse, to be able; perfect stem, **potu-**

I was able, I could, I have been able

fu*ī*	fu*imus*	potu*ī*	potu*imus*
fu*istī*	fu*istis*	potu*istī*	potu*istis*
fu*it*	fu*ērunt*	potu*it*	potu*ērunt*

Note

1. The perfect endings of **esse** and **posse** are the same as those of regular verbs.

2. The perfect stem of the compound verb **abesse** is **āfu-**.

3. The third person of **esse** may sometimes be translated as follows:

fuit	there was
fuērunt	there were

EXERCISES

A. In the space before each verb in column *A*, write the letter of its English equivalent in column *B*.

	Column A		*Column B*
------	**1.** potuit	*a.*	I was absent
------	**2.** potuistī	*b.*	it was near
------	**3.** praefuī	*c.*	he has been
------	**4.** dēfuit	*d.*	could you?
------	**5.** fuēruntne?	*e.*	you were
------	**6.** fuit	*f.*	he was able
------	**7.** adfuimus	*g.*	they were able
------	**8.** fuistī	*h.*	were they able?
------	**9.** āfuimus	*i.*	it was lacking
------	**10.** adfuit	*j.*	we were in charge
------	**11.** potuēruntne?	*k.*	we were away
------	**12.** potuistisne?	*l.*	I was in charge
------	**13.** āfuī	*m.*	we were near
------	**14.** potuērunt	*n.*	have they been?
------	**15.** praefuimus	*o.*	you could

B. Complete the English translation.

1. Nōn potuērunt dormīre. _____ to sleep.

2. Fuistisne miserī? _____ wretched?

3. Nōs, cōnsulēs, dēfuimus.   We, the consuls, _____.

4. Hodiē praefuī.   Today _____.

5. Eō tempore nōn adfuistī.   At that time _____.

6. Āfuit tōtum diem.   _____ the entire day.

7. Cōnsīdere potuimus.   _____ to sit down.

8. Fuērunt multa tēla in castrīs.   _____ many weapons in camp.

9. Solvere potuī.   _____ to set sail.

10. Fuit quondam ista virtūs.   _____ once such courage.

C. Write all the specified forms in the perfect indicative active.

1. *esse* and *posse:* third person plural   _____

2. *adesse* and *posse:* third person singular   _____

3. *praeesse:* first person singular and plural   _____

4. *abesse:* second person singular and plural   _____

5. *deesse:* third person singular and plural   _____

D. Translate into Latin.

1. she has been   _____

2. they could   _____

3. you (sing.) were not in charge   _____

4. we have been away   _____

5. you (pl.) have been wanting   _____

6. I was present   _____

7. Caesar was able   _____

8. Marcus and Sextus have been   _____

9. there was   _____

10. were you (sing.) able?   _____

E. Change the italicized verbs to the perfect.

1. *Possunt* bellum gerere.   _____

2. Pecūnia *deerat.*   _____

3. *Sumus* celerēs.   _____

4. *Aderātisne?*   _____

5. Diū *absum.*   _____

6. Exercituī *praees.*   _____

7. *Erit* in prīmīs.   _____

8. Eum vidēre *poterimus.*   _____

9. *Possum* scrībere.   _____

10. *Erās* vērus amīcus.   _____

Lesson 14—PLUPERFECT INDICATIVE ACTIVE

servāre, to save; perfect stem, **servāv-**

I had saved

servāv*eram*	servāv*erāmus*		
servāv*erās*	servāv*erātis*		
servāv*erat*	servāv*erant*		

vincere, to conquer; perfect stem, **vīc-**

I had conquered

vīc*eram*	vīc*erāmus*
vīc*erās*	vīc*erātis*
vīc*erat*	vīc*erant*

esse, to be; perfect stem, **fu-**

I had been

fu*eram*	fu*erāmus*
fu*erās*	fu*erātis*
fu*erat*	fu*erant*

posse, to be able; perfect stem, **potu-**

I had been able

potu*eram*	potu*erāmus*
potu*erās*	potu*erātis*
potu*erat*	potu*erant*

Note

1. The pluperfect active of all verbs is formed by adding to the perfect stem the following endings:

-eram	-erāmus
-erās	-erātis
-erat	-erant

2. These endings are exactly the same as the imperfect of the verb **esse**.

3. The pluperfect tense represents the time of an action completed before another past event, and is translated by the auxiliary verb *had* plus the past participle.

Caesar Germānōs <u>superāvit</u>; anteā Gallōs
perfect

<u>superāverat</u>.
pluperfect

Caesar <u>defeated</u> the Germans; previously he
past event

had defeated the Gauls.
previous event

EXERCISES

A. In each group there is one verb in the pluperfect tense. Underline it and then write its meaning.

1. sūmpsit, sūmit, sūmpserat, sūmet _____

2. poterant, poterunt, potuērunt, potuerant _____

3. cūrāverās, cūrāvistī, cūrābās, cūrābis _____

4. augēbātis, auxerātis, auxistis, augēbitis _____

5. vertam, verteram, vertēbam, vertī _____

6. scīvimus, sciēbāmus, scīverāmus, sciēmus _____

7. eram, erō, fuī, fueram _____

8. crēdēbat, dēdidit, spexerat, cucurrit _____

9. dōnāverās, impediēbam, valuimus, iēcērunt _____

10. complēbam, pepulit, resistent, iūnxerās _____

B. Write all the specified forms in the pluperfect indicative active.

1. *valēre:* second person singular and plural   --

2. *trahere:* third person singular and plural   --

3. *habitāre:* first person singular and plural   --

4. *esse* and *mūnīre:* third person plural   --

5. *cupere* and *posse:* third person singular   --

C. Translate the English words into Latin.

1. *They had seen* suōs amīcōs.   --

2. *We had been* in nāve.   --

3. *Had you (sing.) burned* frūmentum?   --

4. *I had spent the winter* in Germāniā.   --

5. Iter *you (pl.) had not made.*   --

6. Cūr *had he come* tam tardē?   --

7. Gallī *had abandoned* vīcum.   --

8. *She had told* fābulam bonam.   --

9. *We had not been able* castra pōnere.   --

10. *You (sing.) had undertaken* negōtium.   --

D. Change each verb to the pluperfect.

1. Fossam complēvit.   --

2. Bellum parant.   --

3. Omnēs cōgētis.   --

4. Nūntiābisne hās rēs?   --

5. Cōpiās subsidiō mittimus.   --

6. Reliquōs omnēs coniungam.   --

7. Rōmānī vēra dīcēbant.   --

8. Nōnne audīvistī clāmōrem?   --

9. Tēla movēmus.   --

10. Celeriter sē recipiet.   --

S.P.Q.R.

The initials **S.P.Q.R.** (**senātus populusque Rō-mānus**) were the symbol of Roman power and influence. Even today in Rome this ancient symbol appears on public buildings, street signs, stamps, etc.

Lesson 15—FUTURE PERFECT INDICATIVE ACTIVE

servāre, to save; perfect stem, **servāv-**

I shall (will) have saved

servāv*erō*	servāv*erimus*
servāv*eris*	servāv*eritis*
servāv*erit*	servāv*erint*

vincere, to conquer; perfect stem, **vīc-**

I shall (will) have conquered

vīc*erō*	vīc*erimus*
vīc*eris*	vīc*eritis*
vīc*erit*	vīc*erint*

esse, to be; perfect stem, **fu-**

I shall (will) have been

fu*erō*	fu*erimus*
fu*eris*	fu*eritis*
fu*erit*	fu*erint*

posse, to be able; perfect stem, **potu-**

I shall (will) have been able

potu*erō*	potu*erimus*
potu*eris*	potu*eritis*
potu*erit*	potu*erint*

Note

1. The future perfect active of all verbs is formed by adding to the perfect stem the following endings:

-erō	-erimus
-eris	-eritis
-erit	-erint

2. These endings are the same as the future of the verb **esse,** with the exception of the third person plural where the ending is **-erint** instead of **-erunt.**

3. The future perfect tense represents the time of an action completed before some future event, and is translated by the auxiliary verb *shall have* or *will have* plus the past participle.

Cum tū perveniēs, ego iam **discesserō**.
future — future perfect

When you will arrive, I *shall have departed* already.
future event — previous event

4. Distinguish carefully between verbs ending in **-ērunt, -erant, -erint.**

impedīvēr**u**nt   they hindered or have hindered
impedīver**a**nt   they had hindered
impedīver**i**nt   they will have hindered

EXERCISES

A. Translate the following verbs in the future perfect active.

1. mīserō _____

2. fuerit _____

3. laudāverint _____

4. mānseritis _____

5. mūnīverimus _____

6. iēceris _____

7. vīderitne? _____

8. potuerint _____

9. nōn dederimus _____

10. nōnne postulāveris? _____

B. Write all the specified forms in the future perfect indicative active.

1. *capere:* first person singular and plural _____

2. *dēfendere:* third person singular and plural _____

3. *spērāre:* second person singular and plural _____

4. *timēre* and *scīre:* third person plural _____

5. *esse* and *posse:* third person singular _____

C. In each group there is one verb in the future perfect tense. Underline it and then write its meaning.

1. portāvērunt, portāverint, portāverant _____

2. pepulerās, pepulistī, pepuleris _____

3. ōrāverimus, ōrāverāmus, ōrāvimus _____

4. pāruī, pāruerō, pārueram _____

5. fēcerit, fēcerat, faciēbat _____

D. Translate into Latin.

1. he will have led _____

2. I shall have had _____

3. we shall have written _____

4. they will have been able _____

5. you (sing.) will have put _____

6. you (pl.) will have been _____

7. will they have surrendered? _____

8. I shall have asked _____

9. he will not have heard _____

10. we shall have begun _____

Slave's Collar

A runaway slave suffered very severe punishment in ancient Rome. Besides being branded on his forehead with the letter **F,** for **fugitīvus,** he often had a metal collar riveted around his neck. An inscription bearing his master's name usually appeared on the collar. The nearest modern equivalent would be the manacles placed on African slaves during the slave-trade period.

Lesson 16—REVIEW OF THE PERFECT SYSTEM, ACTIVE

A. Underline the correct English translation.

1. crēdiderat   (he had believed, he believed, he will have believed)

2. locāvērunt   (they had placed, they have placed, they will have placed)

3. mūnīverimus   (we fortified, we had fortified, we shall have fortified)

4. iusserās   (you had ordered, you will have ordered, you ordered)

5. iēcerō   (I have thrown, I had thrown, I shall have thrown)

6. cessistis   (you moved, you will have moved, you had moved)

7. spērāvitne?   (had she hoped?, did she hope?, will she have hoped?)

8. spexerāmus   (we had seen, we shall have seen, we have seen)

9. steterint   (they stood, they will have stood, they had stood)

10. vēneram   (I have come, I had come, I shall have come)

B. In the space before each expression in column *A*, write the letter of its Latin translation in column *B*.

	Column A	*Column B*
------	**1.** we had led	*a.* tardāveram
------	**2.** he has fled	*b.* potuerat
------	**3.** I slowed up	*c.* vīcerant
------	**4.** they will have conquered	*d.* fūgerit
------	**5.** had you (sing.) fallen?	*e.* nōnne rēxistī?
------	**6.** we have led	*f.* dūxerāmus
------	**7.** they had conquered	*g.* ceciderātisne?
------	**8.** he will have fled	*h.* fūgit
------	**9.** she could	*i.* vīcērunt
------	**10.** I had slowed up	*j.* nōn rēxistī
------	**11.** she had been able	*k.* dūximus
------	**12.** you (sing.) have not ruled	*l.* potuit
------	**13.** they have conquered	*m.* ceciderāsne?
------	**14.** haven't you ruled?	*n.* tardāvī
------	**15.** had you (pl.) fallen?	*o.* vīcerint

C. Write all the specified forms in the indicative active.

1. *esse* and *audīre:* pluperfect third plural --

2. *manēre* and *amāre:* perfect second singular --

3. *mittere* and *posse:* future perfect first plural --

4. *suscipere:* perfect and pluperfect third singular --

5. *dīcere:* perfect and future perfect first singular --

D. Complete the English translation.

1. Aedificia cōnspexērunt.   _____ the buildings.
2. Servus fugere temptāverat.   The slave_____ to flee.
3. Eō tempore discesserimus.   At that time _____.
4. Cūr iussistī mīlitēs prōgredī? Why _____ the soldiers to advance?
5. Potestātem accēperam.   _____ power.
6. Iūstitiā rēxistis.   _____ with justice.
7. Victōriam nūntiāverit.   _____ the victory.
8. Suprā dēmōnstrāvimus.   _____ above.
9. Statim responderant.   _____ at once.
10. Cōnstituistīne pugnāre?   _____ to fight?

E. Identify the tense of each verb and then translate it into English.

		TENSE	MEANING
1.	relīquērunt	_____	_____
2.	coniēcerāmus	_____	_____
3.	hiemāverō	_____	_____
4.	cōnsūmpsistis	_____	_____
5.	pāruit	_____	_____
6.	pervēnerās	_____	_____
7.	incenderint	_____	_____
8.	restitimus	_____	_____
9.	effēcit	_____	_____
10.	explōrāverant	_____	_____

F. Rewrite the sentences below, making *all* changes required by the directions in parentheses.

1. Puerī nāvigium *habuērunt.* (substitute equivalent form of *facere*)_____
2. Litterās *scrīpseram.* (change to second person singular)_____
3. *Cōnsul* pervēneris. (substitute *Nōs*)_____
4. Pugnam *vīdit.* (change to the pluperfect)_____
5. Multās rēs *importāvistī.* (change to the plural)_____
6. Respondēre nōn *potuī.* (change to the future perfect)_____
7. Obsidēs *postulāverant.* (substitute equivalent form of *dēfendere*)_____
8. Arma *sūmpsimus.* (change to the singular)_____
9. Dux impetum *nūntiāvit.* (substitute equivalent form of *sustinēre*)_____
10. Prōcesseritne *lēgātus?* (substitute *vōs*)_____

Lesson 17—PRESENT ACTIVE IMPERATIVE

INFINITIVE	PRESENT STEM	IMPERATIVE SINGULAR	IMPERATIVE PLURAL
servāre	servā-	**servā**	**servāte**
monēre	monē-	**monē**	**monēte**
vincere	vince-	**vince**	**vincite**
capere	cape-	**cape**	**capite**
impedīre	impedī-	**impedī**	**impedīte**
esse	es-	**es**	**este**

Note

1. With few exceptions, the imperative singular is the same as the present stem. The plural is formed by adding **-te** to the singular form. However, in third and **-iō** third conjugation verbs the final **e** of the singular form is changed to **i** before **-te** is added.

2. The following verbs drop the final **e** in the imperative singular:

INFINITIVE	PRESENT STEM	IMPERATIVE SINGULAR	IMPERATIVE PLURAL
dīcere	dīce-	**dīc**	**dīcite**
dūcere	dūce-	**dūc**	**dūcite**
facere	face-	**fac**	**facite**

3. The imperative is used in the second person to express a command. The singular is used when addressing one person, the plural when addressing more than one.

Lege fābulam, Iūlia.
singular   singular

Read the story, Julia.

Dēfendite mūrum, mīlitēs.
plural   plural

Defend the wall, soldiers.

EXERCISES

A. Complete the English translation.

1. Coniungite nāvēs. _____ the boats.

2. Postulā iūstitiam. _____ justice.

3. Complēte fossam, servī. _____ the trench, slaves.

4. Dormīte, līberī. _____, children.

5. Dīc mihi. _____ to me.

6. Quā dē causā prōcurre. For this reason _____.

7. Claudite portās, mīlitēs. _____ the gates, soldiers.

8. Ēdūcite cōpiās. _____ the troops.

9. Temptā intellegere. _____ to understand.

10. Cēnā mēcum. _____ with me.

11. Adeste, fidēlēs. _____, O faithful.

12. Amā mē fidēliter. _____ me faithfully.

47

13. Lūdite, amīcī.   _____, friends.

14. Venīte Rōmam.   _____ to Rome.

15. Cavē canem.   _____ the dog.

B. Change each singular imperative to the plural.

1. mitte   _____

2. fac   _____

3. recipe   _____

4. valē   _____

5. audī   _____

C. Write the imperative singular and plural of the following verbs:

	SINGULAR	PLURAL
1. crēdere	_____	_____
2. expugnāre	_____	_____
3. dūcere	_____	_____
4. dēicere	_____	_____
5. manēre	_____	_____

D. Translate the English words into Latin.

1. *Hear* mē, puerī.   _____

2. *Write* litterās, Mārce.   _____

3. *Report* victōriam, serve.   _____

4. *Prevent* impetum, Gallī.   _____

5. *Speak* fortiter, Caesar.   _____

Mottoes on the Great Seal are: **Annuit coeptis,** He (God) has favored our undertakings; **Novus ordo seclorum,** A new world order; **E pluribus unum,** Out of many, one.

Great Seal of the United States

Lesson 18—IRREGULAR, DEFECTIVE, AND IMPERSONAL VERBS

EŌ

PRESENT INFINITIVE	PRESENT STEM	PERFECT STEM
īre, to go	ī-	īv-

PRESENT	
eō	īmus
īs	ītis
it	eunt

IMPERFECT	PLUPERFECT
ībam	īveram or ieram
ībās, etc.	īverās, etc.
FUTURE	**FUTURE PERFECT**
ībō	īverō or ierō
ībis, etc.	īveris, etc.
PERFECT	**IMPERATIVE**
īvī or iī	ī īte
īvistī, etc.	

FERŌ

PRESENT INFINITIVE	PRESENT STEM	PERFECT STEM
ferre, to bear, bring	fer-	tul-

PRESENT	
ferō	ferimus
fers	fertis
fert	ferunt

IMPERFECT	PLUPERFECT
ferēbam	tuleram
ferēbās, etc.	tulerās, etc.
FUTURE	**FUTURE PERFECT**
feram	tulerō
ferēs, etc.	tuleris, etc.
PERFECT	**IMPERATIVE**
tulī	fer ferte
tulistī, etc.	

Compounds of **īre** conjugated similarly are:

    abīre, to go away
    adīre, to go toward
    exīre, to go out
    inīre, to go into
    redīre, to go back
    trānsīre, to go across

Compounds of **ferre** conjugated similarly are:

    cōnferre, to bring together
    īnferre, to bring in
    referre, to bring back

VOLŌ AND *NŌLŌ*

PRESENT INFINITIVE	**velle,** to want		**nōlle,** not to want	
PRESENT STEM	**vel-**		**nōl-**	
PERFECT STEM	**volu-**		**nōlu-**	
PRESENT	**volō**	**volumus**	**nōlō**	**nōlumus**
	vīs	**vultis**	**nōn vīs**	**nōn vultis**
	vult	**volunt**	**nōn vult**	**nōlunt**
IMPERFECT	**volēbam**		**nōlēbam**	
	volēbās, etc.		**nōlēbās,** etc.	
FUTURE	**volam**		**nōlam**	
	volēs, etc.		**nōlēs,** etc.	
PERFECT	**voluī**		**nōluī**	
	voluistī, etc.		**nōluistī,** etc.	
PLUPERFECT	**volueram**		**nōlueram**	
	voluerās, etc.		**nōluerās,** etc.	
FUTURE PERFECT	**voluerō**		**nōluerō**	
	volueris, etc.		**nōlueris,** etc.	

Note

Nōlō is a contraction of **nōn volō.**

COEPĪ

Coepī (I began) is defective in that it exists in the perfect system only.

PERFECT	PLUPERFECT	FUTURE PERFECT
coepī	**coeperam**	**coeperō**
coepistī, etc.	**coeperās,** etc.	**coeperis,** etc.

LICET AND *OPORTET*

Some verbs, because of their meaning, exist only in the third person singular. They are called *impersonal* verbs, since they have no personal subject. In translating into English, the word *it* may be used.

licet present	it is permitted, one may	**oportet** present	it is necessary, one ought
licēbat imperfect	it was permitted	**oportēbat** imperfect	it was necessary
licēbit future	it will be permitted	**oportēbit** future	it will be necessary
licuit perfect	it has been permitted	**oportuit** perfect	it has been necessary

Eīs excēdere **licēbat.**

They were permitted to leave (It was permitted to them to leave).

Oportet mē īre.

I ought to go (It is necessary for me to go).

EXERCISES

A. Write all the specified forms in the indicative active.

1. *ferre* and *velle:* perfect third singular --

2. *īre* and *nōlle:* future first plural --

3. *velle* and *nōlle:* present second singular --

4. *coepī:* pluperfect third singular and plural --

5. *cōnferre* and *abīre:* imperfect first singular --

B. Complete the English translation.

1. Nunc exeunt. -- now.

2. Subsidium tulerās. -- aid.

3. Voluimus remanēre. -- to remain.

4. Coepistisne iter? -- the journey?

5. Oportet tē dormīre. -- for you to sleep.

6. Redīte ad patriam. -- to your country.

7. Impedīmenta cōnferēbant. -- the baggage.

8. Nōlō contendere. -- to fight.

9. Cum amīcīs ībunt. -- with their friends.

10. Quis flūmen trānsierat? Who -- the river?

C. In the space before each expression in column *A*, write the letter of its Latin translation in column *B*.

	Column A	*Column B*
------	**1.** he wanted	*a.* ībunt
------	**2.** they were going	*b.* vult
------	**3.** we had begun	*c.* feretne?
------	**4.** did she bring?	*d.* nōlō
------	**5.** he had wanted	*e.* ībant
------	**6.** I did not want	*f.* coepimus
------	**7.** they will go	*g.* voluit
------	**8.** he wants	*h.* coeperāmus
------	**9.** I do not want	*i.* īte
------	**10.** we have begun	*j.* voluerat
------	**11.** go	*k.* ferēbatne?
------	**12.** they will have gone	*l.* nōlueram
------	**13.** will she bring?	*m.* nōluī
------	**14.** I had not wanted	*n.* tulitne?
------	**15.** was she bringing?	*o.* ierint

D. Draw a line through the form that does *not* belong with the others in each group.

1. ferēmus, ībimus, nōlumus, volēmus

2. coepistis, tulistī, voluistī, īvistī

3. nōluerō, tuleram, ierō, coeperō

4. ferunt, volunt, oportet, nōlet

5. fer, ferte, īte, iit

E. Underline the correct English translation.

1. coeperātis   (you had begun, you began, you will have begun)

2. ferēbat   (she has brought, she was bringing, she will bring)

3. ībimus   (we were going, we are going, we shall go)

4. voluī   (I wanted, I had wanted, I want)

5. nōlunt   (they did not want, they don't want, they will not want)

6. abiit   (he goes away, he will go away, he went away)

7. contulistī   (you brought together, you will bring together, you bring together)

8. ferte   (you bring, you will bring, bring)

9. ierint   (they had gone, they will have gone, they have gone)

10. licēbat   (it was permitted, it is permitted, it will be permitted)

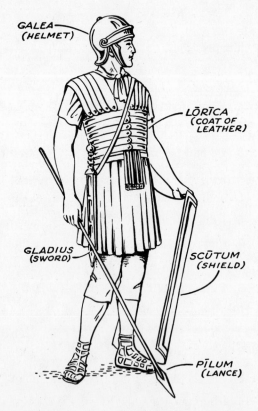

Equipment of the Legionary

Lesson 19—MASTERY EXERCISES ON VERBS, INDICATIVE ACTIVE

A. Write a synopsis (six tenses active) of the following verbs in the form indicated:

1. *dūcere:* 2nd sing.

Pres. _____	*Perf.* _____
Imp. _____	*Plup.* _____
Fut. _____	*Fut. Perf.* _____

2. *esse:* 3rd pl.

Pres. _____	*Perf.* _____
Imp. _____	*Plup.* _____
Fut. _____	*Fut. Perf.* _____

3. *ōrāre:* 1st sing.

Pres. _____	*Perf.* _____
Imp. _____	*Plup.* _____
Fut. _____	*Fut. Perf.* _____

4. *iacere:* 3rd sing.

Pres. _____	*Perf.* _____
Imp. _____	*Plup.* _____
Fut. _____	*Fut. Perf.* _____

5. *ferre:* 1st pl.

Pres. _____	*Perf.* _____
Imp. _____	*Plup.* _____
Fut. _____	*Fut. Perf.* _____

6. *venīre:* 2nd pl.

Pres. _____	*Perf.* _____
Imp. _____	*Plup.* _____
Fut. _____	*Fut. Perf.* _____

7. *īre:* 3rd pl.

Pres. _____	*Perf.* _____
Imp. _____	*Plup.* _____
Fut. _____	*Fut. Perf.* _____

8. *respondēre:* 3rd sing.

Pres. _____	*Perf.* _____
Imp. _____	*Plup.* _____
Fut. _____	*Fut. Perf.* _____

9. *velle:* 1st sing.

Pres. _____	*Perf.* _____
Imp. _____	*Plup.* _____
Fut. _____	*Fut. Perf.* _____

10. *posse:* 1st pl.

Pres. _____	*Perf.* _____
Imp. _____	*Plup.* _____
Fut. _____	*Fut. Perf.* _____

B. In the space before each verb in column *A*, write the letter of its English translation in column *B*.

Column A	*Column B*
_____ **1.** patēbit	*a.* I did not want
_____ **2.** solvērunt	*b.* they will be able
_____ **3.** ostendimus	*c.* we shall show
_____ **4.** nōluistī	*d.* they had set sail
_____ **5.** patēbat	*e.* they were able
_____ **6.** stetistis	*f.* it will extend
_____ **7.** vēnit	*g.* they will have been able
_____ **8.** poterunt	*h.* they set sail
_____ **9.** solverant	*i.* you were standing
_____ **10.** nōluī	*j.* it extended
_____ **11.** potuerint	*k.* he comes
_____ **12.** poterant	*l.* we are showing
_____ **13.** stābātis	*m.* he came
_____ **14.** venit	*n.* you did not want
_____ **15.** ostendēmus	*o.* you stood

C. Change each verb to the plural.

1. fuerat   _____
2. dēdūxistī   _____
3. dormiēbam   _____
4. studēbō   _____
5. speciēs   _____
6. impellit   _____
7. suscēperō   _____
8. vult   _____
9. coepī   _____
10. cūrābisne   _____

D. In each sentence translate the italicized Latin verb into English.

1. Legiōnēs in castra *redūxit.*   _____
2. Magnum spatium *aberant.*   _____
3. Ad eum locum *vēnerāmus.*   _____
4. Aciem *īnstruam.*   _____
5. *Terrēbātisne* nostrōs?   _____
6. Eō tempore *discesseris.*   _____
7. Montem *nōn trānsierant.*   _____

8. Britannī Rōmānōs *circumdabant.* --------------------------------

9. Cūr cōpiās *cōgis?* --------------------------------

10. Spem in virtūte *pōnēbāmus.* --------------------------------

11. Facere pontem *īnstituistī.* --------------------------------

12. Eās rēs in Galliam *tulerat.* --------------------------------

13. Auxilia mittere *audent.* --------------------------------

14. Tardāre hostēs *nōlēbam.* --------------------------------

15. Aciem cōnstituī *iubēbit.* --------------------------------

16. Aeduī bellō *contenderant.* --------------------------------

17. Ea *gerēmus.* --------------------------------

18. Montem circummūnīre *coepērunt.* --------------------------------

19. *Prōcurrite,* virī. --------------------------------

20. Eōdem diē *cēnābō.* --------------------------------

E. Draw a line through the form that does *not* belong with the others in each group.

1. cavēbit, dīvidet, suscipit, hiemābit

2. complēte, dedistis, resiste, cōnfer

3. videō, gerimus, incipiam, cupiētis

4. poterant, iēcerant, prohibuerant, posuerant

5. rēxistī, persuāsistis, dīxī, trādidit

6. erāmus, agēbāmus, movēbimus, poterāmus

7. scītis, dēligis, vincimus, vāstant

8. cognōscō, pellunt, iungēs, vigilāmus

9. pārēbant, praeficiet, impedīvit, crēditis

10. incitat, iit, coepit, oportuit

F. Translate the English words into Latin.

1. *He killed* equum. --------------------------------

2. *Will you (sing.) report* perīculum? --------------------------------

3. *I have ordered* eōs remanēre. --------------------------------

4. *We were working* in agrīs. --------------------------------

5. *They had not understood* rem. --------------------------------

6. *You (pl.) are ruling* bene. --------------------------------

7. *He will have conquered* frūstrā. --------------------------------

8. *Are they able* respondēre? --------------------------------

9. *She will go* statim. --------------------------------

10. *It is permitted* scrībere. --------------------------------

G. Change each verb to the third person, keeping the same tense and number.

1. perspexī   --
2. valēmus   --
3. fīniam   --
4. eris   --
5. potuistis   --
6. interrogāverās   --
7. movēbimus   --
8. caedēbātis   --
9. nōn vīs   --
10. coeperis   --

H. Rewrite the sentences below, making *all* changes required by the directions in parentheses.

1. Iter *tardābant*. (substitute equivalent form of *facere*)

   ----

2. *Cavē* animal. (change to the plural)

   ----

3. Servōs *līberāvimus*. (change to the singular)

   ----

4. Domum *contendō*. (change to the future)

   ----

5. *Virī* tēla iēcerant. (substitute *Vōs*)

   ----

6. Rēx mīlitēs *exercēbit*. (substitute equivalent form of *dūcere*)

   ----

7. Quī bellum *gerunt?* (change to the future perfect)

   ----

8. Tōtum frūmentum *mīsī*. (change to the plural)

   ----

9. *Ego* omnia cognōvī. (substitute *Tū*)

   ----

10. Sextus captīvum *accūsābat*. (substitute equivalent form of *terrēre*)

Unit II—Verbs, Indicative Passive

*Lesson 20—*PRESENT INDICATIVE PASSIVE

FIRST CONJUGATION

servāre, to save; present stem, **servā-**

I am saved, I am being saved

serv*or*	serv*āmur*
serv*āris*	serv*āminī*
serv*ātur*	serv*antur*

SECOND CONJUGATION

monēre, to warn; present stem, **monē-**

I am warned, I am being warned

mon*eor*	mon*ēmur*
mon*ēris*	mon*ēminī*
mon*ētur*	mon*entur*

THIRD CONJUGATION

vincere, to conquer; present stem, **vince-**

I am conquered, I am being conquered

vinc*or*	vinc*imur*
vinc*eris*	vinc*iminī*
vinc*itur*	vinc*untur*

-IŌ THIRD CONJUGATION

capere, to take; present stem, **cape-**

I am taken, I am being taken

cap*ior*	cap*imur*
cap*eris*	cap*iminī*
cap*itur*	cap*iuntur*

FOURTH CONJUGATION

impedīre, to hinder; present stem, **impedī-**

I am hindered, I am being hindered

imped*ior*	imped*īmur*
imped*īris*	imped*īminī*
imped*ītur*	imped*iuntur*

Note

1. The passive personal endings are:

-r	-mur
-ris	-minī
-tur	-ntur

2. These endings are substituted for the active endings of the present tense. However, in the first person singular, the final **o** is kept, making the ending **-or.**

3. In the second person singular of third and **-iō** third conjugation verbs, the final **e** of the present stem is kept and not changed to **i** as in the active voice. Thus,

ACTIVE	PASSIVE
vincis	vinc*eris*
capis	cap*eris*

57

4. The present passive of **facere** is highly irregular, having active endings. The meaning is varied too: *be made, happen, become.*

fīō   (rarely used)

fīs   (rarely used)

fit   fīunt

5. The verb **vidēre** in the passive often means *to seem.*

Puer ab amīcīs **vidētur.**	The boy *is seen* by his friends.
But	
Puer īnfēlīx **vidētur.**	The boy *seems* unhappy.

6. In the active voice, the subject generally performs some action. In the passive voice, the subject is acted upon.

ACTIVE VOICE	PASSIVE VOICE
Servus nāvigium **trahit.**	Nāvigium ā servō **trahitur.**
The slave drags the boat.	The boat is dragged by the slave.
Mīlitēs tēla **iaciunt.**	Tēla ab mīlitibus **iaciuntur.**
The soldiers are throwing weapons.	Weapons are being thrown by the soldiers.
Mittisne nūntiōs?	**Mitterisne** ā cōnsule?
Are you sending messengers?	Are you being sent by the consul?

EXERCISES

A. Complete the English translation.

1. Rēx ab suīs appellātur.   _____ king by his own men.

2. Perīculum augētur.   The danger _____.

3. Iniūriīs prohibēmur.   _____ from injuries.

4. Terrērisne hāc rē?   _____ by this thing?

5. Bella geruntur.   Wars _____.

6. Cūr impedīminī?   Why _____?

7. Omnia temptantur.   All things _____.

8. Ad vīllam addūcor.   _____ to the country house.

9. Ad Caesarem mittuntur.   _____ to Caesar.

10. Rēs vidētur gravis.   The matter _____ serious.

B. Write all the specified forms in the present indicative passive.

1. *audīre* and *exīstimāre:* third person plural _____

2. *petere* and *timēre:* second person singular _____

3. *vulnerāre:* first person singular and plural _____

4. *capere:* second person singular and plural _____

5. *retinēre:* third person singular and plural _____

C. Change each verb from the active to the passive, and then translate each passive form into English.

	PASSIVE	TRANSLATION
1. dōnant	------------------------------	------------------------------
2. iungit	------------------------------	------------------------------
3. tenēmus	------------------------------	------------------------------
4. accipis	------------------------------	------------------------------
5. repellō	------------------------------	------------------------------
6. ēdūcitis	------------------------------	------------------------------
7. occupatne?	------------------------------	------------------------------
8. nōn interficiunt	------------------------------	------------------------------
9. ferimus	------------------------------	------------------------------
10. incitās	------------------------------	------------------------------

D. Underline the verb that correctly translates the italicized English words.

1. *He is sent ahead* cum explōrātōribus.
   (a) Praemittit   (b) Praemittitur   (c) Praemittuntur

2. *We are advised* ā rēge.
   (a) Monēminī   (b) Monēmus   (c) Monēmur

3. Fīlia eius *is seized*.
   (a) capitur   (b) caperis   (c) capior

4. Tū *are not taught* bene.
   (a) nōn docēris   (b) nōn docēs   (c) nōn docēminī

5. Mīlitēs *are enrolled*.
   (a) cōnscrībitur   (b) cōnscrībuntur   (c) cōnscrībimur

6. Ego *am allowed* discēdere.
   (a) permittō   (b) permittor   (c) permittam

7. Vōs *are being chosen*.
   (a) dēligiminī   (b) dēligeris   (c) dēligimur

8. Inter duās aciēs *the battle is being fought*.
   (a) contendit   (b) contenduntur   (c) contenditur

9. *Are* tū *ordered* pugnāre?
   (a) Iubēsne   (b) Iubērisne   (c) Iubetne

10. Omnēs sociī *are being called together*.
    (a) convocant   (b) convocātur   (c) convocantur

E. Change each verb to the plural.

1. suscipitur	------------------------------
2. iūdicor	------------------------------
3. movēris	------------------------------
4. pōneris	------------------------------
5. fit	------------------------------

Lesson 21—IMPERFECT INDICATIVE PASSIVE

FIRST CONJUGATION

servāre, to save; present stem, **servā-**

I was saved, I was being saved

servā*bar*	servā*bāmur*
servā*bāris*	servā*bāminī*
servā*bātur*	servā*bantur*

SECOND CONJUGATION

monēre, to warn; present stem, **monē-**

I was warned, I was being warned

monē*bar*	monē*bāmur*
monē*bāris*	monē*bāminī*
monē*bātur*	monē*bantur*

THIRD CONJUGATION

vincere, to conquer; present stem, **vince-**

I was conquered, I was being conquered

vincē*bar*	vincē*bāmur*
vincē*bāris*	vincē*bāminī*
vincē*bātur*	vincē*bantur*

-IŌ THIRD CONJUGATION

capere, to take; present stem, **cape-**

I was taken, I was being taken

capiē*bar*	capiē*bāmur*
capiē*bāris*	capiē*bāminī*
capiē*bātur*	capiē*bantur*

FOURTH CONJUGATION

impedīre, to hinder; present stem, **impedī-**

I was hindered, I was being hindered

impediē*bar*	impediē*bāmur*
impediē*bāris*	impediē*bāminī*
impediē*bātur*	impediē*bantur*

Note

1. The endings of the imperfect indicative passive for all conjugations are:

-bar	-bāmur
-bāris	-bāminī
-bātur	-bantur

2. These endings are substituted for the active endings of the imperfect.

3. The imperfect passive of **facere** has active endings: **fīēbam, fīēbās,** etc.

EXERCISES

A. Change each verb from the present passive to the imperfect passive, and then translate each new form into English.

	IMPERFECT PASSIVE	TRANSLATION
1. relinqueris	------------------------------	------------------------------
2. ēiciuntur	------------------------------	------------------------------
3. iubeor	------------------------------	------------------------------

60

4. tardātur   _____   _____

5. opprimimur   _____   _____

6 impedīminī   _____   _____

7. putantur   _____   _____

8. nōn moneor   _____   _____

9. audīrisne?   _____   _____

10. vidētur   _____   _____

B. Write all the specified forms in the imperfect indicative passive.

1. *dīcere:* third person singular and plural   _____

2. *pācāre:* first person singular and plural   _____

3. *exercēre:* second person singular and plural   _____

4. *scīre* and *facere:* third person plural   _____

5. *portāre* and *habēre:* third person singular   _____

C. Complete the English translation.

1. Auxilia in Galliam mittēbantur.   Auxiliary troops _____ into Gaul.

2. Dux dēligēbātur.   The leader _____

3. Summam scientiam habēre exīstimābāris.   _____ to have the greatest knowledge.

4. Ex castrīs ēdūcēbāmur.   _____ out of camp.

5. Vigilāre nōn mandābāminī.   _____ to keep awake.

6. Ab prīncipe incitābar.   _____ by the chief.

7. Bellō premēbantur.   _____ by war.

8. Urbs ab incolīs dēfendēbātur.   The city _____ by its inhabitants.

9. Ā Caesare monēbāmur.   _____ by Caesar.

10. Cōgēbārisne ex nāvī ēgredī?   _____ to disembark?

D. Translate the English words into Latin.

1. Rēx *was feared.*   _____

2. Agrī *were being destroyed.*   _____

3. Ā maiōribus cōpiīs *you (pl.) were conquered.*   _____

4. Cūr *were we being driven out?*   _____

5. *I was ordered* prōcurrere.   _____

6. *You (sing.) were not wounded* graviter.   _____

7. Oppidum *was being fortified.*   _____

8. Ā duce *they were praised.*   _____

9. Quis ab cōnsule *was being sought?*   _____

10. *We used to be attacked* nocte.   _____

E. Express the idea of each sentence in the passive voice.

EXAMPLE: Mīlitēs oppidum dēfendēbant.   Oppidum ā mīlitibus dēfendēbātur.

1. Caesar virōs redūcēbat.   Virī ā Caesare _____.

2. Magister puerum docēbat.   Puer ā magistrō _____.

3. Līberī nōs spectābant.   Nōs ā līberīs _____.

4. Hostēs tē prohibēbant.   Tū ab hostibus _____.

5. Homō mē interrogābat.   Ego ab homine _____.

Composition of a Roman Legion

□ = 60 soldiers

1 century (**centuria**)

□ □ = □□ = 120 soldiers

2 centuries   1 maniple (**manipulus**)

□□ □□ □□ = □□□□□□ = 360 soldiers

3 maniples   1 cohort (**cohors**)

10 cohorts

= 3600 soldiers

1 legion (**legiō**)

Lesson 22—FUTURE INDICATIVE PASSIVE

FIRST CONJUGATION

servāre, to save; present stem, **servā-**

I shall (will) be saved

servā*bor*	servā*bimur*
servā*beris*	servā*biminī*
servā*bitur*	servā*buntur*

SECOND CONJUGATION

monēre, to warn; present stem, **monē-**

I shall (will) be warned

monē*bor*	monē*bimur*
monē*beris*	monē*biminī*
monē*bitur*	monē*buntur*

THIRD CONJUGATION

vincere, to conquer; present stem, **vince-**

I shall (will) be conquered

vinc*ar*	vinc*ēmur*
vinc*ēris*	vinc*ēminī*
vinc*ētur*	vinc*entur*

-IŌ THIRD CONJUGATION

capere, to take; present stem, **cape-**

I shall (will) be taken

capi*ar*	capi*ēmur*
capi*ēris*	capi*ēminī*
capi*ētur*	capi*entur*

FOURTH CONJUGATION

impedīre, to hinder; present stem, **impedī-**

I shall (will) be hindered

impedi*ar*	impedi*ēmur*
impedi*ēris*	impedi*ēminī*
impedi*ētur*	impedi*entur*

Note

1. The endings of the future indicative passive are as follows:

1ST AND 2ND CONJUGATIONS		3RD, -IŌ 3RD, AND 4TH CONJUGATIONS	
-bor	-bimur	-ar	-ēmur
-beris	-biminī	-ēris	-ēminī
-bitur	-buntur	-ētur	-entur

2. These endings are substituted for the active endings of the future.

3. The future passive of **facere** has active endings: **fīam, fīēs,** etc.

4. In third conjugation verbs, a long **e** distinguishes the future passive from the present passive in the second person singular.

PRESENT	FUTURE
vinc*e*ris, you are conquered	vinc*ē*ris, you will be conquered

63

5. The future passive of third conjugation verbs is often confused with the present passive of second conjugation verbs because of the similarity of endings. Distinguish the following:

THIRD CONJUGATION		SECOND CONJUGATION	
FUTURE		PRESENT	
vinc*ēris*	you will be conquered	mon*ēris*	you are warned
vinc*ētur*	he will be conquered	mon*ētur*	he is warned
vinc*ēmur*	we shall be conquered	mon*ēmur*	we are warned
vinc*ēminī*	you will be conquered	mon*ēminī*	you are warned
vinc*entur*	they will be conquered	mon*entur*	they are warned

EXERCISES

A. Change each verb from the active to the passive, and then translate each passive form into English.

	PASSIVE	TRANSLATION
1. dēligent	-----------------------------	-----------------------------
2. līberābis	-----------------------------	-----------------------------
3. impediet	-----------------------------	-----------------------------
4. iubēbitis	-----------------------------	-----------------------------
5. mittēmus	-----------------------------	-----------------------------
6. laudābō	-----------------------------	-----------------------------
7. audiēs	-----------------------------	-----------------------------
8. appellābit	-----------------------------	-----------------------------
9. faciam	-----------------------------	-----------------------------
10. exercēbunt	-----------------------------	-----------------------------

B. Write all the specified forms in the future indicative passive.

1. *relinquere:* third person singular and plural   ------------------------------

2. *tenēre:* second person singular and plural   ------------------------------

3. *capere:* first person singular and plural   ------------------------------

4. *locāre* and *iacere:* third person plural   ------------------------------

5. *prohibēre* and *mūnīre:* third person singular   ------------------------------

C. Complete the English translation.

1. Animō regēris.   ------------------------------- by your mind.

2. Mīlitēs discēdere iubēbuntur.   The soldiers ------------------------ to leave.

3. Nōn iam dēfendēminī.   No longer ------------------------------.

4. Praemium Mārcō dabitur.   The prize ------------------------ to Marcus.

5. Ab omnibus recipiēmur.   ------------------------------- by all.

6. Eō tempore nōn pācābor.   At that time ------------------------------.

7. Prīmā lūce interficiētur.   --- at dawn.

8. Mox aedificābuntur.   --- soon.

9. Mittērisne ad Britanniam?   --- to Britain?

10. Ā cōnsule iudicābimur.   --- by the consul.

D. In each group there is one verb in the future passive. Underline it and then write its meaning.

1. petētur, timētur, dēbētur   ---

2. retinēris, capiēris, vidēris   ---

3. mūniuntur, dūcēbantur, vulnerābuntur   ---

4. habēmur, dīcimur, agēmur   ---

5. vincam, portābor, locābō   ---

E. Translate the English words into Latin.

1. Ā nūllō *they will be seen.*   ---

2. *It will not be written* hodiē.   ---

3. Quis *will be named* amīcus?   ---

4. *I shall not be hindered* ā tē.   ---

5. *You will be put,* Iūlia, in magnō perīculō.   ---

6. *We shall be killed* sī manēbimus.   ---

7. *You will be given up,* puerī.   ---

8. *Will they be defeated* in proeliō?   ---

9. Tēla *will be thrown.*   ---

10. Propter vulnera *we shall be delayed.*   ---

Masks

Masks served two very important purposes on the Roman stage. First, they enabled the actors to play many different characters in a single play. Secondly, the peculiar formation of the mask with its wide-open mouth amplified the actor's voice, which would otherwise hardly be heard in a large open-air theater. Occasionally, modern authors like Eugene O'Neill have employed the mask to indicate a dual personality in a character.

Lesson 23—PERFECT INDICATIVE PASSIVE OF FIRST AND SECOND CONJUGATION VERBS

FIRST CONJUGATION

servāre, to save; participial stem, **servāt-**

I was (have been) saved

servāt*us*, -a, -um	{ *sum* *es* *est*	servāt*ī*, -ae, -a	{ *sumus* *estis* *sunt*

SECOND CONJUGATION

monēre, to warn; participial stem, **monit-**

I was (have been) warned

monit*us*, -a, -um	{ *sum* *es* *est*	monit*ī*, -ae, -a	{ *sumus* *estis* *sunt*

Note

1. The perfect passive consists of two parts. The first part is the participial stem plus the endings **-us, -a, -um** for the singular, and **-ī, -ae, -a** for the plural. The second part is the present of the verb **esse.**

2. The first part is called the *perfect passive participle*. Like an adjective, the participle agrees with the subject in gender, number, and case.

Nūntius monit*us est.* The messenger was warned.
<small>masc., sing., nom.</small>

Nūntiī monit*ī sunt.* The messengers were warned.
<small>masc., pl., nom.</small>

Fēmina monit*a est.* The woman was warned.
<small>fem., sing., nom.</small>

Fēminae monit*ae sunt.* The women were warned.
<small>fem., pl., nom.</small>

3. The perfect passive participle of verbs of the first conjugation ends in **-ātus, -a, -um.**

INFINITIVE	PERFECT PASSIVE PARTICIPLE
laudāre	*laudātus*
occupāre	*occupātus*
vāstāre	*vāstātus*

66

4. The perfect passive participle of verbs of the second conjugation ends in **-tus** or **-sus**. However, the spelling of the participial stem varies, as shown in the following list of verbs:

Endings in -tus

INFINITIVE	PERFECT PASSIVE PARTICIPLE
augēre	*auctus*
complēre	*complētus*
dēbēre	*dēbitus*
docēre	*doctus*
exercēre	*exercitus*
habēre (and its compounds)	*habitus*
monēre	*monitus*
movēre (and its compounds)	*mōtus*
tenēre (and its compounds)	*tentus*
terrēre (and its compounds)	*territus*

Endings in -sus

iubēre	*iussus*
respondēre	*respōnsus*
vidēre	*vīsus*

5. Some verbs lack a perfect passive participle and therefore cannot be used in the passive voice. Two such verbs are **manēre** and **studēre**.

EXERCISES

A. Complete the perfect indicative passive of each verb by supplying the correct ending of the participle and the proper form of the verb **esse**.

1. Signum dat _____ _____.

2. Īnsidiae prohibit _____ _____.

3. Nōs iuss _____ _____.

4. Fossa complēt _____ _____.

5. Tū nōn vīs _____ _____.

6. Virī incitāt _____ _____.

7. Proelia nūntiāt _____ _____.

8. Ego retent _____ _____.

9. Servus līberāt _____ _____.

10. Vōs monit _____ _____.

B. Complete the English translation.

1. Clāmōre permōtī sunt.   _____ by the shouting.

2. Appellātus est socius.   _____ an ally.

3. Cūr trāns flūmen portātī estis?   Why _____ across the river?

4. Ab hostibus nōn superātī sumus.   _____ by the enemy.

5. Fugere iussus sum.   _____ to flee.

6. Ā magistrō monita es.   _____ by the teacher.

7. Caesarī nūntiātum est.   _____ to Caesar.

8. Oppida occupāta sunt.   The towns _____.

9. Numquam laudātae sumus.   Never _____

10. Cōpiae hostium vīsae sunt.   The forces of the enemy _____

C. Write all the specified forms in the perfect indicative passive.

1. *augēre:* third person singular and plural   _____

2. *vulnerāre:* first person singular and plural   _____

3. *pācāre:* second person singular and plural   _____

4. *habēre* and *spectāre:* third person plural   _____

5. *putāre* and *movēre:* third person singular   _____

D. Change each verb to the plural.

1. Puer rogātus est.   Puerī _____

2. Ab omnibus vīsa es.   Ab omnibus _____

3. Auxilium nōn retentum est.   Auxilia nōn _____

4. Ā duce incitātus sum.   Ā duce _____

5. Nāvis armāta est.   Nāvēs _____

E. Express the idea of each sentence in the passive voice.

1. Servus equum cūrāvit.   Equus ā servō _____

2. Dux mīlitēs exercuit.   Mīlitēs ā duce _____

3. Tū mē vulnerāvistī.   Ego ā tē _____

4. Vir puellam servāvit.   Puella ā virō _____

5. Nostrī signa vīdērunt.   Signa ā nostrīs _____

Hadrian's Tomb

Erected in the second century A.D. by the emperor Hadrian as a mausoleum for himself and his successors, Hadrian's Tomb remains today a symbol in stone of Rome, the Eternal City. Now the tomb, called Castel Sant'Angelo, is a museum that attracts many tourists.

Lesson 24—PERFECT INDICATIVE PASSIVE OF THIRD CONJUGATION VERBS

vincere, to conquer; participial stem, **vict-**

I was (have been) conquered

vict*us*, -*a*, -*um*	$\begin{cases} sum \\ es \\ est \end{cases}$	vict*ī*, -*ae*, -*a*	$\begin{cases} sumus \\ estis \\ sunt \end{cases}$

Note

1. The perfect passive participle of verbs of the third conjugation ends in **-tus** or **-sus**. However, the spelling of the participial stem varies, as shown in the following list of verbs:

Endings in -tus

INFINITIVE	PERFECT PASSIVE PARTICIPLE
agere (and its compounds)	*āctus*
cognōscere	*cognitus*
contendere	*contentus*
crēdere	*crēditus*
dēdere	*dēditus*
dīcere	*dictus*
dūcere (and its compounds)	*ductus*
gerere	*gestus*
īnstruere	*īnstrūctus*
intellegere	*intellēctus*
iungere (and its compounds)	*iūnctus*
legere (and its compounds)	*lēctus*
ostendere	*ostentus*
petere	*petītus*
pōnere (and its compounds)	*positus*
quaerere	*quaesītus*
reddere	*redditus*
regere	*rēctus*
relinquere	*relictus*
scrībere (and its compounds)	*scrīptus*
solvere	*solūtus*
statuere (and its compounds)	*statūtus*
sūmere (and its compounds)	*sūmptus*
tollere	*sublātus*
trādere	*trāditus*
trahere	*trāctus*
vincere	*victus*

69

Endings in -sus

INFINITIVE	PERFECT PASSIVE PARTICIPLE
caedere	*caesus*
claudere	*clausus*
dēfendere	*dēfēnsus*
dīvidere	*dīvīsus*
incendere	*incēnsus*
lūdere	*lūsus*
mittere	*missus*
pellere	*pulsus*
premere	*pressus*
vertere	*versus*

2. The participial stem of the irregular verb **ferre** is **lāt-**, making the perfect passive participle **lātus, -a, -um.** The perfect passive participle of **cōnferre** is **collātus**; and of **īnferre, illātus.**

EXERCISES

A. Complete the English translation.

1. Bellum diū gestum est.   War _____ for a long time.

2. Ab hostibus pulsī sunt.   _____ by the enemy.

3. Cūr ā mātre relictus es?   Why _____ by your mother?

4. Aequē rēctī sumus.   _____ fairly.

5. Ā praetōre dēfēnsa est.   _____ by the judge.

6. Ad Graeciam missus sum.   _____ to Greece.

7. Ab omnibus nōn intellēctī estis.   _____ by all.

8. Ancorae sublātae sunt.   The anchors _____.

9. Ā tribūnō petītus est.   _____ by the tribune.

10. Ad rēgem adductī sumus.   _____ to the king.

B. Write all the specified forms in the perfect indicative passive.

1. *premere:* second person singular and plural   _____

2. *iungere:* third person singular and plural   _____

3. *ferre:* first person singular and plural   _____

4. *dīcere* and *claudere:* third person plural   _____

5. *vertere* and *sūmere:* third person singular   _____

C. Fill in the blanks with the correct form of the verb in italics.

1. *ductus sum:*   virī _____   puella _____

2. *īnstrūcta est:*   prīma aciēs _____   nōs _____

3. *cōnscrīptus es:*   mīlitēs _____   vōs _____

4. *caesus sum:*   legiōnēs _____   agmen _____

5. *incēnsum est:*   oppida _   vīcus _

6. *trāctus sum:*   tū _   quis _ ?

7. *dīvīsus est:*   Gallia _ _ _ _ _ _ _ _ _ _ _ _ _ _ _ _ _ _   id _

8. *trāditī sunt:*   ego _   cohortēs _ _ _ _ _ _ _ _ _ _ _ _ _ _ _ _ _ _

9. *victus sum:*   Gallī _ _ _ _ _ _ _ _ _ _ _ _ _ _ _ _ _ _ _   nōs _

10. *redditus est:*   tēlum _ _ _ _ _ _ _ _ _ _ _ _ _ _ _ _ _ _   equus cibusque _ _ _ _ _ _ _ _ _ _ _ _ _

D. Translate the English words into Latin.

1. Nāvēs *have been joined.*   _

2. Nōs ad Italiam *were sent.*   _

3. Omne frūmentum *was used up.*   _

4. Nūntiī *have been sent ahead.*   _

5. Ego *was led out.*   _

6. *You (pl.) were not conquered* ab hostibus.   _

7. *It has been decided* ab omnibus.   _

8. Multa bella *were waged.*   _

9. Cūr *have you (sing.) been driven out?*   _

10. *He was shown* imperātōrī.   _

E. Express the idea of each sentence in the passive voice.

1. Imperātor hostēs oppressit.   Hostēs ab imperātōre _ -

2. Puer librum āmīsit.   Liber ā puerō _ -

3. Caesar auxilia remīsit.   Auxilia ā Caesare _ -

4. Adulēscēns sententiam prōposuit.   Sententia ab adulēscente _ -

5. Captīvī portās clausērunt.   Portae ā captīvīs _ -

Triremes

Triremes, war-galleys equipped with three banks of oars, were propelled by oars and sails. They attained a speed nearly equal to that of a modern steamboat. The rostrum, or beak, below the prow was used to ram another vessel.

Lesson 25—PERFECT INDICATIVE PASSIVE OF *-IŌ* THIRD AND FOURTH CONJUGATION VERBS

-IŌ THIRD CONJUGATION

capere, to take; participial stem, **capt-**

I was (have been) taken

FOURTH CONJUGATION

impedīre, to hinder; participial stem, **impedīt-**

I was (have been) hindered

capt*us*, -a, -um	sum / es / est	capt*ī*, -ae, -a	sumus / estis / sunt	impedīt*us*, -a, -um	sum / es / est	impedīt*ī*, -ae, -a	sumus / estis / sunt

Note

1. The perfect passive participle of -iō third conjugation verbs ends in **-tus.** However, the spelling of the participial stem varies, as shown in the following list of verbs:

INFINITIVE	PERFECT PASSIVE PARTICIPLE
capere	*captus*
cupere	*cupītus*
facere	*factus*
iacere	*iactus*
specere (and its compounds)	*spectus*

2. Compounds of **capere, facere,** and **iacere** change the **a** of the stem to **e** in the perfect passive participle.

captus	*but*	acc**e**ptus
factus	*but*	cōnf**e**ctus
iactus	*but*	coni**e**ctus

3. The perfect passive participle of most fourth conjugation verbs ends in **-ītus.** Note the two exceptions in the list below.

INFINITIVE	PERFECT PASSIVE PARTICIPLE
audīre	*audītus*
fīnīre	*fīnītus*
impedīre	*impedītus*
mūnīre	*mūnītus*
scīre (and its compounds)	*scītus*
sentīre	*sēnsus*
venīre (and its compounds)	*ventus*

EXERCISES

A. Change each verb to the plural.

1. Hostis interfectus est.   Hostēs _____.

2. Cūr iactum est tēlum?   Cūr _____ tēla?

3. Ā praesidiō impedīta sum.   Ā praesidiō _____.

4. Ā magistrō cōnspectus es.   Ā magistrō _____.

5. Scūtum inventum est.   Scūta _____.

B. Complete the English translation.

1. Verba vēra audīta sunt.   True words _____ .

2. Quī circumventī sunt?   Who _____ ?

3. Oppidum mūnītum est.   The town _____ .

4. Ab cōnsule acceptus sum.   _____ by the consul.

5. Praefectus es, Mārce.   _____ , Marcus.

6. Fēminae captae sunt.   The women _____ .

7. Captīvus ēiectus est.   The prisoner _____ .

8. Subsidium cupītum est.   Aid _____ .

9. Ā prīncipe cōnspectī sumus.   _____ by the chief.

10. Ubi impedītae estis?   Where _____ ?

C. Write all the specified forms in the perfect indicative passive.

1. *fīnīre:* third person singular and plural   _____

2. *perspicere:* second person singular and plural   _____

3. *audīre:* first person singular and plural   _____

4. *iacere* and *scīre:* third person plural   _____

5. *sentīre* and *interficere:* third person singular _____

D. Translate into Latin.

1. he has been received   _____

2. it was undertaken   _____

3. she was observed   _____

4. we have been heard   _____

5. you (sing.) were put in charge _____

6. I was captured   _____

7. they (n.) have been finished _____

8. you (pl.) were hindered   _____

9. it has been fortified   _____

10. they (f.) were made   _____

E. Express the idea of each sentence in the passive voice.

1. Cōnsul calamitātem sēnsit.   Calamitās ā cōnsule _____ .

2. Barbarī tēla coniēcērunt.   Tēla ā barbarīs _____ .

3. Hostēs vōs impedīvērunt.   Vōs ab hostibus _____ .

4. Ariovistus nōs cēpit.   Nōs ab Ariovistō _____ .

5. Nūntius negōtium suscēpit.   Negōtium ā nūntiō _____ .

Lesson 26—PLUPERFECT AND FUTURE PERFECT INDICATIVE PASSIVE

PLUPERFECT PASSIVE

servāre, to save; participial stem, **servāt-**   **vincere,** to conquer; participial stem, **vict-**

I had been saved   I had been conquered

servāt*us*, -a, -um	$\begin{cases} eram \\ erās \\ erat \end{cases}$	servāt*ī*, -ae, a	$\begin{cases} erāmus \\ erātis \\ erant \end{cases}$	vict*us*, -a, -um	$\begin{cases} eram \\ erās \\ erat \end{cases}$	vict*ī*, -ae, -a	$\begin{cases} erāmus \\ erātis \\ erant \end{cases}$

FUTURE PERFECT PASSIVE

I shall (will) have been saved   I shall (will) have been conquered

servāt*us*, -a, -um	$\begin{cases} erō \\ eris \\ erit \end{cases}$	servāt*ī*, -ae, -a	$\begin{cases} erimus \\ eritis \\ erunt \end{cases}$	vict*us*, -a, -um	$\begin{cases} erō \\ eris \\ erit \end{cases}$	vict*ī*, -ae, -a	$\begin{cases} erimus \\ eritis \\ erunt \end{cases}$

Note

1. The pluperfect indicative passive of all verbs consists of the perfect passive participle plus the imperfect of the verb **esse.**

2. The future perfect indicative passive of all verbs consists of the perfect passive participle plus the future of the verb **esse.**

EXERCISES

A. Change each verb to the plural.

1. praemissus erat _____

2. ductus erō _____

3. vīsus erās _____

4. ācta erit _____

5. līberāta eris _____

6. audītus eram _____

7. fīnītum erat _____

8. lāta erās _____

9. susceptum erit _____

10. dēlēctus eram _____

B. Translate the *rewritten* verbs in Exercise A into English.

1. --
2. --
3. --
4. --
5. --
6. --
7. --
8. --
9. --
10. --

C. Write all the specified forms in the pluperfect and future perfect passive.

1. *vincere:* third person plural   ---------------------------------------
2. *rogāre:* third person singular   ---------------------------------------
3. *iubēre:* first person plural   ---------------------------------------
4. *capere:* second person singular   ---------------------------------------
5. *impedīre:* first person singular   ---------------------------------------

D. Underline the correct English translation.

1. aedificāta erant   (they had been built, they will have been built)
2. positī eritis   (you will have been put, you had been put)
3. mōtī erāmus   (we shall have been moved, we had been moved)
4. interfecta erat   (he had been killed, she had been killed)
5. cōnstitūtum erit   (it will have been decided, it had been decided)

E. Change each verb from the active to the passive.

1. recēperit   ---
2. vulnerāverās   ---
3. rēxerāmus   ---
4. pācāverō   ---
5. vīderant   ---

F. Translate into Latin.

1. they had been saved   -------------------------------------
2. he will have been prevented   -------------------------------------
3. we had been defended   -------------------------------------
4. I had been warned   -------------------------------------
5. you (sing.) will have been sent   -------------------------------------

Lesson 27—MASTERY EXERCISES ON VERBS, INDICATIVE PASSIVE

A. Write a synopsis (six tenses passive) of the following verbs in the form indicated:

1. *vincere:*   3rd pl.   *Pres.* _____   *Perf.* _____

   Imp. _____   *Plup.* _____

   Fut. _____   *Fut. Perf.* _____

2. *movēre:*   1st sing.   *Pres.* _____   *Perf.* _____

   Imp. _____   *Plup.* _____

   Fut. _____   *Fut. Perf.* _____

3. *superāre:*   2nd pl.   *Pres.* _____   *Perf.* _____

   Imp. _____   *Plup.* _____

   Fut. _____   *Fut. Perf.* _____

4. *mūnīre:*   3rd sing.   *Pres.* _____   *Perf.* _____

   Imp. _____   *Plup.* _____

   Fut. _____   *Fut. Perf.* _____

5. *recipere:*   1st pl.   *Pres.* _____   *Perf.* _____

   Imp. _____   *Plup.* _____

   Fut. _____   *Fut. Perf.* _____

6. *amāre:*   2nd sing.   *Pres.* _____   *Perf.* _____

   Imp. _____   *Plup.* _____

   Fut. _____   *Fut. Perf.* _____

7. *ferre:*   3rd pl.   *Pres.* _____   *Perf.* _____

   Imp. _____   *Plup.* _____

   Fut. _____   *Fut. Perf.* _____

8. *mittere:*   1st sing.   *Pres.* _____   *Perf.* _____

   Imp. _____   *Plup.* _____

   Fut. _____   *Fut. Perf.* _____

9. *iubēre:*   2nd pl.   *Pres.* _____   *Perf.* _____

   Imp. _____   *Plup.* _____

   Fut. _____   *Fut. Perf.* _____

10. *facere:*   3rd sing.   *Pres.* _____   *Perf.* _____

   Imp. _____   *Plup.* _____

   Fut. _____   *Fut. Perf.* _____

B. In the space before each verb in column *A*, write the letter of its English translation in column *B*.

	Column A	*Column B*
`------`	**1.** doceor	*a.* you are sought
`------`	**2.** interfectus erat	*b.* we shall have been ruled
`------`	**3.** petēris	*c.* he is being led
`------`	**4.** relinquēbantur	*d.* I was taught
`------`	**5.** rēctī erimus	*e.* he was killed
`------`	**6.** laudābāminī	*f.* I am taught
`------`	**7.** doctus sum	*g.* you will be sought
`------`	**8.** relictī sunt	*h.* he had been killed
`------`	**9.** peteris	*i.* you will be praised
`------`	**10.** dūcētur	*j.* they have been abandoned
`------`	**11.** interfectus est	*k.* he was being led
`------`	**12.** dūcitur	*l.* we had been ruled
`------`	**13.** laudābiminī	*m.* he will be led
`------`	**14.** dūcēbātur	*n.* you were being praised
`------`	**15.** rēctī erāmus	*o.* they were being abandoned

C. Underline the correct English translation.

1. gerēbantur   (they were being waged, they are waged, they have been waged)

2. vulnerāmur   (you are wounded, they are wounded, we are wounded)

3. vocābiminī   (you were called, you are called, you will be called)

4. pulsa est   (he was driven, she was driven, they were driven)

5. factum est   (it happened, it happens, it will happen)

6. audītus erās   (you have been heard, you will have been heard, you had been heard)

7. captī erunt   (they will be taken, they had been taken, they will have been taken)

8. mittarne?   (am I sent?, was I sent?, will I be sent?)

9. prohibēberis   (you are prevented, you will be prevented, you were prevented)

10. dīcitur   (it is said, it has been said, it was said)

D. Change each verb from the active to the passive.

1. vīdī   ------------------------------------

2. interficiet   ------------------------------------

3. vāstant   ------------------------------------

4. trahēbās   ------------------------------------

5. tardāverātis   ------------------------------------

6. armāvimus   ------------------------------------

7. monēbis   ------------------------------------

8. spexerit   ------------------------------------

9. sūmpsērunt _____

10. incitō _____

E. Complete the English translation.

1. Ducēs dēliguntur.   Leaders _____.

2. Agrī cultūra nōn intermittētur.   Cultivation of the field _____.

3. Magnopere perturbābāmur.   _____ greatly _____.

4. Sequī iussī estis.   _____ to follow.

5. Scientiam habēre exīstimābantur.   _____ to have knowledge.

6. Cūr remissus erās?   Why _____?

7. Ab hīs doctus sum.   _____ by them.

8. Cōnsilium cognōscitur.   The plan _____.

9. Animō cōnfīrmātī sunt.   _____ in mind.

10. Perīculum auctum erit.   The danger _____.

F. Change each verb to the plural.

1. collocābitur _____   6. rogārisne _____

2. expelleris _____   7. cōnspecta erit _____

3. impedītus sum _____   8. excipiar _____

4. dēiciēbātur _____   9. complētum est _____

5. exercitus eram _____   10. circumdatur _____

G. Translate into Latin.

1. we were being led _____

2. he had been heard _____

3. they are being prepared _____

4. I have been warned _____

5. you (sing.) will be abandoned _____

6. you (pl.) will have been subdued _____

7. Caesar had been killed _____

8. she has been disturbed _____

9. it was being waged _____

10. they will be cared for _____

H. Express the idea of each sentence in the passive voice.

1. Caesar lēgātōs mīsit.   Lēgātī ā Caesare _____.

2. Rōmānī cōnsulem capient.   Cōnsul ā Rōmānīs _____.

3. Hostēs tē laudāverant.   Tū ab hostibus _____.

4. Omnēs nōs vident.   Nōs ab omnibus _____.

5. Mīlitēs oppidum mūniēbant.   Oppidum ā mīlitibus _____.

6. Germānī vōs petīverint.   Vōs ā Germānīs -- .

7. Servī fēminās servāverant.   Fēminae ab servīs --- .

8. Quis equōs agit?   Ā quō equī -- ?

9. Pater mē tulit.   Ego ā patre --- .

10. Suscipiēbatne Sextus   -- negōtium ā Sextō?
    negōtium?

I. Rewrite the sentences below, making *all* changes required by the directions in parentheses.

1. Ab Gallīs *servātus est*. (substitute equivalent form of *capere*)

----

2. *Ego* dēlēctus eram. (substitute *Nōs*)

----

3. Agrī *vāstantur*. (change to the future)

----

4. In castrīs *relinquēbāris*. (change to the plural)

----

5. Ab omnibus *amātur*. (substitute equivalent form of *petere*)

----

6. Ab hostibus *vīsae sunt*. (change to the singular)

----

7. Pīla *iacta erant*. (change to the present)

----

8. Oppidum *mūnītum est*. (change to the future perfect)

----

9. Arma ā captīvīs *portābuntur*. (substitute equivalent form of *recipere*)

----

10. Nōn *vulnerātus sum*. (change to the second person singular)

Postage Stamps

Roman names and figures appear on the stamps of various countries. **Helvetia,** the ancient name for Switzerland, is found on many Swiss stamps. The figures of **Romulus** and **Remus** being nursed by a wolf frequently appear on Italian stamps.

Unit III—*Principal Parts of Verbs; Infinitives; Participles; Gerund*

Lesson 28—PRINCIPAL PARTS OF VERBS

FIRST CONJUGATION

servō	servāre	servāvī	servātus
I save	to save	I saved	having been saved
	PRESENT STEM	PERFECT STEM	PARTICIPIAL STEM
	servā-	servāv-	servāt-

SECOND CONJUGATION

moneō	monēre	monuī	monitus
I warn	to warn	I warned	having been warned
	PRESENT STEM	PERFECT STEM	PARTICIPIAL STEM
	monē-	monu-	monit-

THIRD CONJUGATION

vincō	vincere	vīcī	victus
I conquer	to conquer	I conquered	having been conquered
	PRESENT STEM	PERFECT STEM	PARTICIPIAL STEM
	vince-	vīc-	vict-

-IŌ THIRD CONJUGATION

capiō	capere	cēpī	captus
I take	to take	I took	having been taken
	PRESENT STEM	PERFECT STEM	PARTICIPIAL STEM
	cape-	cēp-	capt-

FOURTH CONJUGATION

impediō	impedīre	impedīvī	impedītus
I hinder	to hinder	I hindered	having been hindered

PRESENT STEM	PERFECT STEM	PARTICIPIAL STEM
impedī-	impedīv-	impedīt-

Note

1. Most verbs have four principal parts. The first is the present active, first singular; the second is the present active infinitive; the third is the perfect active, first singular; and the fourth is the perfect passive participle. In the case of some verbs that lack a perfect passive participle, the future active participle, ending in **-ūrus, -a, -um,** is given instead.

2. Most first conjugation verbs follow the pattern of **servāre.** Exceptions are:

dō	dare	dedī	datus
stō	stāre	stetī	statūrus
praestō	praestāre	praestitī	praestitus

3. Most second conjugation verbs follow the pattern of **monēre.** The following are exceptions:

augeō	augēre	auxī	auctus
caveō	cavēre	cāvī	cautūrus
compleō	complēre	complēvī	complētus
iubeō	iubēre	iussī	iussus
maneō	manēre	mānsī	mānsūrus
moveō	movēre	mōvī	mōtus
respondeō	respondēre	respondī	respōnsus
sedeō	sedēre	sēdī	sessūrus
suādeō	suādēre	suāsī	suāsūrus
videō	vidēre	vīdī	vīsus

4. The principal parts of third conjugation verbs vary considerably. Below is a list of such verbs, with similarities shown where possible.

agō	agere	ēgī	āctus
cadō	cadere	cecidī	cāsūrus
caedō	caedere	cecīdī	caesus
cēdō	cēdere	cessī	cessūrus
claudō	claudere	clausī	clausus

(like **claudō** are **dīvidō** and **lūdō**)

cognōscō	cognōscere	cognōvī	cognitus
consīdō	consīdere	consēdī	consessūrus
cōnsistō	cōnsistere	cōnstitī	cōnstitūrus

(like **cōnsistō** is **resistō**)

contendō	contendere	contendī	contentus

(like **contendō** are **dēfendō, incendō,** and **ostendō**)

crēdō	crēdere	crēdidī	crēditus

(like crēdō are dēdō, reddō, and trādō)

currō	currere	cucurrī	cursūrus
dīcō	dīcere	dīxī	dictus

(like dīcō are dūcō, īnstruō, intellegō, iungō, regō, and trahō)

gerō	gerere	gessī	gestus
legō	legere	lēgī	lēctus
mittō	mittere	mīsī	missus
pellō	pellere	pepulī	pulsus
petō	petere	petīvī	petītus
pōnō	pōnere	posuī	positus
premō	premere	pressī	pressus
quaerō	quaerere	quaesīvī	quaesītus
relinquō	relinquere	relīquī	relictus
scrībō	scrībere	scrīpsī	scrīptus
solvō	solvere	solvī	solūtus
statuō	statuere	statuī	statūtus
sūmō	sūmere	sūmpsī	sūmptus
tollō	tollere	sustulī	sublātus
vertō	vertere	vertī	versus
vincō	vincere	vīcī	victus

5. In the principal parts of the **-iō** third conjugation verb **capere,** there is a vowel pattern that holds true for two other common verbs of this conjugation, **facere** and **iacere.** This pattern is in the stem of the verb and is as follows:

a	a	ē	a
capiō	capere	cēpī	captus
faciō	facere	fēcī	factus
iaciō	iacere	iēcī	iactus

The *compounds* of these verbs follow a different pattern:

i	i	ē	e
accipiō	accipere	accēpī	acceptus
cōnficiō	cōnficere	cōnfēcī	cōnfectus
coniciō	conicere	coniēcī	coniectus

Other verbs of this conjugation are:

cupiō	cupere	cupīvī	cupītus
fugiō	fugere	fūgī	fūgitūrus
speciō	specere	spexī	spectus

Compounds of **specere,** however, follow the pattern below:

cōnspiciō	cōnspicere	cōnspexī	cōnspectus

6. Most fourth conjugation verbs follow the pattern of **impedīre**. Exceptions are:

sentiō	sentīre	sēnsī	sēnsus
veniō	venīre	vēnī	ventus

7. The irregular verbs below have the following principal parts:

eō	īre	īvī(iī)	itūrus
fero	ferre	tulī	lātus
fīō	fierī	factus sum	——
volō	velle	voluī	——
nōlō	nōlle	nōluī	——

EXERCISES

A. Supply the missing principal part.

	FIRST	SECOND	THIRD	FOURTH
1.	habeō	-------------------	habuī	habitus
2.	dō	dare	-------------------	datus
3.	-------------------	audīre	audīvī	audītus
4.	mittō	mittere	mīsī	-------------------
5.	iaciō	iacere	-------------------	iactus
6.	efficiō	efficere	effēcī	-------------------
7.	-------------------	ēnūntiāre	ēnūntiāvī	ēnūntiātus
8.	maneō	manēre	-------------------	mānsūrus
9.	eō	-------------------	īvī	itūrus
10.	perspiciō	perspicere	perspexī	-------------------

B. All the verbs except one in each group belong to the same conjugation. Draw a line through the one that does *not* belong.

1. rogō, petō, perturbō, vulnerō
2. sentiō, veniō, mūniō, nūntiō
3. recipiō, dēbeō, exerceō, obsideō
4. fugiō, interficiō, conveniō, cupiō
5. trādō, gerō, pācō, dēdō
6. scrīpsī, vīdī, posuī, ēgī
7. mōtus, iussus, doctus, captus
8. tollere, resistere, respondēre, quaerere
9. cōnfēcī, sēdī, incēpī, conspexī
10. rēxī, pugnāvī, stetī, ōrāvī

C. Each verb form below is one of the four principal parts. Indicate which part it is and then translate it into English.

	PRINCIPAL PART	TRANSLATION
EXAMPLE: iactus	4th	having been thrown
1. dīxī		
2. putāre		
3. sciō		
4. monitus		
5. suscipere		
6. habitō		
7. dormīvī		
8. pulsus		
9. patēre		
10. voluī		

D. Write the remaining principal parts of the following verbs:

1. habeō			
2. cōgō			
3. recipiō			
4. audiō			
5. mandō			
6. crēdō			
7. iubeō			
8. faciō			
9. gerō			
10. ferō			

E. Underline the correct Latin translation.

1. to conquer	(vincō, vincere, vīcī, victus)
2. I have placed	(locō, locāre, locāvī, locātus)
3. having been ruled	(regō, regere, rēxī, rēctus)
4. I do not know	(nesciō, nescīre, nescīvī, nescītus)
5. I increased	(augeō, augēre, auxī, auctus)
6. having been taken	(capiō, capere, cēpī, captus)
7. to lead	(dūcō, dūcere, dūxī, ductus)
8. I tell	(nārrō, nārrāre, nārrāvī, nārrātus)
9. I lost	(āmittō, āmittere, āmīsī, āmissus)
10. having been fortified	(mūniō, mūnīre, mūnīvī, mūnītus)

Lesson 29—INFINITIVES

servō

PRESENT STEM	PERFECT STEM	PARTICIPIAL STEM
servā-	**servāv-**	**servāt-**

ACTIVE	PASSIVE
Present: servā*re*, to save	servā*rī*, to be saved
Perfect: servā*visse*, to have saved	servā*tus*, *-a, -um esse*, to have been saved
Future: servāt*ūrus*, *-a, -um esse*, to be about to save	

vincō

PRESENT STEM	PERFECT STEM	PARTICIPIAL STEM
vince-	**vīc-**	**vict-**

ACTIVE	PASSIVE
Present: vince*re*, to conquer	vinc*ī*, to be conquered
Perfect: vīc*isse*, to have conquered	vict*us*, *-a, -um esse*, to have been conquered
Future: vict*ūrus*, *-a, -um esse*, to be about to conquer	

sum   possum

ACTIVE ONLY	
Present: es*se*, to be	pos*se*, to be able
Perfect: fu*isse*, to have been	potu*isse*, to have been able
Future: fut*ūrus*, *-a, -um esse*, to be about to be	

Note

1. Most verbs have six infinitives, three in the active voice and three in the passive. The future passive infinitive, however, is very rarely used, and is therefore not included in the list above.

2. The present active infinitive of all verbs is the second principal part.

3. The present passive infinitive is formed by changing the final **e** of the active infinitive to **ī**. This is true of all verbs except those in the third and **-iō** third conjugation, where the final **ere** is changed to **ī**.

ACTIVE	PASSIVE
servār*e*	servār*ī*
monēr*e*	monēr*ī*
impedīr*e*	impedīr*ī*

But

vinc*ere*	vinc*ī*
cap*ere*	cap*ī*

85

4. The perfect active infinitive is formed by adding the ending **-isse** to the perfect stem.

5. The perfect passive infinitive consists of the fourth principal part plus **esse**.

6. The future active infinitive is formed by adding the endings **-ūrus, -a, -um** to the participial stem plus **esse**.

7. The present passive infinitive of the verb **facere** is **fierī**.

8. The irregular verbs below have the following infinitives:

ACTIVE ONLY			
eō	**volō**	**nōlō**	**coepī**
Present: īre	velle	nōlle	————
Perfect: īvisse (īsse)	voluisse	nōluisse	coepisse
Future: itūrus, -a, -um esse	————	————	————

ferō

	ACTIVE	PASSIVE
Present:	ferre	ferrī
Perfect:	tulisse	lātus esse
Future:	lātūrus, -a, -um esse	

EXERCISES

A. Supply the missing active infinitives.

PRESENT	PERFECT	FUTURE
1. pōnere	----------------------	positūrus esse
2. ----------------------	vēnisse	ventūrus esse
3. clāmāre	clāmāvisse	----------------------
4. vidēre	----------------------	vīsūrus esse
5. ----------------------	cōnfēcisse	cōnfectūrus esse
6. pācāre	pācāvisse	----------------------
7. ----------------------	adfuisse	adfutūrus esse
8. crēdere	----------------------	crēditūrus esse
9. īre	īsse	----------------------
10. fugere	----------------------	fugitūrus esse

B. Change each infinitive from the active to the passive.

1. augēre	----------------------	6. iēcisse	----------------------
2. recēpisse	----------------------	7. interficere	----------------------
3. dīcere	----------------------	8. nūntiāvisse	----------------------
4. cūrāvisse	----------------------	9. impedīre	----------------------
5. mūnīre	----------------------	10. mōvisse	----------------------

C. In the space before each infinitive in column *A*, write the letter of its English translation in column *B*.

	Column A		*Column B*
------	**1.** expellere	*a.*	to have been conquered
------	**2.** locātus esse	*b.*	not to want
------	**3.** vīcisse	*c.*	to have been able
------	**4.** posse	*d.*	to be driven out
------	**5.** velle	*e.*	to have joined
------	**6.** auditūrus esse	*f.*	to be about to place
------	**7.** locātūrus esse	*g.*	to have been
------	**8.** iungī	*h.*	to drive out
------	**9.** potuisse	*i.*	to be about to hear
------	**10.** nōlle	*j.*	to have been placed
------	**11.** expellī	*k.*	to be able
------	**12.** audītus esse	*l.*	to have conquered
------	**13.** iūnxisse	*m.*	to be joined
------	**14.** fuisse	*n.*	to have been heard
------	**15.** victus esse	*o.*	to want

D. Underline the correct Latin translation.

1. to have destroyed   (vāstāre, vāstāvisse, vāstātus esse)

2. to be led   (dūcere, dūcī, dūxisse)

3. to hold   (tenēre, tenērī, tenuisse)

4. to have been praised   (laudārī, laudātus esse, laudāvisse)

5. to be about to see   (vīsus esse, vidērī, vīsūrus esse)

6. to be taken   (sūmere, sūmī, sūmpsisse)

7. to burn   (incendere, incendī, incendisse)

8. to have wished   (cupere, cupītus esse, cupīvisse)

9. to have been loved   (amātus esse, amātūrus esse, amāvisse)

10. to be about to sleep   (dormīre, dormīvisse, dormitūrus esse)

E. Change each infinitive to the perfect tense, keeping the same voice.

1. scīre ---------------------------

2. āctūrus esse ---------------------------

3. līberārī ---------------------------

4. incipere ---------------------------

5. scrībī ---------------------------

6. respōnsūrus esse ---------------------------

7. incitāre ---------------------------

8. habērī ---------------------------

9. discessūrus esse ---------------------------

10. ferre ---------------------------

Lesson 30—PARTICIPLES; GERUND

PARTICIPLES

servāre

<table>
<tr><td align="center">PRESENT STEM</td><td align="center">PARTICIPIAL STEM</td></tr>
<tr><td align="center">servā-</td><td align="center">servāt-</td></tr>
</table>

ACTIVE	PASSIVE
Present: servā**ns**, saving	——
Perfect: ——	servāt**us, -a, -um,** having been saved
Future: servāt**ūrus, -a, -um,** about to save	serva**ndus, -a, -um,** must be saved

capere

<table>
<tr><td align="center">PRESENT STEM</td><td align="center">PARTICIPIAL STEM</td></tr>
<tr><td align="center">cape-</td><td align="center">capt-</td></tr>
</table>

Present: capi**ēns,** taking	——
Perfect: ——	capt**us, -a, -um,** having been taken
Future: capt**ūrus, -a, -um,** about to take	capi**endus, -a, -um,** must be taken

impedīre

<table>
<tr><td align="center">PRESENT STEM</td><td align="center">PARTICIPIAL STEM</td></tr>
<tr><td align="center">impedī-</td><td align="center">impedīt-</td></tr>
</table>

Present: impedi**ēns,** hindering	——
Perfect: ——	impedīt**us, -a, -um,** having been hindered
Future: impedīt**ūrus, -a, -um,** about to hinder	impedi**endus, -a, -um,** must be hindered

Note

1. The present active participle is formed by adding the ending **-ns** to the present stem. However, in **-iō** third conjugation verbs an **i** is inserted before the final **e** of the stem, and in fourth conjugation verbs an **e** is inserted before the **-ns** ending.

2. The future active participle is the same as the future active infinitive without **esse.**

3. The perfect passive participle is the same as the perfect passive infinitive without **esse.**

4. The future passive participle is formed by adding the endings **-ndus, -a, -um** to the present stem. However, in **-iō** third conjugation verbs an **i** is inserted before the final **e** of the stem, and in fourth conjugation verbs an **e** is inserted before the **-ndus** ending. The future passive participle is also known as the gerundive.

5. Latin verbs lack a perfect active and a present passive participle.

6. The irregular verbs below have the following participles:

ACTIVE ONLY				
sum	**possum**	**eō**	**volō**	**nōlō**
Present: ____	potēns	iēns	volēns	nōlēns
Perfect: ____	____		____	____
Future: futūrus, -a, -um	____	itūrus, -a, -um	____	____

ferō

	ACTIVE	PASSIVE
Present: ferēns		____
Perfect: ____		lātus, -a, -um
Future: lātūrus, -a, -um		ferendus, -a, -um

GERUND

	servāre	**capere**	**impedīre**
Genitive:	serva**ndī,** of saving	capie**ndī**	impedie**ndī**
Dative:	serva**ndō,** for saving	capie**ndō**	impedie**ndō**
Accusative:	serva**ndum,** saving	capie**ndum**	impedie**ndum**
Ablative:	serva**ndō,** by saving	capie**ndō**	impedie**ndō**

Note

1. The gerund is a verbal noun. That is to say, it is formed from a verb but functions also as a noun. It exists in the singular only and has no nominative. The gerund should not be confused with the gerundive (future passive participle), such as **servandus, -a, -um.**

2. The gerund is formed by adding the ending **-ndī,** etc., to the present stem. However, in **-iō** third conjugation verbs an **i** is inserted before the final **e** of the stem, and in fourth conjugation verbs an **e** is inserted before the **-ndī** ending.

3. The gerund of **īre** is **eundī** and of **ferre, ferendī.**

EXERCISES

A. Underline the correct English translation.

1. sedēns   (about to sit, sitting, must be seated)

2. missus   (having been sent, sending, about to send)

3. audītūrus   (must be heard, having been heard, about to hear)

4. līberandus   (about to free, must be freed, having been freed)

5. scrībendī   (about to write, of writing, by writing)

6. iaciēns   (throwing, of throwing, by throwing)

7. oppugnātūrus   (must be attacked, having been attacked, about to attack)

8. gerendō   (waging, by waging, of waging)

9. lātus   (having been brought, bringing, about to bring)

10. iēns   (about to go, by going, going)

B. Give the tense and voice of the following participles:

	TENSE	VOICE
1. petītus		
2. mānsūrus		
3. quaerēns		
4. cognōscendus		
5. dēspērāns		
6. solūtūrus		
7. dandum		
8. mūnītus		
9. futūrus		
10. agenda		

C. Write the perfect and future passive participles of the following verbs:

	PERFECT PASSIVE	FUTURE PASSIVE
1. portāre		
2. movēre		
3. mūnīre		
4. dēfendere		
5. cōnficere		
6. occupāre		
7. cōnspicere		
8. iungere		
9. retinēre		
10. ferre		

D. In each group of verb forms there is one gerund. Underline it and then write its meaning.

1. nāvigāns, nāvigandī, nāvigandus   _____

2. dīcendō, dictūrus, dīcendus   _____

3. scienda, scītus, sciendum   _____

4. monendus, monendī, monēns   _____

5. iēns, itūrus, eundō   _____

E. Translate into Latin.

1. having been seen   _____

2. about to ask   _____

3. fleeing --

4. must be done --

5. by destroying --

6. of replying --

7. having been conquered --

8. must be warned --

9. about to choose --

10. seeking --

MASTERY VERB DRILL SHEET

This Verb Drill Sheet can be used with any verb. Write the correct Latin form of the particular verb selected.

1. He will ------------------------------. ------------------------------

2. Have you (sing.) ------------------------------? ------------------------------?

3. They are not ------------------------------ing. ------------------------------

4. We had ------------------------------. ------------------------------

5. I have been ------------------------------. ------------------------------

6. to ------------------------------ ------------------------------

7. Did you (pl.) ------------------------------? ------------------------------?

8. She will have ------------------------------. ------------------------------

9. having been ------------------------------ ------------------------------

10. I am being ------------------------------. ------------------------------

11. They will be ------------------------------. ------------------------------

12. to have been ------------------------------ ------------------------------

13. He was ------------------------------ing. ------------------------------

14. about to ------------------------------ ------------------------------

15. to be ------------------------------ ------------------------------

16. We were being ------------------------------. ------------------------------

17. Sextus had been ------------------------------. Sextus ------------------------------

18. to have ------------------------------ ------------------------------

19. You (sing.) will have been ------------------------------. ------------------------------

20. must be ------------------------------ ------------------------------

21. to be about to ------------------------------ ------------------------------

22. ------------------------------ing ------------------------------

23. by ------------------------------ing ------------------------------

24. They used to ------------------------------. ------------------------------

25. Why does she ------------------------------? Cūr ------------------------------?

Unit IV—*Deponent Verbs*

Lesson 31—DEPONENT VERBS OF THE FIRST AND SECOND CONJUGATIONS

A deponent verb is one that looks passive in form, but is translated as if it were active.

FIRST CONJUGATION   SECOND CONJUGATION

PRINCIPAL PARTS

hortor, hortārī, hortātus sum   **vereor, verērī, veritus sum**

I urge, to urge, I urged   I fear, to fear, I feared

PRESENT			
I urge		I fear	
hort*or*	hort*āmur*	ver*eor*	ver*ēmur*
hort*āris*	hort*āminī*	ver*ēris*	ver*ēminī*
hort*ātur*	hort*antur*	ver*ētur*	ver*entur*

IMPERFECT			
I was urging		I feared (was fearing)	
hortā*bar*	hortā*bāmur*	verē*bar*	verē*bāmur*
hortā*bāris*	hortā*bāminī*	verē*bāris*	verē*bāminī*
hortā*bātur*	hortā*bantur*	verē*bātur*	verē*bantur*

FUTURE			
I shall urge		I shall fear	
hortā*bor*	hortā*bimur*	verē*bor*	verē*bimur*
hortā*beris*	hortā*biminī*	verē*beris*	verē*biminī*
hortā*bitur*	hortā*buntur*	verē*bitur*	verē*buntur*

PERFECT	
I urged	I feared
hortāt*us*, *-a, -um* $\begin{cases} sum \\ es \\ est \end{cases}$ hortātī, *-ae, -a* $\begin{cases} sumus \\ estis \\ sunt \end{cases}$	verit*us*, *-a, -um* $\begin{cases} sum \\ es \\ est \end{cases}$ veritī, *-ae, -a* $\begin{cases} sumus \\ estis \\ sunt \end{cases}$

PLUPERFECT	
I had urged	I had feared
hortāt*us*, *-a, -um* $\begin{cases} eram \\ erās \\ erat \end{cases}$ hortātī, *-ae, -a* $\begin{cases} erāmus \\ erātis \\ erant \end{cases}$	verit*us*, *-a, -um* $\begin{cases} eram \\ erās \\ erat \end{cases}$ veritī, *-ae, -a* $\begin{cases} erāmus \\ erātis \\ erant \end{cases}$

FUTURE PERFECT	
I shall have urged	I shall have feared
hortāt*us*, *-a, -um* $\begin{cases} erō \\ eris \\ erit \end{cases}$ hortātī, *-ae, -a* $\begin{cases} erimus \\ eritis \\ erunt \end{cases}$	verit*us*, *-a, -um* $\begin{cases} erō \\ eris \\ erit \end{cases}$ veritī, *-ae, -a* $\begin{cases} erimus \\ eritis \\ erunt \end{cases}$

INFINITIVES

Present: hortā*rī,* to urge	verē*rī,* to fear
Perfect: hortāt*us, -a, -um esse,* to have urged	verit*us, -a, -um esse,* to have feared
Future: hortāt*ūrus, -a, -um esse,* to be about to urge	verit*ūrus, -a, -um esse,* to be about to fear

PARTICIPLES

Present:	hortā*ns,* urging	verē*ns,* fearing
Perfect:	hortāt*us, -a, -um,* having urged	verit*us, -a, -um,* having feared
Future Active:	hortāt*ūrus, -a, -um,* about to urge	verit*ūrus, -a, -um,* about to fear
Future Passive:	horta*ndus, -a, -um,* must be urged	vere*ndus, -a, -um,* must be feared

GERUND

Genitive:	horta*ndī,* of urging	vere*ndī,* of fearing
Dative:	horta*ndō*	vere*ndō*
Accusative:	horta*ndum*	vere*ndum*
Ablative:	horta*ndō*	vere*ndō*

Note

1. Deponent verbs have three forms, besides the gerund, which are also active in *form* as well as *meaning*. They are the future infinitive and the present and future participles.

2. The future passive participle, also called the *gerundive*, is passive in *meaning* as well as in *form*.

3. With the exception of the gerundive, deponent verbs lack passive meanings. One cannot say in Latin, for example, *he is urged, he was urged,* or *he will be urged,* using the verb **hortor.** A comparison with a regular verb will illustrate this.

REGULAR VERB		DEPONENT VERB	
servō active form	I save active meaning	———	———
servor passive form	I am saved passive meaning	**hortor** passive form	I urge active meaning
servābis	you will save	———	———
servāberis	you will be saved	**hortāberis**	you will urge
servāvit	he saved	———	———
servātus est	he was saved	**hortātus est**	he urged
servātus	having been saved	**hortātus**	having urged

DEPONENT VERBS OF THE FIRST CONJUGATION

arbitror, arbitrārī, arbitrātus sum, think
cōnor, cōnārī, cōnātus sum, try
dominor, dominārī, dominātus sum, rule, hold sway
hortor, hortārī, hortātus sum, urge, encourage
  adhortor, adhortārī, adhortātus sum, urge (strongly)
  cohortor, cohortārī, cohortātus sum, urge (strongly)
mīror, mīrārī, mīrātus sum, wonder at
  admīror, admīrārī, admīrātus sum, wonder at, admire
moror, morārī, morātus sum, delay, stay

DEPONENT VERBS OF THE SECOND CONJUGATION

polliceor, pollicērī, pollicitus sum, promise
vereor, verērī, veritus sum, fear

Note. The principal parts of **audeō** (dare) are **audeō, audēre, ausus sum.**

Audeō is called a *semi-deponent* verb inasmuch as it is deponent in the perfect system only. A synopsis in the third person singular will illustrate this peculiarity.

Present:	**audet**	he dares
Imperfect:	**audēbat**	he dared
Future:	**audēbit**	he will dare

But

Perfect:	**ausus est**	he has dared
Pluperfect:	**ausus erat**	he had dared
Future Perfect:	**ausus erit**	he will have dared

EXERCISES

A. Change each verb to the plural.

1. arbitrātur --
2. ausus sum --
3. verēbāris --
4. pollicēbor --
5. morātus erat --
6. dominātus eris --
7. admīrāta --
8. cohortandus --
9. cōnābitur --
10. adhortābar --

B. In the space before each verb in column *A*, write the letter of its English translation in column *B*.

	Column A	Column B
------	**1.** morābātur	*a.* having urged
------	**2.** pollicitī sumus	*b.* to have wondered at
------	**3.** hortandus	*c.* we thought
------	**4.** mīrātus esse	*d.* he delays
------	**5.** arbitrābāris	*e.* we had promised
------	**6.** morātur	*f.* to be about to wonder at
------	**7.** arbitrābāmur	*g.* must be urged
------	**8.** pollicitī erimus	*h.* he will delay
------	**9.** mīrārī	*i.* you (sing.) thought
------	**10.** hortātus	*j.* we have promised
------	**11.** morābitur	*k.* you (pl.) thought
------	**12.** hortāns	*l.* we shall have promised
------	**13.** arbitrābāminī	*m.* he delayed
------	**14.** pollicitī erāmus	*n.* to wonder at
------	**15.** mīrātūrus esse	*o.* urging

C. Underline the correct form.

1. future third plural: verentur, verēbuntur, verēbantur
2. present infinitive: cōnārī, cōnāns, cōnātus esse
3. imperfect first singular: arbitrābor, arbitror, arbitrābar
4. gerund: dominandī, domināns, dominandus
5. perfect second singular: morātus eris, morātus erās, morātus es
6. present third singular: pollicentur, pollicētur, pollicēris

7. perfect participle: cohortātus, cohortātūrus, cohortandus

8. pluperfect second plural: mīrātus erās, mīrātī erātis, mīrātī eritis

9. perfect infinitive: admīrātus, admīrātus esse, admīrātūrus esse

10. future perfect first plural: ausī eritis, ausī erāmus, ausī erimus

D. Write a synopsis (six tenses) of the following verbs in the form indicated:

1. *vereor:*   3rd sing.   *Pres.* _____   *Perf.* _____

                                Imp. _____   *Plup.* _____

                                Fut. _____   *Fut. Perf.* _____

2. *moror:*   1st pl.   *Pres.* _____   *Perf.* _____

                             Imp. _____   *Plup.* _____

                             Fut. _____   *Fut. Perf.* _____

3. *arbitror:*   2nd sing.   *Pres.* _____   *Perf.* _____

                                  Imp. _____   *Plup.* _____

                                  Fut. _____   *Fut. Perf.* _____

4. *polliceor:*   3rd pl.   *Pres.* _____   *Perf.* _____

                                 Imp. _____   *Plup.* _____

                                 Fut. _____   *Fut. Perf.* _____

5. *cohortor:*   1st sing.   *Pres.* _____   *Perf.* _____

                                  Imp. _____   *Plup.* _____

                                  Fut. _____   *Fut. Perf.* _____

E. Complete the Latin translation.

1. They have dared to leave.   _____ discēdere.

2. Caesar was encouraging his men.   Caesar suōs _____.

3. We are promising money.   Pecūniam _____.

4. You (sing.) had thought he   _____ eum esse servum.
was a slave.

5. You will not delay long,   _____ diū, amīcī.
friends.

6. I fear the gods.   Deōs _____.

7. They used to hold sway   Inter Gallōs _____
among the Gauls.

8. He had admired the buildings.   Aedificia _____.

9. Will she wonder at everything?   _____ omnia?

10. We shall have tried in vain.   Frūstrā _____.

Lesson 32—DEPONENT VERBS OF THE THIRD CONJUGATION

PRINCIPAL PARTS

sequor, sequī, secūtus sum

I follow, to follow, I followed

PRESENT		IMPERFECT		FUTURE	
I follow		I was following		I shall follow	
sequor	sequimur	sequēbar	sequēbāmur	sequar	sequēmur
sequeris	sequiminī	sequēbāris	sequēbāminī	sequēris	sequēminī
sequitur	sequuntur	sequēbātur	sequēbantur	sequētur	sequentur

PERFECT		PLUPERFECT		FUTURE PERFECT	
I followed		I had followed		I shall have followed	
secūtus, -a, -um { sum / es / est		secūtus, -a, -um { eram / erās / erat		secūtus, -a, -um { erō / eris / erit	
secūtī, -ae, -a { sumus / estis / sunt		secūtī, -ae, -a { erāmus / erātis / erant		secūtī, -ae, -a { erimus / eritis / erunt	

INFINITIVES

Present: sequī, to follow
Perfect: secūtus, -a, -um esse, to have followed
Future: secūtūrus, -a, -um esse, to be about to follow

PARTICIPLES

Present: sequēns, following
Perfect: secūtus, -a, -um, having followed
Future Active: secūtūrus, -a, -um, about to follow
Future Passive: sequendus, -a, -um, must be followed

GERUND

Genitive: sequendī, of following
Dative: sequendō
Accusative: sequendum
Ablative: sequendō

97

DEPONENT VERBS OF THE THIRD CONJUGATION

loquor, loquī, locūtus sum, speak
> **colloquor, colloquī, collocūtus sum,** speak with

nancīscor, nancīscī, nactus sum, find, obtain

nāscor, nāscī, nātus sum, be born

proficīscor, proficīscī, profectus sum, set out, depart

sequor, sequī, secūtus sum, follow
> **cōnsequor, cōnsequī, cōnsecūtus sum,** pursue, overtake
> **exsequor, exsequī, exsecūtus sum,** follow up
> **insequor, insequī, insecūtus sum,** follow up, pursue
> **persequor, persequī, persecūtus sum,** follow up, pursue
> **prōsequor, prōsequī, prōsecūtus sum,** follow up, pursue
> **subsequor, subsequī, subsecūtus sum,** follow closely

ūtor, ūtī, ūsus sum, use

EXERCISES

A. Write a synopsis (six tenses) of the following verbs in the form indicated:

1. *ūtor:*   3rd pl.   *Pres.* _____   *Perf.* _____
                             Imp. _____   *Plup.* _____
                             Fut. _____   *Fut. Perf.* _____

2. *loquor:*   1st sing.   *Pres.* _____   *Perf.* _____
                                 Imp. _____   *Plup.* _____
                                 Fut. _____   *Fut. Perf.* _____

3. *nancīscor:*   2nd sing.   *Pres.* _____   *Perf.* _____
                                    Imp. _____   *Plup.* _____
                                    Fut. _____   *Fut. Perf.* _____

4. *proficīscor:*   1st pl.   *Pres.* _____   *Perf.* _____
                                    Imp. _____   *Plup.* _____
                                    Fut. _____   *Fut. Perf.* _____

5. *insequor:*   3rd sing.   *Pres.* _____   *Perf.* _____
                                   Imp. _____   *Plup.* _____
                                   Fut. _____   *Fut. Perf.* _____

B. Underline the correct English translation.

1. loquēbantur   (they were speaking, they had spoken, they have spoken)

2. nāscitur   (he was born, he will be born, he is born)

3. utēmur   (we are using, we shall use, we used)

4. secūtī erātis   (you followed, you have followed, you had followed)

5. nactus es   (I found, you found, he found)

C. Change each verb to the singular.

1. colloquuntur

2. exsequēbāminī

3. profectī sumus

4. ūsa

5. nancīscēmur

6. nātī erant

7. cōnsequendī

8. prōsecūtī eritis

9. locūtae

10. profectūrī

D. Each verb form below is either an infinitive, a participle, or a gerund. Identify each form and then translate it into English.

	IDENTIFICATION	TRANSLATION
1. subsequī		
2. ūtēns		
3. loquendō		
4. nātus		
5. profectus esse		
6. nancīscendus		
7. secūtūrus esse		
8. nāscendī		
9. ūsūrus		
10. locūtus		

E. Complete the Latin translation.

1. He spoke briefly.   Breviter _____.

2. They will set out the next day.   Proximō diē_____.

3. Are you (sing.) using a sword?   _____ gladiō?

4. We were born in Italy.   In Italiā _____

5. Why had you (pl.) followed him?   Cūr eum _____?

6. Having found suitable weather, he   _____ idōneam
   set sail.   tempestātem, solvit.

7. I do not want to set out.   Nōn volō _____.

8. By speaking, he accomplished his   _____ rem cōnfēcit.
   task.

9. We were following the army.   Exercitum _____.

10. I had not used a shield.   _____ scūtō.

Lesson 33—DEPONENT VERBS OF THE -*IŌ* THIRD AND FOURTH CONJUGATIONS

-IŌ THIRD CONJUGATION	FOURTH CONJUGATION
PRINCIPAL PARTS	
gradior, gradī, gressus sum	**experior, experīrī, expertus sum**
I walk, to walk, I walked	I try, to try, I tried

PRESENT			
I walk		I try	
grad*ior*	grad*imur*	exper*ior*	exper*īmur*
grad*eris*	grad*iminī*	exper*īris*	exper*īminī*
grad*itur*	grad*iuntur*	exper*ītur*	exper*iuntur*

IMPERFECT			
I was walking		I was trying	
gradiē*bar*	gradiē*bāmur*	experiē*bar*	experiē*bāmur*
gradiē*bāris*	gradiē*bāminī*	experiē*bāris*	experiē*bāminī*
gradiē*bātur*	gradiē*bantur*	experiē*bātur*	experiē*bantur*

FUTURE			
I shall walk		I shall try	
gradi*ar*	gradi*ēmur*	experi*ar*	experi*ēmur*
gradi*ēris*	gradi*ēminī*	experi*ēris*	experi*ēminī*
gradi*ētur*	gradi*entur*	experi*ētur*	experi*entur*

PERFECT			
I walked		I tried	
gress*us*, -*a, -um* { *sum* *es* *est*	gress*ī*, -*ae, -a* { *sumus* *estis* *sunt*	expert*us*, -*a, -um* { *sum* *es* *est*	expert*ī*, -*ae, -a* { *sumus* *estis* *sunt*

PLUPERFECT			
I had walked		**I had tried**	
gress*us*, -*a*, -*um* {*eram* *erās* *erat*	gress*ī*, -*ae*, -*a* {*erāmus* *erātis* *erant*	expert*us*, -*a*, -*um* {*eram* *erās* *erat*	expert*ī*, -*ae*, -*a* {*erāmus* *erātis* *erant*

FUTURE PERFECT			
I shall have walked		**I shall have tried**	
gress*us*, -*a*, -*um* {*erō* *eris* *erit*	gress*ī*, -*ae*, -*a* {*erimus* *eritis* *erunt*	expert*us*, -*a*, -*um* {*erō* *eris* *erit*	expert*ī*, -*ae*, -*a* {*erimus* *eritis* *erunt*

INFINITIVES

Present: gradī, to walk	experīrī, to try
Perfect: gress*us*, -*a*, -*um esse*, to have walked	expert*us*, -*a*, -*um esse*, to have tried
Future: gress*ūrus*, -*a*, -*um esse*, to be about to walk	expert*ūrus*, -*a*, -*um esse*, to be about to try

PARTICIPLES

Present: gradiē*ns*, walking	experiē*ns*, trying
Perfect: gress*us*, -*a*, -*um*, having walked	expert*us*, -*a*, -*um*, having tried
Future Active: gress*ūrus*, -*a*, -*um*, about to walk	expert*ūrus*, -*a*, -*um*, about to try
Future Passive: gradie*ndus*, -*a*, -*um*, must be walked	experie*ndus*, -*a -um*, must be tried

GERUND

Genitive: gradie*ndī*, of walking	experie*ndī*, of trying
Dative: gradie*ndō*	experie*ndō*
Accusative: gradie*ndum*	experie*ndum*
Ablative: gradie*ndō*	experie*ndō*

DEPONENT VERBS OF THE -IŌ THIRD CONJUGATION

gradior, gradī, gressus sum, walk, go
   aggredior, aggredī, aggressus sum, go to, attack
   ēgredior, ēgredī, ēgressus sum, go out, leave
   prōgredior, prōgredī, prōgressus sum, go forth, advance
morior, morī, mortuus sum, die
patior, patī, passus sum, suffer, allow

Note

The future active participle of **morior** is **moritūrus, -a, -um.**

DEPONENT VERBS OF THE FOURTH CONJUGATION

experior, experīrī, expertus sum, try, test
orior, orīrī, ortus sum, rise
potior, potīrī, potītus sum, take possession of

EXERCISES

A. In the space before each verb in column *A*, write the letter of its English translation in column *B*.

Column A		*Column B*
------	**1.** morī	*a.* having taken possession of
------	**2.** aggressus erat	*b.* we are rising
------	**3.** potītus	*c.* I am dying
------	**4.** orimur	*d.* by allowing
------	**5.** patiēns	*e.* he attacked
------	**6.** aggressus erit	*f.* to die
------	**7.** potītūrus	*g.* we were rising
------	**8.** moriar	*h.* he had attacked
------	**9.** patiendus	*i.* to have taken possession of
------	**10.** oriēmur	*j.* allowing
------	**11.** aggressus est	*k.* I shall die
------	**12.** patiendō	*l.* about to take possession of
------	**13.** morior	*m.* must be allowed
------	**14.** oriēbāmur	*n.* we shall rise
------	**15.** potītus esse	*o.* he will have attacked

B. Change each verb to the plural.

1. ēgrediētur   ------------------------------------
2. gressus sum   ------------------------------------
3. mortuus   ------------------------------------
4. experiēbāris   ------------------------------------
5. potītur   ------------------------------------
6. orta eram   ------------------------------------
7. patiendum   ------------------------------------
8. aggressus erit ------------------------------------
9. moritūrus   ------------------------------------
10. gradiēris   ------------------------------------

C. Write a synopsis (six tenses) of the following verbs in the form indicated:

1. *potior:*   3rd pl.   *Pres.* ....   *Perf.* ....

    Imp. ....   *Plup.* ....

    Fut. ....   *Fut. Perf.* ....

2. *patior:*   3rd sing.   *Pres.* ....   *Perf.* ....

    Imp. ....   *Plup.* ....

    Fut. ....   *Fut. Perf.* ....

3. *ēgredior:*   1st pl.   *Pres.* ....   *Perf.* ....

    Imp. ....   *Plup.* ....

    Fut. ....   *Fut. Perf.* ....

4. *orior:*   2nd sing.   *Pres.* ....   *Perf.* ....

    Imp. ....   *Plup.* ....

    Fut. ....   *Fut. Perf.* ....

5. *experior:*   1st sing.   *Pres.* ....   *Perf.* ....

    Imp. ....   *Plup.* ....

    Fut. ....   *Fut. Perf.* ....

D. Complete the Latin translation.

1. They had attacked the town.   Oppidum ....

2. He will take possession of the camp.   Castrīs ....

3. We did not want to die.   Nōn volēbāmus ....

4. Are you (sing.) allowing him to leave?   .... eum discēdere?

5. I was walking slowly.   Tardē ....

6. Having tested his luck, he ran forward.   .... fortūnam, prōcucurrit.

7. Why were you (pl.) advancing?   Cūr ....?

8. By attacking, they hope for victory.   .... victōriam spērant.

9. I shall not wholly die.   Nōn omnis ....

10. The storm rose quickly.   Tempestās celeriter ....

E. Underline the correct English translation.

1. mortuus est   (he died, he had died, he was dying)

2. potientur   (they take possession of, they took possession of, they will take possession of)

3. patī   (I suffered, to suffer, having suffered)

4. prōgrediendō   (advancing, by advancing, of advancing)

5. expertus   (having tried, to have tried, about to try)

Lesson 34—REVIEW OF DEPONENT VERBS

A. Write a synopsis (six tenses) of the following verbs in the form indicated:

1. *loquor:* 3rd sing.   *Pres.* _____   *Perf.* _____
   Imp. _____   *Plup.* _____
   Fut. _____   *Fut. Perf.* _____

2. *vereor:* 3rd pl.   *Pres.* _____   *Perf.* _____
   Imp. _____   *Plup.* _____
   Fut. _____   *Fut. Perf.* _____

3. *arbitror:* 1st pl.   *Pres.* _____   *Perf.* _____
   Imp. _____   *Plup.* _____
   Fut. _____   *Fut. Perf.* _____

4. *potior:* 2nd sing.   *Pres.* _____   *Perf.* _____
   Imp. _____   *Plup.* _____
   Fut. _____   *Fut. Perf.* _____

5. *patior:* 1st sing.   *Pres.* _____   *Perf.* _____
   Imp. _____   *Plup.* _____
   Fut. _____   *Fut. Perf.* _____

B. Change each verb to the plural.

1. nāscitur _____
2. mīrātus sum _____
3. pollicēbāris _____
4. ortus erat _____
5. persequēris _____
6. hortātus erō _____
7. profecta _____
8. cōnābor _____
9. nancīscendus _____
10. ūtiturne _____

C. Draw a line through the form that does *not* belong with the others in each group.

1. arbitrābitur, potiētur, verētur, pollicēbitur
2. ausī erāmus, prōgrediēbāmur, experīmur, dominābor
3. proficīscentur, verentur, gradiuntur, morantur
4. collocūtus erās, secūtus es, potītus eris, mortuus erat
5. patiēns, cōnandus, locūtūrus, nactus esse
6. experiar, prōsequēmur, hortābor, pollicēmur
7. hortārī, morātus, passus esse, ūsūrus esse
8. ūtēbāmur, prōgressī estis, ortus erat, gradiēminī
9. moritūrus, admīrandus, morātūrus esse, passus
10. insequendus, aggrediendō, mīranda, ūtendus

104

D. In the space before each verb in column *A*, write the letter of its English translation in column *B*.

Column *A*   Column *B*

_____ **1.** dominābuntur   *a.* he will have dared

_____ **2.** ausus est   *b.* by trying

_____ **3.** morātus   *c.* to have delayed

_____ **4.** experiēns   *d.* they are ruling

_____ **5.** sequēmur   *e.* must be tried

_____ **6.** dominābantur   *f.* he dared

_____ **7.** ausus erit   *g.* they will rule

_____ **8.** experiendus   *h.* we were following

_____ **9.** morātus esse   *i.* he had dared

_____ **10.** sequimur   *j.* about to delay

_____ **11.** dominantur   *k.* we are following

_____ **12.** ausus erat   *l.* they were ruling

_____ **13.** sequēbāmur   *m.* we shall follow

_____ **14.** experiendō   *n.* trying

_____ **15.** morātūrus   *o.* having delayed

E. Complete the English translation.

1. Ausī sumus oppugnāre.   _____ to attack.

2. Eōs Rhēnum trānsīre nōn patiētur.   _____ them to cross the Rhine.

3. Hostēs, secūtī, impedīmenta ferēbant.   The enemy, _____, brought the baggage.

4. Illum vulnerātum esse arbitrantur.   _____ that he was wounded.

5. Verēbārisne omnēs deōs?   _____ all the gods?

6. Cum duce collocūtī erātis.   _____ with the leader.

7. Fortūnam experiar.   _____ my luck.

8 Cohortātus suōs proelium commīsit.   _____ his men he joined battle.

9. Paucōs diēs morābimur.   _____ for a few days.

10. Pollicendō omnibus persuādet.   _____ he persuades all.

F. Change each verb to the third person, keeping the same tense and number.

1. ūsus sum   _____

2. hortābāminī   _____

3. expertī erāmus   _____

4. gradiēris   _____

5. nāsceris   _____

6. morātus erō   _____

7. potīmur   _____

8. cōnābiminī   _____

9. passī sumus   --------------------------------

10. proficīscēbar   --------------------------------

G. Translate the italicized words into Latin.

1. *They followed* the enemy.   -------------------------------- hostēs.

2. *He will go forth* at once.   Statim --------------------------------.

3. Caesar *was encouraging* his men.   Caesar suōs --------------------------------.

4. *We are not delaying* long.   -------------------------------- diū.

5. I want *to rule*.   Volō --------------------------------.

6. *Do you (sing.) think* he is going?   -------------------------------- eum īre?

7. *It does not follow* easily.   -------------------------------- facile.

8. *Having spoken*, I left.   --------------------------------, discessī.

9. Why *had you (pl.) admired* him?   Cūr eum --------------------------------?

10. *I shall have used* the sword.   Gladiō --------------------------------.

H. Rewrite the sentences below, making *all* changes required by the directions in parentheses.

1. Caesar suōs *hortātus est*. (substitute equivalent form of *sequor*)

----

2. *Servī* crās proficīscentur. (substitute *Ego*)

----

3. Fugitīvī *prōgrediuntur*. (change to the perfect)

----

4. Nostrī Germānōs *timent*. (substitute equivalent form of *vereor*)

----

5. Celerius *loquēbāminī*. (change to the singular)

----

6. Oppidō *potītus erat*. (change to the plural)

----

7. *Ego* multa pollicitus sum. (substitute *Nōs*)

----

8. Tempestās *orta erit*. (change to the imperfect)

----

9. Obses fugere *temptābit*. (substitute equivalent form of *cōnor*)

----

10. Diū *morantur*. (change to the pluperfect)

Unit V—Subjunctive Mood

Lesson 35—PRESENT SUBJUNCTIVE OF REGULAR VERBS

FIRST CONJUGATION

serv*āre*, to save; present stem, **servā-**

ACTIVE		PASSIVE	
serv*em*	serv*ēmus*	serv*er*	serv*ēmur*
serv*ēs*	serv*ētis*	serv*ēris*	serv*ēminī*
serv*et*	serv*ent*	serv*ētur*	serv*entur*

SECOND CONJUGATION

mon*ēre*, to warn; present stem, **monē-**

ACTIVE		PASSIVE	
mon*eam*	mon*eāmus*	mon*ear*	mon*eāmur*
mon*eās*	mon*eātis*	mon*eāris*	mon*eāminī*
mon*eat*	mon*eant*	mon*eātur*	mon*eantur*

THIRD CONJUGATION

vinc*ere*, to conquer; present stem, **vince-**

vinc*am*	vinc*āmus*	vinc*ar*	vinc*āmur*
vinc*ās*	vinc*ātis*	vinc*āris*	vinc*āminī*
vinc*at*	vinc*ant*	vinc*ātur*	vinc*antur*

-IŌ THIRD CONJUGATION

cap*ere*, to take; present stem, **cape-**

cap*iam*	cap*iāmus*	cap*iar*	cap*iāmur*
cap*iās*	cap*iātis*	cap*iāris*	cap*iāminī*
cap*iat*	cap*iant*	cap*iātur*	cap*iantur*

FOURTH CONJUGATION

imped*īre*, to hinder; present stem, **impedī-**

ACTIVE		PASSIVE	
imped*iam*	imped*iāmus*	imped*iar*	imped*iāmur*
imped*iās*	imped*iātis*	imped*iāris*	imped*iāminī*
imped*iat*	imped*iant*	imped*iātur*	imped*iantur*

Note

1. The sign of the present subjunctive in the first conjugation is **e**. The tense is formed by changing the final **ā** of the present stem to **e**, and adding the personal endings. The complete endings are:

ACTIVE		PASSIVE	
-em	-ēmus	-er	-ēmur
-ēs	-ētis	-ēris	-ēminī
-et	-ent	-ētur	-entur

107

2. The sign of the present subjunctive in all the other conjugations is **a**. The complete endings are:

ACTIVE		PASSIVE	
-am	-āmus	-ar	-āmur
-ās	-ātis	-āris	-āminī
-at	-ant	-ātur	-antur

3. In the second conjugation, the final **e** of the present stem is kept before the endings are added.

4. In the **-iō** third conjugation, the final **e** of the present stem is changed to **i** before the endings are added.

5. In the fourth conjugation, the final **i** of the present stem is kept before the endings are added.

6. In the third, **-iō** third, and fourth conjugations, the present subjunctive first person singular has the same spelling as the future indicative first person singular. Its use in a particular sentence determines which form it is. Compare:

PRESENT SUBJUNCTIVE		FUTURE INDICATIVE	
ACTIVE		*ACTIVE*	
vincam	vincāmus	**vincam**	vincēmus
vincās	vincātis	vincēs	vincētis
vincat	vincant	vincet	vincent
PASSIVE		*PASSIVE*	
vincar	vincāmur	**vincar**	vincēmur
vincāris	vincāminī	vincēris	vincēminī
vincātur	vincantur	vincētur	vincentur

EXERCISES

A. Change each verb from the active to the passive.

1. intellegat ....
2. incipiant ....
3. superem ....
4. iubeātis ....
5. audiāmus ....
6. occupēs ....
7. moveat ....
8. ēdūcam ....
9. iūdicent ....
10. incitēmus ....

B. In each group all the verbs except one are in the present subjunctive. Underline that one, and then change it to the present subjunctive.

1. veniāmus, rogāmus, mittāmus, videāmus ....
2. pācent, collocent, temptent, agent ....
3. mitteris, cōnficiās, vulnerēris, interficiāris ....

4. persuādeat, audiāmur, occupāminī, vincantur   -

5. postulem, dūcās, mandāris, relinquāmur   -

C. Change each verb to the plural.

1. accipiat   -   **6.** petāris   -

2. timeās   -   **7.** superet   -

3. līberer   -   **8.** habeam   -

4. impediam   -   **9.** faciās   -

5. appellētur   -   **10.** laudēris   -

D. Write all the specified forms in the present subjunctive active and passive.

1. *cēdere:* third singular   -

2. *amāre:* second plural   -

3. *recipere:* first singular   -

4. *retinēre:* third plural   -

5. *audīre:* first plural   -

6. *portāre:* second singular   -

7. *servāre:* third singular   -

8. *mūnīre:* third plural   -

9. *intellegere:* second plural   -

10. *movēre:* first singular   -

Peristyle
of a
Roman House

The peristȳlium, or garden court with columns, was located in the rear of the house, and thus afforded greater privacy for the family. Today in Italy, Spain, and our own California, there are gardens, terraces, and patios designed for outdoor living.

Lesson 36—PRESENT SUBJUNCTIVE OF IRREGULAR AND DEPONENT VERBS

IRREGULAR VERBS

sum

sim	sīmus	possim	possīmus
sīs	sītis	possīs	possītis
sit	sint	possit	possint

possum

volō

velim	velīmus	nōlim	nōlīmus
velīs	velītis	nōlīs	nōlītis
velit	velint	nōlit	nōlint

nōlō

eō

eam	eāmus	fīam	fīāmus
eās	eātis	fīās	fīātis
eat	eant	fīat	fīant

fīō (passive of faciō)

ferō

ACTIVE		PASSIVE	
feram	ferāmus	ferar	ferāmur
ferās	ferātis	ferāris	ferāminī
ferat	ferant	ferātur	ferantur

DEPONENT VERBS

FIRST CONJUGATION		SECOND CONJUGATION		THIRD CONJUGATION		-IŌ THIRD CONJUGATION	
horter	hortēmur	verear	vereāmur	sequar	sequāmur	gradiar	gradiāmur
hortēris	hortēminī	vereāris	vereāminī	sequāris	sequāminī	gradiāris	gradiāminī
hortētur	hortentur	vereātur	vereantur	sequātur	sequantur	gradiātur	gradiantur

FOURTH CONJUGATION

experiar	experiāmur
experiāris	experiāminī
experiātur	experiantur

EXERCISES

A. Write the present subjunctive of the verbs **sum** and **eō** in the form determined by the subject.

	sum	eō
1. virī	-------------	-------------
2. ego	-------------	-------------
3. Caesar	-------------	-------------
4. vōs	-------------	-------------
5. ille	-------------	-------------
6. tū	-------------	-------------
7. dux et lēgātus	-------------	-------------
8. nōs	-------------	-------------
9. eī	-------------	-------------
10. Mārcus amīcusque	-------------	-------------

B. Change each verb to the plural.

1. potiātur -----------------------   **6.** nōlīs -----------------------

2. ferās -----------------------   **7.** mīrer -----------------------

3. velim -----------------------   **8.** possit -----------------------

4. vereāris -----------------------   **9.** nāscātur -----------------------

5. fīat -----------------------   **10.** patiar -----------------------

C. In each group all the verbs except one are in the present subjunctive. Underline that one, and then change it to the present subjunctive.

1. sequātur, sit, fit, cōnētur   -----------------------

2. ferēmur, morēmur, prōgrediāmur, eāmus   -----------------------

3. velīs, possīs, arbitrāris, loquāris   -----------------------

4. nōlint, polliceantur, oriantur, hortantur   -----------------------

5. dominer, feram, ūtētur, experiantur   -----------------------

D. Write all the specified forms in the present subjunctive.

1. *eō:* first plural   -----------------------

2. *vereor:* third singular   -----------------------

3. *sum:* second singular   -----------------------

4. *morior:* third plural   -----------------------

5. *nōlō:* first singular   -----------------------

6. *moror:* second plural   -----------------------

7. *fīō:* third singular   -----------------------

8. *proficīscor:* third plural   -----------------------

9. *possum:* first plural   -----------------------

10. *potior:* second singular   -----------------------

Lesson 37—IMPERFECT SUBJUNCTIVE OF REGULAR VERBS

FIRST CONJUGATION

ACTIVE		PASSIVE	
servārem	servārēmus	servārer	servārēmur
servārēs	servārētis	servārēris	servārēminī
servāret	servārent	servārētur	servārentur

SECOND CONJUGATION

ACTIVE		PASSIVE	
monērem	monērēmus	monērer	monērēmur
monērēs	monērētis	monērēris	monērēminī
monēret	monērent	monērētur	monērentur

THIRD CONJUGATION

vincerem	vincerēmus	vincerer	vincerēmur
vincerēs	vincerētis	vincerēris	vincerēminī
vinceret	vincerent	vincerētur	vincerentur

-IŌ THIRD CONJUGATION

caperem	caperēmus	caperer	caperēmur
caperēs	caperētis	capereris	caperēminī
caperet	caperent	caperētur	caperentur

FOURTH CONJUGATION

ACTIVE		PASSIVE	
impedīrem	impedīrēmus	impedīrer	impedīrēmur
impedīrēs	impedīrētis	impedīrēris	impedīrēminī
impedīret	impedīrent	impedīrētur	impedīrentur

Note

The imperfect subjunctive of all verbs is formed by taking the entire present infinitive active and adding the following endings:

ACTIVE		PASSIVE	
-m	-mus	-r	-mur
-s	-tis	-ris	-minī
-t	-nt	-tur	-ntur

EXERCISES

A. Change each verb from the present to the imperfect subjunctive.

1. agat ------------------------------------
2. rogentur ------------------------------------
3. recipiāmus ------------------------------------
4. retineās ------------------------------------
5. audiar ------------------------------------
6. intellegātis ------------------------------------
7. moneātur ------------------------------------
8. laudēmur ------------------------------------

9. scrībam --

10. petant --

B. Write all the specified forms in the imperfect subjunctive active and passive.

1. *dīcere:* third plural --

2. *dōnāre:* second singular --

3. *vidēre:* first plural --

4. *suscipere:* third singular --

5. *mūnīre:* third plural --

6. *armāre:* first singular --

7. *prohibēre:* second plural --

8. *cognōscere:* third singular --

9. *trādere:* first plural --

10. *interficere:* second singular --

C. Give the voice, person, and number of the following imperfect subjunctives:

	VOICE	PERSON	NUMBER
1. resisteret			
2. postulārēmur			
3. cōnspicerēs			
4. sedērent			
5. repellerēminī			
6. dormīrem			
7. audērēmus			
8. ēicerentur			
9. crēderētis			
10. aedificārētur			

D. Change each verb from the active to the passive.

1. pōnerem --

2. incitāret --

3. iubērēmus --

4. impedīrent --

5. reciperēs --

6. audīrētis --

7. cōnstitueret --

8. līberārent --

9. interrogārem --

10. coniungerēmus --

Lesson 38—IMPERFECT SUBJUNCTIVE OF IRREGULAR AND DEPONENT VERBS

IRREGULAR VERBS

sum		volō		eō		fīō	
essem	essēmus	vellem	vellēmus	īrem	īrēmus	fierem	fierēmus
essēs	essētis	vellēs	vellētis	īrēs	īrētis	fierēs	fierētis
esset	essent	vellet	vellent	īret	īrent	fieret	fierent

Note

Irregular verbs form the imperfect subjunctive *regularly*, namely, by adding the personal endings to the present active infinitive. In the case of **fīō** (passive of **faciō**), the passive infinitive **fierī** is changed to **fiere** before the endings are added.

DEPONENT VERBS

FIRST CONJUGATION		SECOND CONJUGATION		THIRD CONJUGATION		**-IŌ** THIRD CONJUGATION	
hortārer	hortārēmur	verērer	verērēmur	sequerer	sequerēmur	graderer	graderēmur
hortārēris	hortārēminī	verērēris	verērēminī	sequerēris	sequerēminī	graderēris	graderēminī
hortārētur	hortārentur	verērētur	verērentur	sequerētur	sequerentur	graderētur	graderentur

FOURTH CONJUGATION

experīrer	experīrēmur
experīrēris	experīrēminī
experīrētur	experīrentur

Note

1. Deponent verbs also form the imperfect subjunctive *regularly*. As in the case of **fīō,** one must not forget to change the passive infinitive to what looks like an active infinitive, before adding the personal endings. Thus:

hortārī	becomes	**hortāre-**
verērī	becomes	**verēre-**
sequī	becomes	**sequere-**
gradī	becomes	**gradere-**
experīrī	becomes	**experīre-**

2. Deponent verbs, being passive in form, have only passive personal endings.

EXERCISES

A. In each group all the verbs except one are in the imperfect subjunctive. Underline that one, and then change it to the imperfect subjunctive.

1. pollicerētur, sequētur, posset, arbitrārētur ______________________
2. nōlīs, ūtererīs, fierēs, morārēris ______________________
3. īrēmus, potīrēmur, ferrēmus, aggrediāmur ______________________
4. cōnārentur, vellent, sint, audērent ______________________
5. loquerer, proficīscēminī, ferrētur, orīrēmur ______________________

B. Write the imperfect subjunctive of the verbs **possum** and **ūtor** in the form determined by the subject.

	possum	**ūtor**
1. Caesar	__________	__________
2. nōs	__________	__________
3. mīlitēs	__________	__________
4. tū	__________	__________
5. ego	__________	__________
6. is	__________	__________
7. vōs	__________	__________
8. pater fīliusque	__________	__________
9. omnēs	__________	__________
10. Sextus et ego	__________	__________

C. Change each verb from the plural to the singular.

1. prōgrederentur ______________
2. trānsīrēmus ______________
3. audērētis ______________
4. mīrārēmur ______________
5. prōsequerēminī ______________
6. ferrent ______________
7. adessēmus ______________
8. vellētis ______________
9. arbitrārentur ______________
10. fierent ______________

D. Change each verb from the present subjunctive to the imperfect subjunctive.

1. patiantur ______________
2. fīās ______________
3. sīmus ______________
4. pollicear ______________
5. nōlit ______________
6. adhortēmur ______________
7. eātis ______________
8. possint ______________
9. nancīscātur ______________
10. cōnferāminī ______________

Lesson 39—PERFECT AND PLUPERFECT SUBJUNCTIVE
OF REGULAR VERBS

PERFECT SUBJUNCTIVE

ACTIVE   PASSIVE

servō, servāre, servāvī, servātus

servāv*erim*	servāv*erīmus*	servāt*us*, -a, -um	$\begin{cases} sim \\ sīs \\ sit \end{cases}$	servāt*ī*, -ae, -a	$\begin{cases} sīmus \\ sītis \\ sint \end{cases}$
servāv*erīs*	servāv*erītis*				
servāv*erit*	servāv*erint*				

vincō, vincere, vīcī, victus

vīc*erim*	vīc*erīmus*	vict*us*, -a, -um	$\begin{cases} sim \\ sīs \\ sit \end{cases}$	vict*ī*, -ae, -a	$\begin{cases} sīmus \\ sītis \\ sint \end{cases}$
vīc*erīs*	vīc*erītis*				
vīc*erit*	vīc*erint*				

PLUPERFECT SUBJUNCTIVE

servāv*issem*	servāv*issēmus*	servāt*us*, -a, -um	$\begin{cases} essem \\ essēs \\ esset \end{cases}$	servāt*ī*, -ae, -a	$\begin{cases} essēmus \\ essētis \\ essent \end{cases}$
servāv*issēs*	servāv*issētis*				
servāv*isset*	servāv*issent*				

vīc*issem*	vīc*issēmus*	vict*us*, -a, -um	$\begin{cases} essem \\ essēs \\ esset \end{cases}$	vict*ī*, -ae, -a	$\begin{cases} essēmus \\ essētis \\ essent \end{cases}$
vīc*issēs*	vīc*issētis*				
vīc*isset*	vīc*issent*				

Note

1. The perfect active subjunctive of all verbs is formed by adding to the perfect stem the following endings:

-erim	-erīmus
-erīs	-erītis
-erit	-erint

2. The perfect active subjunctive resembles the future perfect active indicative in all forms except the first person singular, where the ending is **-erim** instead of **-erō**.

3. The pluperfect active subjunctive is formed by taking the perfect active infinitive and adding to it the personal endings **-m, -s, -t, -mus, -tis, -nt**.

4. The perfect passive subjunctive consists of two parts. The first part is the perfect passive participle, the second the present subjunctive of the verb **esse**.

5. The pluperfect passive subjunctive also consists of two parts. The first part is again the perfect passive participle, the second the imperfect subjunctive of the verb **esse**.

6. The perfect passive participle, like any adjective, agrees with the subject in gender, number, and case.

EXERCISES

A. Change each verb to the plural.

1. mīsisset   _____
2. cūrāverim   _____
3. audītus sit   _____
4. posuerīs   _____
5. monitus esset   _____

6. iūdicāvissem   _____
7. gestum sit   _____
8. locāvissēs   _____
9. trādiderit   _____
10. dēfēnsa essēs   _____

B. Write all the specified forms in the perfect and pluperfect subjunctive.

1. *fugere:* third plural active   _____
2. *amāre:* second singular passive   _____
3. *vidēre:* first plural active   _____
4. *mūnīre:* third singular passive   _____
5. *agere:* second plural active   _____
6. *ōrāre:* first singular active   _____
7. *pellere:* third plural passive   _____
8. *scīre:* third singular active   _____
9. *accipere:* second plural passive   _____
10. *petere:* first plural passive   _____

C. Change each verb from the passive to the active subjunctive.

1. mōtus sīs   _____
2. doctī essent   _____
3. iacta sint   _____
4. impedītus essem _____
5. occupātus sit   _____

6. iussī essēmus   _____
7. relictus sim   _____
8. prohibitus esset _____
9. superātae sītis _____
10. ducta essēs   _____

D. Supply the proper ending to make each subjunctive verb agree with its subject.

1. *sociī:*   gessisse _____
2. *tū:*   vulnerāt _____ sī _____
3. *nōs:*   quaesīt _____ essē _____
4. *Cornēlia:* mānser _____
5. *ego:*   scrīpser _____
6. *omnēs:*   retent _____ esse _____
7. *vōs:*   incēper _____
8. *pater:*   cōnstituisse _____
9. *eī:*   convocāt _____ si _____
10. *puellae:* reduct _____ esse _____

Lesson 40—PERFECT AND PLUPERFECT SUBJUNCTIVE OF IRREGULAR AND DEPONENT VERBS

PERFECT SUBJUNCTIVE

sum			volō	
fuerim	fuerīmus		voluerim	voluerīmus
fuerīs	fuerītis		voluerīs	voluerītis
fuerit	fuerint		voluerit	voluerint

hortor			sequor	
hortātus, -a, -um { sim, sīs, sit	hortātī, -ae, -a { sīmus, sītis, sint		secūtus, -a, -um { sim, sīs, sit	secūtī, -ae, -a { sīmus, sītis, sint

PLUPERFECT SUBJUNCTIVE

sum			volō	
fuissem	fuissēmus		voluissem	voluissēmus
fuissēs	fuissētis		voluissēs	voluissētis
fuisset	fuissent		voluisset	voluissent

hortor			sequor	
hortātus, -a, -um { essem, essēs, esset	hortātī, -ae, -a { essēmus, essētis, essent		secūtus, -a, -um { essem, essēs, esset	secūtī, -ae, -a { essēmus, essētis, essent

Note

The perfect and pluperfect subjunctive of irregular and deponent verbs are formed in regular fashion. Deponent verbs, of course, exist only in the passive.

EXERCISES

A. Write all the specified forms in the perfect and pluperfect subjunctive.

1. *eō:* third plural _____

2. *patior:* first singular _____

3. *possum:* third singular _____

4. *loquor:* second plural _____

5. *nōlō:* second singular _____

  6. *vereor:* first plural   --

  7. *sum:* third singular   --

  8. *cōnor:* third plural   --

  9. *volō:* first singular   --

  10. *ferō:* second singular active --

B. In each group all the verbs except one are either in the perfect or the pluperfect subjunctive. Underline that one.

1. factus esset, voluerō, ūsus sīs, nōluissēmus

2. īvissēs, profectus sim, arbitrātus erat, fuissent

3. mīrātī estis, potuerint, veritus sit, tulerim

4. prōgressī essent, exīverit, fuerīmus, potuerās

5. ausus essem, mortuus erit, facta sit, tulissētis

C. Supply the proper ending to make each subjunctive verb agree with its subject.

  1. *Caesar:*   īvisse ------------

  2. *paucī:*   aus ------------ sī ------------

  3. *tū:*   secūt ------------ esse ------------

  4. *pōns:*   fact ------------ sī ------------

  5. *nōs:*   voluisse ------------

  6. *ego:*   profect ------------ esse ------------

  7. *fēminae:*   morāt ------------ sī ------------

  8. *vōs:*   tuler ------------

  9. *illī:*   potuisse ------------

  10. *praesidium:*   nact ------------ esse ------------

D. Change each verb from the plural to the singular.

  1. pollicitī essent   ---

  2. fuerīmus   ---

  3. expertī sītis   ---

  4. trānsīvissent   ---

  5. ūsī essēmus   ---

  6. lātī sint   ---

  7. coepissētis   ---

  8. potuerītis   ---

  9. voluissēmus   ---

  10. tulerint   ---

Lesson 41—REVIEW OF THE SUBJUNCTIVE MOOD

A. Give the tense and voice of the following subjunctives:

	TENSE	VOICE
1. cōnsisteret	----------------------------------	----------------------------------
2. possint	----------------------------------	----------------------------------
3. missus esset	----------------------------------	----------------------------------
4. vidērēminī	----------------------------------	----------------------------------
5. iusserim	----------------------------------	----------------------------------
6. capiantur	----------------------------------	----------------------------------
7. factum sit	----------------------------------	----------------------------------
8. oppugnārentur	----------------------------------	----------------------------------
9. vīcissēs	----------------------------------	----------------------------------
10. velīmus	----------------------------------	----------------------------------

B. Write a synopsis in the subjunctive (four tenses) of the following verbs in the form indicated:

1. *audiō:* 3rd sing. act. *Pres.* ---------------------- *Perf.* ----------------------
       Imp. ---------------------- *Plup.* ----------------------

2. *parō:* 1st pl. act. *Pres.* ---------------------- *Perf.* ----------------------
       Imp. ---------------------- *Plup.* ----------------------

3. *trādō:* 2nd sing. pass. *Pres.* ---------------------- *Perf.* ----------------------
       Imp. ---------------------- *Plup.* ----------------------

4. *moneō:* 3rd pl. pass. *Pres.* ---------------------- *Perf.* ----------------------
       Imp. ---------------------- *Plup.* ----------------------

5. *iaciō:* 2nd pl. act. *Pres.* ---------------------- *Perf.* ----------------------
       Imp. ---------------------- *Plup.* ----------------------

6. *laudō:* 1st sing. pass. *Pres.* ---------------------- *Perf.* ----------------------
       Imp. ---------------------- *Plup.* ----------------------

7. *volō:* 3rd pl. *Pres.* ---------------------- *Perf.* ----------------------
       Imp. ---------------------- *Plup.* ----------------------

8. *mīror:* 1st pl. *Pres.* ---------------------- *Perf.* ----------------------
       Imp. ---------------------- *Plup.* ----------------------

9. *possum:* 3rd sing. *Pres.* ---------------------- *Perf.* ----------------------
       Imp. ---------------------- *Plup.* ----------------------

10. *vereor:* 2nd pl. *Pres.* ---------------------- *Perf.* ----------------------
       Imp. ---------------------- *Plup.* ----------------------

C. Change each subjunctive to the plural.

1. postulāret
2. vēnissem
3. vidērētur
4. pollicitus sit
5. sustineās
6. secūtus essem
7. potiātur
8. posuerīs
9. potuissēs
10. factum esset

D. Change each verb from the indicative to the corresponding form of the subjunctive.

1. sedēs
2. impediēbat
3. locūtī sunt
4. expugnāveram
5. expellēbantur
6. fēcistis
7. eunt
8. nātus erat
9. mandor
10. fuistī

E. Change each subjunctive from the active to the passive.

1. ēiciant
2. dūxerīs
3. convocēmus
4. ferret
5. prohibuissem
6. relinquerētis
7. pācāverint
8. recēpisset
9. retineās
10. spectārēmus

Unit VI—Nouns

Lesson 42—NOMINATIVE AND ACCUSATIVE OF THE FIRST AND SECOND DECLENSIONS

	FIRST DECLENSION		SECOND DECLENSION	
	terra, land; base, terr-		servus, slave; base, serv-	
	SINGULAR	PLURAL	SINGULAR	PLURAL
Nom.	terra	terrae	servus	servī
Acc.	terram	terrās	servum	servōs

Note

1. Nouns of the first and second declensions have the following endings:

	FIRST DECLENSION		SECOND DECLENSION	
	SINGULAR	PLURAL	SINGULAR	PLURAL
Nom.	-a	-ae	-us	-ī
Acc.	-am	-ās	-um	-ōs

2. Nouns of the first declension are feminine unless they denote males. Thus, **fēmina** (woman) and **terra** (land) are feminine, but **nauta** (sailor) is masculine.

3. Nouns of the second declension ending in **-us** are masculine.

4. The nominative case is used principally as *subject*, the accusative as *direct object* of a verb.

COMMON NOUNS OF THE FIRST DECLENSION

FEMININE

adulēscentia, youth	**dīligentia,** care, diligence	**hōra,** hour
amīcitia, friendship	**disciplīna,** training	**iānua,** door
ancora, anchor	**domina,** lady, mistress	**iniūria,** wrong
aqua, water	**epistula,** letter	**inopia,** lack
aquila, eagle	**fābula,** story	**īnsidiae** (*pl.*), ambush
arēna, sand, arena	**fāma,** report	**īnsula,** island
audācia, boldness	**familia,** household	**īra,** anger
casa, hut	**fēmina,** woman	**lingua,** tongue
causa, reason, cause	**fīlia,** daughter	**littera,** letter
cēna, dinner	**fōrma,** shape, beauty	**lūna,** moon
colōnia, colony	**fortūna,** fortune	**māteria,** timber
contrōversia, dispute	**fossa,** trench	**mātrōna,** wife
cōpia, supply	**fuga,** flight	**memoria,** memory
cūra, care, anxiety	**glōria,** fame	**mēnsa,** table
dea, goddess	**grātia,** gratitude, favor	**mora,** delay

nātūra, nature
opera, work, effort
patria, country
pecūnia, money
poena, punishment
porta, gate
praeda, loot
prōvincia, province
puella, girl
pugna, battle

rēgīna, queen
rīpa, shore
rosa, rose
sagitta, arrow
schola, school
scientia, knowledge
sententia, opinion
silva, forest
statua, statue
taberna, shop

terra, land, earth
toga, toga
tuba, trumpet
tunica, tunic
unda, wave
via, road
victōria, victory
vigilia, watch
vīlla, farmhouse
vīta, life

MASCULINE

agricola, farmer
incola, inhabitant

nauta, sailor

poēta, poet

Note

1. The plural of **cōpia** usually means *troops, forces.*

2. The word **littera** means a *letter* of the *alphabet;* the plural, **litterae**, means a *letter* in the sense of a *communication*, and requires a plural verb.

COMMON NOUNS OF THE SECOND DECLENSION

MASCULINE (-us)

amīcus, friend
animus, mind
annus, year
barbarus, foreigner, native
campus, plain
captīvus, prisoner
carrus, wagon
cibus, food
circus, circle, circus
deus, god
digitus, finger
discipulus, pupil

dominus, master
equus, horse
fīlius, son
fugitīvus, deserter
gladius, sword
lēgātus, envoy, lieutenant
līberī (*pl.*), children
locus, place
lūdus, game, school
modus, manner
mūrus, wall

numerus, number
nūntius, messenger, message
ōceanus, ocean
oculus, eye
populus, people
servus, slave
socius, ally
somnus, sleep
tribūnus, tribune
ventus, wind
vīcus, village

Note

The word **populus** (people) is a collective noun and, being singular, requires a singular verb. The plural form of **populus** is seldom used.

EXERCISES

A. Identify the case and number of the following forms:

1. praedam _____ 6. lēgātī _____
2. servōs _____ 7. portās _____
3. sententiae _____ 8. gladium _____
4. īnsula _____ 9. nautam _____
5. mūrus _____ 10. carrōs _____

B. Change each singular form to the plural.

1. annus   ---------------------------------
2. poenam   ------------------------------
3. littera   --------------------------------
4. nūntium   ------------------------------
5. poēta   ----------------------------------

6. equum   ------------------------------
7. discipulus   --------------------------
8. rīpam   ------------------------------
9. iniūria   -----------------------------
10. deum   --------------------------

C. Write the following specified forms:

1. accusative singular: *numerus, dea, socius*

----

2. nominative plural: *sagitta, amīcus, colōnia*

----

3. accusative plural: *fīlius, incola*

----

4. nominative singular: *silvās, locum*

D. Translate the English words into Latin.

1. *The prisoners* capiuntur.   ---------------------
2. Voluntne *the food?*   ---------------------
3. Vidēmus *the road.*   ---------------------
4. *The land* vidētur.   ---------------------
5. Spectat *the children.*   ---------------------
6. *The girls* manent.   ---------------------
7. *The people* servātur.   ---------------------
8. Cōgēbat *the troops.*   ---------------------
9. *The master* loquitur.   ---------------------
10. Amāmus *the queen.*   ---------------------

Mottoes

Organizations, as well as nations, often find Latin the most suitable medium to express an idea. Note the mottoes: **Semper paratus,** Always ready (United States Coast Guard) and **Semper fidelis,** Always faithful (United States Marine Corps).

Lesson 43—GENITIVE, DATIVE, AND ABLATIVE OF THE FIRST AND SECOND DECLENSIONS

	FIRST DECLENSION		SECOND DECLENSION	
	SINGULAR	PLURAL	SINGULAR	PLURAL
Gen.	terr*ae*	terr*ārum*	serv*ī*	serv*ōrum*
Dat.	terr*ae*	terr*īs*	serv*ō*	serv*īs*
Abl.	terr*ā*	terr*īs*	serv*ō*	serv*īs*

Note

1. Nouns of the first declension have the following endings:

	SINGULAR	PLURAL
Gen.	**-ae**	**-ārum**
Dat.	**-ae**	**-īs**
Abl.	**-ā**	**-īs**

2. The ending **-ae** is the same for the genitive singular, the dative singular, and the nominative plural. The ending **-īs** is the same for the dative and ablative plural. The use of a particular form in a sentence determines its case.

3. The ablative singular is distinguished from the nominative singular by a long mark, or *macron*, over the **ā.**

4. Nouns of the second declension have the following endings:

	SINGULAR	PLURAL
Gen.	**-ī**	**-ōrum**
Dat.	**-ō**	**-īs**
Abl.	**-ō**	**-īs**

5. The ending **-ī** is the same for the genitive singular and the nominative plural. However, nouns ending in **-ius** generally have one **i** in the genitive singular. Thus, the genitive singular of **socius** is **socī,** and the nominative plural **sociī.**

6. The endings for the dative and ablative are the same: **-ō** in the singular and **-īs** in the plural.

7. The ending **-īs** in the dative and ablative plural is the same for both the first and second declensions. However, two nouns of the first declension, **dea** and **fīlia,** have the ending **-ābus** to distinguish them from their male counterparts. Thus:

NOMINATIVE SINGULAR	DATIVE AND ABLATIVE PLURAL
deus	deīs
dea	deābus
fīlius	fīliīs
fīlia	fīliābus

8. The genitive is used principally to show possession (*of, 's*), the dative for the indirect object (*to, for*), and the ablative to express phrases that in English require the prepositions *from, by, with, at, in, on.*

EXERCISES

A. Identify the case(s) and number of the following forms:

1. memoriā ------------------------------
2. deīs ------------------------------
3. vīcōrum ------------------------------
4. vigiliae ------------------------------
5. gladiō ------------------------------

6. silvārum ------------------------------
7. barbarī ------------------------------
8. incolīs ------------------------------
9. prōvinciā ------------------------------
10. equōrum ------------------------------

B. Change each singular form to the plural.

1. carrō ------------------------------
2. linguae ------------------------------
3. undā ------------------------------
4. fugitīvī ------------------------------
5. fīlī ------------------------------

6. sententiae ------------------------------
7. nūntiō ------------------------------
8. oculī ------------------------------
9. iniūriā ------------------------------
10. poētā ------------------------------

C. Underline the correct form.

1. genitive plural: *lēgātī, lēgātōrum, lēgātīs*
2. ablative singular: *fossīs, fossae, fossā*
3. dative singular: *modō, modī, modīs*

4. ablative plural: *nautā, nautīs, nautārum*
5. genitive singular: *vīllārum, fīliō, ventī*

D. Write the following specified forms:

1. ablative plural: *lūdus, cōpia* ------------------------------
2. dative singular: *adulēscentia, socius* ------------------------------
3. genitive plural: *locus, fīlia* ------------------------------
4. ablative singular: *aquila, discipulus* ------------------------------
5. genitive singular: *tribūnus, patria* ------------------------------

Roman
Writing Implements

Tabellae (wax tablets) and a **stilus,** serving as a pencil, were the writing implements used by schoolboys in ancient Rome. Later in their schooling, the pupils were taught to use pen and ink on papyrus. The tabellae were similar to slates used in schools a generation ago, and papyrus gradually developed into our modern paper.

Lesson 44—-ER, -IR, AND NEUTER NOUNS OF THE SECOND DECLENSION

-er

puer, boy; base, **puer-**   **liber,** book; base, **libr-**

	SINGULAR	PLURAL	SINGULAR	PLURAL
Nom.	puer	puer*ī*	liber	libr*ī*
Gen.	puer*ī*	puer*ōrum*	libr*ī*	libr*ōrum*
Dat	puer*ō*	puer*īs*	libr*ō*	libr*īs*
Acc.	puer*um*	puer*ōs*	libr*um*	libr*ōs*
Abl.	puer*ō*	puer*īs*	libr*ō*	libr*īs*

-ir   ### NEUTER

vir, man; base, **vir-**   **tēlum,** weapon; base, **tēl-**

	SINGULAR	PLURAL	SINGULAR	PLURAL
Nom.	vir	vir*ī*	tēl*um*	tēl*a*
Gen.	vir*ī*	vir*ōrum*	tēl*ī*	tēl*ōrum*
Dat.	vir*ō*	vir*īs*	tēl*ō*	tēl*īs*
Acc.	vir*um*	vir*ōs*	tēl*um*	tēl*a*
Abl.	vir*ō*	vir*īs*	tēl*ō*	tēl*īs*

Note

1. Nouns ending in **-er** or **-ir** are declined as if they ended in **-us: puer(us), vir(us).** The gender of these nouns is masculine.

2. The base of a noun is found by dropping the ending of the *genitive singular.* Thus, the base of **puer** is **puer-,** but the base of **liber** is **libr-.**

3. Nouns ending in **-um** are neuter and differ from masculine nouns as follows: in the nominative singular they end in **-um,** and in the nominative and accusative plural they end in **-a.** Observe that the nominative and accusative endings are identical.

4. Nouns ending in **-ium** generally have one **i** in the genitive singular, as is true of **-ius** nouns.

5. Do not confuse a nominative singular of a first declension noun, for example **poena,** with a nominative or accusative plural of a second declension neuter noun, for example **bella.**

COMMON NOUNS OF THE SECOND DECLENSION

MASCULINE (-er, -ir)

ager, agrī, field   **magister (-trī),** teacher   **vesper,** evening
liber, librī, book   **puer,** boy   **vir,** man

Note

The spelling of English derivatives offers a clue to the Latin base. Thus:

DERIVATIVE	LATIN BASE
*agr*iculture	**(agr-)**
*libr*ary	**(libr-)**
*magistr*ate	**(magistr-)**
*puer*ile	**(puer-)**

Neuter (-um)

aedificium, building
arma (*pl.*), arms
ātrium, atrium
auxilium, help
bellum, war
beneficium, kindness
caelum, sky
castra (*pl.*), camp
colloquium, conference
concilium, meeting
cōnsilium, plan
domicilium, home
dōnum, gift
factum, deed
forum, forum
frūmentum, grain

hīberna (*pl.*), winter quarters
impedīmentum, hindrance
imperium, command
initium, beginning
intervāllum, space
iūdicium, judgment, trial
iugum, yoke, ridge
nāvigium, boat
negōtium, task
officium, duty
oppidum, town
perīculum, danger
pīlum, javelin
praemium, reward
praesidium, guard
pretium, price

proelium, battle
rēgnum, kingdom
respōnsum, reply
scūtum, shield
signum, signal
silentium, silence
spatium, space
studium, eagerness
subsidium, aid
tēlum, weapon
templum, temple
tergum, back
theātrum, theater
vāllum, wall
verbum, word

Note

1. The word **castra** (camp) is used practically always in the plural and requires a plural verb. The singular **castrum** (fort) is rarely used.

    Castra **sunt** magna.   The camp *is* large.

2. **Impedīmenta** (the plural of **impedīmentum**) usually means *baggage*.

3. The masculine noun **locus** is neuter in the plural: **locus** (place); **loca** (places).

4. Distinguish between **līberī** (children) and **librī** (books).

EXERCISES

A. Underline the correct form.

1. accusative singular: *virōs, virōrum, virum*

2. nominative singular: *pīla, pīlī, pīlum*

3. dative plural: *magistrō, magistrīs, magistrōrum*

4. ablative plural: *negōtiō, negōtiīs, negōtī*

5. genitive singular: *librōrum, librō, librī*

6. nominative plural: *cōpia, praemium, perīcula*

7. dative singular: *puerō, verbī, vāllīs*

8. genitive plural: *factōrum, praesidium, cōnsilī*

9. ablative singular: *castrīs, forō, tergī*

10. accusative plural: *pugna, imperium, auxilia*

B. Identify the case(s) and number of the following forms:

1. oppidī ....

2. vesperō ....

3. beneficia ....

4. agrōrum ....

5. magister ....

6. officiīs ....

7. dōnum ....

8. librī ....

9. virōs ....

10. puerum ....

C. Write the following specified forms:

1. dative singular: *puer, magister* ....

2. nominative plural: *aedificium, vir* ....

3. accusative plural: *liber, verbum* ....

4. genitive singular and plural: *praesidium* ....

5. ablative singular and plural: *ager* ....

D. Change each singular form to the plural.

1. impedīmentum ....

2. cōnsilī ....

3. magister ....

4. factō ....

5. puerum ....

E. Change each plural form to the singular.

1. signōrum ....

2. colloquia ....

3. agrī ....

4. pīlīs ....

5. virōs ....

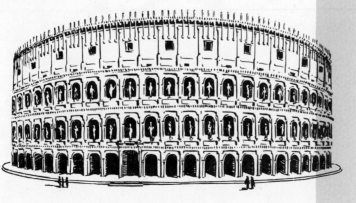

The Colosseum

The Colosseum, the largest amphitheater and most famous building of ancient Rome, was used principally for gladiatorial combats. The arena could also be turned into a lake for mock naval battles. The Colosseum, even today, is sometimes used for outdoor performances of plays and operas.

Lesson 45—VOCATIVE CASE; ENDINGS OF THE FIRST AND SECOND DECLENSIONS

The *vocative* case, used to address a person, has the same form as the nominative, with the following exceptions: second declension nouns ending in **-us** form the vocative singular by changing **-us** to **-e**; nouns ending in **-ius** change **-ius** to **-ī**.

	NOMINATIVE	VOCATIVE
SINGULAR:	domina	domina
PLURAL:	dominae	dominae
SINGULAR:	magister	magister
PLURAL:	magistrī	magistrī

But

dominus	domin*e*
nūntius	nūnt*ī*

Note

Unless used for special emphasis, the vocative never stands first in a sentence.

Portā, **Mārce**, tubam.   Marcus, carry the trumpet.

ENDINGS OF THE FIRST AND SECOND DECLENSIONS

FIRST DECLENSION   SECOND DECLENSION

			MASCULINE		NEUTER	
	SINGULAR	PLURAL	SINGULAR	PLURAL	SINGULAR	PLURAL
Nom.	-a	-ae	-us (-er, -ir)	-ī	-um	-a
Gen.	-ae	-ārum	-ī	-ōrum	-ī	-ōrum
Dat.	-ae	-īs	-ō	-īs	-ō	-īs
Acc.	-am	-ās	-um	-ōs	-um	-a
Abl.	-ā	-īs	-ō	-īs	-ō	-īs

Note

Observe the similarity in the endings of the two declensions:

	FIRST DECLENSION	SECOND DECLENSION
accusative singular:	-am	-um
accusative plural:	-ās	-ōs (masc.)
genitive plural:	-ārum	-ōrum
dative and ablative plural:	-īs	-īs

EXERCISES

A. Identify the case(s) and number of the following forms:

1. praemium _____
2. amīcitiā _____
3. lēgātōs _____
4. captīvī _____
5. templa _____
6. fossa _____
7. silentiō _____
8. oppidī _____
9. īnsidiīs _____
10. vesper _____

11. nūntiōrum _____
12. animum _____
13. undās _____
14. gladiīs _____
15. colōniam _____
16. praedae _____
17. amīce _____
18. litterārum _____
19. modus _____
20. sociī _____

B. Give the Latin vocative for each English noun.

1. Manē diū, *Cornelia.* _____
2. Mē sequere, *Marcus.* _____
3. Ubi sunt discipulī, *teacher?* _____
4. Dēfendite oppidum, *farmers.* _____
5. Properātisne, *allies?* _____
6. Dēlige amīcōs bonōs, *son.* _____
7. Respondēte celeriter, *boys.* _____
8. Cūr discēdis, *lieutenant?* _____
9. Dīc causam, *messenger.* _____
10. Ēdūcite equōs, *slaves.* _____

C. Change each singular form to the plural.

1. sagittam _____
2. oculus _____
3. deō _____
4. perīculī _____
5. via _____

6. ventum _____
7. prōvinciae _____
8. ager _____
9. terrā _____
10. locus _____

D. Draw a line through the form that does *not* belong with the others in each group.

1. carrī, iniūriae, tēla, aquās
2. annōrum, praesidī, puellam, fēminārum
3. pecūniā, virum, poenās, officia
4. populō, deae, statuās, factīs
5. nautīs, familiā, castrīs, mūrī

E. Write the following specified forms:

1. accusative plural: *cōnsilium, vīcus* _____
2. dative singular: *adulēscentia, populus* _____
3. ablative singular: *scūtum, poena* _____
4. genitive plural: *puer, fīlia* _____
5. nominative plural: *pīlum, causa* _____
6. accusative singular: *fuga, magister* _____
7. vocative singular: *nūntius, amīcus* _____
8. ablative plural: *officium, silva* _____
9. dative plural: *dominus, domina* _____
10. genitive singular: *arēna, rēgnum* _____

F. In the space before each noun in column *A*, write the letter of its form in column *B*.

	Column A		Column B
_____	**1.** librōrum	*a.*	accusative singular
_____	**2.** incolīs	*b.*	vocative singular
_____	**3.** fossam	*c.*	genitive singular
_____	**4.** beneficia	*d.*	accusative plural
_____	**5.** proelī	*e.*	dative or ablative singular
_____	**6.** poēta	*f.*	genitive plural
_____	**7.** discipule	*g.*	ablative singular
_____	**8.** fugitīvōs	*h.*	nominative singular
_____	**9.** praedā	*i.*	dative or ablative plural
_____	**10.** captīvō	*j.*	nominative or accusative plural

The Fasces

The Roman fasces, a bundle of rods and an ax all tied together, were
a symbol of supreme authority. The Italian dictator Mussolini revived
the symbol in founding the system of fascism. The fasces, as a symbol
of unity, are stamped on the American dime.

Lesson 46—THIRD DECLENSION NOUNS, MASCULINE AND FEMININE

CONSONANT STEMS

soror, sister; base, **sorōr-**   **eques**, horseman; base, **equit-**

	SINGULAR	PLURAL	SINGULAR	PLURAL
Nom.	soror	sorōr*ēs*	eques	equit*ēs*
Gen.	sorōr*is*	sorōr*um*	equit*is*	equit*um*
Dat.	sorōr*ī*	sorōr*ibus*	equit*ī*	equit*ibus*
Acc.	sorōr*em*	sorōr*ēs*	equit*em*	equit*ēs*
Abl.	sorōr*e*	sorōr*ibus*	equit*e*	equit*ibus*

I-STEMS

hostis, enemy; base, **host-**   **pars**, part; base, **part-**

	SINGULAR	PLURAL	SINGULAR	PLURAL
Nom.	host*is*	host*ēs*	pars	part*ēs*
Gen.	host*is*	host*ium*	part*is*	part*ium*
Dat.	host*ī*	host*ibus*	part*ī*	part*ibus*
Acc.	host*em*	host*ēs* (-*īs*)	part*em*	part*ēs* (-*īs*)
Abl.	host*e*	host*ibus*	part*e*	part*ibus*

IRREGULAR DECLENSIONS

nēmō   **vīs**

	SINGULAR	SINGULAR	PLURAL
Nom.	nēmō	vīs	vīrēs
Gen.	nūllīus	vīs	vīrium
Dat.	nēminī	vī	vīribus
Acc.	nēminem	vim	vīrēs
Abl.	nūllō	vī	vīribus

Note

1. The endings of third declension masculine and feminine nouns are:

	SINGULAR	PLURAL
Nom.	(varies)	-ēs
Gen.	-is	-um (-ium)
Dat.	-ī	-ibus
Acc.	-em	-ēs (-īs)
Abl.	-e	-ibus

133

2. I-stem nouns differ from consonant-stem nouns in the genitive plural, ending in **-ium** instead of **-um.** Also, in some i-stem nouns the accusative plural may end in **-īs** as well as **-ēs,** the ablative singular in **-ī** as well as **-e,** and the accusative singular in **-im** as well as **-em.**

3. Most i-stem nouns can be identified by their endings in the nominative singular: **-is,** as **hostis** and **nāvis;** **-ns,** as **dēns** and **mōns;** and **-rs,** as **mors** and **pars.** It is to be noted that all i-stem nouns end in **-s** except **nox** (originally spelled **nocts**).

4. The following nouns of the third declension are masculine:

   a. Those denoting males: **pater** (father), **rēx** (king).
   b. Abstract nouns ending in **-or: dolor** (grief), **terror** (fright).
   c. Unclassified nouns: **collis, dēns, fīnis, īgnis, mēnsis, mōns, mōs, ōrdō, pēs, pōns, sōl.**

5. The following nouns are feminine:

   a. Those denoting females: **māter** (mother), **soror** (sister).
   b. Those ending in **-iō** as **legiō;** **-rs** as **pars;** **-tās** as **aestās;** **-tūdō** as **fortitūdō;** **-ūs** as **salūs;** **-x** as **pāx.**
   c. Unclassified nouns: **arbor, caedēs, classis, gēns, hiems, laus, mēns, nāvis, plēbs, turris, urbs, vallēs, vīs.**

6. The *genitive* singular of a noun, not the nominative, gives the clue to the rest of the declension. For example:

NOMINATIVE	GENITIVE
ae*tās*	ae*tātis*
du*x*	du*cis*
frā*ter*	frā*tris*
mīl*es*	mīl*itis*
mō*ns*	mo*ntis*
multi*tūdō*	multi*tūdinis*
rē*x*	rē*gis*

COMMON MASCULINE AND FEMININE NOUNS OF THE THIRD DECLENSION

(arranged according to similarity of endings)

MASCULINE

-or, -ōris

amor, love	**gladiātor,** gladiator	**praetor,** praetor, judge
clāmor, shout	**honor,** honor, office	**quaestor,** quaestor
color, color	**imperātor,** general	**senātor,** senator
dēfēnsor, defender	**labor,** work	**terror,** fright
dictātor, dictator	**maiōrēs** (*pl.*), ancestors	**timor,** fear
dolor, pain, grief	**mercātor,** trader	**victor,** conqueror
explorātor, scout	**ōrātor,** speaker	

-is, -is (-ium in the genitive plural)

canis, dog	**fīnis,** boundary; (*pl.*), territory	**īgnis,** fire
cīvis, citizen	**hostis,** enemy	**mēnsis,** month
collis, hill		

-ns, -ntis (-ium)

adulēscēns, young man

cliēns, client

dēns, tooth

mōns, mountain

pōns, bridge

-es, -itis

eques, horseman

mīles, soldier

pedes, infantryman

-er, -ris

frāter, brother

pater, father

-ō, -inis

homō, man

ōrdō, order

-ō, -ōnis

centuriō, centurion

leō, lion

MISCELLANEOUS

ariēs, -ietis, ram, battering ram

cōnsul, -is, consul

dux, ducis, leader

mōs, mōris, custom

nēmō, nūllīus, no one

obses, -idis, hostage

pēs, pedis, foot

prīnceps, -ipis, chief

rēx, rēgis, king

sōl, sōlis, sun

FEMININE

-tās, -tātis

aestās, summer

aetās, age

auctōritās, influence

calamitās, disaster

celeritās, speed

cīvitās, state

cupiditās, desire

difficultās, difficulty

facultās, opportunity

lībertās, freedom

nōbilitās, fame, nobility

potestās, power

tempestās, weather, storm

voluntās, will, wish

-iō, -iōnis

condiciō, terms, agreement

dēditiō, surrender

lēgātiō, embassy

legiō, legion

mūnītiō, fortification

nātiō, tribe

obsidiō, siege

occāsiō, opportunity

oppugnātiō, attack

ōrātiō, speech

possessiō, possession

profectiō, departure

ratiō, plan

regiō, region

suspīciō, suspicion

-tūdō, -tūdinis

altitūdō, height, depth

cōnsuētūdō, custom

fortitūdō, bravery

lātitūdō, width

magnitūdō, size

multitūdō, crowd

-is, -is (-ium)

| classis, fleet | nāvis, ship | turris, tower |

-rs, -rtis (-ium)

| ars, skill, art | mors, death | pars, part |
| cohors, cohort | | |

-s, -is

| hiems, winter | plēbs, common people | urbs (-ium), city |

-x, -cis

| arx, citadel | pāx, peace | vōx, voice |
| lūx, light | | |

-ēs, -is (-ium)

| caedēs, murder | vallēs, valley | |

-ns, -ntis (-ium)

| gēns, clan, race | mēns, mind | |

-or, -oris

| arbor, tree | soror, sister | |

-ūs, -ūtis

| salūs, welfare | virtūs, courage | |

MISCELLANEOUS

| laus, laudis, praise | māter, -tris, mother | vīs, vīs, force |
| lēx, lēgis, law | nox, noctis, night | |

EXERCISES

A. Identify the case(s) and number of the following forms:

1. pedum ---------------------------
2. noctem ---------------------------
3. ducī ---------------------------
4. lēgibus ---------------------------
5. cohortis ---------------------------

6. lībertāte ---------------------------
7. equitēs ---------------------------
8. urbium ---------------------------
9. ōrdō ---------------------------
10. nēmō ---------------------------

B. Underline the correct form.

1. accusative singular: *cīvēs, cīvem, cīvium*
2. ablative plural: *frātribus, frātre, frātris*
3. dative singular: *sorōribus, sorōrī, sorōre*
4. genitive plural: *fīnium, fīnis, fīnibus*
5. nominative plural: *mīles, mīlitis, mīlitēs*
6. accusative plural: *partis, partēs, partem*
7. genitive singular: *virtūtis, virtūs, virtūtī*
8. nominative singular: *vōcēs, urbis, ratiō*
9. dative plural: *vīribus, prīncipī, tempestātēs*
10. ablative singular: *regiōnibus, mente, senātōrī*

C. Change each singular form to the plural.

1. nāvem ---------------------------
2. arbor ---------------------------
3. equitī ---------------------------
4. victōris ---------------------------
5. laude ---------------------------

6. caedis ---------------------------
7. cīvitās ---------------------------
8. nātiōnem ---------------------------
9. obses ---------------------------
10. homine ---------------------------

D. Write the following specified forms:

1. dative singular and plural: *pedes* ---
2. accusative singular and plural: *cohors* ---
3. ablative singular: *condiciō, altitūdō* ---
4. genitive plural: *īgnis, cōnsul* ---
5. nominative plural: *turris, mōs* ---

E. Draw a line through the form that does *not* belong with the others in each group.

1. noctium, hominum, timōrem, frātris
2. magnitūdō, dolōris, suspīciō, classis
3. celeritātis, praetōrum, legiōnibus, hominēs
4. pāce, vī, mercātōre, mīlitī
5. mēns, pōns, nāvis, vallēs
6. fīnis, sōl, dēns, mēnsis
7. auctōritātem, lūcēs, clāmōre, patris
8. urbem, condiciōnēs, hiemis, gentēs
9. maiōribus, cīvī, adulēscentibus, equitis
10. pedes, vōx, hostis, mōns

Lesson 47—THIRD DECLENSION NOUNS, NEUTER

CONSONANT STEMS

nōmen, name; base, **nōmin-**   **iter,** journey; base, **itiner-**

	SINGULAR	PLURAL	SINGULAR	PLURAL
Nom.	nōmen	nōmin*a*	iter	itiner*a*
Gen.	nōmin*is*	nōmin*um*	itiner*is*	itiner*um*
Dat.	nōmin*ī*	nōmin*ibus*	itiner*ī*	itiner*ibus*
Acc.	nōmen	nōmin*a*	iter	itiner*a*
Abl.	nōmin*e*	nōmin*ibus*	itiner*e*	itiner*ibus*

I-STEM

animal, animal; base, **animāl-**

	SINGULAR	PLURAL
Nom.	animal	animāl*ia*
Gen.	animāl*is*	animāl*ium*
Dat.	animāl*ī*	animāl*ibus*
Acc.	animal	animāl*ia*
Abl.	animāl*ī*	animāl*ibus*

Note

1. Neuter nouns of the third declension have the same forms for the nominative and accusative. In the plural these forms end in **-a.**

2. Neuter **i**-stem nouns differ from neuter consonant stems in the ablative singular, which ends in **-ī;** in the genitive plural, which ends in **-ium;** and in the nominative and accusative plural, which end in **-ia.**

3. Neuter nouns of the third declension ending in **-us,** as **tempus,** should not be confused with masculine nouns of the second declension also ending in **-us,** as **populus.** The genitive singular gives the clue to the declension.

	THIRD DECLENSION	SECOND DECLENSION
Nom.	tempus	populus
Gen.	tempor*is*	popul*ī*

COMMON NEUTER NOUNS OF THE THIRD DECLENSION
(arranged according to similarity of endings)

CONSONANT STEMS

-us, -eris

genus, kind, race   **opus,** work   **vulnus,** wound
latus, side

138

-us, -oris

corpus, body   **lītus,** shore   **tempus,** time

-en, -inis

agmen, marching column   **flūmen,** river   **nōmen,** name

MISCELLANEOUS

caput, -itis, head   **iter, itineris,** march   **iūs, iūris,** right

I-STEMS

animal, -is, animal   **mare, -is,** sea

EXERCISES

A. Identify the case(s) and number of the following forms:

1. animālium   _____   6. agminī   _____

2. opus   _____   7. genere   _____

3. flūminis   _____   8. corporum   _____

4. itineribus   _____   9. iūra   _____

5. vulnera   _____   10. marī   _____

B. Change each singular form to the plural.

1. latere   _____   6. animālī   _____

2. nōmen   _____   7. caput   _____

3. corporī   _____   8. tempore   _____

4. iter   _____   9. vulneris   _____

5. lītoris   _____   10. iūre   _____

C. Write the following specified forms:

1. ablative singular: *agmen, mare*   _____

2. genitive plural: *animal, flūmen*   _____

3. accusative singular: *genus, tempus*   _____

4. dative singular: *corpus, nōmen*   _____

5. nominative plural: *latus, iter*   _____

6. genitive singular: *caput, lītus*   _____

7. ablative plural: *iūs, vulnus*   _____

8. accusative plural: *mare, opus*   _____

9. dative plural: *flūmen, corpus*   _____

10. vocative singular and plural: *tempus*   _____

Lesson 48—REVIEW OF THIRD DECLENSION NOUNS

ENDINGS OF THE THIRD DECLENSION

	MASCULINE AND FEMININE		NEUTER	
	SINGULAR	PLURAL	SINGULAR	PLURAL
Nom.	—	-ēs	—	-a(-ia)
Gen.	-is	-um(-ium)	-is	-um(-ium)
Dat.	-ī	-ibus	-ī	-ibus
Acc.	-em	-ēs(-īs)	—	-a(-ia)
Abl.	-e	-ibus	-e(-ī)	-ibus

Note

1. Nouns of the third declension have the same endings in the plural for the nominative and accusative (**-ēs, -a,** or **-ia**), and for the dative and ablative (**-ibus**).

2. Since the base of third declension nouns often differs in spelling from the nominative, the following hint in determining the base will be found useful. Think of an English derivative from the Latin noun. The derivative will usually give a clue to the base. Below are some examples.

NOMINATIVE	ENGLISH DERIVATIVE	LATIN BASE
caput	*capital*	**capit-**
corpus	*corporal*	**corpor-**
dēns	*dentist*	**dent-**
genus	*general*	**gener-**
iter	*itinerary*	**itiner-**
iūs	*jury*	**iūr-**
latus	*lateral*	**later-**
laus	*laudatory*	**laud-**
legiō	*legionary*	**legion-**
lēx	*legal*	**lēg-**
lūx	*lucid*	**lūc-**
mēns	*mental*	**ment-**
mīles	*military*	**mīlit-**
mors	*mortal*	**mort-**
mōs	*moral*	**mōr-**
nōmen	*nominate*	**nōmin-**
nox	*nocturnal*	**noct-**
opus	*operate*	**oper-**
ōrdō	*ordinal*	**ōrdin-**
pāx	*pacify*	**pāc-**
pēs	*pedal*	**ped-**
pōns	*pontoon*	**pont-**
prīnceps	*principal*	**prīncip-**
rēx	*regal*	**rēg-**
salūs	*salutary*	**salūt-**
tempus	*temporary*	**tempor-**
vōx	*vocal*	**vōc-**
vulnus	*vulnerable*	**vulner-**

EXERCISES

A. In the space before each noun in column *A*, write the letter of its form in column *B*.

	Column A		*Column B*
_____	**1.** urbis	*a.*	genitive plural
_____	**2.** genus	*b.*	ablative singular
_____	**3.** obsidem	*c.*	nominative or accusative plural
_____	**4.** sorōrum	*d.*	nominative or accusative singular
_____	**5.** equitī	*e.*	dative or ablative plural
_____	**6.** lēgēs	*f.*	genitive singular
_____	**7.** centuriō	*g.*	accusative plural
_____	**8.** nāvibus	*h.*	dative singular
_____	**9.** voluntāte	*i.*	nominative singular
_____	**10.** hostīs	*j.*	accusative singular

B. Identify the case(s) and number of the following forms:

1. turribus	_____	6. flūmina	_____
2. condiciō	_____	7. tempestātēs	_____
3. nōbilitātis	_____	8. explōrātōre	_____
4. cīvium	_____	9. cōnsuētūdinem	_____
5. hominī	_____	10. iter	_____

C. Underline the correct form.

1. genitive plural: *ratiōnum, ratiōnis, ratiōnēs*
2. accusative singular: *tempora, temporum, tempus*
3. ablative singular: *mare, marī, maris*
4. dative plural: *montī, montibus, montium*
5. nominative plural: *iūra, iūs, iūribus*
6. genitive singular: *caedēs, vulnerī, vīs*
7. accusative plural: *ducem, praetōris, īgnīs*
8. dative singular: *partis, generī, ōrdinibus*
9. nominative singular: *cupiditās, mēnsēs, legiōne*
10. ablative plural: *hiemis, aetāte, cohortibus*

D. Write the following specified forms:

1. accusative plural: *pars, corpus*   _____
2. genitive singular: *multitūdō, opus*   _____
3. ablative singular: *animal, caput*   _____
4. nominative plural: *amor, vulnus*   _____

 5. dative singular: *nātiō, cīvitās*   ---
 6. accusative singular: *genus, prīnceps*   --
 7. ablative plural: *regiō, mōs*   ---
 8. genitive plural: *gēns, lēx*   --
 9. nominative singular: *vōcēs, collium*   --
10. dative plural: *senātor, eques*   ---

E. Change each singular form to the plural.

1. mātris   ---------------------------
2. urbe   -----------------------------
3. nōmen   ---------------------------
4. hominī   --------------------------
5. fīnem   ---------------------------

6. nox   ------------------------------
7. adulēscentis   --------------------
8. animal   --------------------------
9. cōnsulī   -------------------------
10. marī   ---------------------------

A Street in Pompeii

When Vesuvius erupted in 79 A.D., Pompeii was one of the cities completely buried by volcanic ash. Today, through expert excavation, one can again see the city restored to life with everything intact. Many modern shops in Italy resemble those of ancient Pompeii.

Lesson 49—FOURTH DECLENSION NOUNS

impetus, attack; base, **impet-**   **cornū,** horn; base, **corn-**

	MASCULINE		NEUTER	
	SINGULAR	PLURAL	SINGULAR	PLURAL
Nom.	impet*us*	impet*ūs*	corn*ū*	corn*ua*
Gen.	impet*ūs*	impet*uum*	corn*ūs*	corn*uum*
Dat.	impet*uī*	impet*ibus*	corn*ū*	corn*ibus*
Acc.	impet*um*	impet*ūs*	corn*ū*	corn*ua*
Abl.	impet*ū*	impet*ibus*	corn*ū*	corn*ibus*

Note

1. Nouns of the fourth declension have the following endings:

	MASCULINE AND FEMININE		NEUTER	
	SINGULAR	PLURAL	SINGULAR	PLURAL
Nom.	-us	-ūs	-ū	-ua
Gen.	-ūs	-uum	-ūs	-uum
Dat.	-uī	-ibus	-ū	-ibus
Acc.	-um	-ūs	-ū	-ua
Abl.	-ū	-ibus	-ū	-ibus

2. As is true of neuter nouns of the second and third declensions, fourth declension neuters have the same forms for the nominative and accusative. In the plural these forms end in **-ua.**

3. Long marks (macrons) are particularly important in the fourth declension. The ending **-us** indicates the nominative singular, but **-ūs** may be either the genitive singular, nominative plural, or accusative plural.

4. Nouns of the fourth declension ending in **-us** are masculine; those ending in **-ū** are neuter. Feminine by exception are **domus** (home) and **manus** (hand).

5. Fourth declension nouns ending in **-us** are not to be confused with nouns of other declensions also ending in **-us.** The genitive singular ending determines the declension to which a noun belongs. For example:

NOMINATIVE	GENITIVE	DECLENSION
impetus	impet*ūs*	fourth
vulnus	vulner*is*	third
servus	serv*ī*	second

143

COMMON NOUNS OF THE FOURTH DECLENSION

MASCULINE

aditus, approach	**equitātus,** cavalry	**passus,** pace
adventus, arrival	**exercitus,** army	**portus,** harbor
cāsus, chance	**exitus,** outcome, departure	**prīncipātus,** leadership
cōnspectus, sight	**impetus,** attack	**reditus,** return
cōnsulātus, consulship	**magistrātus,** magistrate	**senātus,** senate
currus, chariot	**occāsus,** setting	**ūsus,** use, experience
cursus, running, course		

FEMININE

domus, home   **manus,** hand

NEUTER

cornū, horn, wing

Note

Domus is sometimes declined as a second declension noun.

EXERCISES

A. Underline the correct form.

1. genitive singular: *exercitus, exercitūs, exercituī*

2. accusative plural: *cornū, cornūs, cornua*

3. ablative singular: *passū, passibus, passuī*

4. dative singular: *senātuī, senātū, senātibus*

5. genitive plural: *impetum, impetūs, impetuum*

B. Identify the case(s) and number of the following forms:

1. manū ------------------------------
2. portūs ------------------------------
3. equitātuī ------------------------------
4. reditum ------------------------------
5. passuum ------------------------------
6. magistrātibus ------------------------------
7. cursus ------------------------------
8. cornūs ------------------------------
9. cornua ------------------------------
10. domum ------------------------------

C. Change each singular form to the plural.

1. impetūs ------------------------------
2. exercituī ------------------------------
3. manū ------------------------------
4. currus ------------------------------
5. aditum ------------------------------

D. Write the following specified forms:

1. accusative singular and plural: *manus* ------------------------------
2. genitive singular and plural: *exitus* ------------------------------
3. ablative singular and plural: *cāsus* ------------------------------
4. dative singular: *cōnsulātus, cornū* ------------------------------
5. nominative plural: *cornū, prīncipātus* ------------------------------

Lesson 50—FIFTH DECLENSION NOUNS

rēs, thing; base, **r-**   **aciēs,** battle line; base, **aci-**

	SINGULAR	PLURAL	SINGULAR	PLURAL
Nom.	rēs	rēs	aciēs	aciēs
Gen.	reī	rērum	aciēī	aciērum
Dat.	reī	rēbus	aciēī	aciēbus
Acc.	rem	rēs	aciem	aciēs
Abl.	rē	rēbus	aciē	aciēbus

Note

1. Nouns of the fifth declension have the following endings:

	SINGULAR	PLURAL
Nom.	-ēs	-ēs
Gen.	-eī	-ērum
Dat.	-eī	-ēbus
Acc.	-em	-ēs
Abl.	-ē	-ēbus

2. An **e** appears in the ending of each case without exception.

3. The following endings are identical:

   a. the nominative singular, nominative plural, accusative plural (**-ēs**)
   b. the genitive and dative singular (**-eī**)
   c. the dative and ablative plural (**-ēbus**)

4. Nouns of the fifth declension are feminine. By exception **diēs** (day) and **merīdiēs** (noon) are masculine. However, **diēs** is feminine in the expression **cōnstitūtā diē** (on the appointed day).

COMMON NOUNS OF THE FIFTH DECLENSION

FEMININE	MASCULINE
aciēs, battle line	**diēs,** day
fidēs, faith	**merīdiēs,** noon
rēs, thing	
speciēs, appearance	
spēs, hope	

EXERCISES

A. Identify the case(s) and number of the following forms:

1. diem _____
2. aciērum _____
3. rēbus _____
4. speciēs _____
5. fidē _____

6. merīdiēī _____
7. spem _____
8. aciēs _____
9. rērum _____
10. diē _____

145

B. Write the following specified forms:

1. ablative singular and plural: *rēs*   --
2. genitive singular and plural: *spēs*   --
3. accusative singular and plural: *diēs*   --
4. dative singular and plural: *aciēs*   --
5. nominative plural: *speciēs, fidēs*   --

C. Underline the correct form.

1. accusative singular: *spēs, spem, speī*
2. ablative plural: *diēbus, diē, diēs*
3. genitive plural: *reī, rērum, rem*
4. dative singular: *merīdiē, merīdiem, merīdiēī*
5. ablative singular: *speciē, aciēī, fidēs*

D. Change each singular form to the plural.

1. reī   --------------------------------
2. diē   --------------------------------
3. aciēs   --------------------------------
4. spem   --------------------------------
5. speciē   --------------------------------

Pont du Gard

This is the greatest of the Roman aqueducts, built in the first century A.D. near Nîmes, France. It is a tribute to the engineering genius of Rome that some of its highly developed water systems with their characteristic aqueducts are still in use today.

Lesson 51—REVIEW OF THE FIVE DECLENSIONS

COMPARISON OF NOUN ENDINGS

SINGULAR							
1st Decl.	*2nd Decl.*		*3rd Decl.*		*4th Decl.*		*5th Decl.*
(f.)	(m.)	(n.)	(m. & f.)	(n.)	(m.)	(n.)	(f.)
Nom. a	us(er, ir)	um	—	—	us	ū	ēs
Gen. ae	ī	ī	is	is	ūs	ūs	eī
Dat. ae	ō	ō	ī	ī	uī	ū	eī
Acc. am	um	um	em	—	um	ū	em
Abl. ā	ō	ō	e	e(ī)	ū	ū	ē

PLURAL							
Nom. ae	ī	a	ēs	a(ia)	ūs	ua	ēs
Gen. ārum	ōrum	ōrum	um(ium)	um(ium)	uum	uum	ērum
Dat. īs	īs	īs	ibus	ibus	ibus	ibus	ēbus
Acc. ās	ōs	a	ēs(īs)	a(ia)	ūs	ua	ēs
Abl. īs	īs	īs	ibus	ibus	ibus	ibus	ēbus

Note

1. Observe the following similarities in the endings of the five declensions:

	1ST	2ND	3RD	4TH	5TH
accusative singular:	-am	-um	-em	-um	-em
accusative plural:	-ās	-ōs	-ēs (-īs)	-ūs	-ēs
genitive plural:	-ārum	-ōrum	-um (-ium)	-uum	-ērum

2. The endings of the dative and ablative plural in each declension are identical. Observe also the similarity in the five declensions.

1ST	2ND	3RD	4TH	5TH
-īs	-īs	-ibus	-ibus	-ēbus

3. All neuter nouns, regardless of declension, have the same form for the accusative as the nominative. In the plural these cases always end in **-a**.

147

4. Unless one knows the declension to which a particular noun belongs, errors can easily result. Note the following possibilities of error because of similarity of endings:

FORM	IDENTIFICATION
caus*a*	nom. sing. fem. 1st declension
arm*a*	nom. or acc. pl. neuter 2nd declension
corpor*a*	nom. or acc. pl. neuter 3rd declension
ann*us*	nom. sing. masc. 2nd declension
gen*us*	nom. or acc. sing. neuter 3rd declension
port*us*	nom. sing. 4th declension
pu*er*	nom. sing. 2nd declension
frāt*er*	nom. sing. 3rd declension
ann*ī*	gen. sing. or nom. pl. 2nd declension
duc*ī*	dat. sing. 3rd declension
ann*um*	acc. sing. masc. 2nd declension
fact*um*	nom. or acc. sing. neuter 2nd declension
frātr*um*	gen. pl. 3rd declension
port*um*	acc. sing. 4th declension
frātr*em*	acc. sing. 3rd declension
aci*em*	acc. sing. 5th declension
duc*ēs*	nom. or acc. pl. 3rd declension
aci*ēs*	nom. sing., nom. pl., acc. pl. 5th declension
caus*īs*	dat. or abl. pl. 1st declension
ann*īs*	dat. or abl. pl. 2nd declension
nāv*īs*	acc. pl. 3rd declension
aet*ās*	nom. sing. 3rd declension
caus*ās*	acc. pl. 1st declension
sal*ūs*	nom. sing. 3rd declension
port*ūs*	gen. sing., nom. pl., acc. pl. 4th declension
nāt*iō*	nom. sing. 3rd declension
nūnt*iō*	dat. or abl. sing. 2nd declension

EXERCISES

A. Identify the case(s) and number of the following forms:

1. urbium _____
2. currum _____
3. hīberna _____
4. vigiliā _____
5. mūrōs _____
6. diērum _____
7. incolae _____
8. vesper _____
9. vulneris _____
10. exercitibus _____

11. praesidī _____
12. plēbī _____
13. cīvēs _____
14. obsidum _____
15. auctōritāte _____
16. occāsū _____
17. grātiās _____
18. lēgāte _____
19. caput _____
20. reī _____

B. In the space before each noun in column *A*, write the letter of its form in column *B*.

	Column A	*Column B*
_ _ _ _ _	**1.** itinere	*a.* genitive plural
_ _ _ _ _	**2.** senātum	*b.* accusative plural
_ _ _ _ _	**3.** perīculōrum	*c.* vocative singular
_ _ _ _ _	**4.** litterīs	*d.* ablative singular
_ _ _ _ _	**5.** equōs	*e.* genitive or dative singular
_ _ _ _ _	**6.** virō	*f.* accusative singular
_ _ _ _ _	**7.** fideī	*g.* nominative singular
_ _ _ _ _	**8.** dēditiō	*h.* genitive singular
_ _ _ _ _	**9.** amīce	*i.* dative or ablative singular
_ _ _ _ _	**10.** mercātōris	*j.* dative or ablative plural

C. Change each singular form to the plural.

1. flūmen _ 6. prōvinciā _ _ _ _ _ _ _ _ _ _ _ _ _ _ _ _ _

2. adventus _ 7. vīcī _

3. diē _ 8. virum _

4. hominis _ 9. animālis _ _ _ _ _ _ _ _ _ _ _ _ _ _ _ _ _ _

5. cohortī _ 10. factō _

D. Change each plural form to the singular.

1. auxilia _ 6. tubārum _ _ _ _ _ _ _ _ _ _ _ _ _ _ _ _ _ _

2. rīpās _ 7. fīliī _

3. magistrīs _ 8. tempora _ _ _ _ _ _ _ _ _ _ _ _ _ _ _ _ _ _

4. tribūnōs _ 9. passuum _ _ _ _ _ _ _ _ _ _ _ _ _ _ _ _ _ _

5. aciēbus _ 10. īgnīs _

E. Draw a line through the noun in each group that is *not* in the same *number* as the others.

1. iūra, arborēs, tempestās, manūs, poenās

2. modō, genera, urbem, audācia, mare

3. equitēs, imperiō, mīlitis, cōnsulātū, fortitūdō

4. cīvēs, prīncipātus, bella, diēs, barbarī

5. portae, impetūs, amōrēs, lītora, potestās

F. Draw a line through the noun in each group that is *not* in the same *case* as the others.

1. agminibus, victōrī, oppidīs, fīnīs, rēbus

2. frūmentum, īnsidiās, opus, labōrem, facultās

3. sorōrī, scūtō, lībertāte, exercitibus, sagittā

4. passuum, locīs, virtūtis, ducum, ūsūs

5. vōcēs, numerus, spatiō, hiems, regiō

G. Underline the correct form.

1. accusative singular: *ducum, collium, genus*

2. ablative plural: *tēlīs, studiō, cīvīs*

3. dative singular: *ōrātiō, mīlitī, operis*

4. nominative plural: *cōnsilia, cōpia, legiōnī*

5. genitive plural: *occāsum, subsidium, mentium*

6. ablative singular: *corporī, marī, imperātōrī*

7. accusative plural: *adventus, aciēs, partis*

8. dative plural: *aedificiīs, īgnīs, adulēscentis*

9. nominative singular: *impedīmentō, caedis, mūnītiō*

10. genitive singular: *senātūs, oculus, cōnsulī*

H. Write the following specified forms:

1. ablative plural: *socius, diēs*   --

2. genitive singular: *nōmen, equitātus*   --

3. dative singular: *proelium, agricola*   --

4. nominative plural: *negōtium, condiciō*   --

5. accusative plural: *iter, prīnceps*   --

6. genitive plural: *classis, rēs*   --

7. ablative singular: *multitūdō, cursus*   --

8. dative plural: *littera, homō*   --

9. accusative singular: *virtūs, vīs*   --

10. vocative singular: *fīlia, amīcus*   --

I. In the following sentences substitute, in the proper form, the noun in parentheses for the noun in italics:

1. Mārcus *tēlum* dēicit. (rēs)   -----------------------------

2. Magnus numerus *virōrum* convēnit. (homō)   -----------------------------

3. *Vulnera* sunt in capite. (Oculus)   -----------------------------

4. Puerī *īgnēs* vīdērunt. (aquila)   -----------------------------

5. Dux *mīlitī* negōtium dedit. (exercitus)   -----------------------------

6. *Viā* prohibitus est. (Iter)   -----------------------------

7. Causam *senātūs* laudāmus. (lībertās)   -----------------------------

8. Fābulam *nautīs* nārrō. (soror)   -----------------------------

9. Magnitūdinem *aciērum* timent. (cornū)   -----------------------------

10. Omnēs ē *nāve* ēgressī sunt. (castra)   -----------------------------

J. In the following list, indicate the declension of each noun by putting the number *1* for a noun of the first declension, the number *2* for a noun of the second declension, etc.

1. populus	------		**11.** fidēs	------	
2. diēs	------		**12.** castra	------	
3. lēx	------		**13.** flūmen	------	
4. verbum	------		**14.** cōpia	------	
5. multitūdō	------		**15.** magister	------	
6. exercitus	------		**16.** respōnsum	------	
7. nauta	------		**17.** frāter	------	
8. salūs	------		**18.** mōs	------	
9. caput	------		**19.** cornū	------	
10. adventus	------		**20.** spēs	------	

K. In the following list, indicate the gender of each noun by putting the letter *m* for a masculine noun, the letter *f* for a feminine noun, and the letter *n* for a neuter noun.

1. dea	------		**11.** gladius	------	
2. imperium	------		**12.** manus	------	
3. corpus	------		**13.** mōns	------	
4. impetus	------		**14.** liber	------	
5. nōmen	------		**15.** mare	------	
6. virtūs	------		**16.** celeritās	------	
7. hiems	------		**17.** aciēs	------	
8. arma	------		**18.** legiō	------	
9. pēs	------		**19.** impedīmentum	------	
10. rēs	------		**20.** agricola	------	

The Ides of March

Caesar was assassinated on the Ides of March (March 15), 44 B.C., while presiding over a meeting of the Roman Senate. Ever since that fatal day, the Ides of March have come to mean any day of impending disaster.

Unit VII—Adjectives, Numerals, and Adverbs

Lesson 52—FIRST AND SECOND DECLENSION ADJECTIVES

	SINGULAR			PLURAL		
	(m.)	*(f.)*	*(n.)*	*(m.)*	*(f.)*	*(n.)*
Nom.	nōt**us**	nōt**a**	nōt**um**	nōt**ī**	nōt**ae**	nōt**a**
Gen.	nōt**ī**	nōt**ae**	nōt**ī**	nōt**ōrum**	nōt**ārum**	nōt**ōrum**
Dat.	nōt**ō**	nōt**ae**	nōt**ō**	nōt**īs**	nōt**īs**	nōt**īs**
Acc.	nōt**um**	nōt**am**	nōt**um**	nōt**ōs**	nōt**ās**	nōt**a**
Abl.	nōt**ō**	nōt**ā**	nōt**ō**	nōt**īs**	nōt**īs**	nōt**īs**

Note

1. The masculine and neuter forms of the adjective are declined like nouns of the second declension; the feminine forms like nouns of the first declension.

2. Some adjectives end in **-er** in the masculine nominative singular. Otherwise they are declined like **nōtus, -a, -um.**

>   *Nom.*   **līber, lībera, līberum**
>   *Gen.*   **līberī, līberae, līberī,** etc.

3. Most adjectives ending in **-er** in the masculine nominative singular drop the **e** in all other forms.

>   *Nom.*   **aeger, aegra, aegrum**
>   *Gen.*   **aegrī, aegrae, aegrī,** etc.

4. An adjective agrees with its noun in gender, number, and case.

>   **mūrus altus   fortūnam malam   cīvibus bonīs**

5. In agreeing with its noun, an adjective need not have the same ending as the noun, nor be in the same declension as the noun.

>   **regiō clāra   mīlitum miserōrum**
>   **poētam vērum   rēs magnās**

6. Except for emphasis or contrast, an adjective generally follows its noun.

>   **manus dextra,** the right hand
>   **dextra manus,** the *right* hand (not the left)

152

7. An adjective may be used without a noun when the noun is clearly understood. This occurs mostly in the plural. If the adjective is masculine, it refers to people; if neuter, to things.

Paucī mānsērunt.   A few (men) remained.
masculine

Omnēs vīdī.   I saw everyone (all men).
masculine

Omnia agenda erant.   Everything (all things) had to be done.
neuter

Multa deerant.   Many things were lacking.
neuter

8. The vocative of adjectives is formed the same way as for nouns. Thus, the vocative of **clāra** is **clāra**, but the vocative of **clārus** is **clāre**. **Meus** has a special form, **mī**.

9. An adjective can often furnish a clue in identifying a noun whose form is otherwise uncertain. For example, in the combination **obsidēs reliquōs, obsidēs** may be either nominative or accusative plural. The obvious case of **reliquōs**, however, informs us that in this instance **obsidēs** must be accusative plural.

COMMON FIRST AND SECOND DECLENSION ADJECTIVES

(-us, -a, -um)

aequus, equal, fair	**grātus,** pleasing	**paucī** (*pl.*), few
altus, high, deep	**hūmānus,** human	**posterus,** following
amīcus, friendly	**idōneus,** suitable	**propinquus,** near
amplus, large	**ignōtus,** unknown	**proximus,** nearest
angustus, narrow	**incertus,** uncertain	**pūblicus,** public
apertus, open	**inimīcus,** unfriendly	**quantus,** how great
barbarus, foreign	**inīquus,** unequal	**rēctus,** straight
bonus, good	**lātus,** wide	**reliquus,** remaining
certus, certain	**longus,** long	**salvus,** safe
cēterī (*pl.*), the rest	**magnus,** great	**singulī** (*pl.*), one at a time
clārus, clear	**malus,** bad	**summus,** highest
commodus, suitable	**maritimus,** of the sea	**superus,** upper
continuus, successive	**medius,** middle	**suus,** his (her, their) own
cupidus, desirous	**meus,** my	**tantus,** so great
ēgregius, outstanding	**multus,** much	**tardus,** slow, late
extrēmus, farthest	**necessārius,** necessary	**timidus,** fearful
falsus, false	**nōtus,** known	**tuus,** your
fīnitimus, neighboring	**novus,** new	**vacuus,** empty, free
fīrmus, strong	**opportūnus,** suitable	**validus,** strong
frīgidus, cold	**parātus,** prepared	**vērus,** true
frūmentārius, fertile	**parvus,** small	**vīvus,** alive, living

(-er, -era, -erum)

līber, free   **miser,** poor, unfortunate

(-er, -ra, -rum)

aeger, sick	**pulcher,** beautiful
dexter, right	**sinister,** left
integer, whole	**vester,** your
noster, our	

EXERCISES

A. Underline the correct form of the adjective.

1. accusative singular feminine: *amplum, amplās, amplam*
2. nominative plural neuter: *falsa, falsae, falsī*
3. genitive singular masculine: *nostrōrum, nostrī, nostrō*
4. ablative singular feminine: *tarda, tardā, tardae*
5. dative plural neuter: *paucī, pauca, paucīs*
6. vocative singular masculine: *nōtus, nōte, nōtī*
7. genitive plural feminine: *suārum, suae, suōrum*
8. accusative plural neuter: *tantōs, tanta, tantum*
9. dative singular masculine: *fīrmīs, fīrmī, fīrmō*
10. ablative plural neuter: *aegrīs, summa, extrēmō*

B. Identify the case(s), number, and gender of the following forms:

1. pulchrā _____
2. integrīs _____
3. pūblicī _____
4. novōs _____
5. grāta _____
6. vīvōrum _____
7. līberō _____
8. medium _____
9. timidae _____
10. meārum _____

C. In the space before each noun in column *A*, write the letter of its modifying adjective in column *B*.

	Column A	Column B
_____	**1.** cohortem	*a.* validīs
_____	**2.** fidē	*b.* miserōs
_____	**3.** exercitibus	*c.* longōrum
_____	**4.** iter	*d.* ēgregius
_____	**5.** diērum	*e.* cēterae
_____	**6.** mīles	*f.* integram
_____	**7.** incolās	*g.* incerta
_____	**8.** tempestās	*h.* multārum
_____	**9.** sorōrēs	*i.* bonā
_____	**10.** manuum	*j.* magnum

D. Underline the noun in parentheses with which the adjective agrees.

1. nova   (cōnsilia, mēnsis, silvae)

2. grātīs   (rēs, classis, lēgibus)

3. vestrārum   (impetuum, līberōrum, legiōnum)

4. quantae   (fortūna, caedis, itineris)

5. proximōs   (fīnēs, pontis, arborēs)

6. suā   (fossa, auxilia, speciē)

7. aequī   (animō, lateris, gentēs)

8. timidō   (equitī, senātūs, ducis)

9. miserās   (animālia, agricolās, mātrēs)

10. tantum   (pedum, opus, calamitātem)

E. Make each adjective agree with the noun in italics.

1. *altitūdō*—parvus ....

6. *nāvibus*—reliquus ....

2. *prōvinciā*—noster ....

7. *aciem*—parātus ....

3. *locum*—medius ....

8. *hīberna*—commodus ....

4. *impetū*—magnus ....

9. *cīvitātis*—līber ....

5. *mīlitum*—integer ....

10. *exercituī*—validus ....

The Appian Way

Perhaps the most famous road in antiquity was the Appian Way, the "Rēgīna Viārum" (Queen of Roads). Begun in the fourth century B.C., it ultimately extended from Rome to Brundisium, 350 miles to the south. The road was constructed of immense blocks of stone laid with such perfect exactness that it is still used after 2,000 years of traffic.

Lesson 53—THIRD DECLENSION ADJECTIVES

THREE ENDINGS

	SINGULAR			PLURAL		
	(m.)	(f.)	(n.)	(m.)	(f.)	(n.)
Nom.	ācer	ācris	ācre	ācrēs	ācrēs	ācria
Gen.	ācris	ācris	ācris	ācrium	ācrium	ācrium
Dat.	ācrī	ācrī	ācrī	ācribus	ācribus	ācribus
Acc.	ācrem	ācrem	ācre	ācrēs (-īs)	ācrēs (-īs)	ācria
Abl.	ācrī	ācrī	ācrī	ācribus	ācribus	ācribus

TWO ENDINGS

	SINGULAR		PLURAL	
	(m. & f.)	(n.)	(m. & f.)	(n.)
Nom.	levis	leve	levēs	levia
Gen.	levis	levis	levium	levium
Dat.	levī	levī	levibus	levibus
Acc.	levem	leve	levēs (-īs)	levia
Abl.	levī	levī	levibus	levibus

ONE ENDING

	SINGULAR		PLURAL		SINGULAR		PLURAL	
	(m. & f.)	(n.)	(m. & f.)	(n.)	(m. & f.)	(n.)	(m. & f.)	(n.)
Nom.	audāx	audāx	audācēs	audācia	potēns	potēns	potentēs	potentia
Gen.	audācis	audācis	audācium	audācium	potentis	potentis	potentium	potentium
Dat.	audācī	audācī	audācibus	audācibus	potentī	potentī	potentibus	potentibus
Acc.	audācem	audāx	audācēs (-īs)	audācia	potentem	potēns	potentēs (-īs)	potentia
Abl.	audācī	audācī	audācibus	audācibus	potentī	potentī	potentibus	potentibus

Note

1. Third declension adjectives follow the general pattern of third declension i-stem nouns. Note particularly that the ablative singular of all genders ends in **-ī** and the genitive plural in **-ium**. Also, the accusative plural may end in **-īs** as well as **-ēs**.

2. Like neuter nouns, the accusative forms of neuter adjectives are the same as the nominative. In the plural, these forms end in **-ia**.

3. The present participle in Latin serves as an adjective and is declined like **potēns**. The ablative singular, however, usually ends in **-e**. For example: **vocāns, vocantis, vocantī, vocantem, vocante**.

COMMON THIRD DECLENSION ADJECTIVES

THREE ENDINGS

(-er, -ris, -re)

ācer, sharp

(er, -eris, -ere)

celer, swift

TWO ENDINGS

(-is, -e)

brevis, short	**facilis,** easy	**levis,** light
cīvīlis, civil	**fidēlis,** faithful	**mīlitāris,** military
commūnis, common	**fortis,** brave	**nōbilis,** noble
cōnsulāris, consular	**gravis,** heavy, severe	**omnis,** all
difficilis, difficult	**immortālis,** immortal	**similis,** similar, like
dissimilis, unlike	**incolumis,** unharmed	**ūtilis,** useful

ONE ENDING

(-x, genitive -cis)

audāx, daring
fēlīx, happy
īnfēlīx, unhappy

(-ēns, genitive -entis)

dīligēns, careful
potēns, powerful
recēns, recent

pār, equal

EXERCISES

A. Identify the case(s), number, and gender of the following forms:

1. omne _____

2. celerēs _____

3. pārī _____

4. gravia _____

5. fidēlibus _____

6. facilium _____

7. ācrem _____

8. dīligentis _____

9. nōbilīs _____

10. fēlīx _____

B. Underline the correct form of the adjective.

1. accusative singular feminine: *recēns, recentia, recentem*

2. ablative plural neuter: *celeribus, celerī, celeria*

3. genitive plural masculine: *brevis, brevium, brevem*

4. dative singular neuter: *cīvīlī, cīvīlis, cīvīlīs*

5. nominative plural feminine: *ācria, ācris, ācrēs*

6. accusative plural masculine: *similīs, similem, similis*

7. genitive singular neuter: *potēns, potentium, potentis*

8. dative plural feminine: *nōbilī, nōbilibus, nōbilīs*

9. ablative singular masculine: *ūtilibus, ūtilīs, ūtilī*

10. nominative singular neuter: *facilis, pār, gravia*

C. Make each adjective agree with the noun in italics.

1. *prōvinciam*—omnis ....
2. *deīs*—immortālis ....
3. *tempore*—brevis ....
4. *prīncipēs*—potēns ....
5. *rērum*—ūtilis ....

6. *impetum*—ācer ....
7. *bellō*—cīvilis ....
8. *līberōs*—dīligēns ....
9. *mātrī*—īnfēlīx ....
10. *aetātis*—pār ....

D. Underline the noun in parentheses with which the adjective agrees.

1. omne   (corpore, corporī, corpus)
2. fēlīcem   (puerum, puerōrum, puer)
3. recentibus   (annōs, annīs, annōrum)
4. celeris   (sagittīs, sagittā, sagitta)
5. facilia   (negōtium, negōtī, negōtia)
6. commūnium   (spem, spērum, spēs)
7. gravī   (impetuī, impetus, impetūs)
8. mīlitārīs   (ratiōnis, ratiōnibus, ratiōnēs)
9. ācer   (proelium, ōrātiō, gladiātor)
10. potentēs   (hostis, sociī, agmina)

E. Translate each English adjective into Latin, making it agree with the accompanying noun.

1. brave   mīlitum   ....
2. easy   aditum   ....
3. similar   pontis   ....
4. equal   cōnsiliīs   ....
5. daring   peditī   ....
6. swift   tempus   ....
7. short   aciē   ....
8. all   perīcula   ....
9. careful   līberōrum   ....
10. unhappy   terrā   ....

Lesson 54—IRREGULAR ADJECTIVES; NUMERALS

Some adjectives are irregular in the genitive and dative singular only. The genitive ends in **-īus** and the dative in **-ī** in all genders. The plural is regularly declined like **nōtus, -a, -um** (see page 152).

	SINGULAR		
	(m.)	*(f.)*	*(n.)*
Nom.	alius	alia	aliud
Gen.	*alīus*	*alīus*	*alīus*
Dat.	*aliī*	*aliī*	*aliī*
Acc.	alium	aliam	aliud
Abl.	aliō	aliā	aliō

Adjectives declined in this way are:

alius, alia, aliud, other, another
alter, altera, alterum, the other (of two)
neuter, neutra, neutrum, neither (of two)
nūllus, nūlla, nūllum, no, none
sōlus, sōla, sōlum, alone, only

tōtus, tōta, tōtum, whole
ūllus, ūlla, ūllum, any
uter, utra, utrum, which (of two)
uterque, utraque, utrumque, each

Note

The combination **nōn nūllī** (*pl.*) means *some* (people).

CARDINAL NUMBERS

ūnus, one
duo, two
trēs, three
quattuor, four

quīnque, five
sex, six
septem, seven
octō, eight
novem, nine

decem, ten
vīgintī, twenty
centum, one hundred
mīlle, one thousand

ORDINAL NUMBERS

prīmus, first
secundus, second
tertius, third

quārtus, fourth
quīntus, fifth
sextus, sixth
septimus, seventh

octāvus, eighth
nōnus, ninth
decimus, tenth

ROMAN NUMERALS

I = 1   **V** = 5   **X** = 10   **L** = 50   **C** = 100   **D** = 500   **M** = 1000

ūnus

	(m.)	(f.)	(n.)
Nom.	ūnus	ūna	ūnum
Gen.	*ūnīus*	*ūnīus*	*ūnīus*
Dat.	*ūnī*	*ūnī*	*ūnī*
Acc.	ūnum	ūnam	ūnum
Abl.	ūnō	ūnā	ūnō

Note

Ūnus is declined like **alius**.

duo　　　　　　　　　trēs　　　　mīlle

	(m.)	(f.)	(n.)	(m. & f.)	(n.)	SINGULAR	PLURAL
Nom.	duo	du*ae*	duo	tr*ēs*	tr*ia*	mīlle	mīl*ia*
Gen.	du*ōrum*	du*ārum*	du*ōrum*	tr*ium*	tr*ium*	mīlle	mīl*ium*
Dat.	du*ōbus*	du*ābus*	du*ōbus*	tr*ibus*	tr*ibus*	mīlle	mīl*ibus*
Acc.	du*ōs*	du*ās*	duo	tr*ēs*	tr*ia*	mīlle	mīl*ia*
Abl.	du*ōbus*	du*ābus*	du*ōbus*	tr*ibus*	tr*ibus*	mīlle	mīl*ibus*

Note

1. Cardinal numbers from *four* to *one hundred* are not declined.

2. Numerals are adjectives, and as such agree with their nouns. One exception, however, is **mīlia,** the plural of **mīlle. Mīlia** is a neuter noun followed by the genitive.

mīlle sociī　　　　　　a thousand allies
nominative

tria mīlia sociōrum　　　three thousand allies
nominative　　genitive

3. Ordinal numbers are declined like **nōtus, -a, -um.**

EXERCISES

A. Make each adjective or number agree with the noun in italics.

1. *ratiōnem*—ūllus　_ _ _ _ _ _ _ _ _ _ _
2. *prīncipum*—duo　_ _ _ _ _ _ _ _ _ _ _
3. *passūs*—mīlle　_ _ _ _ _ _ _ _ _ _ _
4. *aedificī*—tōtus　_ _ _ _ _ _ _ _ _ _ _
5. *senātuī*—sōlus　_ _ _ _ _ _ _ _ _ _ _

6. *diē*—quīntus　_ _ _ _ _ _ _ _ _ _ _
7. *praesidia*—trēs　_ _ _ _ _ _ _ _ _ _ _
8. *hominibus*—alius　_ _ _ _ _ _ _ _ _ _ _
9. *cōnsulis*—ūnus　_ _ _ _ _ _ _ _ _ _ _
10. *sorōrī*—neuter　_ _ _ _ _ _ _ _ _ _ _

B. Give the English equivalent of the Roman numerals.

1. LXX mīlitēs   _____ soldiers
2. XII negōtia   _____ tasks
3. vāllum pedum XV   a wall of _____ feet
4. IX nāvēs   _____ ships
5. DC obsidēs   _____ hostages
6. MCCLVI armātī   _____ armed soldiers
7. DCCC mīlia passuum   _____ miles
8. XLVII diēs   _____ days
9. XIV equitēs   _____ horsemen
10. CXLIV hōrae   _____ hours

C. Identify the case(s), number, and gender of the following forms:

1. duābus _____
2. ūnī _____
3. decimō _____
4. mīlium _____
5. alterīus _____
6. tria _____
7. secundam _____
8. aliī _____
9. ūllōrum _____
10. tōtīus _____

D. Underline the adjective or number in parentheses that agrees with the noun.

1. flūmina   (duōs, duās, duo)   6. magistrātuī   (neutrī, neutrīus, neutrō)
2. lēx   (uter, utra, utrum)   7. discipulī   (mīlle, mīlia, mīlium)
3. lateris   (quārtī, quārtīs, quārtae)   8. nūntī   (ūnī, ūnō, ūnīus)
4. pedum   (trēs, tria, trium)   9. vir   (decem, decimō, decimus)
5. cīvitātis   (alterae, alterīus, alterīs)   10. aciē   (prīma, prīmae, prīmā)

E. Complete the English translation.

1. alter vir   _____ man   6. ūllum genus   _____ kind
2. nōn nūllī stābant _____ were standing 7. centum diēs   _____ days
3. novem servī   _____ slaves   8. vīgintī nāvēs _____ ships
4. octāvus mēnsis   _____ month   9. nūllus victor _____ conqueror
5. utraque arbor   _____ tree   10. quīnta nox   _____ night

Lesson 55—REVIEW OF DECLENSION OF ADJECTIVES AND NUMERALS

A. Identify the case(s) and number of the following forms:

1. omnibus urbibus ....
2. suō nōmine ....
3. reliquōs Gallōs ....
4. legiō ūna ....
5. prōvinciae tōtī ....
6. latere apertō ....
7. alterīus partis ....
8. recentī victōriā ....
9. nōn nūllīs nātiōnibus ....
10. XXV mīlia ....

11. ācrī impetū ....
12. tantam multitūdinem ....
13. duās aciēs ....
14. reliquārum rērum ....
15. ūllam condiciōnem ....
16. reī mīlitāris ....
17. equitēs nostrī ....
18. quārtae cohortis ....
19. magnō ūsuī ....
20. cīvitātum potentium ....

B. In the space before each noun in column A, write the letter of its modifying adjective in column B.

	Column A	Column B
....	**1.** regiōnem	*a.* prīmō
....	**2.** vulnus	*b.* duābus
....	**3.** maris	*c.* omnium
....	**4.** impetū	*d.* nostra
....	**5.** obsidum	*e.* grave
....	**6.** calamitātī	*f.* potentēs
....	**7.** oppida	*g.* ūllī
....	**8.** fēminīs	*h.* fīnitimam
....	**9.** colōniae	*i.* fortīs
....	**10.** barbarōs	*j.* tōtīus

C. For each noun write the proper form of **certus** and **omnis**.

	CERTUS	OMNIS		CERTUS	OMNIS
1. magistrōs	....	....	6. cīve	....	....
2. portum	....	....	7. praesidī	....	....
3. rēbus	....	....	8. nātiōnī	....	....
4. līberī	....	....	9. nautā	....	....
5. portārum	....	....	10. genus	....	....

D. Underline the correct case and number of the following:

1. mīlitēs fortīs   (nominative plural, accusative plural)
2. ūnī officiō   (dative singular, ablative singular)
3. adventūs celeris   (genitive singular, nominative plural)
4. frātrēs nostrī   (nominative plural, accusative plural)
5. aciēs longa   (nominative singular, nominative plural)
6. exercitūs parvōs   (nominative plural, accusative plural)
7. cīvis sōlīus   (nominative singular, genitive singular)
8. viae brevis   (genitive singular, dative singular)
9. manūs nostrae   (nominative plural, accusative plural)
10. diēī tōtī   (genitive singular, dative singular)

E. Each group in parentheses contains one form that does *not* agree with the noun. Rewrite it correctly.

1. praetōrum   (duōrum, reliquum, nōbilium)   ----------------------------
2. fidem   (bonam, commūnem, novum)   ----------------------------
3. annō   (tōtī, longō, breve)   ----------------------------
4. caedīs   (gravis, multōs, recentēs)   ----------------------------
5. incolae   (validae, alīus, timidī)   ----------------------------

F. Underline the adjective in parentheses that agrees with the noun.

1. ōrātiō   (longō, longā, longa)
2. maris   (tōtīus, tōtō, tōtīs)
3. verba   (trium, trēs, tria)
4. aciem   (tertium, tertiam, tertia)
5. impetuum   (ācrium, ācrem, ācre)

G. Write the following specified forms:

1. accusative plural: *fīnis extrēmus, deus immortālis*

----

2. ablative singular: *negōtium difficile, fāma bona*

----

3. dative plural: *exercitus tuus, eques celer*

----

4. genitive singular: *vōx similis, iniūria ūlla*

----

5. nominative plural: *captīvus īnfēlīx, proelium ācre*

----

6. dative singular: *patria utra, puer dīligēns*

----

7. accusative singular: *aciēs secunda, condiciō commūnis*

----

8. genitive plural: *tria nāvigia, senātor fortis*

----

9. ablative plural: *mīlle hominēs, iter magnum*

----

10. vocative singular: *meus fīlius, amīcus bonus*

H. Translate the following expressions into English:

1. LX virī   -------------------------   6. octō hōrae   -------------------------

2. tria mīlia mīlitum   ------------------   7. XIX pedēs   -------------------------

3. alter puer   --------------------------   8. CLIV nāvēs --------------------------

4. duārum legiōnum   ------------------   9. neutra via   -------------------------

5. septimō diē   ------------------------   10. alia nox   -------------------------

I. Rewrite the sentences below, making *all* changes required by the directions in parentheses.

1. Iūlius *meam* tubam habet. (substitute equivalent form of *noster*)

----

2. Equī *validī* currēbant. (substitute equivalent form of *celer*)

----

3. *Multōs* amīcōs habeō. (substitute the opposite)

----

4. Cōnsilium *ūtile* capiēbant. (substitute equivalent form of *magnus*)

----

5. Erat puer *fēlīx*. (substitute the negative form)

----

6. In *certō* perīculō erāmus. (substitute equivalent form of *gravis*)

----

7. Ā *dextrō* cornū pugnātum est. (substitute the opposite)

----

8. *Duo* mīlia passuum prōgressī sunt. (change to the next higher number)

----

9. Ā ducibus *barbarīs* victī erant. (substitute equivalent form of *potēns*)

----

10. Tuam virtūtem, *mīles*, admīrāmur. (change to *mīlitēs*)

Lesson 56—COMPARISON OF ADJECTIVES

REGULAR COMPARISON

POSITIVE	COMPARATIVE	SUPERLATIVE
	(m. & f.) *(n.)*	*(m.)* *(f.)* *(n.)*
alt*us*, -*a*, -*um*	alt*ior*, alt*ius*	alt*issimus*, -*a*, -*um*
fort*is*, -*e*	fort*ior*, fort*ius*	fort*issimus*, -*a*, -*um*
audā*x*	audā*cior*, audā*cius*	audā*cissimus*, -*a*, -*um*
potē*ns*	potent*ior*, potent*ius*	potent*issimus*, -*a*, -*um*
līber, -er*a*, -er*um*	līber*ior*, līber*ius*	līber*rimus*, -*a*, -*um*
ācer, -cr*is*, -cr*e*	ācr*ior*, ācr*ius*	ācer*rimus*, -*a*, -*um*
facil*is*, -*e*	facil*ior*, facil*ius*	facil*limus*, -*a*, -*um*

Note

1. The comparative degree is formed by adding **-ior** to the base of the positive for the masculine and feminine, and **-ius** for the neuter.

2. The superlative is formed by adding **-issimus, -a, -um** to the base of the positive, with two exceptions:

    a. Adjectives ending in **-er** (regardless of declension) add **-rimus, -a, -um** to the *nominative singular masculine.*

POSITIVE	SUPERLATIVE
līber	līber*rimus*
ācer	ācer*rimus*

    b. Four adjectives ending in **-lis** (facilis, difficilis, similis, dissimilis) add **-limus, -a, -um** to the base of the positive.

POSITIVE	SUPERLATIVE
facilis	facil*limus*

3. Superlative degree adjectives are all declined like **altus, -a, -um**. The declension of comparatives will be discussed in the next lesson.

IRREGULAR COMPARISON

POSITIVE	COMPARATIVE	SUPERLATIVE
	(m. & f.) *(n.)*	*(m.)* *(f.)* *(n.)*
bon*us*, -*a*, -*um*	mel*ior*, mel*ius*	opt*imus*, -*a*, -*um*
mal*us*, -*a*, -*um*	pe*ior*, pe*ius*	pess*imus*, -*a*, -*um*
magn*us*, -*a*, -*um*	ma*ior*, ma*ius*	max*imus*, -*a*, -*um*
parv*us*, -*a*, -*um*	min*or*, min*us*	min*imus*, -*a*, -*um*
mult*us*, -*a*, -*um*	——, plūs	plū*rimus*, -*a*, -*um*

Note

1. The comparative degree is translated as follows:

altior, -ius, higher, rather high, too high

audācior, -ius, more daring

2. The superlative degree is translated as follows:

altissimus, -a, -um, highest, very high

audācissimus, -a, -um, most or very daring

3. The following adjectives are really comparatives whose positives either do not exist or are rarely used:

citerior, nearer	**īnferior,** lower	**superior,** higher
complūrēs (*pl.*), several	**prior,** former	**ulterior,** farther
exterior, outer		

EXERCISES

A. Identify the degree of each adjective by putting a check in the appropriate column.

	POSITIVE	COMPARATIVE	SUPERLATIVE
1. grātior	-------	-------	-------
2. clārissimus	-------	-------	-------
3. facilius	-------	-------	-------
4. commūnis	-------	-------	-------
5. simillimus	-------	-------	-------
6. minor	-------	-------	-------
7. pessimus	-------	-------	-------
8. celeris	-------	-------	-------
9. pulcherrima	-------	-------	-------
10. idōneus	-------	-------	-------

B. Make each adjective agree with the noun in italics.

1. *fossam*—lātissimus ....
2. *dominus*—gravior ....
3. *adituum*—facilis ....
4. *tempus*—brevior ....
5. *celeritāte*—maximus ....

6. *operis*—difficillimus ....
7. *rēbus*—miserrimus ....
8. *praetōrem*—potēns ....
9. *multitūdinī*—minimus ....
10. *ratiō*—dīligentior ....

C. Underline the correct English translation.

1. clārior   (clear, clearer, clearest)
2. celerrima   (swift, swifter, very swift)
3. optimum   (good, better, best)
4. inimīcus   (unfriendly, more unfriendly, most unfriendly)

5. simillimus   (similar, more similar, very similar)

6. minus   (small, smaller, smallest)

7. ulterior   (far, farther, farthest)

8. idōneus   (suitable, more suitable, most suitable)

9. plūrimus   (much, more, most)

10. peior   (bad, worse, worst)

D. Compare the following adjectives:

	COMPARATIVE	SUPERLATIVE
1. certus	-----------------------------	-----------------------------
2. fortis	-----------------------------	-----------------------------
3. ācer	-----------------------------	-----------------------------
4. miser	-----------------------------	-----------------------------
5. magnus	-----------------------------	-----------------------------
6. difficilis	-----------------------------	-----------------------------
7. bonus	-----------------------------	-----------------------------
8. fēlīx	-----------------------------	-----------------------------
9. recēns	-----------------------------	-----------------------------
10. multus	-----------------------------	-----------------------------

Roman Dress

The toga, the formal garment of the Romans, has become associated with tradition, dignity, and authority. Today the academic gowns worn at commencement exercises and the judicial robes worn in court are reminiscent of the Roman toga.

Lesson 57—DECLENSION OF COMPARATIVES

	SINGULAR		PLURAL	
	(m. & f.)	*(n.)*	*(m. & f.)*	*(n.)*
Nom.	gravior	gravius	graviōr**ēs**	graviōr**a**
Gen.	graviōr**is**	graviōr**is**	graviōr**um**	graviōr**um**
Dat.	graviōr**ī**	graviōr**ī**	graviōr**ibus**	graviōr**ibus**
Acc.	graviōr**em**	gravius	graviōr**ēs**	graviōr**a**
Abl.	graviōr**e**	graviōr**e**	graviōr**ibus**	graviōr**ibus**

Note

1. All comparatives, whether formed from adjectives of the first and second or third declension, are declined like third declension consonant-stem nouns.

2. Observe the following differences in declining a positive adjective of the third declension and a comparative:

	POSITIVE	COMPARATIVE
ablative singular:	grav**ī**	graviōr**e**
genitive plural:	grav**ium**	graviōr**um**
nominative or accusative plural neuter:	grav**ia**	graviōr**a**

3. **Plūs** (more), the comparative of **multus,** is a neuter noun. The plural (*more, many, several*), however, is used as an adjective. The complete declension follows:

	SINGULAR	PLURAL	
	(n.)	*(m. & f.)*	*(n.)*
Nom.	plūs	plūr**ēs**	plūr**a**
Gen.	plūr**is**	plūr**ium**	plūr**ium**
Dat.	————	plūr**ibus**	plūr**ibus**
Acc.	plūs	plūr**ēs** (-**īs**)	plūr**a**
Abl.	plūr**e**	plūr**ibus**	plūr**ibus**

EXERCISES

A. Underline the comparative in each group of adjectives.

1. facilium, facillimum, faciliōrum
2. longiōra, longa, longissima
3. ūtilī, ūtiliōre, ūtile
4. aegerrima, aegra, aegriōra
5. plūribus, plūrimīs, multīs

6. pessimō, peiōre, malō
7. potentis, potentissimī, potentiōris
8. minus, minimum, parvum
9. celerēs, celerrimī, celeriōrēs
10. audāciōrem, audācem, audācissimum

B. Make each comparative agree with the noun in italics.

1. *equitem*—altior ....
2. *legiōnēs*—fortior ....
3. *terrā*—melior ....
4. *spērum*—maior ....
5. *nōmen*—longior ....

6. *exercituī*—potentior ....
7. *fīliīs*—īnfēlīcior ....
8. *dōnum*—ūtilior ....
9. *poētās*—nōbilior ....
10. *cīvitās*—fīrmior ....

C. In the space before each noun in column *A*, write the letter of its modifying comparative in column *B*.

	Column A	*Column B*
......	**1.** lēgātum	*a.* maius
......	**2.** īnsulīs	*b.* vēriōrēs
......	**3.** iter	*c.* graviōra
......	**4.** rērum	*d.* difficiliōris
......	**5.** magistrātuī	*e.* pulchriōribus
......	**6.** vōcēs	*f.* melior
......	**7.** officia	*g.* audāciōre
......	**8.** causa	*h.* dīligentiōrem
......	**9.** cōnsilī	*i.* grātiōrī
......	**10.** proeliō	*j.* similiōrum

Interior of a Roman Home

As one entered the home of a wealthy Roman, one found himself in a large reception room, the atrium, flanked by various rooms and leading to the peristyle in the rear. The spaciousness and openness of the atrium have been copied by designers of modern villas in Italy, Spain, and other Mediterranean countries.

Lesson 58—FORMATION AND COMPARISON OF ADVERBS

FORMATION OF ADVERBS FROM ADJECTIVES

ADJECTIVE	ADVERB	ADJECTIVE	ADVERB
clārus	clārē	brevis	breviter
aequus	aequē	ācer	ācriter
miser	miserē	fēlīx	fēlīciter
pulcher	pulchrē	dīligēns	dīligenter

Note

1. Adverbs are formed from first and second declension adjectives by adding -ē to the base.

ADJECTIVE	BASE	ADVERB
clārus	clār-	clārē
pulcher	pulchr-	pulchrē

2. Adverbs are formed from third declension adjectives by adding **-iter** to the base. However, adjectives ending in **-ēns** (genitive, **-entis**) add **-er** to the base.

ADJECTIVE	BASE	ADVERB
brevis	brev-	breviter
fēlīx	fēlīc-	fēlīciter
dīligēns	dīligent-	dīligenter

3. The following adjectives form their adverbs irregularly:

ADJECTIVE	ADVERB
audāx	audācter
bonus	bene
facilis	facile
magnus	magnopere
malus	male
multus	multum
parvus	parum

4. The adverb from the adjective **firmus** is found in two forms, **firmē** and **firmiter**.

COMPARISON OF ADVERBS

POSITIVE	COMPARATIVE	SUPERLATIVE
ample	amplius	amplissimē
breviter	brevius	brevissimē
audācter	audācius	audācissimē
dīligenter	dīligentius	dīligentissimē
miserē	miserius	miserrimē
ācriter	ācrius	ācerrimē
facile	facilius	facillimē
bene	melius	optimē
male	peius	pessimē
magnopere	magis	maximē
parum	minus	minimē
multum	plūs	plūrimum

Note

1. Except for **magis,** the comparative form of an adverb is the same as the neuter comparative form of the adjective.

2. Except for **plūrimum,** the superlative of an adverb is formed from the superlative of the adjective by changing **-us** to **-ē.** For example:

ADJECTIVE	ADVERB
brevissimus	**brevissimē**
ācerrimus	**acerrimē**
facillimus	**facillimē**
minimus	**minimē**

3. The three degrees are translated as follows:

POSITIVE	COMPARATIVE	SUPERLATIVE
tardē, slowly	**tardius,** more slowly	**tardissimē,** most or very slowly
male, badly	**peius,** worse	**pessimē,** worst

4. The adverbs **diū** and **saepe** have no corresponding adjectives. They are compared as follows:

POSITIVE	COMPARATIVE	SUPERLATIVE
diū, a long time	**diūtius,** a longer time	**diūtissimē,** a very long time
saepe, often	**saepius,** more often	**saepissimē,** most or very often

5. The adverbs **magis** (more) and **maximē** (most) are used to compare adjectives ending in **-us** preceded by **e** or **i.** For example:

POSITIVE	COMPARATIVE	SUPERLATIVE
idōneus, suitable	*magis* **idōneus,** more suitable	*maximē* **idōneus,** most or very suitable
ēgregius, remarkable	*magis* **ēgregius,** more remarkable	*maximē* **ēgregius,** most or very remarkable

EXERCISES

A. Form the adverb from each of the following adjectives:

1. timidus _____   6. īnfēlīx _____
2. levis _____   7. aeger _____
3. recēns _____   8. bonus _____
4. līber _____   9. ācer _____
5. celer _____   10. magnus _____

B. Translate into English the following adverbs:

1. clārē _____   6. līberrimē _____
2. facilius _____   7. graviter _____
3. fortissimē _____   8. minus _____
4. pūblicē _____   9. audācter _____
5. saepius _____   10. simillimē _____

C. Identify the degree of each adverb by putting a check in the appropriate column.

	POSITIVE	COMPARATIVE	SUPERLATIVE
1. melius	-------	-------	-------
2. plūrimum	-------	-------	-------
3. grātē	-------	-------	-------
4. pulcherrimē	-------	-------	-------
5. facile	-------	-------	-------
6. apertissimē	-------	-------	-------
7. nōbilius	-------	-------	-------
8. peius	-------	-------	-------
9. difficillimē	-------	-------	-------
10. breviter	-------	-------	-------

D. Compare the following:

	COMPARATIVE	SUPERLATIVE
1. fīrmē	----------------	----------------
2. fortiter	----------------	----------------
3. magnopere	----------------	----------------
4. miserē	----------------	----------------
5. dīligenter	----------------	----------------
6. audācter	----------------	----------------
7. facile	----------------	----------------
8. diū	----------------	----------------
9. necessārius	----------------	----------------
10. aegrē	----------------	----------------

Lesson 59—REVIEW OF COMPARISON OF ADJECTIVES AND ADVERBS

A. Underline the correct English translation.

1. potentior   (powerful, more powerful, more powerfully)

2. diūtius   (a long time, a longer time, a very long time)

3. pulcherrima   (beautiful, most beautiful, very beautifully)

4. inimīcī   (unfriendly, more unfriendly, very unfriendly)

5. ūtilissimum   (useful, rather useful, most useful)

6. facillimē   (easiest, very easy, very easily)

7. magnopere   (great, greater, greatly)

8. minus   (little, less, least)

9. certiōribus   (certain, certainly, more certain)

10. līberrimē   (very freely, rather freely, too freely)

B. Supply the missing form for each adjective or adverb.

POSITIVE	COMPARATIVE	SUPERLATIVE
1. gravis	gravior	--------------------
2. celeriter	--------------------	celerrimē
3. --------------------	audācior	audācissimus
4. malus	--------------------	pessimus
5. saepe	saepius	--------------------
6. --------------------	altius	altissimē
7. miser	miserior	--------------------
8. bene	melius	--------------------
9. idōneus	--------------------	maximē idōneus
10. --------------------	levius	levissimē

C. Underline the correct translation of the italicized words.

1. *a very light* toga   (levior, levissima)

2. *better* cibus   (melior, melius)

3. *more swiftly* cucurrit   (celerior, celerius)

4. *most carefully* labōrābat (dīligentissimus, dīligentissimē)

5. *the worst* cōnsilium   (peius, pessimum)

6. *a more suitable* tempus   (opportūnior, opportūnius)

7. *least* timēbant   (minimus, minimē)

8. *more fiercely* pugnāvit   (ācrior, ācrius)

9. *a suitable* locus   (idōneus, magis idōneus)

10. *recently* vēnērunt   (recenter, recentius)

173

D. In the space before each noun in column *A*, write the letter of its modifying adjective in column *B*.

Column A	Column B
------ **1.** bellī	*a.* meliōrum
------ **2.** cohortem	*b.* ācriōre
------ **3.** diērum	*c.* potentiōrēs
------ **4.** agmen	*d.* plūrimīs
------ **5.** impetū	*e.* fortissimam
------ **6.** cīvitātis	*f.* fīrmissimā
------ **7.** mīlitibus	*g.* celerius
------ **8.** deōs	*h.* audāciōrī
------ **9.** portā	*i.* longissimī
------ **10.** ducī	*j.* optimae

E. Check the appropriate columns below to indicate (*a*) whether each form is an adjective, an adverb, or both; (*b*) the degree of each form.

	ADJECTIVE	ADVERB	POSITIVE	COMPARATIVE	SUPERLATIVE
1. nōbilior	-------	-------	-------	-------	-------
2. aegerrimē	-------	-------	-------	-------	-------
3. īnfēlīciter	-------	-------	-------	-------	-------
4. apertē	-------	-------	-------	-------	-------
5. brevius	-------	-------	-------	-------	-------
6. optimē	-------	-------	-------	-------	-------
7. dissimillimus	-------	-------	-------	-------	-------
8. saepius	-------	-------	-------	-------	-------
9. fīnitimus	-------	-------	-------	-------	-------
10. vērissimus	-------	-------	-------	-------	-------

F. For each of the following nouns, write the correct form of the adjective:

1. silvās	(comparative of *lātus*)	----------------------------------
2. lēx	(superlative of *aequus*)	----------------------------------
3. agmen	(superlative of *novus*)	----------------------------------
4. aditum	(superlative of *difficilis*)	----------------------------------
5. peditum	(comparative of *tardus*)	----------------------------------
6. carrīs	(comparative of *parvus*)	----------------------------------
7. vī	(superlative of *magnus*)	----------------------------------
8. hominī	(superlative of *integer*)	----------------------------------
9. sorōris	(comparative of *pulcher*)	----------------------------------
10. speciē	(comparative of *fēlīx*)	----------------------------------

G. Write the following specified forms:

1. accusative plural: *cīvis timidissimus* _____
2. ablative singular: *salūs maior* _____
3. dative plural: *prīnceps validus* _____
4. nominative plural: *praemium grātius* _____
5. genitive singular: *aciēs simillima* _____
6. ablative plural: *iter angustius* _____
7. accusative singular: *poena gravissima* _____
8. dative singular: *socius amīcior* _____
9. genitive plural: *liber audācissimus* _____
10. nominative singular: *portum minōrem* _____

H. Rewrite the sentences below, making *all* changes required by the directions in parentheses.

1. *Rēctā* viā discessērunt. (change to the superlative)

_____

2. Rhēnus erat *altissimus*. (substitute equivalent form of *lātus*)

_____

3. Eīs *facile* persuāsit. (change to the comparative)

_____

4. Orgetorīx *nōbilis* fuit. (change to the superlative)

_____

5. Nāvibus *multīs* factīs, domum nāvigābant. (change to the comparative)

_____

6. Ā prōvinciā *longē* absunt. (change to the superlative)

_____

7. Locum *idōneum* dēlēgērunt. (change to the comparative)

_____

8. Amīcōrum *magnum* numerum habēbat. (change to the superlative)

_____

9. *Optimōs* carrōs fēcērunt. (change to the positive)

_____

10. Agricolae *minimē* labōrābant. (substitute equivalent form of *dīligēns*)

_____

Unit VIII—Pronouns

Lesson 60—DEMONSTRATIVE PRONOUNS

is

	SINGULAR			PLURAL		
	(m.)	(f.)	(n.)	(m.)	(f.)	(n.)
Nom.	is	ea	id	eī	eae	ea
Gen.	eius	eius	eius	eōrum	eārum	eōrum
Dat.	eī	eī	eī	eīs	eīs	eīs
Acc.	eum	eam	id	eōs	eās	ea
Abl.	eō	eā	eō	eīs	eīs	eīs

hic

	SINGULAR			PLURAL		
	(m.)	(f.)	(n.)	(m.)	(f.)	(n.)
Nom.	hic	haec	hoc	hī	hae	haec
Gen.	huius	huius	huius	hōrum	hārum	hōrum
Dat.	huic	huic	huic	hīs	hīs	hīs
Acc.	hunc	hanc	hoc	hōs	hās	haec
Abl.	hōc	hāc	hōc	hīs	hīs	hīs

ille

	SINGULAR			PLURAL		
	(m.)	(f.)	(n.)	(m.)	(f.)	(n.)
Nom.	ille	illa	illud	illī	illae	illa
Gen.	illīus	illīus	illīus	illōrum	illārum	illōrum
Dat.	illī	illī	illī	illīs	illīs	illīs
Acc.	illum	illam	illud	illōs	illās	illa
Abl.	illō	illā	illō	illīs	illīs	illīs

īdem

	SINGULAR			PLURAL		
	(m.)	(f.)	(n.)	(m.)	(f.)	(n.)
Nom.	īdem	eadem	idem	eīdem	eaedem	eadem
Gen.	eiusdem	eiusdem	eiusdem	eōrundem	eārundem	eōrundem
Dat.	eīdem	eīdem	eīdem	eīsdem	eīsdem	eīsdem
Acc.	eundem	eandem	idem	eōsdem	eāsdem	eadem
Abl.	eōdem	eādem	eōdem	eīsdem	eīsdem	eīsdem

Note

1. **Is, hic,** and **ille** may be used both as pronouns and as adjectives. As pronouns their meanings are:

> **is, hic, ille** = he
> **ea, haec, illa** = she
> **id, hoc, illud** = it

As adjectives, their meanings are:

> **is, ea, id** = this, that (*plural*, these, those)
> **hic, haec, hoc** = this (*plural*, these)
> **ille, illa, illud** = that (*plural*, those)

2. **Īdem,** meaning *the same*, is a compound of **is** plus the indeclinable suffix **-dem.** It follows the declension of **is** with a few changes in spelling, especially the change of **m** to **n** before the letter **d.**

eum, eam	*but*	**eundem, eandem**
acc. sing.		acc. sing.

eōrum, eārum	*but*	**eōrundem, eārundem**
gen. pl.		gen. pl.

3. Demonstrative adjectives are generally placed before the nouns they modify.

EXERCISES

A. Identify the case(s), number, and gender of the following forms:

1. hōs _____
2. illō _____
3. eius _____
4. eīsdem _____
5. hanc _____
6. eōrum _____
7. illae _____
8. idem _____
9. huic _____
10. illīus _____

B. Underline the demonstrative in parentheses that agrees with the noun.

1. hiemem   (illam, illārum, illum)
2. urbis   (hae, huic, huius)
3. pīlum   (id, eum, eam)
4. rērum   (eiusdem, eārundem, eōrundem)
5. pugnā   (haec, hōc, hāc)
6. fugitīvōs   (eīsdem, eōsdem, eiusdem)
7. equitātuī   (huic, eius, illō)

8. partibus   (huius, illās, eīsdem)

9. pedem   (eīdem, illam, eum)

10. nūntiī   (ille, eīdem, huic)

C. In the space before each noun in column *A*, write the letter of its modifying demonstrative in column *B*.

	Column A	*Column B*
_____	**1.** cōnsilium	*a.* illīus
_____	**2.** gentis	*b.* eīs
_____	**3.** equitātuī	*c.* illam
_____	**4.** temporibus	*d.* id
_____	**5.** aciem	*e.* hāc
_____	**6.** labōrem	*f.* illa
_____	**7.** legiōnum	*g.* eōsdem
_____	**8.** grātiā	*h.* hunc
_____	**9.** lībertās	*i.* eārundem
_____	**10.** vīcōs	*j.* eīdem

D. Make each demonstrative agree with the noun in italics.

1. *dominum*—hic _____

2. *mortis*—ille _____

3. *passuum*—is _____

4. *quaestōrī*—īdem _____

5. *iūs*—ille _____

6. *diē*—is _____

7. *vīllīs*—hic _____

8. *vim*—īdem _____

9. *captīvōs*—ille _____

10. *castrōrum*—īdem _____

E. Each group in parentheses contains one incorrect form. Rewrite it correctly.

1. genitive plural feminine   (eōrum, hārum, illārum)   _____

2. ablative singular neuter   (eō, eōdem, hoc)   _____

3. dative singular masculine   (illī, huius, eīdem)   _____

4. accusative plural neuter   (illa, ea, hae)   _____

5. nominative plural feminine   (eadem, eae, illae)   _____

6. ablative plural masculine   (eōsdem, hīs, illīs)   _____

7. genitive singular feminine   (eī, illīus, huius)   _____

8. accusative singular neuter   (illud, eum, idem)   _____

9. dative plural feminine   (hīs, eāsdem, eīs)   _____

10. nominative singular masculine (idem, hic, ille) _____

Lesson 61—PERSONAL, REFLEXIVE, AND INTENSIVE PRONOUNS

PERSONAL PRONOUNS

	FIRST PERSON		SECOND PERSON	
	SINGULAR	PLURAL	SINGULAR	PLURAL
Nom.	ego (*I*)	nōs (*we*)	tū (*you*)	vōs (*you*)
Gen.	meī	nostrum (-trī)	tuī	vestrum (-trī)
Dat.	mihi	nōbīs	tibi	vōbīs
Acc.	mē	nōs	tē	vōs
Abl.	mē	nōbīs	tē	vōbīs

Note

1. For the third person, the demonstrative pronouns **is, hic,** and **ille** are used.

Eam (**hanc, illam**) vīdimus.	We saw her.
Eī (**huic, illī**) librum dedī.	I gave the book to him.

2. Personal pronouns are not needed as subject except for emphasis or contrast.

Praemium accēpimus.	We received the prize.
Nōs praemium accēpimus.	*We* received the prize.

REFLEXIVE PRONOUN

	SINGULAR	PLURAL
Nom.	—	—
Gen.	suī	suī
Dat.	sibi	sibi
Acc.	sē (sēsē)	sē (sēsē)
Abl.	sē (sēsē)	sē (sēsē)

Note

1. The reflexive pronoun **suī** is a third person pronoun. For the first and second persons, the proper forms of the personal pronouns are used.

Puer **sē** vulnerāvit.	The boy wounded himself.
Mē accūsō.	I accuse myself.
Vidētisne **vōs?**	Do you see yourselves?

2. The meaning of **suī** is determined by the subject.

Mīles sē dēfendit.	The soldier defends *himself.*
Rēgīna sē dēfendit.	The queen defends *herself.*
Sociī sē dēfendunt.	The allies defend *themselves.*

179

INTENSIVE PRONOUN

ipse, self

	SINGULAR			PLURAL		
	(m.)	*(f.)*	*(n.)*	*(m.)*	*(f.)*	*(n.)*
Nom.	ipse	ipsa	ipsum	ipsī	ipsae	ipsa
Gen.	ipsīus	ipsīus	ipsīus	ipsōrum	ipsārum	ipsōrum
Dat.	ipsī	ipsī	ipsī	ipsīs	ipsīs	ipsīs
Acc.	ipsum	ipsam	ipsum	ipsōs	ipsās	ipsa
Abl.	ipsō	ipsā	ipsō	ipsīs	ipsīs	ipsīs

Note

1. Since **ipse** and **suī** both mean *self*, it is important to distinguish between them. **Ipse** is used to intensify or emphasize a particular noun or pronoun, expressed or understood. **Suī** is used to refer back to the subject of a sentence or clause.

Cōnsul **ipse** locūtus est. <small>intensive</small>	The consul himself spoke.
Ipse locūtus est. <small>intensive</small>	He himself spoke.

But

Cōnsul **sē** trādidit. <small>reflexive</small>	The consul surrendered himself.

2. **Ipse** has a full declension, but **suī** lacks a nominative case.

EXERCISES

A. Put a check in the proper column to indicate whether a form of **suī** or of **ipse** is to be used.

	SUĪ	IPSE
1. Caesar *himself* declared war.	-------	-------
2. She taught *herself* to drive.	-------	-------
3. They heard the president *himself*.	-------	-------
4. They convinced *themselves* he was right.	-------	-------
5. She wrote it *herself*.	-------	-------

B. Identify the case(s) and number of the following forms:

1. ipsīus _____   **6.** nostrum _____

2. sibi _____   **7.** sēsē _____

3. nōbīs _____   **8.** ipsīs _____

4. tē _____   **9.** vōs _____

5. ipsārum _____   **10.** mihi _____

C. Each group in parentheses contains one incorrect form. Rewrite it correctly.

1. dative singular   (suī, mihi, ipsī)   ---------------------
2. genitive plural   (vestrum, nostrī, ipsīus)   ---------------------
3. accusative singular   (mē, vōs, sēsē)   ---------------------
4. nominative plural   (ipsa, vōs, meī)   ---------------------
5. ablative plural   (sē, ipsīus, nōbīs)   ---------------------
6. genitive singular   (ipsī, suī, tuī)   ---------------------
7. accusative plural   (sēsē, ipsās, nostrum)   ---------------------
8. nominative singular   (ego, tē, ipsum)   ---------------------
9. dative plural   (ipsīs, sibi, mihi)   ---------------------
10. ablative singular   (sibi, ipsā, tē)   ---------------------

D. Write the following specified forms:

1. accusative plural: *suī, tū*   --------------------------------------
2. ablative singular: *ipse, ego*   --------------------------------------
3. dative plural: *ego, suī*   --------------------------------------
4. genitive singular: *tū, ipsa*   --------------------------------------
5. nominative plural: *ego, tū*   --------------------------------------

E. Complete each sentence with the accusative case of the proper reflexive.

1. Mīles ------------ interfēcit.

2. Tū ------------ nōn vidēs.

3. Parātisne ------------?

4. ------------ laudāre nōn possumus.

5. Ego ------------ scīre dēbeō.

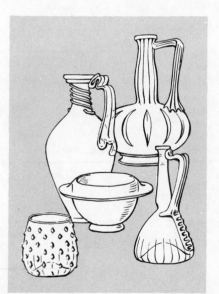

Glassware

The Romans had no superiors in ornamental glassmaking. The vases found in Pompeii are excellent examples of delicate beauty and superb workmanship. Today most glassware is made by machine, but the original Roman designs are still sometimes reproduced.

Lesson 62—RELATIVE, INTERROGATIVE, AND INDEFINITE PRONOUNS

RELATIVE PRONOUN

quī, who, which

	SINGULAR			PLURAL		
	(m.)	*(f.)*	*(n.)*	*(m.)*	*(f.)*	*(n.)*
Nom.	quī	quae	quod	quī	quae	quae
Gen.	cuius	cuius	cuius	quōrum	quārum	quōrum
Dat.	cui	cui	cui	quibus	quibus	quibus
Acc.	quem	quam	quod	quōs	quās	quae
Abl.	quō	quā	quō	quibus	quibus	quibus

INTERROGATIVE PRONOUN

quis, who?; **quid,** what?

	SINGULAR		PLURAL		
	(m. & f.)	*(n.)*	*(m.)*	*(f.)*	*(n.)*
Nom.	quis	quid	quī	quae	quae
Gen.	cuius	cuius	quōrum	quārum	quōrum
Dat.	cui	cui	quibus	quibus	quibus
Acc.	quem	quid	quōs	quās	quae
Abl.	quō	quō	quibus	quibus	quibus

Note

1. The relative pronoun refers back to an antecedent; the interrogative pronoun is a question word.

RELATIVE PRONOUN:	Iūlia est puella **quam** amō.	Julia is the girl *whom* I love.
INTERROGATIVE PRONOUN:	**Quem** amās?	*Whom* do you love?

2. The interrogative pronoun may also be used as an adjective. As such, it is declined like the relative pronoun **quī, quae, quod.**

INTERROGATIVE PRONOUN:	**Quis** mē vocat?	*Who* is calling me?
INTERROGATIVE ADJECTIVE:	**Quī** puer mē vocat?	*What* boy is calling me?

3. The genitive of both the relative and the interrogative—**cuius** (sing.), **quōrum** (pl.)—is best translated *whose.*

RELATIVE PRONOUN:	Puer **cuius** librum habeō abest.	The boy *whose* book I have is absent.
INTERROGATIVE ADJECTIVE:	**Quōrum** agrī vāstantur?	*Whose* fields are being destroyed?

182

INDEFINITE PRONOUNS

aliquis, someone; aliquid, something

	(m. & f.)	(n.)	(m.)	(f.)	(n.)
	SINGULAR		PLURAL		
Nom.	aliquis	aliquid	aliquī	aliquae	aliqua
Gen.	alicuius	alicuius	aliquōrum	aliquārum	aliquōrum
Dat.	alicui	alicui	aliquibus	aliquibus	aliquibus
Acc.	aliquem	aliquid	aliquōs	aliquās	aliqua
Abl.	aliquō	aliquō	aliquibus	aliquibus	aliquibus

Note

1. **Aliquis** is a compound of **quis** plus the indeclinable prefix **ali-**.

2. **Aliquis** may also be used as an adjective. As such, the declension starts **aliquī, aliqua, aliquod**.

PRONOUN: **Aliquis** locūtus est.   *Someone* spoke.

ADJECTIVE: **Aliquī** puer locūtus est.   *Some* boy spoke.

quīdam, a certain one

	(m.)	(f.)	(n.)	(m.)	(f.)	(n.)
	SINGULAR			PLURAL		
Nom.	quīdam	quaedam	quiddam	quīdam	quaedam	quaedam
Gen.	cuiusdam	cuiusdam	cuiusdam	quōrundam	quārundam	quōrundam
Dat.	cuidam	cuidam	cuidam	quibusdam	quibusdam	quibusdam
Acc.	quendam	quandam	quiddam	quōsdam	quāsdam	quaedam
Abl.	quōdam	quādam	quōdam	quibusdam	quibusdam	quibusdam

Note

1. **Quīdam** is a compound of **quī** plus the indeclinable suffix **-dam**.

2. The letter **m** is changed to **n** before **d**.

quem, quam   *but*   que**n**dam, qua**n**dam
acc. sing.   acc. sing.

quōrum, quārum   *but*   quōru**n**dam, quāru**n**dam
gen. pl.   gen. pl.

3. **Quīdam** may also be used as an adjective. As such, the declension starts **quīdam, quaedam, quoddam**.

PRONOUN: **Quiddam** rogāvit.   He asked for *a certain thing*.

ADJECTIVE: **Quoddam** cōnsilium rogāvit.   He asked for *a certain* plan.

quisque, each one; **quidque**, each thing

	SINGULAR	
	(m. & f.)	*(n.)*
Nom.	quisque	quidque
Gen.	cuiusque	cuiusque
Dat.	cuique	cuique
Acc.	quemque	quidque
Abl.	quōque	quōque

Note

1. **Quisque** is a compound of **quis** plus the indeclinable suffix **-que**. The plural is rarely used.

2. **Quisque** may also be used as an adjective. As such, the declension starts **quisque, quaeque, quodque.**

PRONOUN:	Cavē **quidque**.	Beware of *each thing*.
ADJECTIVE:	Cavē **quodque** perīculum.	Beware of *each* danger.

EXERCISES

A. Identify the case(s) and number of the following forms:

1. cui ----------------------------------
2. aliquem ----------------------------------
3. quibusdam ----------------------------------
4. quisque ----------------------------------
5. aliquārum ----------------------------------

6. quōs ----------------------------------
7. alicuius ----------------------------------
8. quāsdam ----------------------------------
9. quōdam ----------------------------------
10. cuique ----------------------------------

B. Make each adjective agree with the noun in italics.

1. *virtūs*—quī ----------------------------
2. *prīncipem*—aliquī ----------------------------
3. *tēlum*—quisque ----------------------------
4. *formās*—quīdam ----------------------------
5. *equīs*—aliquī ----------------------------

6. *aciē*—quisque ----------------------------
7. *nāvium*—quī· ----------------------------
8. *proelia*—quīdam ----------------------------
9. *flūminis*—aliquī ----------------------------
10. *senātuī*—quī ----------------------------

C. Underline the adjective in parentheses that agrees with the noun.

1. spem   (quem, quam, quod)
2. condiciōnēs   (aliquās, alicuius, aliquōs)
3. vir   (cuidam, quoddam, quīdam)
4. fīlī   (quisque, cuiusque, cuique)
5. iūra   (quae, aliquae, quoddam)
6. cāsum   (quodque, quandam, aliquem)
7. fortūnā   (quādam, quaeque, aliquō)

8. explōrātōrī   (aliquī, cui, cuiusque)
9. generibus   (quibusdam, alicuius, cuique)
10. honōrum   (quārum, aliquōrum, quaedam)

D. Write the following specified forms:

1. accusative singular: *quis, quīdam*   ---
2. ablative plural: *quīdam, aliquis*   ---
3. genitive singular: *quisque, quaedam*   ---
4. dative singular: *aliquid, quiddam*   ---
5. nominative plural: *quod, aliqua*   ---

Battle Formation of a Roman Legion

Aciēs Triplex

1 cohort

360 soldiers

PRĪMA ACIĒS
(experienced soldiers)

SECUNDA ACIĒS

TERTIA ACIĒS

Lesson 63—REVIEW OF PRONOUNS

A. In the space before each form in column *A*, write the letter of the noun it modifies in column *B*.

	Column A		Column B
------	**1.** hunc	*a.*	iūdiciīs
------	**2.** cuius	*b.*	ratiō
------	**3.** eōrundem	*c.*	mūrōs
------	**4.** quibusdam	*d.*	locō
------	**5.** quaeque	*e.*	caedis
------	**6.** illud	*f.*	lūce
------	**7.** eī	*g.*	maiōrum
------	**8.** aliquā	*h.*	vīrēs
------	**9.** ipsōs	*i.*	labōrem
------	**10.** quās	*j.*	corpus

B. Identify the case(s) and number of the following forms:

1. tibi ---------------------------------

2. nostrum -----------------------------

3. sēsē ---------------------------------

4. mē -----------------------------------

5. quāsdam ------------------------------

6. vōbīs ----------------------------------

7. eārundem ------------------------------

8. cui ------------------------------------

9. quisque --------------------------------

10. alicuius -------------------------------

C. Underline the correct form.

1. ablative plural: *illīus, quibusdam, vōs*

2. genitive singular: *eiusdem, tibi, cuidam*

3. nominative plural: *sibi, quisque, eīdem*

4. dative singular: *cui, meī, eōdem*

5. accusative plural: *quaedam, eum, aliquam*

6. nominative singular: *mē, suī, quid*

7. ablative singular: *alicui, ipsā, vōbīs*

8. dative plural: *eīs, quisque, illīus*

9. accusative singular: *īdem, quendam, ipsās*

10. genitive plural: *vestrī, sibi, quandam*

D. Each group in parentheses contains one form that does *not* agree with the noun. Rewrite it correctly.

1. hominis   (eius, cuique, ipsīus, huius)   -------------------

2. multitūdinem   (quaedam, illam, aliquam, eandem)   -------------------

3. rēbus   (eīsdem, ipsōs, quibusdam, illīs)   -------------------

4. viārum   (hārum, quārum, aliquārum, eōrundem)   -------------------

186

5. currū   (eō, quōdam, huic, aliquō)   ----------------------

6. subsidium   (hōc, quoddam, illud, ipsum)   ----------------------

7. barbarōs   (aliquōs, eāsdem, quōsdam, eōs)   ----------------------

8. legiōnī   (huic, cuique, eī, illō)   ----------------------

9. cīvēs   (eī, quīdam, ipsīs, eīdem)   ----------------------

10. ōrātiō   (haec, quae, quaeque, aliquae)   ----------------------

E. Underline the correct translation of the italicized words.

1. The boy sailed the boat *himself*.   (sē, ipse)

2. *Who* wrote the speech?   (Quis, Quid)

3. They warned *us* to leave.   (nōs, vōs)

4. He arrived at *that* time.   (hōc, illō)

5. We heard *the same* story.   (eam, eandem)

6. *Each one* brought a gift.   (Quisque, Aliquis)

7. *A certain* woman gave us the letter.   (Quīdam, Quaedam)

8. They blamed *themselves* for the accident.   (eōs, sē)

9. This is the book *that* I wanted.   (quem, illum)

10. Everyone found *something*.   (aliquem, aliquid)

F. Write the following specified forms:

1. accusative singular: *illa lēx, ego, suī*

    ----

2. ablative plural: *quīdam numerus, haec littera*

    ----

3. genitive singular: *quod oppidum, aliquī ōrdō*

    ----

4. nominative plural: *is impetus, tū, ego*

    ----

5. dative singular: *eadem classis, imperātor ipse*

    ----

6. ablative singular: *ea fidēs, quī incola*

    ----

7. accusative plural: *quoddam flūmen, aliqua urbs*

    ----

8. dative plural: *īdem hostis, suī, tū*

    ----

9. genitive plural: *hoc nāvigium, quis, ipsa*

    ----

10. ablative singular and plural: *ego, tū*

G. Rewrite the sentences below, making *all* changes required by the directions in parentheses.

1. *Hoc* cōnsilium iniit. (substitute equivalent form of *Is*)

---

2. *Illum* vīdimus. (change to the plural)

---

3. *Aliquibus* victōriam nūntiāvī. (substitute equivalent form of *Quīdam*)

---

4. Lēgātus *vōs* laudāvit. (change to the singular)

---

5. *Quemque* spectāvimus. (change to the neuter)

---

6. *Quem* docuistī? (change to the plural)

---

7. Frūmentum ab *homine* ipsō parātum est. (change to *hominibus*)

---

8. *Eques* fortiter sē *dēfendit*. (change to *Equitēs . . . dēfendērunt*)

---

9. Virī eiusdem *vīcī* convēnērunt. (change to *vīcōrum*)

---

10. Poēta *mihi* locūtus est. (change to the reflexive)

Vercingetorix, an Arvernian, who became commander-in-chief of all the Gallic forces, unsuccessfully challenged Caesar's supremacy in Gaul in 52 B.C. The surrender of Vercingetorix at Alesia marked the end of the Gallic War. Because of his ability to unify the various Gallic tribes, and his heroic resistance to Roman rule, Vercingetorix is regarded as the first national hero of France.

Surrender of Vercingetorix

Unit IX—Prepositions

Lesson 64

PREPOSITIONS WITH THE ACCUSATIVE

ad, to, toward
ante, before, in front of
apud, among, in the presence of
circum, around
contrā, against, opposite
extrā, outside of, beyond

in, into, against
inter, between, among
intrā, within
ob, on account of
per, through
post, after, behind

praeter, besides, beyond
propter, on account of
sub, under (with verbs of motion)
super, above
trāns, across

PREPOSITIONS WITH THE ABLATIVE

ā, ab, from, by
cum, with
dē, down from, concerning

ē, ex, out of, from
in, in, on
prō, in front of, in behalf of

sine, without
sub, under (with verbs of rest)

Note

1. The forms **ā** and **ē** are used before words beginning with a consonant, **ab** and **ex** before words beginning with a vowel or a consonant.

Ā *or* **Ab** patriā fugit.	*But*	**Ab** īnsulā fugit.
Ē *or* **Ex** fossā vēnit.	*But*	**Ex** agrō vēnit.

2. Distinguish between the use of prepositions that sometimes take the ablative and sometimes the accusative.

ABLATIVE (WITH VERBS OF REST)

In aquā est.
　He is in the water.

Sub arbore sedēbat.
　He was sitting under a tree.

ACCUSATIVE (WITH VERBS OF MOTION)

In aquam contendit.
　He hurried into the water.

Sub arborem cucurrit.
　He ran under a tree.

EXERCISES

A. Translate into English.

1. inter nōs   --

2. dē monte   --

3. ante castra   --

4. ob perīculum   --

5. sine amīcīs   --

6. intrā vālla   --

7. apud hostēs   --

8. prō patriā   --

9. super omnia   _____

10. circum urbem   _____

B. Select the correct preposition.

1. _____ Genavam pervenit.   (Ab, Ad)

2. Hī sunt _____ prōvinciam.   (ex, extrā)

3. Locūtus est _____ hīs.   (per, prō)

4. _____ Italiam contendit.   (In, Dē)

5. Habitant _____ flūmen.   (trāns, prō)

6. Pugnātum est _____ utrīsque ācriter.   (ā, ab)

7. _____ omnibus cōpiīs proficīscitur.   (Cum, Circum)

8. _____ eōs fuit rēx Dīviciācus.   (Ab, Apud)

9. Suōs _____ agrīs dēdūcunt.   (ē, ex)

10. _____ multitūdinem hostium proeliō abstinuit.   (Praeter, Propter)

C. Underline the expression in parentheses that makes the sentence grammatically correct.

1. Ob (eam causam, eā causā) discessit.

2. In (fīnēs, fīnibus) hostium pervēnērunt.

3. Sine (vulnera, vulneribus) fūgērunt.

4. Sub (nāvem, nāve) dormiēbat.

5. Post (castra, castrīs) aciem īnstrūxit.

6. Praeter (spem, spē) erant omnēs.

7. Dē (nōs, nōbīs) fābulam nārrāvit.

8. Sub (arborem, arbore) contendit.

9. Ē (dentēs, dentibus) armātī oriēbantur.

10. In (oppidum, oppidō) diū mānsērunt.

D. Translate into Latin.

1. by Marcus   _____

2. in the place   _____

3. between friends   _____

4. toward the forest   _____

5. without help   _____

6. through the land   _____

7. outside of the camp   _____

8. opposite Italy   _____

9. with love   _____

10. out of danger   _____

E. Rewrite the sentences below, making *all* changes required by the directions in parentheses.

1. *Circum* īnsulam nāvigābant. (substitute *Ab*)

----

2. Puerī in aquā *sunt*. (change to *contendunt*)

----

3. *Cum* amīcīs iter fēcērunt. (substitute the opposite)

----

4. *Ob* perīculum nōn manent. (substitute a synonym)

----

5. Agricola sub pontem *properāvit*. (change to *habitāvit*)

----

6. Castra fēcērunt *intrā* mūrōs. (substitute the opposite)

----

7. Gallī *ex* silvīs fugiēbant. (substitute *per*)

----

8. *Ante* castra cōnstitit. (substitute a synonym)

----

9. Rēx multa *dē* exercitū dīxit. (substitute *apud*)

----

10. Hostēs *ad* montem currēbant. (substitute *dē*)

Wrestling

In the games of ancient Greece and Rome, wrestling occupied a very important place. Today, with the advent of television, wrestling has become popular as an exhibition rather than a sport.

Unit X—*Idioms*

Lesson 65

An idiom is a use of words peculiar to a particular language. The following examples will illustrate:

1. **Dare** normally means *to give;* used with **poenam**, it means *to suffer.*

Mihi librum **dedit.**	He *gave* me the book.
Poenam **dedit.**	He *suffered* punishment.
<small>idiom</small>	

2. **Capere** normally means *to take* or *seize;* used with **cōnsilium,** it means *to form.*

Obsidem **cēpērunt.**	They *seized* the hostage.
Cōnsilium **cēpērunt.**	They *formed* a plan.
<small>idiom</small>	

VERBAL IDIOMS

agere

    grātiās agere, to thank
        Nōbīs **grātiās ēgērunt.**   They thanked us.

    vītam agere, to live a life
        Bonam **vītam ēgit.**   He lived a good life.

capere (and compound)

    cōnsilium capere, to form a plan
        Cōnsilium melius **cēpimus.**   We formed a better plan.

    sē recipere, to retreat
        Hostēs **sē recēpērunt.**   The enemy retreated.

committere

    proelium committere, to begin or join battle
        Caesar **proelium committet.**   Caesar will join battle.

conicere

    in fugam conicere, to put to flight
        Gallōs **in fugam coniēcimus.**   We put the Gauls to flight.

dare

    in fugam dare, to put to flight
        Eōs **in fugam dedit.**   He put them to flight.

    in fugam sēsē dare, to flee
        Omnēs **in fugam sēsē dedērunt.**   They all fled.

    inter sē dare, to exchange
        Inter sē obsidēs **dedērunt.**   They exchanged hostages.

    iter dare, to give the right of way
        Caesar eīs **iter** nōn **dedit.**   Caesar did not give them the right of way.

    poenam dare, to suffer punishment or pay the
    penalty
        Poenam nōn **dabunt.**   They will not suffer punishment.

dīcere

    causam dīcere, to plead a case
      Causam dīcere nōluit.   He did not want to plead his case.

dūcere (and compounds)

    bellum dūcere, to prolong the war
      Dūcene **bellum** imperātor?   Will the general prolong the war?

    in mātrimōnium dūcere, to marry
      Iūliam **in mātrimōnium dūxit.**   He married Julia.

    mūrum perdūcere, to construct a wall
      Caesar **mūrum** X pedum **perdūxit.**   Caesar constructed a 10-foot wall.

    nāvem dēdūcere, to launch a ship
      Argonautae **nāvem dēdūxērunt.**   The Argonauts launched the ship.

facere and **fierī**

    certiōrem facere, to inform
      Rēgem **certiōrem fēcit.**   He informed the king.

    certior fierī, to be informed
      Rēx **certior fīēbat.**   The king was informed.

    imperāta facere, to obey commands
      Captīvus omnia **imperāta fēcit.**   The prisoner obeyed all the commands.

    iter facere, to march
      Exercitus mīlle passūs **iter fēcerat.**   The army had marched a mile.

    potestātem facere, to give an opportunity
      Eīs discēdendī **potestātem fēcit.**   He gave them the opportunity of leaving.

    proelium facere, to engage in battle
      Germānī cum Rōmānīs **proelium fēcērunt.**   The Germans engaged in battle with the Romans.

    verba facere, to speak
      Prō hīs prīnceps **verba facit.**   The chief speaks in their behalf.

    vim facere, to use force
      Helvētiī **vim facere** cōnantur.   The Helvetians try to use force.

ferre (and compounds)

    aegrē ferre, to be annoyed at
      Rem **aegrē ferēbat.**   He was annoyed at the matter.

    signa ferre, to advance
      Cohortēs **signa tulērunt.**   The cohorts advanced.

    sē cōnferre, to proceed
      Tardē **sē cōnferēbant.**   They proceeded slowly.

    bellum īnferre, to make war
      Bellum īnferre cōnstituimus.   We decided to make war.

    grātiam referre, to show gratitude
      Dēbēs **grātiam referre.**   You ought to show gratitude.

    pedem referre, to retreat
      Dux **pedem refert.**   The leader is retreating.

    sē referre, to go back, return
      Ad castra **sē referunt.**   They are returning to camp.

habēre

    grātiam habēre, to feel grateful
        Omnēs **grātiam habēmus.**   We all feel grateful.

    in animō habēre, to intend
        Vincere **in animō habet.**   He intends to conquer.

    ōrātiōnem habēre, to deliver a speech
        Cicerō longam **ōrātiōnem habuit.**   Cicero delivered a long speech.

īre

    pedibus īre, to go on foot, walk
        Pedibus īre volumus.   We want to walk.

movēre

    castra movēre, to break camp
        Rōmānī hodiē **castra movēbunt.**   The Romans will break camp today.

mūnīre

    viam mūnīre, to build a road
        Iussī sunt **viam mūnīre.**   They were ordered to build a road.

pōnere

    castra pōnere, to pitch camp
        Trāns flūmen **castra posuērunt.**   They pitched camp across the river.

posse

    plūrimum posse, to be very powerful
        Rēx Haeduōrum **plūrimum poterat.**   The king of the Haeduans was very powerful.

solvere

    nāvem solvere, to set sail
        Mediā nocte **nāvem solvit.**   He set sail at midnight.

tenēre

    memoriā tenēre, to remember
        Nihil **memoriā tenēbat.**   He remembered nothing.

vertere

    terga vertere, to turn and flee
        Hostēs **terga vertērunt.**   The enemy turned and fled.

OTHER IDIOMS

ā dextrō cornū, on the right wing

ā sinistrō cornū, on the left wing

in summō monte, on top of the mountain

magnum iter, a forced march

mīlle passūs, a mile

mīlia passuum, miles

multā nocte, late at night

nāvis longa, a battleship

nāvis onerāria, a transport

nē . . . quidem, not even

nōn iam, no longer

nōn modo . . . sed etiam, not only . . . but also

nōn nūllī, some

nōn numquam, sometimes

novissimum agmen, the rear

prīmum agmen, the van

prīmā lūce, at dawn

quā de causā, for this reason

quam celerrimē, as quickly as possible

quam prīmum, as soon as possible

rēs frūmentāria, grain supply

rēs gestae, deeds, achievements

rēs mīlitāris, military science

rēs novae, a revolution

rēs pūblica, government, state

simul atque (ac), as soon as

sōlis occāsū, at sunset

sub monte, at the foot of the mountain

EXERCISES

A. Underline the word in parentheses that is properly used with the word on the left.

1. nāvem   (īvit, solvit, potuit)

2. nē . . .   (quidem, idem, quīdam)

3. certiōrem   (habēbant, ferēbant, faciēbant)

4. iter   (dedī, posuī, iēcī)

5. simul   (et, quī, atque)

6. memoriā   (fit, tenet, agit)

7. bellum   (pōnimus, dīcimus, dūcimus)

8. quam   (prīmum, prīmus, prīmō)

9. terga   (pōnuntne, vertuntne, dantne)

10. multā   (nox, noctem, nocte)

B. Complete the English translation.

1. Mīles imperāta fēcit.   The soldier _____ the commands.

2. Mihi grātiās ēgērunt.   _____ me.

3. Quā dē causā discessit.   _____ he left.

4. Rēs gestae erant maximae.   _____ were very great.

5. Hostēs vim fēcērunt.   The enemy _____.

6. Legiō signa ferēbat.   The legion _____.

7. Ā sinistrō cornū impetum fēcit.   He made an attack _____.

8. Moram aegrē ferēbāmus.   _____ the delay.

9. Equitēs pedibus nōn ībunt.   The cavalry _____.

10. Ad flūmen sē contulit.   _____ to the river.

11. Manēre in animō habēmus.   _____ to stay.

12. Proelium nōtum memoriā tenēbat.   _____ the famous battle.

13. Prīmā lūce convēnērunt.   They came together _____.

14. Circum montem viam mūnīverant.   _____ around the mountain.

15. Sōlis occāsū dēdidimus.   We surrendered _____.

16. Germānī in fugam sēsē dedērunt.   The Germans _____.

17. Dux sub monte cōnsēdit.   The leader encamped _____.

18. Omnēs ad silvam sē recēpērunt.   All _____ to the forest.

19. Rem frūmentāriam parāvit.   He prepared _____.

20. Frūstrā causam dīxistī.   _____ in vain.

C. Translate the English words into Latin.

1. Vēnit *as quickly as possible.*   _____

2. Dux *feels grateful.*   _____

3. Hostēs *joined battle.*   _____

4. *No longer* timent. --

5. Voluit *to prolong the war.* --

6. Rōmānī *were pitching camp.* --

7. *Two miles* ambulāvit. --

8. Imperātor *is very powerful.* --

9. Persequēbātur *the rear* hostium. ------------------------------------

10. *A forced march* fēcērunt. ---

D. Rewrite the sentences below, making *all* changes required by the directions in parentheses.

1. Līberī *fugiunt.* (substitute an idiomatic synonym)

----

2. Nostrī *mīlle passūs* prōgressī erant. (change to *six miles*)

----

3. In *prīmum agmen* impetum fēcērunt. (substitute the opposite)

----

4. Nūntius rūrsus *locūtus est.* (substitute an idiomatic synonym)

----

5. Imperātor *nāvēs onerāriās* removet. (change to *battleships*)

----

6. Mīlitēs *prōcēdere* incipiunt. (substitute an idiomatic synonym)

----

7. *Sōlis occāsū* abierant. (substitute the opposite)

----

8. Fēminae *ambulāre* cōnstituērunt. (substitute an idiomatic synonym)

----

9. Argonautae *nāvigant.* (substitute an idiomatic synonym)

----

10. Caesarem *certiōrem faciunt.* (change to the passive, starting with *Caesar*)

Roman Coins

Most Roman coins, not unlike those of today, were made of silver or copper of varied design. Among the favorite figures on Roman coins were the head of Jupiter, the head of Rome with a helmet, and chariots drawn by two or four horses.

Unit XI—*Grammatical Structures*

Lesson 66—THE NOMINATIVE AND ACCUSATIVE CASES

THE NOMINATIVE CASE

Uses of the Nominative

1. *Subject* of a verb:

   Discipulī stābant.   The pupils were standing.

   Note

   The subject of an infinitive is in the accusative case.

2. *Predicate noun* or *predicate adjective* (one used with the verb **sum** or a verb in the passive):

   Caesar erat **cōnsul.**   Caesar was consul.
   Liber est **gravis.**   The book is heavy.
   Appellātus est **amīcus** populī Rōmānī.   He was called a friend of the Roman people.

THE ACCUSATIVE CASE

Uses of the Accusative

1. *Direct object* of a verb:

   Amor **omnia** vincit.   Love conquers everything.
   Cavē **canem!**   Beware of the dog!
   Quem vīdistī?   Whom did you see?

2. After certain *prepositions*, such as **ad, ante, apud, circum, contrā, inter, ob, per, post, propter, trāns:**

   Ante merīdiem discessit.   He left before noon.
   Ob perīculum fūgērunt.   On account of the danger they fled.

3. *Duration of time* (how long?):

   Paucās hōrās nāvigāvērunt.   They sailed for a few hours.
      how long

4. *Extent of space* (how far?):

   Duo mīlia passuum prōgressus est.   He advanced two miles.
      how far

5. *Place to which* (with the preposition **ad** or **in**):

   Caesar **ad Galliam** contendit.   Caesar hastened toward Gaul.
   In fīnēs Belgārum eum mīsērunt.   They sent him into the land of the Belgians.

Note

The preposition is omitted when **domus** is used, and with *names of towns*.

Domum properāvit.	He hurried home.
Rōmam iter fēcērunt.	They traveled to Rome.
Athēnās īmus.	We are going to Athens.

6. *Subject* of an *infinitive:*

Suōs convenīre iussit.	He ordered his men to assemble.
Gallōs appropinquāre audīvit.	He heard that the Gauls were approaching.

EXERCISES

A. In each sentence indicate which word is the subject and which the direct object.

	SUBJECT	DIRECT OBJECT
1. Caesar mīlitēs hortātus est.	---------------------	---------------------
2. Virī perīculum vīdērunt.	---------------------	---------------------
3. Quem vulnerāvit gladiātor?	---------------------	---------------------
4. Cūr Iāsōn Mēdēam relīquit?	---------------------	---------------------
5. Suscipit rem dux.	---------------------	---------------------
6. Obsidēs Sēquanī dant.	---------------------	---------------------
7. Coēgitne familiam Orgetorīx?	---------------------	---------------------
8. Multitūdō tēla coniēcit.	---------------------	---------------------
9. Id Belgae oppugnāre coepērunt.	---------------------	---------------------
10. Nostrī in hostēs impetum fēcērunt.	---------------------	---------------------

B. Underline all the words that go in the accusative, and then translate them into Latin.

1. Marcus rescued the horse.   ---
2. They sailed for six days.   ---
3. He ran a great distance.   ---
4. The general said that the army had left.   -------------------------------
5. He led the soldiers across the river.   ----------------------------------
6. We all hurried home.   ---
7. They threw the swords into the water.   --------------------------------
8. What did the consul say?   ---
9. He compelled the Gauls to surrender.   ---------------------------------
10. Did the leader decide to capture the town?   ----------------------------

C. Underline the word or expression in parentheses that makes the sentence grammatically correct.

1. Coēgit (virī, virōs) properāre.
2. (Rōmam, Ad Rōmam) rediērunt.
3. Discipulī erant (tardī, tardōs).
4. (Quis, Quem) vocāvistī?

5. Ībunt (Germāniam, ad Germāniam).

6. Audīvimus (Caesar, Caesarem) pervēnisse.

7. (Duo diēs, Duōs diēs) exspectābam.

8. Orgetorīx dēligitur (dux, ducem).

9. Contendērunt (domum, ad domum).

10. Sextus erat (meus amīcus, meum amīcum).

D. Translate the italicized words into Latin.

1. She ran *into the street*.   --

2. *The horses* were led away.   --

3. Galba was made *king*.   --

4. He arranged *the battle line*.   --

5. They stayed *many months*.   --

6. We shall sail *to the island*.   --

7. He ordered *the men* to defend *Rome*.   --

8. The swords are *new*.   --

9. They built the wall *a few feet* long.   --

10. Is *the farmer* walking *through the fields?*   --

Centurion

A centurion in the Roman army was a non-commissioned officer in command of a century (originally 100 men). Usually of humble origin, the centurion rose from the ranks through sheer bravery and ability. His pay was double that of an ordinary soldier. The rank of sergeant in a modern army corresponds to the Roman centurion.

Lesson 67—THE GENITIVE AND DATIVE CASES

THE GENITIVE CASE

Uses of the Genitive

1. To show *possession*:

Vīs **hostium** nōs perterruit.   The violence of the enemy alarmed us.
Mīlitis equus vulnerātus est.   The soldier's horse was wounded.

2. To *describe* another noun:

Erat vir **magnae auctōritātis.**   He was a man of great influence.

3. To denote a *part* (*partitive genitive*):

Partem **annī** labōrābant.   They worked part of the year.

Exception. With cardinal numbers and words such as **paucī** (a few) and **quīdam** (certain), the ablative with **ex** or **dē** is regularly used.

Ūnus ē fīliīs captus est.   One of his sons was captured.
Paucī dē nostrīs prōgressī sunt.   A few of our men advanced.

4. With *certain adjectives* (**cupidus**):

Cupidus **laudis** erat.   He was desirous of praise.

5. With *certain ablatives* (**causā, grātiā**):

Amīcitiae causā adulēscentem   He defended the youth for the sake of
  dēfendit.   friendship.
Ars **artis grātiā.**   Art for art's sake.

Note

The genitive always precedes the ablative.

THE DATIVE CASE

Uses of the Dative

1. *Indirect object:*

Cōnsulī calamitātem nūntiāvit.   He reported the disaster to the consul.
Mihi praemium dedērunt.   They gave me the reward.

Note

Do not confuse the dative of the indirect object (used with verbs of giving, telling, and showing) with the accusative of place to which (used with verbs of motion). Compare the following sentences:

INDIRECT OBJECT	PLACE TO WHICH (TO WHOM)
Amīcīs fābulam nārrāvit. He told a story to his friends.	**Ad amīcōs** properāvit. He hurried to his friends.
Lēgātīs pecūniam dedimus We gave money to the envoys.	**Ad lēgātōs** pecūniam mīsimus. We sent money to the envoys.

2. With *certain adjectives* (**aequus, amīcus, inimīcus, fīnitimus, grātus, idōneus, pār, propinquus, proximus, similis, dissimilis**):

Omnibus amīcus erat.	He was friendly to all.
Locus est idōneus **lūdō**.	The place is suitable for a school.

3. With *special verbs* (**crēdō, imperō, noceō, pāreō, persuādeō, resistō, studeō**):

Nūntiō crēdimus.	We believe the messenger.
Hostibus restitērunt.	They resisted the enemy.

4. With some *compound verbs* (**adsum, dēsum, praesum, īnferō, praeficiō, praestō**):

Labiēnus **castrīs** praeerat.	Labienus was in charge of the camp.
Omnibus ducibus praestitit.	He surpassed all the leaders.

Note

Some compounds take an accusative (direct object) as well as a dative.

Caesarem cōpiīs praefēcērunt.	They put Caesar in charge of the troops.
dir. obj. ind. obj.	
Bellum Germānīs intulit.	He waged war upon the Germans.
dir. obj. ind. obj.	

5. *Purpose:*

Locum **castrīs** dēlēgērunt.	They chose a place for a camp.

6. *Reference* (often used together with a dative of purpose in a double dative construction):

Nōbīs auxiliō erat.	He was of help to us.
reference purpose	
Castra erant **praesidiō oppidō**.	The camp was a protection to the town.
purpose reference	

7. *Possession* (with the verb **esse** to denote the possessor):

Mihi est cōnsilium.	I have a plan. (There is to me a plan.)

8. *Agency* (used with the gerundive to indicate the person by whom an action *must* be performed):

Caesarī omnia *erant agenda*.	Everything had to be done by Caesar.
gerundive	
Prōvincia **incolīs** *dēfendenda est*.	The province must be defended by the inhabitants.
gerundive	

EXERCISES

A. Underline the correct translation of the italicized words.

1. He was speaking *to his son*.   (fīliō, ad fīlium)

2. They gave *him* the kingdom.   (eī, ad eum)

3. Are you going *to Italy?*   (Italiae, ad Italiam)

4. *Whose* pen is this?   (Quī, Cuius)

5. We persuaded *the general*.   (imperātōrī, imperātōrem)

6. Seek a suitable spot *for a bridge*.   (pontī, prō ponte)

7. *To whom* did you show the plan?   (Quibus, Ad quōs)

8. She believes *no one*.   (nēminī, nēminem)

9. They will travel *to the kingdom*.   (rēgnō, ad rēgnum)

10. Marcus told *us* everything.   (nōs, nōbīs)

B. Translate the English words into Latin.

1. spēs *of victory* --

2. *example* grātiā --

3. *the consul's* auctōritās --

4. praeerat *the town* --

5. cōnficiendum est *by Quintus* --

6. studēbant *war* --

7. *the slaves'* officium --

8. vir *of great courage* --

9. lēgātum *the cohort* praefēcērunt --

10. sunt proximī *the Germans* --

C. Check the appropriate column to indicate whether you might expect a genitive or a dative with the following Latin words:

	GENITIVE	DATIVE
1. resistere	-------	-------
2. cupidus	-------	-------
3. causā	-------	-------
4. proximus	-------	-------
5. ostendere	-------	-------
6. praestāre	-------	-------
7. pars	-------	-------
8. imperāre	-------	-------
9. grātiā	-------	-------
10. capiendus	-------	-------

D. Translate into English.

1. Caesarī nūntiāvērunt --

2. eōrum imperātor --

3. Allobrogibus imperāvit --

4. prīmī cīvitātis --

5. nōbīs est lēx --

6. quōrum arma --

7. erat impedīmentō exercituī --

8. ōrātiō omnibus audienda est --

9. mē hībernīs praefēcit --

10. eius labor --

Lesson 68—THE ABLATIVE CASE

Uses of the Ablative

1. After certain *prepositions*, such as **ab, cum, dē, ex, prō, sine**:

Prō patriā mortuī sunt.	They died for their country.
Sine praesidiō vēnit.	He came without a guard.

2. *Accompaniment* (with the preposition **cum**):

Cum tribus legiōnibus prōgressus est.	He advanced with three legions.

Note

When **cum** is used with a pronoun, it is attached to it as an enclitic: **mēcum** (with me), **nōbīscum** (with us), **quōcum** (with whom), etc.

Quibuscum bellum gerēbant?	With whom were they waging war?

3. *Means* (without a preposition; used with things):

Gladiō vulnerātus est.	He was wounded with a sword.

4. *Personal agent* (with the preposition **ā** or **ab** and a passive verb; used with persons):

Ā mīlite vulnerātus est.	He was wounded by the soldier.

5. *Place where* or *in which* (with the preposition **in**):

In Italiā habitant.	They live in Italy.
Labōrāsne **in agrīs?**	Are you working in the fields?

   Exceptions: **Rōmae** (in Rome); **domī** (at home).

Rōmae habitābāmus.	We used to live in Rome.
Domī erat.	He was at home.

6. *Place from which* (with the prepositions **ab, dē,** or **ex**):

Dē monte cucurrit.	He ran down the mountain.
Ē portū nāvigant.	They are sailing out of the harbor.

Note

The preposition is omitted with *names of towns* and **domus**.

Rōmā profectī sunt.	They set out from Rome.
Domō excessit.	He left home.

7. *Time when* or *within which* (without a preposition):

Prīmā lūce nāvigāvērunt. _{at what time}	They sailed at dawn.
Tribus diēbus proficīscēmur. _{within what time}	We shall set out within three days.

8. *Manner* (with the preposition **cum**):

Cum virtūte pugnābātis.	You fought with courage.

Note

Cum may be omitted if an adjective modifies the noun. If expressed, **cum** generally stands between the adjective and the noun.

Magnā (cum) virtūte pugnābātis. | You fought with great courage.

9. *Specification* or *respect* (without a preposition):

Cēterōs celeritāte superat. | He surpasses the others in speed.

10. *Separation* (with or without the preposition **ab** or **ex**):

Horātius hostēs ā ponte prohibuit. | Horatius kept the enemy from the bridge.
Thēseus patriam perīculō līberāvit. | Theseus freed his country from danger.

11. *Description* (with a modifying adjective):

Vir magnā auctōritāte erat. | He was a man of great influence.

12. *Cause* (usually without a preposition):

Timōre commōtī, fūgērunt. | Moved by fear, they fled.
Multīs dē causīs bellum intulit. | He waged war for many reasons.

13. With **ūtor** and **potior**:

Hōc cōnsiliō ūtētur. | He will use this plan.
Rōmānī castrīs potītī sunt. | The Romans took possession of the camp.

14. *Ablative absolute.* (This construction is used to denote the *time* or *circumstances* of an action. The construction consists of a noun or pronoun in the ablative, with a participle, adjective, or another noun agreeing with it. The translation into English varies.)

Proeliō factō, hostēs sē trādidērunt. | After the battle was fought, the enemy surrendered.

Caesare cōnsule, Rōma potentissima erat. | When Caesar was consul, Rome was very powerful.

Frūmentō cōnsūmptō, concilium habēbant. | Since the grain had been used up, they held a meeting.

EXERCISES

A. In each sentence underline all the words that are in the ablative, and then translate them into English. If there are any accompanying prepositions, include them in your translation.

1. Flūmen prōvinciam ab Helvētiīs dīvidit. --

2. Diē cōnstitūtā convēnērunt. --

3. Legiōnēs ex hībernīs ēdūcit. --

4. Eōs suīs fīnibus prohibent. --

5. In Italiam magnīs itineribus contendit. --

6. Erat in Galliā ulteriōre legiō ūna. --

7. Diēs quam cōnstituit cum lēgātīs vēnit. --

8. Omnibus rēbus comparātīs, solvērunt. --

9. Animō incertō eius reditum exspectant. --

10. Hī omnēs linguā lēgibusque inter sē differunt. --

11. Ā cōnsulibus laudātī sunt. --

12. Ībuntne tēcum amīcī? --

13. Cornēlia erat mātrōna magnā virtūte. -----------------------------

14. Certīs dē causīs bellum nōn gerēbant. ----------------------------

15. Tribus hōrīs nāvigāre cōnstituērunt. -----------------------------

B. Underline the word or expression in parentheses that makes the sentence grammatically correct.

1. (Exercitū, Cum exercitū) iter fēcit.

2. Sextus (amīcō, ab amīcō) servātus est.

3. Captīvī (Rōmā, ex Rōmā) fūgērunt.

4. (Germāniā, In Germāniā) manēbāmus.

5. Hostēs (eō tempore, in eō tempore) aggressī sunt.

6. (Armīs, Ab armīs) sē dēfendērunt.

7. Omnēs (altitūdine, in altitūdine) superābat.

8. Contendimus (fortitūdine, cum fortitūdine).

9. (Rōmae, In Rōmā) morātī sunt.

10. Excessistīne (domō, ex domō)?

11. (Oppidum, Oppidō) potītī sunt.

12. Currēbant (monte, dē monte).

13. (Britanniā, Ā Britanniā) nāvigant.

14. (Aestāte, In aestāte) nōn labōrō.

15. (Scūtum, Scūtō) ūsus est.

C. Translate the following ablatives absolute into idiomatic English:

1. hāc rē nūntiātā --

2. nāvibus iūnctīs --

3. eō opere perfectō --

4. hīs pulsīs ---

5. agmine factō ---

6. M. Messālā, M. Pisōne cōnsulibus ----------------------------------

7. locīs superiōribus occupātīs ---------------------------------------

8. oppidīs suīs vīcīsque incēnsīs -------------------------------------

9. carrīs complūribus factīs --

10. hōc audītō --

D. Translate the italicized words into Latin.

1. They decided to remain *in camp*. ---------------------------------

2. *On the same day* he demanded hostages. ---------------------------

3. He received the envoys *from the province*. -----------------------

4. Help was given *by the Germans*. ----------------------------------

5. The whole country was conquered *within a few years.* --

6. *After the towns had been captured,* the war ended. --

7. The army advanced *with great speed.* --

8. He stayed here *with all his friends.* --

9. They crossed the river *by boats.* --

10. He surpassed all *in height.* --

11. He summoned his troops *without delay.* --

12. She refused to stay *at home.* --

13. It was a matter *of great difficulty.* --

14. Stirred *by the speech,* the soldiers enlisted. --

15. He will return *with you,* citizens. --

Jupiter, or Jove, identified by the Romans with the Greek Zeus, was king of the gods. He was worshipped as the god of rain, storms, thunder, and lightning. His name was usually associated with the words "Optimus Maximus," signifying that he was the highest and most powerful among the gods.

Lesson 69—REVIEW OF ALL CASES

A. Underline the correct translation of the italicized words.

1. *A Roman citizen* sum.   (Cīvis Rōmānus, Cīvem Rōmānum)

2. Crēdidit *the people*.   (populō, populum)

3. Discessērunt sine *hope*.   (spem, spē)

4. *With whom* ībis?   (Cum quō, Quōcum)

5. *In winter* labōrāre nōn potuit.   (Hieme, In hieme)

6. Iter fēcimus *for six days*.   (sex diēs, sex diēbus)

7. Praeerat *the camp*.   (castrīs, castra)

8. Scīvit *that the prisoners* sequī.   (captīvī, captīvōs)

9. *To winter quarters* properāvit.   (Hībernīs, Ad hīberna)

10. Exspectāvit *the journey's* fīnem.   (itineris, itinera)

11. *By a weapon* interfectus est.   (Tēlō, Ab tēlō)

12. Victōriam *to the allies* nūntiāvī.   (sociīs, ad sociōs)

13. Ūsī erant *arrows*.   (sagittās, sagittīs)

14. Fossam *three feet* lātam fēcērunt.   (trēs pedēs, tribus pedibus)

15. Aciēs *by Caesar* īnstruenda erat.   (Caesarī, ab Caesare)

16. Collis nōn erat idōneus *for a battle*.   (proeliō, prō proeliō)

17. *From Rome* profectī erāmus.   (Rōmā, Ex Rōmā)

18. Brūtus *consul* factus est.   (cōnsul, cōnsulem)

19. Audīvimus *the gods'* imperium.   (deī, deōrum)

20. Erās *of help* barbarīs.   (auxilī, auxiliō)

B. Translate into English.

1. in flūmine

2. ex nāvibus proximīs

3. domī esse

4. multitūdō hostium

5. Caesaris adventū

6. hōc modō

7. maximā virtūte

8. inimīcus nēminī

9. annō quārtō

10. patrum memoriā

11. paucī numerō   --

12. in ūnum locum   --

13. post eius mortem   --

14. hōrā tertiā   --

15. timōre permōtī   --

16. Rōmulō rēge   --

17. prīmō bellō Pūnicō   --

18. pecūniae cupidus   --

19. eādem dē causā   --

20. nōbīs ūsuī est   --

C. Translate the English words into Latin.

1. Exspectāvērunt *for many hours.*   --

2. *Into our province* vēnerat.   --

3. Lēgātī *of the Germans* missī sunt.   --

4. Caesar *across the river* contendit.   --

5. Iter faciet *with you,* mīlitēs.   --

6. Rōmānōs *on that day* vīcit.   --

7. *To the city* rediit.   --

8. *In our fields* mānsimus.   --

9. Paucī *by the Gauls* interfectī erant.   --

10. Prōgressī sunt *with great speed.*   --

11. Frūmentum *to the troops* datum est.   --

12. Id *before night* fēcērunt.   --

13. Profectī erant *with their families.*   --

14. Dīxit *that the Gauls* oppugnāre   --

15. *From the harbor* nāvigant.   --

16. *Because of great fear* fūgimus.   --

17. Persuāsit *three cohorts* ut exīrent.   --

18. Equitēs *with swords* sē dēfendēbant.   --

19. Dux hostēs *from the territory* expulit.   --

20. Caesar Labiēnum *the army* praefēcit.   --

D. Using the ablative absolute construction, express the following in Latin:

1. after the messenger had been sent   --

2. after capturing many towns   --

3. when all Gaul had been conquered   --

4. having led the soldiers out   --

5. when Caesar and Bibulus were consuls ---------------------------------

6. since the hostages had been killed ---------------------------------

7. after aid had been given ---------------------------------

8. having found out this matter ---------------------------------

9. with you as leader ---------------------------------

10. although the battle had been fought ---------------------------------

E. In the space provided, write the *number* of the word or expression which, when inserted in the blank, makes each sentence grammatically correct.

1. Lēgātus cōpiās ex _____ ēdūxit.

   (1) castra   (2) castrīs   (3) castrōrum   (4) castrum

2. Puer altissimus _____ factus est.

   (1) prīncipem   (2) prīncipis   (3) prīncipī   (4) prīnceps

3. Omnēs _____ ūsī sunt.

   (1) gladiīs   (2) gladiōrum   (3) gladiōs   (4) gladiī

4. Pater _____ iter fēcit.

   (1) fīliō   (2) fīlium   (3) cum fīliō   (4) fīlius

5. Multās hōrās _____ manēbant.

   (1) in forō   (2) in forum   (3) forō   (4) forum

6. Hostēs _____ nōn praestitērunt.

   (1) Rōmānī   (2) Rōmānōs   (3) Rōmānōrum   (4) Rōmānīs

7. Dīximus _____ monitōs esse.

   (1) puerum   (2) puerī   (3) puerōs   (4) puerīs

8. Vēnit opere _____.

   (1) perfectus   (2) perfectī   (3) perfectum   (4) perfectō

9. Labiēnus _____ praeest.

   (1) cōpiīs   (2) cōpiās   (3) cōpiārum   (4) cōpiam

10. Quaerō cūr fēminae _____ persuādeant.

    (1) ducem   (2) ducī   (3) duce   (4) ducis

F. Rewrite the sentences below, making *all* changes required by the directions in parentheses.

1. Imperātor pācem *cupit*. (substitute *studet*)

   ----

2. Iūlius prīncipem *vocat*. (substitute *est*)

   ----

3. Hominēs *Rōmam* fūgērunt. (change to *the city*)

   ----

4. Oppidum *ab incolīs* dēfēnsum est. (change to *a wall*)

----

5. *Diū* in aquā manēbāmus. (change to *three hours*)

----

6. *Tum* nōn labōrābātis. (change to *summer*)

----

7. Ad suōs amīcōs *contendit*. (substitute *locūtus est*)

----

8. Omnēs *in castrīs* sunt. (change to *home*)

----

9. *Ab Italiā* profectus sum. (change to *Rome*)

----

10. Oppidum *aggressī sunt*. (substitute *potītī sunt*)

----

11. Id fēcerant *ob* honōrem. (substitute *causā*)

----

12. Mīlitēs *hortātus est*. (substitute *persuāsit*)

----

13. *Ibi* nōn habitant. (change to *Rome*)

----

14. Lēgātus exercitum *prōsecūtus est*. (substitute *praefuit*)

----

15. Legiō ā Caesare *ēducta est*. (substitute *ēdūcenda est*)

----

16. In silvīs *morātī sunt*. (substitute *properāvērunt*)

----

17. *Ad* montem currimus. (substitute *Dē*)

----

18. Iter facient cum *barbarīs*. (change to *us*)

----

19. Vāllum *longē* patēbat. (change to *100 feet*)

----

20. Castra *īnsidiīs* capta sunt. (change to *the enemy*)

Lesson 70—AGREEMENT

1. A *verb* agrees with its *subject* in person and number.

Agricolae in agrīs **labōrābant.**

3rd pers. pl.   3rd pers. pl.

The farmers were working in the fields.

Quis cāsum **vīdit?**

3rd pers.   3rd pers.

sing.   sing.

Who saw the accident?

Note

A. When there are two or more singular subjects, the verb is plural.

Iūlia et Clāra **clāmant.**

Julia and Clara are shouting.

B. When the subjects are of different *persons*, the first person takes precedence over the second and third, and the second person takes precedence over the third.

Ego et *tū* iter **faciēmus.**

1st   2nd   1st

pers.   pers.   pers.

You and I will march.

Ego et *frāter* **valēmus.**

1st   3rd   1st

pers.   pers.   pers.

My brother and I are well.

Tū et *amīcus* **dēlēctī estis.**

2nd   3rd   2nd

pers.   pers.   pers.

You and your friend have been chosen.

2. An *adjective* or *participle* agrees with its *noun* or *pronoun* in gender, number, and case.

Prīmam nostram *aciem* aggrediēbantur.

fem., sing.,   fem., sing.,   fem., sing.,

acc.   acc.   acc.

They attacked our first battle line.

Ē castrīs **ēgressī,** *hominēs* ad Rhēnum

      masc., pl.,   masc., pl.,

      nom.   nom.

contendērunt.

Having left camp, the men hastened toward the Rhine.

Note

In the passive of the perfect system, the *participle* agrees with the *subject*.

Mīlitēs **circumventī** sunt.

masc., pl.,   masc., pl.,

nom.   nom.

The soldiers were surrounded.

Tēla **coniecta** erant.

neut., pl.,   neut., pl.,

nom.   nom.

Weapons had been thrown.

3. A *predicate noun* or *predicate adjective* (one used with the verb **sum** or a verb in the passive) is in the same case as the *subject*.

Cornēlia erat **māter** Gracchōrum.

nominative   nominative

Cornelia was the mother of the Gracchi.

Scīmus *eum* esse **incolumem.**

     accusative   accusative

We know that he is unharmed.

4. A noun used in *apposition* with another noun agrees with it in case.

Rhēnus, **flūmen** altissimum, Helvētiam ā

nominative nominative

   Germānīs dīvidit.

The Rhine, a very deep river, separates Helvetia from the Germans.

Vīdistīne *Viam Appiam,* **rēgīnam** viārum?   Did you see the Appian Way, the queen of
      <small>accusative</small>   <small>accusative</small>   roads?

5. A *relative pronoun* agrees with its *antecedent* in gender and number; its case, however, depends
on its use in its own clause.

Ea *diēs* **quam** cōnstituerat vēnit.   That day which he had decided upon came.
   <small>fem. fem.</small>
   <small>sing. sing.</small>

Virō **quī** aderat dīximus.   We spoke to the man who was present.
<small>masc. masc.</small>
<small>sing. sing.</small>

6. The possessive adjective **suus, -a, -um** is reflexive; that is, it refers back to the subject but
agrees with the word it modifies in gender, number, and case. Its *meaning* is determined by the subject.

Puer **suam** sorōrem amat.   The boy loves *his* sister.
   <small>refers to</small>
  <small>agrees with</small>

Puella **suam** sorōrem amat.   The girl loves *her* sister.
   <small>refers to</small>
  <small>agrees with</small>

Līberī **suam** sorōrem amant.   The children love *their* sister.
  <small>refers to</small>
 <small>agrees with</small>

Note

When the genitive of the pronouns **is, hic,** or **ille** is used, then someone other than the subject
is indicated.

Puer **eius** sorōrem amat.   The boy loves his or her (*someone else's*)
     sister.

Puella **illīus** domum admīrātur.   The girl admires his or her (*someone else's*)
     home.

Virī **hōrum** pecūniam postulant.   The men are demanding their (*not their own*)
     money.

EXERCISES

A. Underline the correct translation of the italicized words.

1. He followed *his own* cōnsilium.   (suum, eius)

2. They found *his* togam.   (suam, illīus)

3. Caesar encouraged *his* virōs.   (eōs, suōs)

4. He saw *her* perīculum.   (eius, id)

5. The leader accepted *their* subsidium.   (suum, eōrum)

6. He will lead out *his* legiōnem.   (suum, suam)

7. They admired *her* fortitūdinem.   (huius, suam)

8. She reported *his* mortem.   (suam, eius)

9. They loved *their* rēgem.   (eōrum, suum)

10. They spoke to *his* magistrō.   (suō, illīus)

B. Each group in parentheses contains one form that does *not* agree with the noun. Rewrite that
form correctly.

1. fortūnam   (nostram, bonam, commūnis, meliōrem)   -

2. iter   (illud, magnō, longius, difficile)   -

3. sociōrum   (vestrōrum, fortium, nōtum, hōrum)   --------------------------------

4. exercitū   (forte, ūnō, maiōre, eō)   --------------------------------

5. rēbus   (multīs, duōbus, difficilis, omnibus)   --------------------------------

6. officia   (mea, aliquae, certissima, eadem)   --------------------------------

7. magister   (grātus, dīligentior, nōbilis, potentis)   --------------------------------

8. legiōnī   (integrō, fīrmiōre, ācrī, maximō)   --------------------------------

9. hostēs   (paucōs, ipsīs, celerēs, fortīs)   --------------------------------

10. hominis   (novīs, inimīcī, similis, brevissimī)   --------------------------------

C. In the following clauses translate into Latin the relative pronoun in italics:

1. vir *who* praemium obtinuit   --------------------------------

2. Iāsōn *whom* Mēdēa amāvit   --------------------------------

3. mīlitēs *to whom* dux imperāta dedit   --------------------------------

4. fēminae *by whom* līberī servābantur   --------------------------------

5. oppidum *in which* nātus sum   --------------------------------

6. rēx *before whom* stetimus   --------------------------------

7. īnsidiae *into which* Rōmānī cecidērunt   --------------------------------

8. Germānī *whom* omnēs timēbant   --------------------------------

9. urbs *from which* multī fūgērunt   --------------------------------

10. Hannibal *with whom* pācem voluērunt   --------------------------------

D. Rewrite each of the following sentences, changing the subject as directed and making all other necessary changes:

1. *Hostis* expulsus erat.   Hostēs   --------------------------------

2. *Senātus* bellum parāvit.   Rōmānī   --------------------------------

3. *Rēx* in rēgnum receptus est.   Rēgīna   --------------------------------

4. *Bellum* illātum erit.   Bella   --------------------------------

5. *Rōmānī* lēgēs cōnstituērunt.   Rōmulus   --------------------------------

6. *Mīles*, vulnerātus, fugere   Mīlitēs,   --------------------------------
   nōn poterat.

7. Timōre permōtī, *cōnsulēs*   --------------------------------, cōnsul   --------------------------------
   domī manēbant.

8. *Fīlia* fugiēns servāta est.   Fīliae   --------------------------------

9. *Explōrātor*, quī praemissus   Explōrātōrēs   --------------------------------
   erat, locum dēlēgit.

10. *Nōs* amīcī appellātī erāmus.   Ego   --------------------------------

E. Translate into Latin the words in apposition.

1. Vercingetorīx, *a very brave general*, captus est.   --------------------------------

2. Ariovistum, *king* Germānōrum, timēbāmus.   --------------------------------

3. Imperium Mariō, *the consul*, datum erat.   ------------------------------------

4. Lēgī dē Cicerōne, *father* patriae.   ------------------------------------

5. Māter Cornēlī, *our friend*, pervēnit.   ------------------------------------

F. Rewrite the sentences below, making *all* changes required by the directions in parentheses.

1. *Tribūnus* captus est. (change to *Tribūnī*)

----

2. *Germānī* fortēs erant. (substitute *Praesidia*)

----

3. Ariovistum audīvimus. (add the word *rēx* in apposition)

----

4. *Adulēscēns* quī aderat praemium accēpit. (substitute *Puella*)

----

5. Gāius *suum* frātrem timet. (substitute *someone else's*)

----

6. Mārcus domō proficīscitur. (add *sororque* after *Mārcus*)

----

7. Ego prīncipem monēbō. (add *et Cornēlius* after *Ego*)

----

8. *Fossa* erat lātior. (substitute *Flūmen*)

----

9. *Senātor* ab cōnsule laudātus erat. (substitute *Poetae*)

----

10. *Nāvis* quam vīdistī erat mea. (substitute *Opus*)

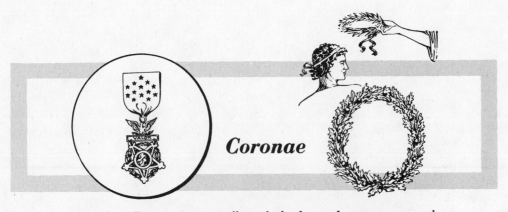

Coronae

Awards in Roman times usually took the form of crowns or wreaths made of acorns, oak leaves, laurel leaves, or olive leaves. The corōna cīvica, corresponding roughly to the Congressional Medal of Honor, was given as a reward for saving a citizen's life in battle. Similar crowns were awarded for excellence in the arts, literature, and athletics.

Lesson 71—THE INDICATIVE AND THE SUBJUNCTIVE

THE INDICATIVE

INDEPENDENT CLAUSES

The indicative mood is used to state a fact in a declarative sentence, or to ask a question in an interrogative sentence.

DECLARATIVE	INTERROGATIVE
Multōs librōs **habeō.**	**Habēsne** multōs librōs?
I have many books.	Have you many books?

DEPENDENT, OR SUBORDINATE, CLAUSES

The indicative is used in the following types of clauses:

1. *Relative Clauses*—introduced by the relative pronoun **quī, quae, quod** (who, that).

Eī **quī** domum **rediērunt** servātī sunt.	Those who returned home were saved.
Auxilium **quod mīsistī** satis erat.	The help that you sent was enough.

2. *Adverbial Clauses*—introduced by the following conjunctions: **antequam** and **priusquam** (before), **dum** (while), **postquam** (after), **quod** (because), **simul atque (ac)** (as soon as), **ubi** (when), **ut** (as).

Antequam (Priusquam) discessit, litterās scrīpsit.	Before he left, he wrote a letter.
Dum haec **geruntur,** Iāsonem exspectābant.	While this was going on, they waited for Jason.

Note. **Dum** (while) always takes the present tense.

Postquam pervēnit, mē monuit.	After he arrived, he warned me.
Domī manēbam **quod** aeger **eram.**	I stayed home because I was ill.
Simul ac mē **vīdit,** fūgit.	As soon as he saw me, he fled.
Ubi locūtus est, omnēs audīvērunt.	When he spoke, all listened.
Omnis Gallia, **ut dīxit** Caesar, in partēs trēs dīvīsa est.	All Gaul, as Caesar said, was divided into three parts.

THE SUBJUNCTIVE

Whereas the indicative is the mood of fact, the subjunctive in Latin is used idiomatically to express a wish, doubt, purpose, mild command, condition, etc.

In English the subjunctive is rare, in Latin fairly common. The Latin subjunctive is translated into English in several ways: by means of the auxiliaries *may, might, should, would;* by the indicative; by the infinitive; by the imperative.

The subjunctive is found in independent, but principally in dependent, clauses.

INDEPENDENT CLAUSES

Hortatory Subjunctive—used mostly in the first person plural, in the present tense, to express an *exhortation*. The negative is introduced by **nē.**

Ducem **sequāmur.**	Let us follow the leader.
Nē diū **maneāmus.**	Let us not stay long.

215

DEPENDENT CLAUSES

1. *Purpose*—introduced by **ut** or **utī** (affirmative) and **nē** (negative). In English purpose is usually expressed by the infinitive.

Properat <u>ut</u> familiam **videat**. <small>aff.</small>	He is hurrying to see his family.
Fūgērunt <u>nē</u> **caperentur**. <small>neg.</small>	They fled in order not to be captured.

Note

A. **Quī** is sometimes substituted for **ut** in a *relative* clause of purpose.

Mīsit lēgātōs **quī** omnia **cognōscerent**.	He sent the envoys to find out everything.

B. Some verbs, such as **hortor** (urge), **imperō** (command), and **persuādeō** (persuade) take as object a *substantive* clause of purpose.

Suōs hortātur **ut prōcēdant**.	He urges his men to advance.
Prīncipī persuāsit **nē manēret**.	He persuaded the chief not to remain.

C. The action in purpose clauses is always incomplete; hence, the *present* subjunctive is used for primary sequence, the *imperfect* for secondary.

2. *Result*—introduced by **ut** (affirmative) and **ut nōn** (negative). The main clause usually contains one of the following clue words:

ita		**tālis**, such	
sīc	so	**tantus**, so great	
tam		**tot**, so many	

Tantā virtūte pugnāverant <u>ut</u> Gallōs in fugam **darent**. <small>aff.</small>	They had fought with such great valor that they put the Gauls to flight.
Vāllum **tam** longē pertinet <u>ut</u> fīnem vidēre **nōn possīmus**. ↑——— negative ———↑	The wall extends so far that we cannot see the end of it.

Note

In result clauses the *present* subjunctive is generally used for primary sequence, the *imperfect* for secondary.

3. **Cum** *Circumstantial*—introduced by **cum** meaning *when* or *while*, to indicate the circumstances under which an action took place in the past. The *imperfect* subjunctive is used for incomplete action, the *pluperfect* for completed action.

Cum virī <u>convenīrent</u>, tempestās orta est. <small>incomplete action</small>	While the men were assembling, a storm arose.
Cum Caesar <u>pervēnisset</u>, hostēs pācem <small>completed action</small> petēbant.	When Caesar (had) arrived, the enemy sought peace.

Note

When the **cum** clause emphasizes the time element, rather than the circumstances, it is called **cum** *temporal* and takes the indicative.

Cum **mortuus est,** adfuī.	When he died, I was present. <small>(at the time when)</small>

4. **Cum** *Causal*—introduced by **cum** meaning *since*. The tense of the subjunctive is determined by the rule for the sequence of tenses.

Cum mē iam <u>vīderit,</u> nōn manēbō. <small>completed primary</small> <small>action sequence</small>	Since he has already seen me, I shall not stay.

Deīs grātiās ēgērunt, **cum** in perīculō
secondary
sequence

nōn iam **essent.**
incomplete
action

They thanked the gods, since they were no longer in danger.

5. *Cum Concessive*—introduced by **cum** meaning *although*. The tense of the subjunctive is determined by the rule for the sequence of tenses. A sentence containing a concessive clause usually has the word **tamen.**

Cum calamitātem nostram **vīdisset,**
completed
action

tamen nihil **fēcit.**
secondary
sequence

Although he had seen our misfortune, still he did nothing.

Cum aeger **sit,** *tamen* labōrāre in
incomplete
action

animō **habet.**
primary
sequence

Although he is ill, he still intends to work.

6. *Indirect Question*—introduced by an interrogative word or expression after a verb of mental action, such as knowing, asking, seeing. The tense of the subjunctive is determined by the rule for the sequence of tenses.

DIRECT QUESTION (INDICATIVE)

Cūr properās?

Why are you hurrying?

Quis litterās mīserat?

Who had sent the letter?

INDIRECT QUESTION (SUBJUNCTIVE)

Sciō **cūr properēs.**
primary   incomplete
sequence   action

I know why you are hurrying.

Rogāvērunt **quis** litterās **mīsisset.**
secondary   completed
sequence   action

They asked who had sent the letter.

SEQUENCE OF TENSES

There are four tenses in the subjunctive mood. The tense to be used in a particular sentence depends upon the rules for the sequence of tenses, shown in the diagram below:

	MAIN VERB	SUBJUNCTIVE VERB	
		INCOMPLETE ACTION	COMPLETED ACTION
PRIMARY	*Present* *Future* *Future Perfect*	Present	Perfect
SECONDARY	*Imperfect* *Perfect* *Pluperfect*	Imperfect	Pluperfect

The *main* verb is also called the *independent* verb; the *subjunctive* verb is the *dependent,* or *subordinate,* verb.

Incomplete means that the action of the subjunctive verb takes place at the *same time as* or *after* that of the main verb.

Completed means that the action of the subjunctive verb took place *before* that of the main verb.

EXAMPLES OF SEQUENCE OF TENSES

Sciō quid agant.

primary   incomplete
sequence   action

I know what they are doing.

Sciō quid ēgerint.

primary   completed
sequence   action

I know what they have done.

Scīvī quid agerent.

secondary   incomplete
sequence   action

I knew what they were doing.

Scīvī quid ēgissent.

secondary   completed
sequence   action

I knew what they had done.

EXERCISES

A. Translate the italicized clauses into English.

1. Pervenit *ut praemium accipiat.*   ------------------------------------

2. Rogāvērunt *quid vīdisset.*   ------------------------------------

3. Tam perterritus est *ut nōn loquerētur.*   ------------------------------------

4. Fortiter pugnābimus *nē capiāmur.*   ------------------------------------

5. *Cum id audīvissem,* discēdere cōnstituī.   ------------------------------------

6. Athēniēnsibus persuāsit *ut classem aedificārent.*   ------------------------------------

7. Tantum est perīculum *ut incolae fugiant.*   ------------------------------------

8. Helvētiī lēgātōs mīserant *quī pācem peterent.*   ------------------------------------

9. *Cum prīma aciēs īnstruerētur,* tamen nōn parātī erant.   ------------------------------------

10. Iam sciēmus *cūr pervēnerit.*   ------------------------------------

11. Mārcus domī remanēbit, *cum nōn valeat.*   ------------------------------------

12. *Cum bellum gererētur,* nēmō domō excessit.   ------------------------------------

13. Pater nescīvit *quō fīlius īret.*   ------------------------------------

14. *Oppidum relinquāmus.*   ------------------------------------

15. *Cum id nūntiātum esset,* Caesar Rōmam contendit.   ------------------------------------

B. In each sentence underline the term that will make the sentence grammatically correct.

1. Rogat ubi discipulī (sint, essent).

2. Flūmen tam lātum erat (nē, ut nōn) trānsīre posset.

3. Vēnērunt ut amīcōs (videant, vidērent).

4. Cum nūntius (missus sit, missus esset), respōnsum exspectāvit.

5. Suīs imperābit ut castra (pōnant, pōnerent).

6. Scīvimus cūr līberī nōs (sequantur, sequerentur).

7. Cum hostem (vīcerit, vīcisset), nōn iam pugnābit.

8. Explōrātōrēs mīserat quī locum idōneum (invenīrent, invēnissent).

9. Duās legiōnēs cōnscrībet (nē, ut nōn) premātur.

10. Cum īnsidiās (timeat, timēret), tamen iter fēcit.

C. Each sentence below illustrates a use of the subjunctive. Place one line under the main verb and two lines under the subordinate verb in each sentence. Then enter in the proper column the sequence (primary or secondary) and the action (incomplete or completed).

	SEQUENCE	ACTION
1. Julia is coming to see the fair.		
2. We asked him what he was doing.		
3. Since we had finished our work, we took a trip.		
4. He will persuade the citizens not to choose a leader.		
5. The shield is so heavy that he cannot carry it.		
6. The soldiers were sent to destroy the fields.		
7. Aid arrived while the enemy were throwing weapons.		
8. Although I have been wounded, I will not surrender.		
9. We know why they are being attacked.		
10. After hostages had been given, he dismissed the army.		

D. In the sentences above (Exercise C), translate into Latin all the verbs that go in the subjunctive. Include in your answer the words that introduce the subjunctive.

1. _____

2. _____

3. _____

4. _____

5. _____

6. _____

7. _____

8. _____

9. _____

10. _____

E. Rewrite the sentences below, making *all* changes required by the directions in parentheses.

1. Barbarī oppidum relinquunt. (start the sentence with *Scit cūr*)

_____

2. *Signō datō*, ducem secūtī sumus. (change to a *cum* circumstantial clause)

----

3. *Mittunt* magistrum quī līberōs doceat. (change to *Mīserant*)

----

4. Nōbīs dīxit ubi *essent*. (change to completed action)

----

5. Virōs hortātur *ut pugnent*. (make the subjunctive clause negative)

----

6. Suīs *persuāsit* ut viam mūnīrent. (change to *persuādēbit*)

----

7. Flūmen altum est. Trānsīre nōn possumus. (add *tam* and combine into one sentence)

----

8. *Iussit* eōs vāllum dēfendere. (substitute *Imperāvit*)

----

9. Cognōscisne quō modō castra *posita sint?* (change to incomplete action)

----

10. Nūntiāvit *rēgem* mortuum esse. (substitute *quis*)

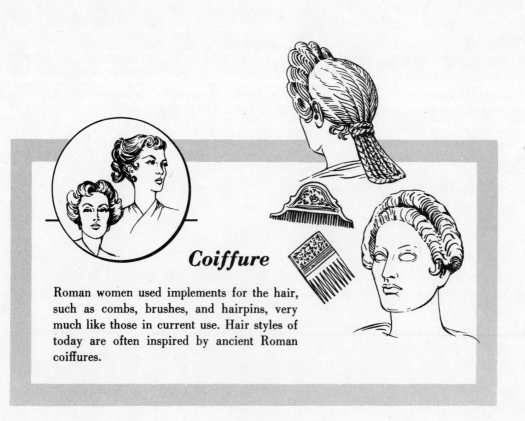

Coiffure

Roman women used implements for the hair, such as combs, brushes, and hairpins, very much like those in current use. Hair styles of today are often inspired by ancient Roman coiffures.

Lesson 72—INFINITIVES

1. *Complementary Infinitive*—after certain verbs, such as **cōnor** (try), **cōnstituō** (decide), **incipiō** (begin), **possum** (be able), **volō** (want), which require an infinitive to complete their meaning. The subject for both verbs is the same.

Caesar **solvere** cōnstituit.	Caesar decided to set sail.
Līberī **scrībere** nōn possunt.	The children are not able to write.

2. *Subject Infinitive*—used as subject of:

   a. the verb **est.**

Vidēre est crēdere.	Seeing is believing. (To see is to believe.)
Errāre hūmānum est.	To err is human.

   b. impersonal verbs, such as **licet** (it is permitted) and **oportet** (it is necessary).

Licet **convenīre.**	To assemble is permitted. (It is permitted to assemble.)
Tē **properāre** oportēbat.	It was necessary that you hurry.

Note

The subject of an infinitive is in the accusative case.

3. *Object Infinitive*—after certain verbs, such as **cōgō** (compel), **iubeō** (order), **prohibeō** (forbid). Each verb has a different subject, with the subject of the infinitive in the accusative case.

Caesar suōs **prōgredī** iussit.	Caesar ordered his men to advance.
Prohibuī Mārcum **scrībere.**	I forbade Marcus to write.

Note

A. Some verbs may take both a complementary and an object infinitive.

Volō <u>**dīcere.**</u>   I want to speak.
  <small>complementary infinitive</small>

Volō eum <u>**dīcere.**</u>   I want him to speak.
  <small>object infinitive</small>

B. Complementary, subject, and object infinitives are used principally in the *present* tense.

4. *Indirect Statement*—after verbs of saying, knowing, thinking, perceiving, with the subject of the infinitive in the accusative case.

An *indirect* statement reports something *indirectly* (not in quotation marks). The English word *that* is not translated into Latin.

Nūntius dīxit <u>**lēgātum**</u> <u>**pervēnisse.**</u>   The messenger said *that the ambassador had*
  <small>accusative infinitive</small>   *arrived.*

A *direct* statement reports something *directly* (in quotation marks).

Nūntius dīxit, **"Lēgātus pervēnit."**   The messenger said, *"The ambassador has*
  <small>nominative indicative</small>   *arrived."*

221

TENSES OF THE INFINITIVE

1. The *present* infinitive is used if the action takes place *at the same time* as that of the main verb.

Scit mē **discēdere.**	He knows that I am leaving.
Scīvit mē **discēdere.**	He knew that I was leaving.

2. The *perfect* infinitive is used if the action took place *before* that of the main verb.

Scit mē **discessisse.**	He knows that I left.
Scīvit mē **discessisse.**	He knew that I had left.

3. The *future* infinitive is used if the action takes place *after* that of the main verb. Note in the following examples that **discessūrum** has an accusative singular masculine ending to agree with **mē.**

Scit mē **discessūrum esse.**	He knows that I will leave.
Scīvit mē **discessūrum esse.**	He knew that I would leave.

Note

A. When the subject of an infinitive is the same as the subject of the main verb, the reflexive **sē** is used. When the subject is different, the accusative of **is, hic,** or **ille** is used. Note also in the following examples that **līberātum** has an accusative singular masculine ending to agree with **sē** and **eum.**

Servus spērat **sē** līberātum esse. ↑——— refers to	The slave hopes that he has been freed.
Servus spērat **eum** (amīcum) refers to ———↑ līberātum esse.	The slave hopes that he (his friend) has been freed.

B. Distinguish between an indirect question and an indirect statement. Both begin with a verb of mental action. An indirect question has an interrogative word and the subjunctive; an indirect statement has a subject accusative and the infinitive.

INDIRECT QUESTION	INDIRECT STATEMENT
Scit **ubi virī labōrent.** 　interr.　　subj.	Scit **virōs labōrāre.** 　acc.　　inf.
He knows where the men are working.	He knows that the men are working.
Cognōvērunt **quō modō vulnerātus esset.** 　　interr.　　　subj.	Cognōvērunt **eum vulnerātum esse.** 　　acc.　　　inf.
They found out how he had been wounded.	They found out that he had been wounded.

EXERCISES

A. Translate the English words into Latin.

1. Miser nōn potest *to see.* -------------------------------------

2. Incolās *to flee* coēgit. -------------------------------------

3. Arbitrātus est tempus *was* bonum. -------------------------------------

4. Terram *to destroy* nōn dēbent. -------------------------------------

5. Caesar putat hostēs *are following.* -------------------------------------

6. Nūntiat Gallōs *have been defeated.* -------------------------------------

7. Equitēs *to advance* iussit. -------------------------------------

8. Scīvit discipulōs *had finished* negōtium. -------------------------------------

9. Audīvit Caesarem auxilium *would send*.   --

10. Dīcit captīvōs *are being warned*.   --

B. Rewrite each sentence, changing the tense of the infinitive as required by the verb in parentheses.

1. Exīstimat exercitum *oppugnāre*. (has attacked)

----

2. Audīmus captīvōs *līberārī*. (have been freed)

----

3. Dīcunt multitūdinem *convenīre*. (will come together)

----

4. Sēnsit rem difficilem *fuisse*. (was)

----

5. Intellegō sōlem *orīrī*. (has risen)

----

6. Cōnfīrmant sē hostēs *impedīvisse*. (are hindering)

----

7. Scīsne bellum *gestum esse?* (is being waged)

----

8. Respondit eōs sine nōbīs *nāvigāre*. (would sail)

----

9. Scrīpsistī castra *mūnīrī*. (had been fortified)

----

10. Putāvit cōnsulem *perventūrum esse*. (had arrived)

C. Complete the English translation.

1. Cōnstituērunt nōbīscum īre.   They decided ------------------------- with us.

2. In eās partēs Galliae venīre audet.   He dares ------------- into those parts of Gaul.

3. Caesar dīxit sē posteā respōnsūrum esse.   Caesar said that he ------------------ later.

4. Resistere potuit nēmō.   No one was able ----------------------------.

5. Lēgātōs ad sē revertere iussit.   He ordered the envoys --------------- to him.

6. Memoriā tenēbat cōnsulem occīsum esse.   He remembered that the consul ----------------.

7. Ad hostēs redīre nōlēbant.   They did not want -------------- to the enemy.

8. Caesarem certiōrem fēcērunt agrōs vāstārī.   They informed Caesar that their fields ----------.

9. Ostendit sē eōs prohibitūrum esse.   He pointed out that he --------------- them.

10. Scīvit mīlitēs profectōs esse.   He knew that the soldiers ----------------.

11. Germānōs sē trādere coēgit.   He compelled the Germans ----------------.

12. Audīvimus barbarōs oppidum relīquisse.   We heard that the natives ------------ the town.

13. Omnēs incolae portās claudere coepērunt.   All the inhabitants began _ _ _ _ _ _ _ _ _ _ _ _ _ the gates.

14. Nūntiātum est equitēs accēdere.   It was reported that the horsemen _ _ _ _ _ _ _ _ _ _ _ _ _ .

15. Dīxērunt eum diū morārī.   They said that he _ _ _ _ _ _ _ _ _ _ _ _ _ _ _ a long time.

D. In each sentence an infinitive is required in translating into Latin. Underline the English words requiring the infinitive, and then write the correct Latin infinitive with its subject, if there is one.

1. They are trying to sleep.   _

2. He wanted them to remain.   _

3. I hope that the camp is being defended.   _

4. Who said that the Romans had been conquered?   _

5. We think that you are in danger.   _

6. Why did Caesar compel his men to flee?   _

7. Marcus wrote that he had arrived home.   _

8. We knew that they feared war.   _

9. They hoped that the king would rule fairly.   _

10. I heard that the Aedui were being oppressed.   _

E. Rewrite the sentences below, making *all* changes required by the directions in parentheses.

1. *Prōcēdere* nōn poterant. (substitute equivalent form of *Sequor*)

_ _

2. Mārcus dīcit sē equum *velle*. (change to past time)

_ _

3. Puerōs *loquī* prohibuit. (substitute equivalent form of *abeō*)

_ _

4. Scīmus imperātōrem terram *vāstāre*. (change to future time)

_ _

5. Hostēs pācem petunt. (start the sentence with *Cognōvit*)

_ _

6. Putāsne *viam* apertam esse? (change to *viās*)

_ _

7. Sēnsit Gallōs *oppugnāre*. (change to the passive)

_ _

8. Exīstimō omnēs *audītōs esse*. (change to the active)

_ _

9. *Dēbēmus* contendere. (substitute *Oportet*)

_ _

10. Scit cūr barbarī perturbentur. (change to indirect statement, omitting *cūr*)

_ _

Lesson 73—PARTICIPLES; GERUND AND GERUNDIVE

PARTICIPLES

A *participle* is a verbal adjective. As an adjective it agrees in gender, number, and case with the noun or pronoun it modifies; as a verb it has tense and voice, and may take an object. There are four participles: a present and future participle in the active voice, and a perfect and future participle in the passive voice. There is no present passive or perfect active participle. The participle is often best translated into English by a clause expressing time, cause, condition, etc.

ACTIVE PARTICIPLES

1. The *present participle* denotes action occurring *at the same time* as that of the main verb.

Virum **currentem** per agrum vīdī.	I saw the man running through the field.
Duōbus **pugnantibus,** omnēs cōnspiciēbant.	While the two were fighting, all looked on.

2. The *future active participle* is generally used with some form of the verb **esse** to express a future or intended action. It is declined like **altus, -a, -um** and agrees with the noun it modifies in gender, number, and case.

Cōnsul **profectūrus est.**	The consul is about to set out.
Rogāvit quot hominēs **perventūrī essent.**	He asked how many men intended to arrive.

PASSIVE PARTICIPLES

1. The *perfect participle* denotes action occurring *before* that of the main verb.

Timōre **permōtī,** multī sēsē in fugam dedērunt.	Alarmed through fear, many fled.
Victōriā **nūntiātā,** virī clāmābant.	After the victory had been announced, the men shouted.

Note

The perfect participle of a deponent verb is *active* in meaning.

Caesar **cohortātus** suōs proelium commīsit.	Having encouraged his men, Caesar joined battle.
Multa mīlia passuum **prōgressī,** cōnstitērunt.	After advancing many miles, they came to a halt.

2. The *future passive participle,* or *gerundive,* is discussed below.

GERUND AND GERUNDIVE

1. The *gerund* is a verbal noun, declined like a second declension noun. It has no nominative and no plural. Its endings are:

-ndī	genitive
-ndō	dative
-ndum	accusative
-ndō	ablative

In English the gerund ends in *-ing*.

Erat cupidus **scrībendī.** genitive	He was desirous of *writing*.
Dīcendō multitūdinem addūxit. ablative	By *speaking*, he influenced the crowd.

2. The *gerundive* (future passive participle) is a verbal adjective and agrees with its noun in gender, number, and case. It has as many forms as **altus, -a, -um.** It is used principally:

a. to express *purpose*, modifying a noun in the accusative with **ad** or a noun in the genitive with **causā** or **grātiā.**

Vēnērunt ad pācem **cōnfīrmandam.**   They came to establish peace.
         ↑
       fem., sing., acc.
          agrees with

Frūmentī **petendī** causā manēbāmus.   We remained for the purpose of seeking grain.
genitive
depends on ──┘

b. to express *obligation* or *necessity* with some form of **esse.** In this use the person by whom the action must be done is put in the dative case (*dative of agent*).

Lēgēs **cōnsulibus cōnservandae** sunt.   The laws must be preserved by the consuls. (The
     dative of agent   consuls must preserve the laws.)

Castra **mīlitibus pōnenda** erant.   Camp had to be pitched by the soldiers. (The
     dative of agent   soldiers had to pitch camp.)

EXERCISES

A. In each sentence underline the participle or gerund, and then translate the *entire sentence* into English.

1. Imperātor spēs patriae līberandae habēbat.

----

2. Ars scrībendī nōn est facilis. ---

3. Exercitus profectūrus est. --

4. Caesar suōs hortātus proelium commīsit.

----

5. Dux oppidum paucīs dēfendentibus expugnāre nōn potuit.

----

6. Prīncipe vulnerātō, omnēs fūgērunt. -----------------------------------

7. Iūra cīvium cōnservanda erunt.

----

8. Urbem summā vī oppugnātam capere nōn potuimus.

----

9. Praesidium oppidī dēfendendī causā comparābant.

----

10. Locus ad aciem īnstruendam idōneus erat.

----

11. Sociī imperātōrī hortandī erant.

----

12. Ibi pugnāns mīles fortis interfectus est.

----

13. Nactus tempestātem idōneam, profectus est. ---

14. Caesarī omnia ūnō tempore erant agenda.

----

15. Amīcī nostrī auxilium petitūrī sunt. ---

B. Underline the correct translation in parentheses.

1. the hope of winning   spēs (vincendī, vincentis)

2. Marcus is about to leave.   Mārcus (discēdendus, discessūrus) est.

3. This must be done.   Hoc (factūrum, faciendum) est.

4. having followed them   (secūtus, secūtūrus) eōs

5. We saw him working.   Eum (labōrātum, labōrantem) vīdimus.

6. after praising the children   līberīs (laudantibus, laudātīs)

7. They intend to run.   (Cursūrī, Currendī) sunt.

8. for preparing grain   ad frūmentum (parātum, parandum)

9. the plan to seize the city   cōnsilium urbis (capiendae, capientis)

10. While fighting, he fell.   (Pugnāns, Pugnandus) cecidit.

C. Rewrite the sentences below, making *all* changes required by the directions in parentheses.

1. Vēnērunt *ut pugnārent.* (substitute *ad* with the gerund)

----

2. *Cum proelium factum esset*, domum rediērunt. (change to an ablative absolute)

----

3. Castra *mūniuntur.* (change to the gerundive denoting necessity)

----

4. Virī in agrō *labōrantes*, gladium invēnērunt. (change to the future)

----

5. Omnēs loquī *cupiunt.* (substitute *cupidī sunt* and the gerund)

----

6. Hostēs sequimur *ut aggrediāmur.* (substitute *causā* and the gerund)

----

7. *Cum rēx dūcat*, vincēmus. (change to an ablative absolute)

----

8. Agrī ab sociīs *vāstābuntur.* (change to the gerundive denoting obligation)

----

9. Caesar *prōcessūrus* Rōmam revertere cōnstituit. (change to the present)

----

10. Prōgressī sunt *ut nāvēs parārent.* (substitute *grātiā* and the gerundive)

Lesson 74—REVIEW OF GRAMMATICAL STRUCTURES

A. Underline the word or expression in parentheses that makes the sentence grammatically correct.

GROUP I

1. Rōmānī in Galliā (multōs annōs, multīs annīs) pugnābant.

2. Multī (eō diē, in eō diē) profectī erant.

3. Gallī (castra, castrīs) potīrī nōn poterant.

4. Caesar lēgātum (cohortēs, cohortibus) praefēcit.

5. Rogāvimus quis librum (legēbat, legeret).

6. Dux (suō amīcō, ad suum amīcum) gladium dederat.

7. Perīculum tantum erat ut hominēs (timēbant, timērent).

8. Vir (quī, quem) audīvistis est prīnceps.

9. Negōtium (servīs, ā servīs) cōnfectum est.

10. Putāvit hostēs (discessisse, discessissent).

GROUP II

11. Monuit captīvōs (nē, ut nōn) fugerent.

12. Gallī (tēlīs magnīs, tēla magna) ūtēbantur.

13. Nūntius dīxit (virī, virōs) convēnisse.

14. Rōmānī fugitīvōs (capere, ut caperent) nōn poterant.

15. (Populum, Populō) persuādēre potuit.

16. Dux audit mīlitēs fortiter (pugnent, pugnāre).

17. Peditēs (virtūte, cum virtūte) pugnābant.

18. Mīles fūgerat nē (interficiātur, interficerētur).

19. Paucī in (castra, castrīs) venient.

20. Hostēs in Italiam prōcessērunt (ad Rōmam capiendam, Rōmam capere).

GROUP III

21. Cum tempus (erat, esset) breve, mīlitēs iter fēcērunt.

22. Servōs in (agrīs, agrōs) relīquērunt.

23. Rogat cūr castra (oppugnent, oppugnārent).

24. Puerī (vīllae, ad vīllam) contendērunt.

25. Cōnsilium (ducī, ā duce) capiendum erat.

26. Dēbēmus dīligenter (labōrāre, ut labōrēmus).

27. Imperātor legiōnem (pugnāre, ut pugnāret) iussit.

28. Rōmānī (captīvīs, captīvōs) nōn nocuērunt.

29. Ad Graeciam nāvigābat ad urbēs clārās (vidēre, videndās).

30. Germānī in Galliam (pugnandī, pugnandōrum) causā vēnērunt.

GROUP IV

31. Hostēs tam ācriter pugnāvērunt ut nōn (vincantur, vincerentur).

32. Mīlitēs ad castra (īvisse, īvissent) cognōvī.

33. Labiēnus (legiōnī decimae, legiōnem decimam) praefectus est.

34. Quaesīvit quis litterās (tulerat, tulisset).

35. Agricolae (Rōmā, ex Rōmā) profectī sunt.

36. Equitēs (magnō auxiliō, magnum auxilium) ducī erant.

37. Caesar in hōc bellō (nāvēs, nāvibus) ūsus erat.

38. Brūtus (cōnsul, cōnsulem) factus est.

39. Rēx (Rōmānīs, ad Rōmānōs) nōn grātus erat.

40. Omnēs servī (hieme, in hieme) labōrābant.

GROUP V

41. Duo mīlia (mīlitēs, mīlitum) prōgressī sunt.

42. Lēgātus (virīs ut castra pōnerent, virōs castra pōnere) imperāvit.

43. Cōnsul (ipse, sē) mihi locūtus est.

44. Prīnceps nāvēs vīdit (quae, quās) removēbantur.

45. Nūntius quaesīvit quis ē castrīs (vēnerat, vēnisset).

46. Mercātōrēs properābant ut gentēs (videant, vidērent).

47. Tam celeriter currit ut agricolae capere (nē, nōn) possint.

48. Cōpiae (multa tēla, multīs tēlīs) ūtēbantur.

49. Exercitus (Caesare, ā Caesare) missus erit.

50. Legiō auxilium (ferre, ut ferret) nōn poterat.

B. Translate into English.

1. vir magnā fortitūdine _____

2. Caesaris adventū _____

3. amīcōrum causā _____

4. hōc modō _____

5. multitūdō hominum _____

6. spē adductus _____

7. sine ullō perīculō _____

8. laudis cupidus _____

9. prō lībertāte _____

10. scrīptūrus est _____

11. nē fugiāmus _____

12. quam ob rem   --

13. hōc audītō   --

14. loquendī grātiā   --

15. calamitās nōn ferenda est   ------------------------------------

16. ad aciem īnstruendam   --------------------------------------

17. Cicerōne cōnsule   --

18. castrīs praeerat   --

19. quae cum ita sint   --

20. in petendā pāce   --

C. Rewrite the sentences below, making *all* changes required by the directions in parentheses.

1. In flūmen *contendunt.* (substitute *stant*)

    ----

2. *Magnā* virtūte pugnābat. (omit *Magnā*)

    ----

3. *Homō* auxilium petit. (change to the plural)

    ----

4. *Nāvigiō* servātus sum. (substitute *a friend*)

    ----

5. Quis discēdit? (start the sentence with *Scīmus*)

    ----

6. Ad *Italiam* properābunt. (substitute *Rome*)

    ----

7. Dīxit omnēs pācem *petere.* (change to past time)

    ----

8. *Veniunt* ut oppidum dēfendant. (change to *Vēnērunt*)

    ----

9. Hostis gladium *capit.* (substitute the equivalent form of *ūtor*)

    ----

10. *Cum nāvēs iūnctae essent*, discessimus. (change to the ablative absolute)

    ----

11. Mīlitēs *mīlle passūs* prōgressī erant. (change to *three miles*)

    ----

12. Puer ā patre in castra *missus est.* (express the same idea in the active voice)

    ----

13. Gallī *ad urbem occupandam* vēnērunt. (substitute an *ut* clause)

    ----

14. Ad ducem frūmentum *portāvit*. (substitute the equivalent form of *dō*)

---

15. Caesar exercitum dūcit. (start the sentence with *Audīvimus*)

---

16. *Statim* cōpiae iter fēcērunt. (substitute the proper form of *id tempus*)

---

17. Rogat quis bellum *gerat*. (change to completed action)

---

18. Suōs amīcōs *videt*. (substitute *crēdit*)

---

19. Virōs *hortātus est* ut aciem īnstruerent. (change to *hortābitur*)

---

20. *Sociī* victōriam nūntiātūrī sunt. (change to the singular)

D. Combine the two sentences into one sentence according to the instructions. Make *all* necessary changes.

EXAMPLE: *Use the proper form of the relative pronoun:*

Caesar erat imperātor. Caesar bellum gessit.

ANSWER: Caesar quī erat imperātor bellum gessit.

1. *Use an ablative absolute:*

Proelium cōnfectum erat. Mīlitēs ad castra rediērunt.

---

2. *Change to an indirect statement:*

Puerī labōrant. Hoc audīvimus.

---

3. *Use the proper form of the relative pronoun:*

Urbs Rōma appellāta est. Rōma nōta est.

---

4. *Use a complementary infinitive:*

Mox incipient. Mox ducem sequentur.

---

5. *Use a present participle:*

Puer currit. Puer cecidit.

---

6. *Use a noun in apposition:*

Brūtum vīdimus. Brūtus cōnsul erat.

---

7. *Change to an **ut** clause of purpose:*

Mīlitibus persuāsit. Mīlitēs convenient.

---

8. *Use a participle:*

Paucī permovēbantur. Paucī fūgērunt.

---

9. *Change to an indirect question:*

Cūr pugnāvērunt? Nōn scīmus.

---

10. *Change to a result clause:*

Mūrus tam longus est. Mūrus dēfendī nōn potest.

E. Underline the correct Latin translation of each English expression.

1. like his father (similis patrem, similis patrī, similis patre).

2. the soldier's shield (mīlitis scūtum, mīles scūtum, mīlitis scūtī)

3. with whom (cum quō, cum quā, quibuscum)

4. in Britain (Britanniā, in Britanniā, in Britanniam)

5. within six hours (sex hōrīs, sex hōrās, sex hōrae)

6. in order to see (vidēre, ut videndum, ut vidēret)

7. at all times (omnia tempora, omnium temporum, omnibus temporibus)

8. he must be freed (līberātus est, līberandus est, līberātūrus est)

9. by doing (agendō, actō, agente)

10. having sent aid (auxilium missus, auxiliō missus, auxiliō missō)

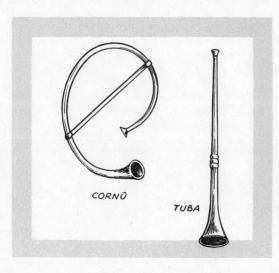

CORNŪ

TUBA

To Give Signals

Roman musical instruments, such as the **cornū** (horn) and the **tuba** (trumpet), were used chiefly for signalling in battle. Modern armies have used similar instruments, as well as drums and whistles, to give signals to their men.

Unit XII—*Passages for Translation and Comprehension*

Lesson 75

GROUP I

Translate the following passages into English:

A

[The Romans forestall possible trouble among the Carnutes, only to be faced
with hostility from another tribal chief, Ambiorix.]

Erat in Carnūtibus quīdam rēx, Tasgetius nōmine. Huic rēgī Caesar multa beneficia dederat, quod
Tasgetius auxilium ad eum mīserat. Tertiō annō rēgnī suī ab inimīcīs Tasgetius interfectus est. Ea rēs
Caesarī nūntiātur. Statim ille L. Plancum cum legiōne ex fīnibus Belgārum in Carnūtēs proficīscī iubet,
nē contrā Rōmānōs cōnsilia faciant. Adventū Rōmānōrum eī quī rēgem interfēcerant captī sunt et ad
Caesarem missī sunt. Hōc factō, legiō Plancī hīberna in fīnibus Carnūtum mūnīvit. In aliā parte Galliae,
tamen, Ambiorīx contrā legiōnem Sabīnī Cottaeque cōpiās suās dūxit. Cum Gallī hōc tempore repulsī
essent, dux Ambiorīx rogāvit ut ūnus ex lēgātīs Rōmānīs ad colloquium venīret.

B

[Acco, a leader of the Senones, decides to cooperate with Caesar.]

Cognitō Caesaris adventū, Accō, quī prīnceps in eō cōnsiliō fuerat, iubet in oppida sua multitūdinem Senonum statim convenīre ante adventum Rōmānōrum omnium. Cum nūntiātum esset Rōmānōs
pervēnisse, Accō ad Caesarem lēgātōs dē pāce mittit. Per Aeduōs, quī omnī tempore in amīcitiā
Caesaris fuerant, Accō et Senonēs condiciōnēs pācis ab Caesare obtinuērunt. Obsidibus multīs trāditīs,
et hāc parte Galliae superātā, Caesar in animō habēbat bellum contrā Trēverōs et Menapiōs gerere.
Ipse cum legiōnibus quīnque in fīnēs Menapiōrum proficīscitur, et prīncipem Senonum cum equitātū
sēcum proficīscī iubet ut bellum celeriter cōnficeret. Hōc cōnsiliō captō, tōtius exercitūs impedīmenta
ad Labiēnum mittit quī hīberna nōndum relīquerat.

C

[Sentiment in Spain swings in favor of Caesar and against Varro, Pompey's lieutenant.]

Itaque, duābus legiōnibus missīs in ulteriōrem Hispāniam cum Q. Cassiō, Caesar ipse cum equitibus
DC magnīs itineribus prōgreditur et nūntium praemittit ad magistrātūs prīncipēsque omnium cīvitātum
in illā regiōne. Nūntiō audītō, diē posterō hī ad urbem Cordubam vēnērunt. Simul senātus Cordubae
portās oppidī contrā Varrōnem clausit, mīlitēs in turribus mūrōque disposuit, et cohortēs duās ad
urbem dēfendendam tenuit. Eōdem tempore cīvēs Carmōnae, quae est cīvitās maxima tōtius prōvinciae
et amīcissima Rōmānīs, cohortēs trēs Varrōnis expulērunt. Itaque Varrō magnā celeritāte cum legiōnibus
suīs contendit nē cohortēs ab hostibus caperentur et interficerentur. In multīs locīs prōvinciae Caesar
amīcitiam inter hōs barbarōs invēnit.

D

[A sneak attack on the Romans is repulsed.]

Cum Gallī dē ācrī proeliō audīrent, maxima pars Aquītāniae Crassō sē dēdere cōnstituit. Crassus
obsidēs quam celerrimē ad sē mittī iussit. In aliā parte paucae nātiōnēs hoc nōn fēcērunt quod hiems
aderat (*was at hand*).

Eōdem tempore in aliā parte Galliae Caesar exercitum ad Morinōs Menapiōsque dūxit quī lēgātōs
dē pāce nōn mīserant. Cum intellegerent maximās nātiōnēs Gallicās ā Rōmānīs pulsās superātāsque esse,
Menapiī et Morinī in silvās suās contendērunt. Cum Caesar pervēnisset et castra mūnīre coepisset,
subitō ex omnibus partibus silvārum in Rōmānōs impetum fēcērunt. Nostrī quī fortissimē pugnābant
hostēs in silvās repellere potuērunt.

E

[Caesar has difficulty getting troops across the Adriatic.]

Caesar, XI diēs in urbe Rōmā morātus, cum praesidiō parvō ad urbem Brundisium profectus est. Legiōnēs XII equitātumque omnem eō venīre iusserat. Hic portus nōn longē ā Graeciā aberat, ubi Pompeius cum maximīs cōpiīs in castrīs erat. Postquam Brundisium vēnit, ex hībernīs legiōnēs equitēsque convocāvit, ut trāns mare celeriter nāvigārent. Postrīdiē septem legiōnēs ad Graeciam trānsportātae sunt et omnēs mīlitēs sine perīculō in terram ēgressī sunt. Eādem nocte nāvēs ad portum Brundisium ā Caesare remittuntur ut reliquae legiōnēs equitātusque trānsportārī possent. Ipse in Graeciā remanet. Calēnum lēgātum, quī nāvibus praepositus erat, hanc rem cōnficere magnā cum celeritāte iussit. Sed Bibulus, lēgātus Pompeī, XXX nāvēs capere potuit. Nāvēs omnēs incendit eōdemque igne nautās interfēcit.

GROUP II

Do *not* write a translation of the following passages; read them through carefully several times and then answer in English the questions below. Use *everything* in the text that will make your answers clear and complete.

F

[Scipio, while arranging to confiscate wealth at Ephesus, receives urgent orders from Pompey to go to Macedonia. Caesar meanwhile dispatches forces into Thessaly.]

Ephesī (*at Ephesus*), Scīpiō iubēbat pecūniam ā templō Diānae removērī. Diē cōnstitūtā, cum prīncipēs quōs Scīpiō vocāverat in templum convēnissent, Scīpiō litterīs ā Pompeiō certior factus est Caesarem cum legiōnibus mare trānsisse. Pompeius hortābātur ut Scīpiō ad sē cum exercitū venīre contenderet. Hīs litterīs acceptīs, Scīpiō iter in Macedoniam parāre incipit paucīsque post diēbus profectus est. Caesar, cum lēgātī ad eum ex Thessaliā vēnissent quī pollicerentur sē imperāta factūrōs esse, L. Cassium Longīnum cum legiōne atque CC equitibus in Thessaliam mīsit.

1. What order did Scipio give at Ephesus? _____

_____

2. On the appointed day, who had gathered in the temple? _____

_____

3. What message reached Scipio concerning Caesar? How did Scipio get this information? _____

_____

4. What did Pompey urge Scipio to do? _____

_____

5. What did Scipio begin to do after receiving the letter? _____

_____

6. When did Scipio set out? _____

_____

7. Who came to Caesar? What did they promise? _____

_____

8. What forces accompanied Lucius Cassius Longinus into Thessaly? _____

_____

G

[After driving the Germans back across the Rhine, Caesar determines
to make use of psychological warfare.]

Germānicō bellō cōnfectō, Caesar cōnstituit trānsīre Rhēnum. Cum vidēret Germānōs tam facile addūcī ut in Galliam venīrent, voluit eōs timēre cum intellegerent exercitum populī Rōmānī et posse et audēre trānsīre Rhēnum. Caesar prīmō ad Germānōs mīsit nūntiōs quī postulārent ut sibi dēderent eōs, quī sibi Galliaeque bellum intulissent. Germānī respondērunt Rhēnum esse fīnem (*boundary*) imperī populī Rōmānī. Ubiī autem magnam cōpiam nāvium ad trānsportandum exercitum pollicēbantur sed Caesar arbitrābātur nōn esse satis tūtum (*safe*) trānsīre nāvibus. Itaque exercitum ponte trādūcere cōnstituit, etsī difficultās faciendī pontem erat summa propter lātitūdinem, celeritātem, altitūdinemque flūminis.

1. What did Caesar determine to do after the war with the Germans was finished? _____

_____

2. What did Caesar see the Germans were easily influenced to do? Since Caesar wished the Germans

to be afraid, what did he want them to understand? _____

_____

_____

3. What did Caesar do first? Whose surrender did he demand from the Germans? _____

_____

_____

4. What was the reply of the Germans? _____

_____

5. What assistance did the friendly Ubii offer Caesar? _____

_____

6. Why did Caesar refuse their offer? _____

_____

7. How did Caesar decide to cross the Rhine? _____

_____

8. State *two* characteristics of the Rhine that presented difficulty. _____

_____

H

[Caesar's men put the soldiers of Pompey to flight but later ran short of grain.]

Caesar signum tubā darī atque in hostēs impetum fierī iussit. Mīlitēs legiōnis nōnae subitō pīla coniēcērunt et Pompeiānōs (*the soldiers of Pompey*) fugere coēgērunt sed fossae magnō impedīmentō eīs fuērunt. Nostrī vērō, complūribus hostium interfectīs, quīnque omnīnō suōrum āmissīs, sē recēpērunt et mūnītiōnēs perfēcērunt. Posteā mīlitēs Caesaris, omnibus frūmentīs longē lātēque cōnsūmptīs, erant in summō perīculō sed haec magnā patientiā (*patience*) ferēbant.

1. What *two* orders did Caesar give? _____

_____

2. What *two* things did the soldiers of the ninth legion then do? _____

_____

3. How did the trenches affect those fleeing? _____

_____

4. State the losses incurred by both sides. _____

_____

5. What did our men do after they withdrew? _____

_____

6. Why were Caesar's soldiers afterward in very great danger? How did they react to these perils?

_____

_____

I

[Diviciacus, the Haeduan, after telling Caesar how the Germans under Ariovistus
had invaded Gaul, explained the sad fate of the Sequani.]

Hāc ōrātiōne ab Dīviciācō habitā, omnēs, quī aderant, magnō flētū (*weeping*) auxilium ā Caesare petere coepērunt. Caesar animadvertit Sēquanōs nihil eārum rērum facere quās reliquī facerent sed terram spectāre. Quaesīvit quae causa eius reī esset. Sēquanī nihil respondērunt sed tacitī (*silent*) mānsērunt. Prō hīs Dīviciācus respondit: "Fortūna Sēquanōrum est miserior et gravior quam reliquō-rum, quod neque querī (*to complain*) neque auxilium ōrāre audent."

1. After Diviciacus' speech, what did all those present do? In what manner? _____

_____

2. What *two* things did Caesar notice about the Sequani? _____

_____

3. What did Caesar then ask the Sequani? _____

_____

4. How did the Sequani then act? _____

_____

5. According to Diviciacus, how did the fortune of the Sequani compare with that of the remaining

Gallic tribes? _____

_____

6. What *two* things did the Sequani not dare to do? _____

_____

J

[Caesar advances to Corfinium, one of Pompey's strongholds.]

Caesar ad oppidum Corfīnium cōnstitit et iūxtā (*next to*) mūrum castra posuit. Rē cognitā, Do-mitius ad Pompeium in Āpūliam explōrātōrēs mittit, quī petant atque ōrent ut auxilium ferat. Dīcit Caesarem hostium exercitū et locōrum angustiīs facile posse frūmentō prohibērī. Quod nisi fēcerit, etiam dīcit sē magnumque numerum equitum Rōmānōrum in perīculum ventūrum esse. Interim suōs cohortātus, auxilia in mūrīs pōnit et mīlitibus certās partēs urbis ad dēfendendum attribuit (*he assigns*).

1. Where did Caesar halt and then what did he do? _____

_____

2. In view of this, what does Domitius do and why? --

----

3. State the inconvenience that Domitius says Caesar can easily suffer. Give the *two* means by which

this can be accomplished. --

----

4. If this should not be done, what, according to Domitius, will result? --------------------------

----

5. State *two* things that Domitius does after encouraging his men. ------------------------------

----

GROUP III

Read the following passages carefully, but do *not* write a translation. Below each passage you will find a series of incomplete statements. Select the answer that best completes *each* statement *on the basis of the information given in the passage.*

K

[Vercingetorix retires to Alesia, which Caesar determines to besiege.]

Omnibus equitibus pulsīs, Vercingetorīx cōpiās suās redūxit quās prō castrīs collocāverat, et statim Alesiam quod est oppidum Mandūbiōrum, iter facere coepit; celeriterque impedīmenta ex castrīs ēdūcī et sē subsequī iussit. Caesar, impedīmentīs in proximum collem ductīs, duābus legiōnibus praesidiō relictīs, hostēs persecūtus est dīligentissimē. Circiter tribus mīlibus hostium ex novissimō agmine interfectīs, posterō diē castra ad Alesiam fēcit.

Perspectā urbis regiōne, perterritīsque hostibus, quod equitātus, in quā parte exercitūs maximam fidem habēbant, erat pulsus, Caesar, hortātus mīlitēs ad labōrem, circum Alesiam mūnītiōnēs facere īnstituit.

Oppidum ipsum erat in tam altissimō locō ut expugnārī nōn posset. Id obsidēre necesse erat. Campum omnem ante oppidum cōpiae Gallōrum complēverant fossamque et vāllum in altitūdinem VI pedum praedūxerant (*they had built*). Ea mūnītiō quae ab Rōmānīs īnstituēbātur spatium XI mīlia passuum patēbat. Castra idōneīs locīs erant posita quōrum portae dīligenter interdiū vigilābantur nē impetus subitō fieret; haec eadem praesidiīs fīrmīs noctū tenēbantur.

1. Vercingetorīx, postquam cōpiās suās redūxit,

    1 equitēs reppulit   3 Alesiam sine morā iit
    2 mīlitēs prō castrīs collocāvit   4 oppidum Mandūbiōrum oppugnāvit

2. Vercingetorīx impedīmenta imperāvit ut

    1 celeriter excēderent   3 prō castrīs collocārentur
    2 sē sequerentur   4 cōpiās suās redūcerent

3. Caesar prīmō

    1 impedīmenta in propinquum montem dūxit   3 impedīmenta in colle relīquit
    2 impedīmenta secūtus est   4 impedīmenta in colle cēpit

4. Deinde Caesar relīquit

    1 duo praesidia impedīmenta dēfendentia   3 praesidium hostibus
    2 praesidium duābus legiōnibus   4 duās legiōnēs ut impedīmenta dēfenderent

5. In eō proeliō Caesar

1 novissimum agmen interfēcit
2 tria mīlia hostium occīdit

3 castra ad Alesiam occupāvit
4 circiter tria mīlia passuum prōgressus est

6. Hostēs perterritī sunt quod

1 exercitus Rōmānus maximus erat
2 regiō urbis dēfendī nōn potuit

3 equitēs eōrum victī erant
4 equitātus fidem maximam habēbat

7. Mīlitibus ad labōrem incitātīs,

1 Caesar circum Alesiam oppugnāre īnstituit
2 mūnītiōnēs circum Alesiam relictae sunt

3 exercitus circum Alesiam pulsus erat
4 Caesar mūnītiōnēs facere incēpit

8. Oppidum obsidēre necesse erat cum

1 cōpiae Rōmānōrum oppugnāre nōn parātae essent
2 propter altitūdinem locī expugnārī nōn posset

3 cōpiae Gallōrum ante oppidum essent
4 oppidum fossam vāllumque habēret

9. Mūnītiō ab Rōmānīs facta

1 pertinuit undecim mīlia passuum
2 patēbat in altitūdinem sex pedēs

3 fossam vāllumque habēbat
4 omnem campum complēverat

10. In castrīs Rōmānōrum

1 impetus subitō factus est
2 praesidia fīrma oppugnābantur

3 portae interdiū noctūque vigilābantur
4 idōnea loca dīligenter tenēbantur

L

[Alcibiades is condemned for an act of sacrilege.]

Alcibiadēs, Athēniēnsis, in cīvitāte summus erat. Propter cōnsilium atque auctōritātem eius, Athēniēnsēs bellum contrā Syrācūsānōs gerere cōnstituērunt. Ad hoc bellum gerendum Alcibiadēs ipse dux dēlēctus est. Cum nāvēs parātae in portū essent, ūnā nocte multae statuae deōrum in urbe Athēnīs fractae (*broken*) sunt et ab hominibus malīs in terrā relictae sunt. Propter hoc factum timor magnus in populō erat. Hominēs dīxērunt Alcibiadem hanc rem fēcisse. Nāvēs tamen illō tempore ad Siciliam nāvigāvērunt. Siciliā victā, cum magistrātūs Athēnārum ducem domum venīre iussissent, ille id nōn facere cōnstituit. Itaque magistrātūs illum absentem damnāvērunt. Tum ad urbem Spartam īvit, et in hōc locō paucōs annōs manēbat. Tandem ad suam urbem redīre potuit et Athēniēnsēs domum eī dedērunt.

1. Athēniēnsēs bellum contrā Syrācūsānōs gerere cōnstituērunt quod

1 Alcibiadēs erat vir summus
2 Alcibiadī erat auctōritās et cōnsilium

3 putāvērunt sē Syrācūsānōs vincere posse
4 Syrācūsānī Athēnās oppugnāvērunt

2. Alcibiadēs dux dēlēctus est

1 cum nāvēs in portū parāvisset
2 quod multās statuās deōrum cōnstituerat

3 ut statuās deōrum frangeret
4 ut bellum gereret

3. Populus perterritus est quod

1 statuae deōrum fractae et in terrā relictae sunt
2 hominēs malī in terrā relictī sunt
3 ūnā nocte Athēnīs multae statuae deōrum vīsae sunt
4 nāvēs ab hominibus malīs fractae sunt

4. Magistrātūs Alcibiadem damnāvērunt cum

1 ad Siciliam nāvigāvisset
2 hominēs dīcerent Alcibiadem hanc rem fēcisse

3 hic nōn fēcisset quod illī postulāvissent
4 ille cōnstituisset domum venīre

5. In urbe Spartā Alcibiadēs

1 domum accēpit
2 statim ad suam urbem redīre voluit

3 ab magistrātibus damnātus est
4 paucōs annōs manēbat

M

[The theater of war shifts from the Greek mainland to Egypt, where an event occurs which marks a turning point in the war.]

Caesar, paucōs diēs in Asiā morātus, audīvit Pompēium in īnsulā Cyprō vīsum esse. Itaque arbitrātus est Pompēium in Aegyptum iter facere. Statim cum legiōne ūnā ex Thessaliā et cum alterā ex Achaiā atque cum equitibus DCCC nāvibusque longīs X ad urbem Alexandrīam pervēnit. In hīs legiōnibus erant sōlum tria mīlia et CC hominum, quod multī mīlitēs vulnera in proeliīs accēperant et Caesar iusserat eōs in castrīs manēre. Propter hanc causam hī ex Achaiā et Thessaliā cōnsequī nōn potuerant. Caesar, tamen, proficīscī cum hīs cōpiīs minimīs cōnstituit. Paucīs diēbus dē morte Pompēī in Aegyptō cognōscit.

1. Caesar putāvit Pompēium in Aegyptum iter facere quod

1 Pompēius paucōs diēs in Asiā morātus est
2 Pompēius dīxit sē eō iter facere

3 cognōvit Pompēium in īnsulā Cyprō fuisse
4 Pompēius iter facere vīsus est

2. Caesar ad urbem Alexandrīam pervēnit

1 cum duābus legiōnibus, octingentīs equitibus et decem nāvibus
2 cum legiōne ūnā, octingentīs equitibus et decem nāvibus
3 cum duābus legiōnibus, octōgintā equitibus et decem nāvibus
4 cum legiōne ūnā, octō mīlia equitum et decem nāvibus

3. In legiōnibus Caesaris erant

1 tria mīlia hominum
2 ducentī hominēs

3 tria mīlia et ducentī hominum
4 tria mīlia et centum hominum

4. Vulneribus acceptīs, multī mīlitēs

1 in castrīs nōn manēbant
2 in proeliīs pugnāre iussī sunt

3 cōnsequī nōn poterant
4 propter hanc causam auxilium rogābant

5. Posteā Caesar audīvit Pompēium

1 cum copiīs minimīs proficīscī
2 mortuum esse

3 in Aegyptō esse
4 paucīs diēbus proficīscī cōnstituisse

N

[Transportation problems put Caesar at a disadvantage in his campaign in Greece.]

Caesar, postquam ipse et Pūblius Servīlius cōnsulēs dēlēctī sunt, contrā Pompēium tempore brevī fīnem bellī facere cōnstituit. Itaque ab urbe proficīscitur ut ad Graeciam īret et per Viam Appiam ad urbem Brundisium pervēnit. Ad hunc portum legiōnēs XII equitātumque omnem venīre iusserat, sed tam paucae erant nāvēs ut cum difficultāte XV mīlia mīlitum et DC equitēs trānsportārī possent. Eōdem tempore Pompēius legiōnēs novem in Graeciā habēbat, et magnum numerum nāvium ab Asiā, Aegyptō et multīs īnsulīs cōnferēbat. Multī rēgēs sē Pompēiō pecūniam multam datūrōs esse pollicitī sunt. Caesar igitur intellēxit hoc bellum futūrum esse longum—nōn breve, ut (as) spērāverat.

1. Caesar cōnstituit

1 dēligere cōnsulēs tempore brevī
2 cōnficere bellum contrā Pompēium sine morā

3 bellum gerere contrā Pompēium
4 dēligere Pūblium Servīlium cōnsulem

2. Caesar Rōmā profectus est et

1 ad Graeciam pervēnit
2 ad Viam Appiam pervēnit

3 ad urbem Appiam vēnit
4 Brundisium vēnit

3. Ad portum Brundisium pervēnērunt

1 quīndecim mīlia mīlitum et sescentī equitēs
2 duodecim legiōnēs equitātumque omnem

3 omnēs mīlitēs quōs Caesar iusserat venīre
4 omnēs nāvēs cum difficultāte

4. Pompēius habēbat

1 multās legiōnēs et paucās nāvēs
2 legiōnēs nāvēsque ab Graeciā

3 novem legiōnēs et multās nāvēs
4 legiōnēs nāvēsque ab Asiā, Aegyptō et multīs īnsulīs

5. Caesar scīvit bellum longum futūrum esse quod

1 Pompēius ab multīs rēgibus auxilium acceptūrus est
2 multī rēgēs dīxērunt sē mīlitēs datūrōs esse
3 Pompēius spērāverat bellum breve futūrum esse
4 Pompēius ab multīs īnsulīs magnum numerum nāvium cōnferēbat

O

[In spite of a generally friendly spirit between the two armies,
a truce talk is interrupted by hostile action.]

Inter castra Pompēī atque Caesaris tantum (*only, nothing but*) erat flūmen Apsus, multaque inter sē colloquia mīlitēs habēbant; nūllum tēlum multōs diēs trāns flūmen iactum est. Caesar lēgātum P. Vatīnium ad rīpam ipsam flūminis mittit quī magnā vōce dē pāce loquerētur. Dīxit, "Cīvēs ad aliōs cīvēs de pāce et de omnium salūte lēgātōs mittere dēbent." Vatīnius cum silentiō ā mīlitibus et Pompēī et Caesaris audītus est. Quīdam mīles ab alterā rīpā respondit Aulum Varrōnem ad concilium cum Vatīniō ventūrum esse. Cum lēgātī duo posterō diē vēnissent, magna multitūdō quoque (*also*) convēnit. Tum T. Labiēnus prōgreditur et cum Vatīniō īrātē (*angrily*) dīcere incipit. Subitō undique tēla missa sunt; vulnerātī sunt complūrēs mīlitēs et trēs centuriōnēs. Tum Labiēnus clāmāvit, "Nunc nūlla pāx esse potest."

1. Multōs diēs inter castra Pompēī et Caesaris

1 tēlum trāns flūmen iactum est
2 flūmen Apsus trānsitum est

3 nūllum proelium factum est
4 mīlitēs inter sē pugnābant

2. Caesar Vatīnium mīsit

1 ut ad rīpam flūminis clāmāret dē pāce
2 ut loquerētur dē tēlīs iactīs

3 ut dīceret cōpiās Pompēī discēdere dēbēre
4 ut pācem salūtemque rogāret

3. Vatīniō audītō,

1 concilium cōnstitūtum est inter Varrōnem Vatīniumque
2 cōnsilium ā mīlitibus cum silentiō captum est
3 mīles ab alterā rīpā respondit sē ventūrum esse
4 quīdam mīles respondit sē cum Vatīniō ventūrum esse

4. Concilium malum fīnem habuit quod

1 duo lēgātī īrātē dīcere incēpērunt
2 multī mīlitēs ad concilium quoque convēnērunt

3 Titus Labiēnus posterō diē prōgressus est
4 magna multitūdō īrātē dīcēbat

5. In proeliō quod secūtum est

1 ex ūnā parte tēla subitō missa sunt
2 complūrēs mīlitēs et trēs centuriōnēs interfectī sunt
3 Labiēnus dīxit pācem nūllam tum esse posse
4 vulnerātī sunt paucī mīlitēs centuriōnēsque

Unit XIII—Oral Latin for the Classroom

Lesson 76—ORAL EXPRESSIONS AND AUDITORY COMPREHENSION

I. QUESTION WORDS

ENGLISH	LATIN
who	quis (pl. quī)
what	quid (pl. quae)
whose	cuius (pl. quōrum)
to whom	cui (pl. quibus)
whom	quem (pl. quōs)
by *or* with what	quō (pl. quibus)
by whom	ā quō (pl. ā quibus)
with whom	quōcum (pl. quibuscum)
where (in what place)	ubi
where (to what place)	quō
where (from what place)	unde
why	cūr / quā rē / quam ob rem
how	quō modō
how great	quantus
how long	quam diū
how many	quot
how often	quotiēns
what kind of	quālis
when	quandō
which (of two)	uter

II. VOCABULARY FOR CLASSROOM CONVERSATION

ENGLISH	LATIN
answer	respōnsum
assignment	pēnsum
blackboard	tabula
book	liber
bookcase	armārium
chalk	crēta
clock	hōrologium
door	iānua, porta
eraser	ērāsūra
locker	capsa
map	tabula geōgraphica
paper	charta
pen	penna
pencil	stilus
picture	pīctūra
principal	prīnceps
principal's office	locus prīncipis
pupil	discipulus (discipula)
question	interrogātiō
room	camera, cella
school	lūdus, schola
seat	sella

story	fābula
table	mēnsa
teacher	magister (magistra)
window	fenestra
word	verbum

III. CLASSROOM DIRECTIONS

ENGLISH	LATIN
come in, enter	inī (inīte); venī (venīte); intrā (intrāte)
go out, leave	exī (exīte)
go	ī (īte)
come here	venī (venīte) hūc
stand up	surge (surgite)
sit down	cōnsīde (cōnsīdite)
open the door	aperī iānuam
close the door	claude iānuam
listen	attende (attendite); audī (audīte)
be quiet	tacē (tacēte)
go on, continue	perge (pergite)
stop that	mitte haec
look here, here is	ecce
put down	pōne
come on	age
take	cape, sūme
read	lege
recite, read aloud	recitā
repeat	repete
answer in English	respondē Anglicē
answer in Latin	respondē Latīnē
translate into English	verte Anglicē
translate into Latin	verte Latīnē

IV. COMMON EXPRESSIONS

ENGLISH	LATIN
hello, good morning (afternoon)	salvē (salvēte)
good-bye	valē (valēte)
how are you?	quid agis?
pretty well	satis bene
yes	sīc; ita; vērō; certē
no	minimē
please	quaesō; si tibi placet
thank you	tibi grātiās agō
excuse me	mihi īgnōsce
sir	domine
madame (ma'am)	domina
what time is it?	quota hōra est?
how is the weather today?	quaenam est tempestās hodiē?
the sun is shining	sōl lūcet
it is raining	pluit
it is snowing	ningit
I shall say it in Latin	Latīnē dīcam
let's talk Latin	Latīnē colloquāmur
you have answered correctly	rēctē respondistī
all right	fīat; licet

V. SAMPLE DIALOGUE

QUESTION OR STATEMENT	ANSWER
Salvēte, discipulī!	Salvē, magister.
Ubi est Mārcus?	Hīc ego sum; adsum.
Ubi est Anna?	Anna abest.
Quis est Paulus?	Ego sum Paulus.
Quae rēs est, Carole?	Est iānua, fenestra, etc.
Estne hic liber?	Ita, est liber.
Estne haec penna?	Minimē, est crēta.
Scrībe in tabulā, Philippe.	In tabulā scrībō.
Claude iānuam, quaesō.	Iānuam claudō.
Ubi est Italia?	Italia in Eurōpā est.

VI. QUESTIONS AND ANSWERS ABOUT CAESAR

QUESTION	ANSWER
In quā terrā nātus est Caesar?	Caesar in Italiā nātus est.
Quod erat praenōmen Caesaris?	Praenōmen Caesaris erat Gāius.
Quod erat nōmen Caesaris?	Nōmen Caesaris erat Iūlius.
Quod erat nōmen fīliae Caesaris?	Nōmen fīliae Caesaris erat Iūlia.
Quae erant uxōrēs (wives) Caesaris?	Uxōrēs Caesaris erant Cornēlia, Pompeia, Calpurnia.
Ubi gerēbat bellum Caesar?	Caesar bellum in Galliā gerēbat.
Quō modō mortuus est Caesar?	Caesar interfectus est.
Quae erant ultima (last) verba Caesaris?	Ultima verba Caesaris erant "Et tū, Brūte!"
Quid dīxit Caesar, cum Rubicōnem trānsisset?	Cum Caesar Rubicōnem trānsisset, dīxit "Ālea iacta est."
Cui dedit in mātrimōnium Caesar fīliam suam?	Caesar Pompeiō fīliam suam in mātrimōnium dedit.

EXERCISES

A. Answer the following questions orally in complete Latin sentences:

1. Quod est tuum nōmen?
2. Quod est nōmen tuī magistrī?
3. Quid agis hodiē?
4. Potesne legere Latīnē?
5. Quot librōs portās?
6. Cōnfēcistīne pēnsum?
7. Vīsne fābulam nārrāre?
8. Quam diū fuistī in illā scholā?
9. Quō potes scrībere?
10. Quis est prīnceps tuae scholae?

B. Carry out the following directions orally in complete Latin sentences:

1. Greet your friend Marcus.
2. Say good-bye to your friends.
3. Ask Sextus to close the door.
4. Ask the girls to open the windows.
5. Ask someone to please repeat the question.
6. Ask Cornelia to answer in Latin.
7. Ask Quintus to translate into English.
8. Offer an apology to your teacher.
9. Tell the students to keep quiet.
10. Ask Julius to read the story.

C. Formulate oral questions in Latin to which the following statements are answers:

1. Meam patriam amō.
2. Ita, est crēta.
3. Georgius abest.
4. Minimē, Italia nōn est lāta.
5. Hodiē pluit.
6. Quattuor pennās habeō.
7. Vērō; iam exeō.
8. Est tertia hōra.
9. Cum meō amīcō manēbō.
10. Ad Graeciam iter facimus.

D. In complete Latin sentences, answer orally the following questions based on Roman background:

1. In quā terrā erat Caesar prōcōnsul?
2. Quis erat cōnsul cum Caesare?
3. Quem superāvit Caesar in Bellō Cīvīlī?
4. Quae erat prīma uxor Caesaris?
5. Quod fēcit Caesar in flūmine Rhēnō?
6. Quis erat Apollōnius Molō?
7. Quid dīxit Caesar cum in Asiā victōriam celerrimam obtinuisset?
8. Quis erat inimīcus Sullae?
9. Quam ob rem obtinuit Caesar corōnam cīvicam?
10. Quae erat prīma nātiō quam Caesar vīcit in Bellō Gallicō?
11. Quōs vīcit Caesar in librō secundō Bellī Gallicī?
12. Quis erat prīnceps nōtus Germānōrum?
13. Quī lēgātus in Bellō Gallicō prīmō amīcus, deinde inimīcus Caesarī erat?
14. Quī lēgātus in Bellō Gallicō frātrem, ōrātōrem nōtissimum, habuit?
15. Quis erat ultimus hostis Caesaris in Bellō Gallicō?
16. Quod erat nōmen Latīnum flūminis "Rhone"?
17. Quod erat nōmen Latīnum terrae "Switzerland"?
18. In quot collibus erat locāta urbs Rōma?
19. Quis erat prīmus rēx Rōmānōrum?
20. Quis erat ultimus rēx Rōmānōrum?
21. Quālis deus erat Mārs?
22. Quis erat dux nōtus Carthāginiēnsis?
23. Quae erat māter frātrum Gracchōrum?
24. Quis fēcit Rēgīnam Viārum?
25. Quī in Colosseō pugnābant?

VII. AUDITORY COMPREHENSION

The following statements are based on a story read to you slowly by your teacher. You do not see the passage; you hear it. After you have heard the passage read twice, you are then to complete each statement below by underlining the best answer of the four alternatives given. (A copy of the passages is available to the teacher on request.)

A. The Story of Hercules

1. Nārrātur Herculem fuisse

   1 altissimum.
   2 amīcissimum.
   3 validissimum.
   4 celerrimum.

2. Iūnō voluit Herculem interficere quod

   1 mātrem eius nōn amābat.
   2 Alcmēna erat inimīca.
   3 puer erat fortissimus.
   4 potestātem rēgīnae habēbat.

3. Ut interficeret Herculem, Iūnō

   1 scūtum cēpit.
   2 mediā nocte vēnit.
   3 frātrem eius mīsit.
   4 serpentibus ūsa est.

4. Puerī ē somnō excitātī sunt quod

   1 in scūtō dormiēbant.
   2 scūtum ā serpentibus movēbātur.
   3 perterritī sunt.
   4 serpentēs appropinquābant.

5. Dēnique serpentēs

   1 Herculem interfēcērunt.
   2 ā frātre Herculis interfectī sunt.
   3 oppressī manibus Herculis interfectī sunt.
   4 magnā vī puerōs occupāvērunt.

B. Alexander's Horse Bucephalus

1. Prīmus dominus equī erat

  1 Alexander.

  2 Philippus.

  3 Charēs.

  4 Būcephalus.

2. Būcephalus ad proelium parātus permīsit in sē sedēre

  1 nēminem.

  2 sōlum rēgēs.

  3 sōlum Alexandrum.

  4 omnēs mīlitēs.

3. Ōlim in Bellō Indicō Alexander in equō sedēns

  1 in gravissimō perīculō erat.

  2 undique tēla coniciēbat.

  3 ab hostibus gravissimē vulnerātus est.

  4 vulneribus paene mortuus est.

4. Būcephalus mortuus est postquam vīdit Alexandrum

  1 nōn iam salvum incolumemque esse.

  2 in terram cecidisse.

  3 tēla extulisse.

  4 nōn iam in perīculō esse.

5. Bellō Indicō cōnfectō,

  1 Alexander in honōre acceptus est.

  2 equus in eīsdem locīs nactus est.

  3 oppidum Būcephalum appellātum est.

  4 Alexander Būcephalum fortissimum vocāvit.

C. Julius Caesar

1. Bibulus in senātum nōn vēnit quod

  1 cursum honōrum obtinuit.

  2 timōre captus est.

  3 aliquī aliquid scrībēbant.

  4 auctōritātem nūllam habēbat.

2. "Iūliō et Caesare" vērō erant

  1 ūnus īdemque cōnsul.

  2 duo cōnsulēs.

  3 Bibulus et Caesar.

  4 Gāius et Mārcus.

3. Cum Caesar in Galliā esset,

  1 pōns trāns Rhēnum ā Germānīs factus est.

  2 Britannī Rōmānīs nōtī erant.

  3 pecūniam obsidēsque Britannīs dedit.

  4 Gallī Germānīque superātī sunt.

4. Bellum Cīvīle inceptum est tum cum

  1 Bellum Gallicum cōnfectum est.

  2 Pompēius dīxit, "Ālea iacta est."

  3 Caesar trāns Rubicōnem exercitum trādūxit.

  4 Pompēius imperātor factus est.

5. Tria verba, "Vēnī, vīdī, vīcī," nūntiāta sunt postquam

  1 rēx Pontī superātus est.

  2 Pompēius cōnsulēsque Brundisium cōnfūgerant.

  3 Pompēius occīsus est.

  4 Caesar plūrimās urbēs occupāverta.

D. Afranius, Caesar's Opponent, Is Kept From Octogesa

1. Afrānius vīdit cōpiās Caesaris

  1 ante sē īnstrūctas esse.

  2 in colle quōdam cōnstitisse.

  3 ab equitātū premī.

  4 ante novissimum agmen esse.

2. Quattuor cohortēs missae sunt

  1 ex eō colle ad Afrānium.

  2 ab altissimō cōnspectū ad montem.

  3 ad Afrānium altissimum in cōnspectū.

  4 ex eō colle ab Afrāniō ad montem.

3. Afrānius montem occupārī iussit quod

  1 mīlitēs Caesaris eōdem properābant.

  2 Caesar ipse cum omnibus cōpiīs fugiēbat.

  3 voluit Octogēsam pervenīre.

  4 cōpiae Caesaris Octogēsam occupāverant.

4. Mīlitēs Afrānī ad montem prōcēdentēs

  1 in equitātum Caesaris impetum fēcērunt.
  2 ab equitibus Caesaris oppugnātī sunt.
  3 in peditēs Caesaris impetum fēcērunt.
  4 ab peditibus Caesaris oppugnātī sunt.

5. In eō proeliō equitēs Caesaris

  1 ab hostibus circumventī sunt.
  2 in conspectū utrīusque exercitūs interfectī sunt.
  3 omnēs quattuor cohortēs occīdērunt.
  4 vim hostium sustinēre nōn potuērunt.

E. Regulus, a Roman Hero

1. Carthāginiēnsēs voluērunt Regulum

  1 Rōmā proficīscī.
  2 sē facere captīvum.
  3 ad captīvōs redīre.
  4 pācem inter sē Rōmānōsque cōnfīrmāre.

2. Regulus cum Rōmam redīsset

  1 senātum monuit nē pācem cōnfīrmāret.
  2 dīxit quod Rōmānī exspectābant.
  3 senātuī persuāsit ut pācem faceret.
  4 nihil exspectābat.

3. Regulus dīxit sē nōn esse Rōmānum quod

  1 Carthāginiēnsēs potestātem habērent.
  2 Rōmae habitāret.
  3 līber nōn esset.
  4 Rōmam profectus esset.

4. Regulus hoc cōnsilium senātōribus dedit

  1 nē spem habērent.
  2 nē captīvōs redderent.
  3 nē resisterent propter sē.
  4 nē retinērent tot mīlia captīvōrum.

5. Posteā Regulus

  1 ad hostēs rediit et occīsus est.
  2 in urbe cum honōre habitābat.
  3 ad Āfricam revertit et līberātus est.
  4 Rōmae remanēre poterat.

The Pantheon

The Pantheon represents the supreme triumph of Roman engineering, and remains one of the architectural wonders of the world. This well-preserved temple with its famous dome has served as the model of some of the most noted buildings in the world. Among them are St. Peter's in Rome, the Capitol in Washington, and the National Gallery of Art in Washington.

Unit XIV—Derivation and Word Study

Lesson 77—PREFIXES AND VERB FAMILIES

Compound verbs in Latin are formed by adding prefixes, many of which are prepositions, to simple verbs. For example:

$$\underset{\substack{\text{away} \quad \text{to go} \quad \text{to go away}}}{\underline{ab+\bar{\imath}re=ab\bar{\imath}re}}$$

$$\underset{\substack{\text{back} \quad \text{to drive} \quad \text{to drive back}}}{\underline{re+pellere=repellere}}$$

In most cases there is no change in spelling, but, for ease of pronunciation, the following changes do occur:

1. *Assimilation.* The final letter of a prefix may change to the first letter of the simple verb. The letter **n** before **p** is changed to **m**. These changes in spelling are also reflected in English derivatives.

$$con + mittere = \text{co}mmittere \text{ (English } commit)$$
$$ad + c\bar{e}dere = ac\text{c}\bar{e}dere \text{ (English } accede)$$
$$in + pellere = i\text{m}pellere \text{ (English } impel)$$

2. *Contraction.* A letter may be completely dropped.

$$co + agere = \underset{a \text{ is dropped}}{\underline{c\bar{o}gere}}$$

$$d\bar{e} + iacere = \underset{a \text{ is dropped}}{\underline{d\bar{e}icere}}$$

3. *Weakening of vowel.* The vowel **a** or **e** of the simple verb is weakened to **i** in the compound.

$$in + capere = inc\textit{i}pere$$
$$ob + ten\bar{e}re = obt\textit{i}n\bar{e}re$$

Note

A. A compound verb may undergo *two* changes in spelling, one in assimilation and one in weakening of vowel.

$$ex + facere = e\textit{ff}ic\textit{e}re$$
$$ad + capere = ac\textit{ci}pere$$

B. The purpose of a prefix is to give added meaning to the simple verb.

dūcere, to lead; **ēdūcere,** to lead out; **redūcere,** to lead back

C. Sometimes a compound verb takes on a completely new meaning.

facere, to make, do	**interficere,** to kill
mittere, to send	**committere,** to join, entrust

D. Some verbs are found principally in the compound form, the simple verb being rarely used.

cōnspicere (to observe) from the rare **specere** (to see)
relinquere (to leave behind) from the rare **linquere** (to leave)

E. Prefixes may be attached to other parts of speech besides verbs.

perfacilis (very easy) from the prefix **per** (thoroughly or very) and the adjective **facilis** (easy)
biennium (two years) from the prefix **bi** (two) and the noun **annus** (year)

PREFIXES

Below is a list of common prefixes, their meanings, examples of their use to form Latin compounds, and examples of their use in English.

PREFIX	MEANING	USE IN LATIN	USE IN ENGLISH
ab- (ā-)	from, away	abducō, āvertō	abduct, avert
ad-	to, toward, near	admittō	admit
ambi-	both, around	ambiō	ambidextrous
ante-	before	antecēdō	antecedent
bene-	well	beneficium	benefit
bi-	two, twice	biennium	biennial
circum-	around	circumveniō	circumvent
con- (co-, com-)	with, together, deeply, completely	conveniō, cōgō, comparō	convene, cogent, compare
contrā-	against	contrādīcō	contradict
dē-	from, down	dēscendō	descend
dis- (dī-)	apart, away	distrahō, dīgredior	distract, digress
ex- (ē-)	out	expellō, ēmittō	expel, emit
extrā-	outside, beyond	extraōrdinārius	extraordinary
in-	in, on, upon	indūcō	induce
in-	not, without	inimīcus	inimical
inter-	between, among	intercipiō	intercept
intrā- (intrō-)	within, inside	intrāmūrānus, intrōspectō	intramural, introspective
male-	badly	maledīcō	malediction
ne-, nōn-	not, without	nesciō, nōndum	nefarious, nonentity
ob-	against, toward	observō	observe
per-	through, thoroughly	perficiō	perfect
post-	after, behind	postpōnō	postpone
prae-	ahead	praedīcō	predict
prō-	forth, before	prōpellō	propel
quadr-	four	quadrupēs	quadruped
re- (red-)	back, again	recurrō, redimō	recur, redemption
retrō-	backwards, back	retrōversus	retrogress
sē- (sēd-)	apart, away	sēcēdō, sēditiō	secede, sedition
sēmi-	half	sēmideus	semicircle
sub- (sus-)	under, up from under	subsequor, sustineō	subsequent, sustain
super-	over, beyond	superfluō	superfluous
trāns- (trā-)	across, over	trānsferō, trādūcō	transfer, traduce
tri-	three	tridēns	trident

COMMON VERB FAMILIES

agō, drive
  cōgō, drive together, gather

cadō, fall
  accidō, befall, happen

caedō, cut
  occīdō, cut down, kill

capiō, take
  accipiō, receive
  excipiō, receive
  incipiō, take on, begin

recipiō, take back
  suscipiō, undertake

cēdō, go, retreat
  accēdō, go to
  concēdō, yield
  discēdō, go away
  excēdō, go out
  prōcēdō, go forth

citō, rouse
  incitō, urge on

currō, run
  prōcurrō, run forward

dō, give
  circumdō, surround
  dēdō, give up
  reddō, give back
  trādō, hand over

dūcō, lead
  addūcō, lead to, influence
  dēdūcō, lead down
  ēdūcō, lead out
  prōdūcō, lead forth
  redūcō, lead back
  trādūcō, lead across

eō, go
  abeō, go away
  adeō, go toward
  exeō, go out
  ineō, go into
  redeō, go back
  trānseō, go across

faciō, make, do
  cōnficiō, do completely, finish
  dēficiō, fail, revolt
  efficiō, bring about
  interficiō, kill
  perficiō, do thoroughly, finish
  praeficiō, put in charge

ferō, bring
  cōnferō, bring together
  īnferō, bring in
  referō, bring back

gradior, step, go
  aggredior, go to, attack
  ēgredior, go out
  prōgredior, go forth

habeō, have, hold
  prohibeō, keep off, prevent

hortor, urge
  adhortor, urge on
  cohortor, urge on

iaciō, throw
  coniciō, throw together
  dēiciō, throw down
  ēiciō, throw out

iungō, join
  coniungō, join together

legō, choose, read
  dēligō, choose (from), select
  intellegō, understand

linquō, leave
  relinquō, leave behind

locō, put
  collocō, put together

loquor, speak
  colloquor, speak with

maneō, remain
  remaneō, remain

mīror, wonder at
  admīror, admire

mittō, send, let go
  āmittō, send away, lose
  committō, bring together, join, entrust
  dīmittō, send off, dismiss
  intermittō, interrupt, stop
  permittō, let go, allow, entrust
  praemittō, send ahead
  remittō, send back

mōnstrō, show
  dēmōnstrō, point out

moveō, move
  commoveō, move deeply, alarm
  permoveō, move thoroughly, alarm
  removeō, move back, withdraw

nūntiō, report
  ēnūntiō, speak out, proclaim
  renūntiō, bring back word

parō, get, prepare
  comparō, get together, arrange

pellō, drive
  expellō, drive out
  impellō, drive on
  repellō, drive back

pōnō, put
  expōnō, put out, set forth
  prōpōnō, set forth, offer

portō, carry, bring
  comportō, bring together
  importō, bring in
  trānsportō, carry across

premō, press
  opprimō, press against, crush

pugnō, fight
  expugnō, capture
  oppugnō, attack

rogō, ask
  interrogō, question

sciō, know
  nesciō, not know

scrībō, write
  cōnscrībō, enlist, enroll

sedeō, sit
  cōnsīdō, sit down, encamp
  obsideō, sit down, besiege

sequor, follow
  cōnsequor, follow up, overtake
  exsequor, follow up
  īnsequor, pursue
  persequor, follow up
  prōsequor, pursue
  subsequor, follow closely

servō, keep, save
  cōnservō, keep together, preserve

speciō, see
  cōnspiciō, observe
  perspiciō, see clearly

spectō, look at
  exspectō, look out for, await

spērō, hope
  dēspērō, give up hope, despair

statuō, decide
  cōnstituō, set up, determine
  īnstituō, decide upon

stō (sistō), stand
  cōnsistō, stand still
  praestō, stand before, excel
  resistō, stand against, resist

struō, erect
  īnstruō, draw up

suādeō, advise
  persuādeō, persuade, convince

sum, be
  absum, be away
  adsum, be near
  dēsum, be lacking, be wanting
  possum, be able
  praesum, be at the head of

sūmō, take
  cōnsūmō, use up

tendō, stretch
  contendō, strive
  ostendō, stretch out, show

teneō, hold
  contineō, hold together
  obtineō, obtain, hold
  pertineō, pertain, extend
  retineō, hold back
  sustineō, hold up

terreō, scare
  perterreō, alarm greatly

turbō, disturb
  perturbō, disturb greatly

veniō, come
  circumveniō, surround
  conveniō, come together
  inveniō, come upon, find
  perveniō, arrive, reach

vertō, turn, change
  animadvertō, turn the mind
    to, notice
  revertō, return

vocō, call
  convocō, call together

EXERCISES

A. Separate the following compound verbs into their component parts (prefix and simple verb), and give the meaning of each part:

	PREFIX	MEANING	SIMPLE VERB	MEANING
1. permoveō				
2. redūcō				
3. suscipiō				
4. prōcurrō				
5. circumveniō				
6. absum				
7. praestō				
8. nesciō				
9. discēdō				
10. ēgredior				

B. Using your knowledge of prefixes, write the meaning of the following compound verbs:

1. abiciō _____
2. sēdūcō _____
3. revocō _____
4. dēcidō _____
5. distrahō _____
6. compellō _____
7. perlegō _____
8. intrōspiciō _____
9. adveniō _____
10. subscrībō _____
11. trānsferō _____
12. prōdō _____
13. praepōnō _____
14. superstō _____
15. intercēdō _____
16. ingredior _____
17. circumsedeō _____
18. antecapiō _____
19. concurrō _____
20. exigō _____

C. Form compound verbs by combining the following prefixes and simple verbs. Be sure to make changes in spelling where necessary.

1. ex + tollō _____
2. in + mittō _____
3. post + pōnō _____
4. per + capiō _____
5. con + mūniō _____
6. ad + faciō _____
7. ob + iaciō _____
8. dis + ferō _____
9. dē + teneō _____
10. re + cadō _____

D. Give the meaning of the following English compound words, all derived from Latin:

1. progress   ---------------------------
2. impatient   ---------------------------
3. circumscribe   ---------------------------
4. conjuncture   ---------------------------
5. reject   ---------------------------
6. contradict   ---------------------------
7. seclude   ---------------------------
8. perturb   ---------------------------
9. interpose   ---------------------------
10. avert   ---------------------------
11. incredible   ---------------------------
12. advent   ---------------------------
13. premonition   ---------------------------

14. antecedent   ---------------------------
15. execute   ---------------------------
16. dispel   ---------------------------
17. renascent   ---------------------------
18. malevolent   ---------------------------
19. retrospect   ---------------------------
20. ambient   ---------------------------
21. quadruped   ---------------------------
22. intramural   ---------------------------
23. supervise   ---------------------------
24. semilunar   ---------------------------
25. bilateral   ---------------------------

Roman Baths

Thermae or **balneae**, as Roman baths were called, were elaborate and luxurious establishments designed for the pleasure-seeking citizen. Besides pools of various types, the baths offered gymnasiums, exercise grounds, libraries—in fact practically everything that a modern country club provides for its members.

Lesson 78—COMMON LATIN ROOTS IN ENGLISH WORDS

ROOT	MEANING	EXAMPLE
aequ (*equ*)	even, just	equality
ag, act	do, perform	agent, action
ama	love	amatory
aqu	water	aqueous
aud	dare	audacity
audi	hear	audience
bene	well	benefit
cad, cid, cas	fall, happen	cadence, incident, occasion
cap, cip, cept	take, seize	captive, recipient, accept
capit	head	capital
cede (*ceed*), cess	move, yield	recede, proceed, concession
cid, cis	cut, kill	suicide, incision
clud, clus	shut, close	include, conclusion
corp, corpor	body	corps, corporal
cred	believe, trust	credit
cup	desire, wish	cupidity
curr, curs	run	current, cursory
de	god	deity
dict	say, speak	diction
doc, doct	teach	docile, doctor
duce, duct	lead	induce, product
fac, fic, fact, fect	do, make	facility, efficient, factor, effect
fer, lat	bear, bring, carry	transfer, relate
fid	trust, belief	fidelity
fin	end	infinite
grad, gress	step, move, go	gradual, congress
grat	pleasing	gratitude
hab, hib	have, hold	habit, prohibit
habit	live, dwell	habitation
iect (*ject*)	throw	reject
iur (*jur*), iust (*just*)	right, law	jury, justice
leg, lect	read, choose	legible, elect
liber	free	liberate
libr	book	library
loca	place	locate
loqu, locut	speak, talk	loquacious, elocution
luc	light	lucid
magn	large, great	magnitude
mal	bad	malice
mitt, miss	send, let go	remittance, mission
monstra	show, point out	demonstrate
mort	death	mortal
mov, mot	move	remove, motion
mult	much, many	multitude
naut	sailor	nautical
nav	ship	naval
nomin	name	nominate
nov	new	novelty
omn	all	omnibus
ped	foot	pedal

pell (*pel*), puls	drive	repellent, compel, compulsive
pet	seek, ask	compete
pon, pos, posit	put, place	component, compose, position
port	carry	import
press	press	oppression
pug, pugn	fight	pugilist, pugnacious
reg, rig, rect	guide, rule	regent, dirigible, erect
sci	know	science
scrib, script	write	describe, scripture
sed, sid, sess	sit	sedentary, assiduous, session
sequ, secut	follow, pursue	sequence, consecutive
serv	save	preserve
simil	like	simile
spec, spic, spect	look	specimen, despicable, inspect
sta, sist	stand	constant, insist
stru, struct	build	instrument, construct
tempor	time	temporary
ten (*tain*), tin, tent	hold	tenure, retain, continent, content
tim	fear	timid
tract	pull, draw, drag	contract
un	one	unify
urb	city	urban
ven, vent	come	convene, convent
ver	true	verify
vert, vers	turn	convert, reverse
vid, vis	see	evident, revise
vinc, vict	conquer	invincible, victor
vit	life	vital
viv	live	vivacious
voc (*voke*), vocat	call	vocal, convoke, vocation

EXERCISES

A. For each English derivative, give the Latin root and the meaning of the root.

	LATIN ROOT	MEANING
1. elocution	---------------	---------------
2. translate	---------------	---------------
3. inhibit	---------------	---------------
4. revive	---------------	---------------
5. precursor	---------------	---------------
6. prospectus	---------------	---------------
7. impugn	---------------	---------------
8. contemporary	---------------	---------------
9. inversion	---------------	---------------
10. evocative	---------------	---------------
11. compulsive	---------------	---------------
12. consequence	---------------	---------------
13. excessive	---------------	---------------

14. audition   ----------------   ----------------

15. indoctrinate   ----------------   ----------------

16. incorporate   ----------------   ----------------

17. infidel   ----------------   ----------------

18. retraction   ----------------   ----------------

19. impediment   ----------------   ----------------

20. lucidity   ----------------   ----------------

B. For each of the following sentences, (*a*) write a Latin word with which the italicized word is associated by derivation, and (*b*) underline the word or expression in the accompanying list that best expresses the meaning of the italicized word.

1. They introduced an *innovation* at the prom.   ------------------

    (*a*) outsider   (*b*) program   (*c*) skit   (*d*) novelty

2. The audience was *visibly* moved.   ------------------

    (*a*) strangely   (*b*) deeply   (*c*) slightly   (*d*) noticeably

3. His *circumspect* behavior puzzled the hostess.   ------------------

    (*a*) cautious   (*b*) rude   (*c*) odd   (*d*) aggressive

4. The guest delivered an *extemporaneous* speech.   ------------------

    (*a*) exceedingly long   (*b*) unplanned   (*c*) solemn   (*d*) pretentious

5. Silas Marner worked at his *vocation* near the village of Raveloe.   ------------------

    (*a*) free time   (*b*) loom   (*c*) machine   (*d*) calling

6. The progress of the Renaissance in England was *incredibly* rapid.   ------------------

    (*a*) hardly   (*b*) insufficiently   (*c*) unbelievably   (*d*) definitely

7. Emily Dickinson is known to have lived a life of *seclusion*.   ------------------

    (*a*) meditation   (*b*) isolation   (*c*) frustration   (*d*) unhappiness

8. The lawyer was known for his *veracity*.   ------------------

    (*a*) stubbornness   (*b*) preciseness   (*c*) truthfulness   (*d*) clearness

9. It was suggested that the Geneva conference be *convened*.   ------------------

    (*a*) assembled   (*b*) disbanded   (*c*) postponed   (*d*) formed

10. The poem "*Invictus*" was written by William Ernest Henley.   ------------------

    (*a*) unconquered   (*b*) unseen   (*c*) deceased   (*d*) reborn

C. Next to each Latin word are four English words, of which three are derivatives. Draw a line through the one that does *not* belong in the group.

1. *tempus:*   temporal, extempore, temperate, contemporary

2. *regō:*   rigorous, dirigible, rectify, regent

3. *pōnō:*   deponent, position, repose, pony

4. *lūx:*   translucent, luxury, lucid, elucidate

5. *aequus:*   equal, equivalent, equine, equinox

6. *audiō:*   audible, audience, audition, audacious

7. *dūcō:*   ductile, docile, reduce, induction

8. *fidēs:*   fiddle, confide, fidelity, confident

9. *timeō:*   timid, time, timorous, timidity

10. *trahō:*   tractor, tractable, contract, track

D. In the space before each word in column *A*, write the letter of its equivalent in column *B*.

Column A	*Column B*
_____ **1.** audacious	*a.* talkativeness
_____ **2.** egress	*b.* following in order
_____ **3.** habitation	*c.* shut out
_____ **4.** loquacity	*d.* likeness
_____ **5.** coincident	*e.* trusting
_____ **6.** incursion	*f.* clearness
_____ **7.** exclude	*g.* able to be drawn out
_____ **8.** incision	*h.* doing good
_____ **9.** credulous	*i.* bold
_____ **10.** regulate	*j.* speak ill of
_____ **11.** sequential	*k.* keep within limits
_____ **12.** tractile	*l.* dwelling
_____ **13.** revert	*m.* cut
_____ **14.** vivid	*n.* happening at the same time
_____ **15.** similitude	*o.* bodily
_____ **16.** malign	*p.* exit
_____ **17.** confine	*q.* lively
_____ **18.** corporeal	*r.* direct by rule
_____ **19.** beneficent	*s.* turn back
_____ **20.** lucidity	*t.* raid

Catapult

For laying siege to a town, the Romans made effective use of various types of **tormenta** (artillery), such as the **catapulta,** the **scorpiō,** and the **ballista,** all used for shooting or hurling arrows, javelins, and stones. With the invention of gunpowder, the tormenta disappeared from the modern military scene.

Lesson 79—SUFFIXES

Whereas prefixes appear at the beginning of words, suffixes are attached to the ending. A suffix generally serves two purposes: it indicates what part of speech a word is, and also gives a clue to its meaning. Thus,

> **cupidus** is an adjective, and means *pertaining to or having a desire;*
> **cupiditās** is a noun, and means the *condition or act of desiring.*

By learning the meaning of common suffixes, we can arrive at the meaning of new words, both Latin and English, based on familiar stems. Below is a list of common Latin suffixes with their English equivalents in parentheses, followed by examples:

SUFFIXES FORMING NOUNS

-ia (*-y*), **-tās** (*-ty*), **-tia** (*-ce, -cy*), **-tūdō** (*-tude*), denote quality, condition, act of

victor **ia**	victor *y*	act of conquering
veri **tās**	veri *ty*	condition of being true
dīligen **tia**	diligen *ce*	quality of being careful
alti **tūdō**	alti *tude*	condition of being high

-iō (*-ion*), **-tiō** (*-tion*), denote an act or the result of an act

suspīc **iō**	suspic *ion*	act of suspecting
mūnī **tiō**	muni *tion*	result of fortifying

-or (*-or*), denotes physical or mental state

terr **or**	terr *or*	state of fright

-tor (*-tor*), denotes one who does something

gladiā **tor**	gladia *tor*	one who fights with a sword

-mentum (*-ment*), denotes the means or result of an action

impedī **mentum**	impedi *ment*	means of hindering

DIMINUTIVES

-ellus, -olus, denote small, little
ag **ellus** (ager + ellus) = a small field
fīli **olus** (fīlius + olus) = a little son

SUFFIXES FORMING ADJECTIVES

-ālis (*-al*), **-ānus** (*-an*), **-āris** (*-ar, -ary*), **-ārius** (*-ary*), **-ēlis** (*-el*), **-icus** (*-ic, -ical*), **-idus** (*-id*), **-īlis** (*-il, -ile*), **-ius** (*-ious*), **-ter** (*-trian*), **-timus** (*-time*), denote belonging to, pertaining to

mort **ālis**	mort *al*	pertaining to death
urb **ānus**	urb *an*	belonging to a city
cīv **īlis**	civ *il*	pertaining to a citizen
mari **timus**	mari *time*	pertaining to the sea

-ilis (*-ile*), **-bilis** (*-ble*), denote able to be, worthy of being

| fac **ilis** | fac *ile* | able to be done |
| nō **bilis** | no *ble* | worthy of being known |

-ōsus (*-ous*, *-ose*), denotes full of, abounding in

| perīcul **ōsus** | peril *ous* | full of danger |
| verb **ōsus** | verb *ose* | abounding in words |

SUFFIXES FORMING VERBS

-tō denotes repeated or intense action

$$\text{iac } \mathbf{t\bar{o}} \text{ (iaci\bar{o} + t\bar{o}) = keep on throwing}$$

EXERCISES

A. Separate the following Latin words into their component parts (stem and suffix), and give the meaning of each part:

	STEM	MEANING	SUFFIX	MEANING
1. ūtilis				
2. celeritās				
3. magnitūdō				
4. agitō				
5. bellicōsus				
6. dēditiō				
7. amīcitia				
8. victor				
9. frūmentārius				
10. equester				
11. timor				
12. gladiolus				
13. amābilis				
14. audācia				
15. vītālis				

B. Underline the correct Latin translation.

1. able to be taught — (doctor, docilis, docilitās)
2. a lover — (amātor, amātiō, amor)
3. hear often — (audītiō, audientia, audītō)
4. pertaining to a soldier — (mīlitia, mīlitāris, mīlitō)
5. act of desiring — (cupiditās, cupītor, cupidus)

C. Using your knowledge of suffixes, give the meaning of the following Latin words:

1. populāris _____
2. scrīptor _____
3. hūmānitās _____
4. studiōsus _____
5. crēdibilis _____
6. pedester _____
7. libellus _____
8. rēgius _____
9. fortitūdō _____
10. nāvālis _____
11. aquāticus _____
12. captō _____
13. pueritia _____
14. dictiō _____
15. dolor _____

16. montānus _____
17. levitās _____
18. cōnsulāris _____
19. fēlīcitās _____
20. viator _____
21. senātōrius _____
22. hostīlis _____
23. dormītō _____
24. nātūrālis _____
25. lātitūdō _____
26. familiāris _____
27. ūtilitās _____
28. obsidiō _____
29. dēbitor _____
30. officiōsus _____

D. Give the meaning of the following English words, paying particular attention to suffixes:

1. lucidity _____
2. navigator _____
3. bellicose _____
4. temporal _____
5. magnitude _____
6. maritime _____
7. vulnerable _____
8. verity _____
9. animation _____
10. terrestrial _____
11. pugnacious _____
12. timidity _____
13. insular _____
14. penal _____
15. tempestuous _____
16. adolescence _____
17. sentiment _____
18. riparian _____
19. celerity _____
20. digital _____

Lesson 80—RELATED WORDS

The following list contains groups of words related in meaning and resembling one another in spelling:

ācer, sharp; ācriter, sharply; aciēs, sharp edge, battle line

adulēscēns, young man; adulēscentia, youth

aedificō, build; aedificium, building

aequus, even; inīquus (in + aequus), uneven

altus, high; altitūdō, height

amīcus, friend; amīcitia, friendship; inimīcus (in + amīcus), unfriendly

amō, love; amor, love

ante, before; anteā, previously; antequam, before

armō, arm; arma, arms

audāx, bold; audācter, boldly; audācia, boldness; audeō, be bold, dare

cadō, fall; cāsus, chance; occāsus, setting; occāsiō, opportunity

caedō, cut, kill; caedēs, murder

capiō, take; captīvus, taken in war, prisoner

celer, swift; celeritās, swiftness; celeriter, swiftly

centum, a hundred; centuriō, leader of a hundred men, centurion

circum, around; circiter, about

cīvis, citizen; cīvitās, citizenship, state; cīvīlis, civil

clāmō, shout; clāmor, shouting

cognōscō, know; nōtus, well-known; nōbilis, noble; nōbilitās, nobility

cōnsul, consul; cōnsulātus, consulship; cōnsulāris, consular

cupiō, desire; cupidus, desirous; cupiditās, desire

cūrō, care for; cūra, care

currō, run; cursus, running; currus, chariot

decem, ten; decimus, tenth

dēfendō, defend; dēfēnsor, defender

diēs, day; hodiē (hōc diē), today; merīdiēs (medius diēs), midday, noon; postrīdiē, the day after; prīdiē, the day before

dīligēns, careful; dīligentia, care

disciplīna, training; discipulus, pupil

dō, give; dēdō, give up; dēditiō, surrender; dōnō, give a gift; dōnum, gift

domus, home; domicilium, home; domina, mistress; dominus, master; dominor, rule

dūcō, lead; dux, leader

eō, to that place; eōdem, to the same place

eō, go; exitus, outcome; initium, going into, beginning; reditus, return

equus, horse; eques, horseman; equitātus, cavalry

exerceō, train; exercitus, trained body, army

explōrō, spy; explōrātor, spy, scout

extrā, outside; extrēmus, outermost

faciō, do; facultās, ability to do, opportunity; facilis, able to be done, easy; facile, easily; difficilis (dis + facilis), not able to be done, difficult; difficultās, difficulty; beneficium, good deed, kindness; factum, deed

fidēs, faith; fidēlis, faithful

fīlius, son; fīlia, daughter

fīnis, boundary; fīnitimus, neighboring, bordering; fīniō, limit, end

fīrmus, strong; cōnfīrmō, strengthen

fortis, brave; fortiter, bravely; fortitūdō, bravery

frūmentum, grain; frūmentārius, pertaining to grain

fugiō, flee; fuga, flight; fugitīvus, deserter

gladius, sword; gladiātor, swordsman

grātus, pleasing; grātia, favor, influence

hiems, winter; **hiemō**, spend the winter; **hīberna**, winter quarters

homō, man; **nēmō (nē + homō)**, no one

imperium, command; **imperātor**, commander; **imperō**, order

inter, between; **interim**, time between, meanwhile; **intereā**, meanwhile

ita, so; **itaque**, and so; **item**, likewise

iūdicō, judge; **iūdicium**, judgment

labōrō, work; **labor**, work

lātus, wide; **lātitūdō**, width

laudō, praise; **laus**, praise

līber, free; **līberō**, set free; **lībertās**, freedom; **līberī**, (freeborn) children

locō, place; **locus**, place

loquor, speak; **colloquium**, conversation

magnus, great; **magnopere**, greatly; **magnitūdō**, greatness; **magis**, in a greater degree; **magister**, one
   with greater learning, teacher; **magistrātus**, magistrate

mare, sea; **maritimus**, pertaining to the sea

mīles, soldier; **mīlitāris**, military

morior, die; **mors**, death; **immortālis**, immortal

moror, delay; **mora**, delay

multus, much; **multitūdō**, great number

mūniō, fortify; **mūnītiō**, fortification

nāvis, ship; **nāvigō**, sail; **nāvigium**, boat; **nauta**, sailor

necesse, necessary; **necessārius**, necessary

nōn, not; **nōndum**, not yet

novem, nine; **nōnus**, ninth

nūntiō, report; **nūntius**, messenger

octō, eight; **octāvus**, eighth

ōrō, speak, plead; **ōrātiō**, speech; **ōrātor**, speaker

pācō, pacify; **pāx**, peace

pater, father; **patria**, fatherland

paulō, a little; **paulum**, a little

pēs, foot; **pedes**, foot soldier; **impediō**, hinder; **impedīmentum**, hindrance

petō, seek, attack; **impetus**, attack

possum, have power, be able; **potēns**, powerful; **potestās**, power

post, after; **posteā**, afterwards; **posterus**, following; **postquam**, after

praeter, beyond; **praetereā**, besides

prīmus, first; **prīmō**, at first; **prīmum**, at first; **prīnceps (prīmus + capiō)**, holding first place, leader;
   prīncipātus, first place; **prior**, previous; **priusquam**, before

prope, near; **propinquus**, near

propter, because of; **proptereā**, for this reason

puer, boy; **puella**, girl

pugnō, fight; **pugna**, fight

quattuor, four; **quārtus**, fourth

quīnque, five; **quīntus**, fifth

relinquō, leave behind; **reliquus**, remaining

respondeō, reply; **respōnsum**, reply

rēx, king; **rēgīna**, queen; **rēgnum**, kingdom; **regō**, rule

salūs, safety; **salvus**, safe

sciō, know; **scientia**, knowledge; **nesciō**, not to know

sedeō, sit; **obsideō**, sit down, besiege; **praesidium**, guard; **subsidium**, line of reserve, aid

senātor, senator; **senātus**, senate

sentiō, feel; **sententia**, feeling, opinion

septem, seven; **septimus**, seventh

sex, six; **sextus**, sixth

sī, if; **nisi**, if not

sōlus, alone; **sōlum**, only

spectō, look at; **cōnspectus**, sight; **speciō**, see; **speciēs**, appearance

spērō, hope; **spēs**, hope; **dēspērō**, give up hope

stō, stand; **cōnsistō**, stand still

studeō, be eager for; **studium,** eagerness
super, above; **suprā,** above; **superus,** upper; **superior,** upper; **superō,** surpass
tardō, slow up; **tardus,** slow
terreō, frighten; **terror,** fright
timeō, fear; **timor,** fear; **timidus,** fearful
trēs, three; **tertius,** third
ūllus, any; **nūllus,** none
ūnus, one; **ūnā,** together
ūtor, use; **ūtilis,** useful; **ūsus,** use
valeō, be strong; **validus,** strong
vāllum, wall; **intervāllum,** space between
veniō, come; **adventus (ad + veniō),** coming, arrival
vertō, turn; **animadvertō,** turn the mind to, notice
vērus, true; **vērō,** truly; **vērum,** but in truth
videō, see; **prūdēns (prō + vidēns),** foreseeing, wise
vigilō, watch; **vigilia,** watch
vincō, conquer; **victor,** conqueror; **victōria,** victory
vir, man; **virtūs,** manliness
vīta, life; **vīvus,** alive
vocō, call; **vōx,** voice
volō, want; **voluntās,** will; **nōlō,** not to want
vulnerō, wound; **vulnus,** wound

EXERCISES

A. In each group, draw a line through the word *not* related to the word in italics.

1. *domus*   (dominus, dōnum, dominor, domicilium)

2. *sedeō*   (sed, subsidium, obsideō, praesidium)

3. *diēs*   (postrīdiē, merīdiēs, deus, hodiē)

4. *audeō*   (audācia, audāx, audācter, audītiō)

5. *ūtor*   (ūsus, uter, ūtilis, ūtilitās)

6. *post*   (posteā, postquam, postulō, posterus)

7. *spectō*   (spēs, cōnspectus, speciēs, speciō)

8. *līber*   (līberō, līberī, liber, lībertās)

9. *magnus*   (magis, magister, manus, magnopere)

10. *super*   (suprā, suspīciō, superō, superior)

B. In each group, there is *one* word that is related to the word in italics. Underline that word and give its meaning.

1. *fortis*   (fortūna, fortitūdō, forum, fōrma)   -

2. *lātus*   (laus, latus, laudō, lātitūdō)   -

3. *spēs*   (speciēs, spectō, dēspērō. spatium)   -

4. *aequus*   (eques, inīquus, equus, equitātus)   -

5. *cūra*   (cūrō, cūr, currō, currus)   -

6. *valeō*   (vāllum, vallēs, vel, validus)   -

7. *possum*   (potēns, postquam, pōnō, posterus)   -

8. *petō*   (pēs, perturbō, pertineō, impetus)   -

9. *videō*   (vigilia, vīs, prūdēns, vīcus)   -

10. *homō*   (nēmō, honor, hortor, hŏra)   -

C. In each group, complete the second pair of words to make them bear the same relationship as the first pair.

EXAMPLE: *dūcō* is to *dux* as *nūntiō* is to *nūntius*

1. *trēs* is to *tertius* as *quattuor* is to   -

2. *pēs* is to *pedes* as *equus* is to   -

3. *post* is to *posteā* as *ante* is to   -

4. *magister* is to *magistrātus* as *cōnsul* is to   -

5. *magnus* is to *magnopere* as *ācer* is to   -

6. *amō* is to *amor* as *laudō* is to   -

7. *labor* is to *labōrō* as *ōrātiō* is to   -

8. *amīcus* is to *amīcitia* as *celer* is to   -

9. *ūtor* is to *ūtilis* as *timeō* is to   -

10. *sī* is to *nisi* as *spērō* is to   -

D. In the space before each word in column *A*, write the letter of its related word in column *B*.

Column A	Column B
------ **1.** nauta	*a.* mora
------ **2.** rēx	*b.* impediō
------ **3.** morior	*c.* nōlō
------ **4.** pēs	*d.* dōnum
------ **5.** eō	*e.* nāvigium
------ **6.** loquor	*f.* cognōscō
------ **7.** faciō	*g.* immortālis
------ **8.** voluntās	*h.* regō
------ **9.** cadō	*i.* cursus
------ **10.** moror	*j.* potestās
------ **11.** nōtus	*k.* colloquium
------ **12.** currō	*l.* prīnceps
------ **13.** dō	*m.* occāsiō
------ **14.** prīmus	*n.* beneficium
------ **15.** possum	*o.* initium

Lesson 81—SYNONYMS

VERBS

accēdō, adeō, appropinquō, approach
accidō, fīō, happen
aggredior, oppugnō, attack
agō, faciō, do
agō, pellō, drive
appellō, vocō, call
arbitror, exīstimō, putō, think
caedō, interficiō, occīdō, kill
capiō, expugnō, occupō, seize
circumdō, circumveniō, surround
coepī, incēpī, began
cognōscō, inveniō, find out
cōgō, cōnferō, bring together
committō, mandō, entrust

cōnor, temptō, try
cōnspiciō, videō, see
contendō, properō, hurry
contendō, pugnō, fight
cupiō, volō, want
dēdō, trādō, surrender
dēficiō, dēsum, be wanting, fail
dēmōnstrō, ostendō, show
dīcō, loquor, nārrō, say, tell
dō, dōnō, give
ēgredior, excēdō, exeō, leave
ferō, patior, suffer, bear
ferō, portō, carry
habeō, teneō, have
impediō, prohibeō, prevent

imperō, iubeō, mandō, order
īnstituō, īnstruō, arrange
locō, pōnō, put
obsideō, oppugnō, besiege
obtineō, parō, get
pācō, superō, vincō, subdue, conquer
pateō, pertineō, extend
patior, permittō, allow
permoveō, perterreō, terrify
petō, quaerō, rogō, ask
praestō, superō, surpass
prōcēdō, prōgredior, advance
timeō, vereor, fear

NOUNS

aditus, adventus, approach
ager, campus, field
amīcus, socius, friend
animus, mēns, mind
arma, tēla, weapons
auctōritās, grātia, influence
auxilium, subsidium, aid
beneficium, grātia, favor
cāsus, fortūna, chance
cīvitās, rēs pūblica, state
collis, mōns, mountain
cōnsilium, ratiō, plan
cōnsuētūdō, mōs, custom

cūra, dīligentia, care
disciplīna, scientia, knowledge
domicilium, domus, home
dux, imperātor, general
epistula, litterae, letter
equitātus, equitēs, cavalry
fāma, glōria, reputation
fīnēs, terra, land
fortitūdō, virtūs, courage
gēns, nātiō, populus, people
homō, vir, man
hostis, inimīcus, enemy
imperium, potestās, power

impetus, vīs, force
iter, via, way
iūs, lēx, law
labor, opera, opus, work
līberī, puerī, children
lītus, rīpa, shore
lūdus, schola, school
modus, ratiō, manner
mūrus, vāllum, wall
nāvigium, nāvis, ship
oppidum, urbs, town
praesidium, vigilia, guard
proelium, pugna, battle

PRONOUNS

hic, ille, is, he

ADJECTIVES

aequus, pār, equal
altus, superus, high
amplus, magnus, large
cēterī, reliquī, the rest
clārus, nōbilis, nōtus, famous
commūnis, pūblicus, public

complūrēs, multī, many
fīnitimus, propinquus, neighboring
fīrmus, fortis, validus, strong
hic, is, this
ille, is, that

incolumis, integer, whole
īnfēlīx, miser, unhappy
necessārius, necesse, necessary
novus, recēns, new
omnis, tōtus, whole
posterus, proximus, next

ADVERBS

iam, nunc, now
intereā, interim, meanwhile

ita, sīc, tam, so
modo, sōlum, only

prīmō, prīmum, at first
quidem, vērō, indeed

PREPOSITIONS

ab, dē, ex, from   apud, inter, among
ante, prō, before   ob, propter, on account of

CONJUNCTIONS

antequam, priusquam, before   aut . . . aut, vel . . . vel,   cum, ubi, when
at, autem, sed, but   either . . . or   enim, nam, for
atque, et, -que, and   autem, sed, but, however   igitur, itaque, therefore
aut, vel, or

EXERCISES

A. In the space before each word in column *A*, write the letter of its synonym in column *B*.

	Column A	Column B
_____	**1.** nāvis	*a.* vērō
_____	**2.** mūrus	*b.* locō
_____	**3.** temptō	*c.* cēterī
_____	**4.** quidem	*d.* fortitūdō
_____	**5.** arma	*e.* multī
_____	**6.** reliquī	*f.* vāllum
_____	**7.** pōnō	*g.* proximus
_____	**8.** litterae	*h.* ostendō
_____	**9.** complūrēs	*i.* nāvigium
_____	**10.** modo	*j.* incolumis
_____	**11.** rīpa	*k.* tēla
_____	**12.** dēmōnstrō	*l.* impetus
_____	**13.** igitur	*m.* epistula
_____	**14.** ratiō	*n.* magnus
_____	**15.** integer	*o.* incēpī
_____	**16.** virtūs	*p.* cōnor
_____	**17.** amplus	*q.* itaque
_____	**18.** coepī	*r.* cōnsilium
_____	**19.** vīs	*s.* lītus
_____	**20.** posterus	*t.* sōlum

B. In each sentence replace the word in italics with a Latin synonym.

1. Caesar erat *dux* nōtissimus.   _____

2. Sociī *subsidium* tulērunt.   _____

3. Rōmānī impetum fortiter *prohibuērunt*.   _____

4. *Antequam* pervenīret, castra posuērunt.   _____

5. *Viam* per silvās invēnimus.   _____

6. Omnēs quidem *permōtī* erant.   ----------------------------------

7. *Aditum* hostium exspectābat.   ----------------------------------

8. Pōns *propinquus* erat.   ----------------------------------

9. *Ob* perīculum puerī fūgērunt.   ----------------------------------

10. Aquītānia ad montēs *patet.*   ----------------------------------

C. Underline the synonym of the italicized word.

1. *enim:* vel, nam, at

2. *imperium:* potestās, iūdicium, cōnsilium

3. *volō:* nōlō, cupiō, cēdō

4. *nunc:* iam, prīmō, tum

5. *novus:* nōtus, alter, recēns

6. *inter:* sine, cum, apud

7. *fīō:* faciō, accidō, accipiō

8. *mōns:* collis, classis, fīnis

9. *superus:* suprā, lātus, altus

10. *vereor:* teneō, timeō, praestō

D. In each group, draw a line through the word that is *not* a synonym of the italicized word.

1. *caedō*   (interficiō, accidō, occīdō)

2. *sīc*   (aut, ita, tam)

3. *nōtus*   (nōbilis, clārus, parvus)

4. *populus*   (homō, gēns, nātiō)

5. *exeō*   (excēdō, appropinquō, ēgredior)

6. *exīstimō*   (possum, putō, arbitror)

7. *ab*   (dē, ex, propter)

8. *loquor*   (pōnō, nārrō, dīcō)

9. *autem*   (sed, nam, at)

10. *occupō*   (capiō, orior, expugnō)

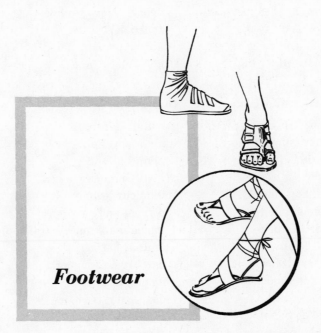

Footwear

The Romans wore sandals indoors and high shoes outdoors. Footwear was usually made of leather or cork. Modern shoe stylists have often adapted the Roman sandal in footwear for both men and women.

Lesson 82—ANTONYMS

VERBS

adsum, be present	**absum,** be away
appropinquō, approach	**excēdō,** leave
cōnservō, preserve	**vāstō,** destroy
cōnsistō, stand still	**ambulō,** walk
dō, give	**accipiō,** receive
dūcō, lead	**sequor,** follow
eō, go	**veniō,** come
incipiō, begin	**cōnficiō,** finish
interrogō, ask	**respondeō,** answer
inveniō, find	**āmittō,** lose
labōrō, work	**lūdō,** play
nāscor, be born	**morior,** die
oppugnō, attack	**dēfendō,** defend
orior, rise	**cadō,** fall
proficīscor, set out	**perveniō,** arrive
prōgredior, advance	**pedem referō,** retreat
sciō, know	**nesciō,** not know
spērō, hope	**dēspērō,** give up hope
stō, stand	**sedeō,** sit
vigilō, keep awake	**dormiō,** sleep
volō, want	**nōlō,** not want

NOUNS AND PRONOUNS

aditus, approach	**exitus,** departure
aestās, summer	**hiems,** winter
aliquid, something	**nihil,** nothing
aliquis, someone	**nēmō,** no one
amīcus, friend	**inimīcus,** enemy
animus, mind	**corpus,** body
auxilium, help	**impedīmentum,** hindrance
beneficium, kindness	**iniūria,** harm
cīvis, citizen	**barbarus,** foreigner
cōpia, abundance	**inopia,** scarcity
deus, god	**dea,** goddess
diēs, day	**nox,** night
dominus, master	**domina,** mistress
fīlius, son	**fīlia,** daughter
frāter, brother	**soror,** sister
hic, this	**ille,** that
homō, person	**rēs,** thing
initium, beginning	**fīnis,** end
labor, work	**lūdus,** play

266

mōns, mountain   vallēs, valley
pater, father   māter, mother
pāx, peace   bellum, war
pedes, infantryman   eques, cavalryman
praemium, reward   poena, punishment
puer, boy   puella, girl
rēx, king   rēgīna, queen
silentium, silence   clāmor, noise
socius, ally   hostis, enemy
terra, land   mare, sea
victor, conqueror   captīvus, prisoner
vir, man   fēmina, woman
virtūs, courage   timor, fear
vīta, life   mors, death

ADJECTIVES

aequus, even   inīquus, uneven
amīcus, friendly   inimīcus, unfriendly
angustus, narrow   lātus, wide
bonus, good   malus, bad
brevis, short   longus, long
celer, fast   tardus, slow
certus, certain   incertus, uncertain
citerior, nearer   ulterior, farther
dexter, right   sinister, left
facilis, easy   difficilis, hard
fēlīx, happy   īnfēlīx, unhappy
fortis, brave   timidus, cowardly
levis, light   gravis, heavy
nōtus, known   ignōtus, unknown
parvus, small   magnus, large
paucī, few   multī, many
prior, previous   posterus, following
similis, like   dissimilis, unlike
ūllus, any   nūllus, none
validus, healthy   aeger, sick
vērus, true   falsus, false

ADVERBS

anteā, previously   posteā, afterwards
bene, well   male, badly
hīc, here   eō, there
iam, already   nōndum, not yet
minimē, least of all maximē, most of all
nunc, now   tum, then
prīdiē, the day before postrīdiē, the next day
prope, near   longē, far
semper, always   numquam, never

PREPOSITIONS

ad, to	**ab**, from
ante, before	**post**, after
cum, with	**sine**, without
in, into	**ex**, out of
intrā, inside	**extrā**, outside
prō, for	**contrā**, against
sub, under	**super**, above

CONJUNCTIONS

antequam, before	**postquam**, after
et, and	**neque**, and not
sī, if	**nisi**, if not
ut, in order that	**nē**, in order that not

EXERCISES

A. Underline the word that is most nearly the opposite of the word in italics.

1. *timor:* timidus, virtūs, vereor, fortis

2. *brevis:* longus, magnus, nōtus, cupidus

3. *incipiō:* dō, eō, capiō, cōnficiō

4. *prō:* dē, ad, contrā, sub

5. *lūdō:* lūdus, labōrō, laudō, līberō

6. *prope:* longē, intrā, prīdiē, propinquus

7. *barbarus:* deus, alius, cīvitās, cīvis

8. *ut:* at, neque, nē, quō

9. *initium:* inter, fīnis, concilium, subsidium

10. *tardus:* fēlīx, ācriter, celer, validus

B. In each sentence replace the word in italics with a Latin antonym.

1. Via erat *angusta.* --------------------------

2. *Volēbat* hodiē discēdere. --------------------------

3. Opus *bene* factum erat. --------------------------

4. *Sine* amīcīs iter fēcimus. --------------------------

5. Mīles *timidus* erat. --------------------------

6. Omnēs *bellum* cupiēbant. --------------------------

7. *Antequam* pervēnit, trādidimus. --------------------------

8. Nūntius litterās *āmīsit.* --------------------------

9. Servus *aliquid* rogābat. --------------------------

10. Respōnsum fuerat *falsum.* --------------------------

C. In the space before each word in column *A*, write the letter of its antonym in column *B*.

	Column A	*Column B*
`------`	**1.** eō	*a.* nisi
`------`	**2.** vīta	*b.* prior
`------`	**3.** levis	*c.* vigilō
`------`	**4.** sī	*d.* sub
`------`	**5.** posterus	*e.* validus
`------`	**6.** semper	*f.* mors
`------`	**7.** super	*g.* cōnservō
`------`	**8.** dormiō	*h.* captīvus
`------`	**9.** praemium	*i.* gravis
`------`	**10.** aditus	*j.* maximē
`------`	**11.** vāstō	*k.* cadō
`------`	**12.** aeger	*l.* veniō
`------`	**13.** minimē	*m.* numquam
`------`	**14.** victor	*n.* poena
`------`	**15.** orior	*o.* exitus

D. Write the feminine antonym of each of the following:

1. dominus `-------------------`   **4.** fīlius `-------------------`

2. deus `-------------------`   **5.** frāter `-------------------`

3. vir `-------------------`

E. Write the antonym of the following Latin words, and translate each answer:

	ANTONYM	TRANSLATION
1. multī	`-------------------`	`-------------------`
2. absum	`-------------------`	`-------------------`
3. homō	`-------------------`	`-------------------`
4. tum	`-------------------`	`-------------------`
5. sciō	`-------------------`	`-------------------`
6. clāmor	`-------------------`	`-------------------`
7. amīcus	`-------------------`	`-------------------`
8. ante	`-------------------`	`-------------------`
9. cōpia	`-------------------`	`-------------------`
10. nox	`-------------------`	`-------------------`

Lesson 83—WORDS OFTEN CONFUSED

ab, by, from
ob, on account of

accēdō, approach
accidō, happen

aeger, sick
ager, field

aestās, summer
aetās, age

alius, another
alter, the other
altus, high

audeō, dare
audiō, hear

aut, or
autem, however

cadō, fall
caedō, cut
cēdō, yield

cīvis, citizen
cīvitās, state

cognōscō, learn
cōgō, collect

cohors, cohort
cohortor, encourage

concilium, meeting
cōnsilium, plan

cum, with, when
dum, while
tum, then

cūrō, take care
currō, run

currus, chariot
cursus, running

deus, god
diēs, day

fīnēs, territory
fīnitimus, neighboring

gēns, clan, nation
genus, race, kind

grātia, favor
grātus, pleasing

hic, this
hīc, here

ibi, there
ubi, where

īdem, the same
idōneus, suitable

inter, between
intrā, within

latus, side
lātus, wide

lēgātus, lieutenant
legiō, legion

liber, book
līber, free
līberī, children

maneō, remain
moneō, advise
mūniō, fortify

mēns, mind
mēnsa, table
mēnsis, month

mīles, soldier
mīlia, thousands

morior, die
moror, delay

mors, death
mōs, custom

nancīscor, find
nāscor, be born

nōtus, well-known
novus, new

pār, equal
pars, part

pāreō, obey
parō, prepare

pater, father
patria, country

pedes, foot soldier
pedēs, feet

porta, gate
portus, harbor

posuī, I put
potuī, I could

praemium, reward
praesidium, protection
proelium, battle

quīdam, certain
quidem, indeed

reddō, give back
redeō, go back

regiō, region
rēgnum, kingdom
regō, rule

saepe, often
semper, always

sī, if
sīc, so

sōl, sun
sōlus, alone

summus, highest
sumus, we are

suscipiō, undertake
suspīciō, suspicion

tam, so
tamen, still, however

tot, so many
tōtus, whole

utī, that, in order that
ūtī, use

venit, he comes
vēnit, he came

vir, man
vīs, force

EXERCISES

A. Underline the correct English translation.

1. moneō   (advise, remain, fortify)

2. caedō   (fall, cut, yield)

3. praesidium   (reward, battle, protection)

4. dum   (when, then, while)

5. mēnsis   (month, table, mind)

6. līber   (children, book, free)

7. alter   (another, the other, high)

8. autem   (however, or, thus)

9. regiō   (rule, kingdom, region)

10. vīs   (life, man, force)

B. Underline the word in parentheses that you would use to translate the italicized English word.

1. They *ran* toward the river.   (cūrō, currō)

2. That *summer* there was no work.   (aetās, aestās)

3. There was commotion *within* the walls.   (intrā, inter)

4. The messenger *came* to tell the news.   (venit, vēnit)

5. The soldiers *obeyed* the general.   (pāreō, parō)

6. *Where* is the camp situated?   (Ibi, Ubi)

7. *I could* see the battle from the tower.   (Posuī, Potuī)

8. *Certain* envoys delivered the message.   (Quīdam, Quidem)

9. The prisoner tried *to use* the sword.   (utī, ūtī)

10. They closed the *gate* at night.   (portam, portum)

C. In the space before each word in column *A*, write the letter of its meaning in column *B*.

	Column A	Column B
_____	**1.** semper	*a.* delay
_____	**2.** lātus	*b.* dare
_____	**3.** cohors	*c.* encourage
_____	**4.** pedes	*d.* often
_____	**5.** reddō	*e.* running
_____	**6.** morior	*f.* feet
_____	**7.** suscipiō	*g.* always
_____	**8.** audeō	*h.* cohort
_____	**9.** saepe	*i.* side
_____	**10.** currus	*j.* suspicion
_____	**11.** tam	*k.* die
_____	**12.** moror	*l.* foot soldier
_____	**13.** pedēs	*m.* go back
_____	**14.** tamen	*n.* hear
_____	**15.** latus	*o.* wide
_____	**16.** cursus	*p.* so
_____	**17.** redeō	*q.* however
_____	**18.** audiō	*r.* chariot
_____	**19.** suspīciō	*s.* undertake
_____	**20.** cohortor	*t.* give back

Lesson 84—SPELLING OF ENGLISH WORDS

Since English has borrowed so heavily from Latin, it is not surprising that the *spelling* of English words derived from Latin is determined to so great an extent by the Latin spelling. Below are a few guides that can help the student immeasurably in the spelling of English words.

1. In the case of English words derived from Latin nouns or adjectives, it is the *stem*, rather than the nominative singular, that furnishes a clue to the correct spelling. The stem, of course, is found in the genitive singular.

ENGLISH WORD	LATIN NOMINATIVE	LATIN GENITIVE	LATIN STEM
nominate	nōmen	nōminis	nōmin-
corporal	corpus	corporis	corpor-
militia	mīles	mīlitis	mīlit-
general	genus	generis	gener-
diligent	dīligēns	dīligentis	dīligent-

2. In the case of English words derived from Latin verbs, the second and fourth principal parts determine the spelling. If the fourth principal part ends in **-tus,** the English noun ends in *-tion;* if in **-sus,** the English word ends in *-sion.*

ENGLISH WORD	2ND PRINCIPAL PART	4TH PRINCIPAL PART
reduce reduction	dūcere (stem **dūce-**)	ductus (stem **duct-**)
inscribe inscription	scrībere (stem **scrībe-**)	scrīptus (stem **scrīpt-**)
compete competition	petere (stem **pete-**)	petītus (stem **petīt-**)
provide provision	vidēre (stem **vidē-**)	vīsus (stem **vīs-**)
convert conversion	vertere (stem **verte-**)	versus (stem **vers-**)

3. Students are often puzzled as to whether an English word ends in *-ant* or *-ent*. Again Latin comes to the rescue. If the English word is derived from a Latin verb of the first conjugation, then in all probability it ends in *-ant;* otherwise in *-ent*. Actually the English word is spelled exactly the same as the stem of the present participle.

ENGLISH WORD	PRESENT PARTICIPLE	GENITIVE	STEM	CONJUGATION
occupant	occupāns	occupantis	occupant-	1st
student	studēns	studentis	student-	2nd
agent	agēns	agentis	agent-	3rd
incipient	incipiēns	incipientis	incipient-	-iō 3rd
convenient	conveniēns	convenientis	convenient-	4th

Note

Some English words of Latin derivation have come into our language indirectly via Norman French. These words, according to French formation, all end in *-ant* regardless of the conjugation of the Latin verb. For example:

tenant from **tenēre** (2nd conjugation)

defendant from **dēfendere** (3rd conjugation)

4. To determine whether an English word ends in *-able* or *-ible*, apply the same rule as in 3. If it comes from a first conjugation verb, it most likely ends in *-able;* otherwise in *-ible*.

ENGLISH WORD	LATIN VERB	CONJUGATION
navigable	nāvigāre	1st
visible	vidēre	2nd
defensible	dēfendere	3rd
audible	audīre	4th

5. The problem of whether a particular English word is spelled with a single or double consonant can usually be solved by referring to the Latin. The following English words illustrate spelling with double consonants because the Latin words from which they are derived have double consonants.

ENGLISH WORD	LATIN WORD
occupy	occupāre (2 *c*'s)
difficulty	difficultās (2 *f*'s)
belligerent	bellum (2 *l*'s)
summit	summus (2 *m*'s)
current	currere (2 *r*'s)

Note

An English word that would normally be spelled with a double consonant (because of the Latin) generally drops one at the end of the word. For example:

Latin **mittere** gives us *remittance,* but *remit.*
2 *t*'s   2 *t*'s   1 *t*

Latin **currere** gives us *concurrent,* but *concur.*
2 *r*'s   2 *r*'s   1 *r*

EXERCISES

A. Below appear ten Latin words whose stems are the source of many English words. With the help of these stems write the correct spelling of the English words that fit the definitions.

EXAMPLE: lēx   (pertaining to the law)   legal
_____

1. mēns   (pertaining to the mind)   _____

2. tempus   (for the time being)   _____

3. genus   (opposite of specific)   _____

4. vulnus   (able to be wounded)   _____

5. caput   (chief city)   _____

6. corpus   (pertaining to the body)   _____

7. iter   (route of a trip)   _____

8. latus   (coming from the side)   _____

9. pōns   (bridge of boats)   _____

10. salūs   (pertaining to health)   _____

B. Paying close attention to Latin stems, complete the spelling of the following English words by underlining the correct missing letter or letters in parentheses:

1. audi—ion (s, t)
2. laud—ble (a, i)
3. recipi—nt (a, e)
4. port—ble (a, i)
5. arbitra—ion (s, t)
6. permi—ion (s, ss)
7. persua—ion (s, t)
8. cog—nt (a, e)
9. la—itude (t, tt)
10. invinc—ble (a, i)
11. peti—ion (s, t)
12. admir—ble (a, i)
13. convic—ion (s, t)
14. compon—nt (a, e)
15. ingredi—nt (a, e)
16. incred—ble (a, i)
17. vi—ion (s, ss)
18. po—ible (s, ss)
19. co—odious (m, mm)
20. perman—nt (a, e)
21. compa—ion (s, ss)
22. infi—ite (n, nn)
23. di—iculty (f, ff)
24. tradi—ion (s, t)
25. egre— (s, ss)

26. co—it (m, mm)
27. cu—ent (r, rr)
28. sep—rate (a, e)
29. ma—ual (n, nn)
30. nu—ify (l, ll)
31. incorp—rate (e, o)
32. mil—tary (e, i)
33. lib—ary (r, er)
34. vo—ition (l, ll)
35. oppre—ive (s, ss)
36. a—ressive (g, gg)
37. admoni—ion (s, t)
38. su—it (m, mm)
39. incompar—ble (a, i)
40. bia—ual (n, nn)
41. rever—nt (a, e)
42. a—ien (l, ll)
43. di—imilar (s, ss)
44. alt—rnate (a, e)
45. repugn—nt (a, e)
46. princ—ple (e, i)
47. insuper—ble (a, e)
48. co—oquial (l, ll)
49. tim—rous (e, o)
50. nasc—nt (a, e)

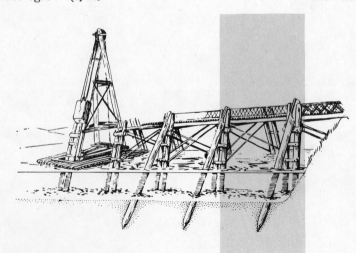

Bridging the Rhine

In 55 B.C., Caesar decided to invade Germany by building a bridge over the wide and swift river Rhine. The bridge, a marvel of engineering skill, was made entirely of wood and completed within ten days. In Book IV of the *Gallic War*, Caesar gives a full description of the bridge, enabling us today to reproduce it in miniature.

Lesson 85—REVIEW OF DERIVATION AND WORD STUDY

A. In the space *before* each word in column *A*, write the letter of its definition in column *B*. Then in the space *after* each word in column *A*, give a Latin word associated with it by derivation.

Column A

------ **1.** elucidate   ----------------------------

------ **2.** malediction   ----------------------------

------ **3.** incredible   ----------------------------

------ **4.** belligerent   ----------------------------

------ **5.** appellation   ----------------------------

------ **6.** veracity   ----------------------------

------ **7.** salutary   ----------------------------

------ **8.** somnolent   ----------------------------

------ **9.** diminutive   ----------------------------

------ **10.** decapitate   ----------------------------

------ **11.** audacity   ----------------------------

------ **12.** laudable   ----------------------------

------ **13.** loquacious   ----------------------------

------ **14.** perturbation   ----------------------------

------ **15.** sedentary   ----------------------------

------ **16.** tenacious   ----------------------------

------ **17.** copious   ----------------------------

------ **18.** docile   ----------------------------

------ **19.** puerile   ----------------------------

------ **20.** nullity   ----------------------------

Column B

a. warlike

b. praiseworthy

c. truthfulness

d. constantly sitting

e. of small size

f. make clear

g. boldness

h. disturbance

i. abundant

j. curse

k. childish

l. holding fast

m. name

n. easily taught

o. talkative

p. sleepy

q. nothingness

r. unbelievable

s. behead

t. healthful

B. Following each Latin word are four English words, of which three are derivatives. Draw a line through the one that does *not* belong in each group.

1. *premō:*   premise, oppress, compression, pressure

2. *medius:*   medium, medieval, meditate, mediate

3. *ūtor:*   utilize, utility, utopia, utensil

4. *veniō:*   convene, veneer, advent, prevention

5. *alius:*   alien, alibi, alias, alive

6. *valeō:*   valise, valid, valiant, invalid

7. *locō:*   locate, local, elocution, dislocation

8. *sequor:*   sequence, consequently, consecutive, section

9. *ōrō:*   oration, orator, ore, oratory

10. *integer:*   integrate, interchange, integrity, disintegrate

11. *mīror:*   mire, admire, miracle, mirage

12. *volō:*   volume, volunteer, volition, voluntary

13. *minor:*   diminish, minus, miner, minute

14. *ūnus:*   unify, unit, union, uneven

15. *ferō:*   infer, conference, ferocious, transfer

C. Underline the Latin word with which each of the following English words is associated by derivation:

1. INFINITE
   īnferō, fīnis, fīrmus

2. DEPOSE
   pōnō, dēspērō, possum

3. IMPEDIMENT
   pēs, impellō, imperium

4. ADMONITION
   adventus, mūniō, moneō

5. CONSECUTIVELY
   cōnsistō, sequor, cōnspiciō

6. IMPERTURBABLE
   turbō, impetus, importō

7. PARRICIDE
   caedō, cadō, parō

8. SINECURE
   sinister, cūrō, currō

9. INADVERTENT
   adventus, vertō, ineō

10. PERFIDIOUS
   perficiō, fīō, fidēs

D. Each of the following English words contains within it a complete Latin word. Find the Latin word and give its meaning.

	LATIN WORD	MEANING
1. bilingual		
2. effeminate		
3. repugnant		
4. subterranean		
5. disparity		
6. annihilate		
7. redundant		
8. ameliorate		
9. confabulation		
10. exacerbate		

E. Underline the correct meaning in parentheses of each of the capitalized English words, and give a Latin word associated with it by derivation.

1. (neat, active, watchful)   VIGILANT   ----------------

2. (destroy, invest, occupy)   DEVASTATE   ----------------

3. (wealthy, sharp, stingy)   ACRIMONIOUS   ----------------

4. (daring, proud, helping)   AUXILIARY   ----------------

5. (supply, fat, dead)   CORPULENT   ....

6. (delay, cemetery, debt)   MORATORIUM   ....

7. (sleeping, suffering, constant)   DORMANT   ....

8. (name, opening, approach)   APERTURE   ....

9. (stopping, size, fewness)   PAUCITY   ....

10. (wordiness, bitterness, readiness)   VERBOSITY   ....

F. Each of the following English words is formed from two Latin words. Write the Latin words and their meanings.

	LATIN WORD	MEANING	LATIN WORD	MEANING
1. cornucopia	....	....	....	....
2. sinecure	....	....	....	....
3. equanimity	....	....	....	....
4. regicide	....	....	....	....
5. omniscient	....	....	....	....
6. soliloquy	....	....	....	....
7. facsimile	....	....	....	....
8. somnambulist	....	....	....	....
9. vociferous	....	....	....	....
10. unilateral	....	....	....	....

G. Show your knowledge of the influence of Latin on English by completing each of the following statements. Your answers should explain the italicized words.

1. We employed a *domestic* in our ....

2. By *alleviating* the burden, he made it ....

3. My *maternal* uncle is related to me on my ....'s side.

4. An *equestrian* travels on a ....

5. The *decimal* system is based on the number ....

6. A *peninsula* is almost an ....

7. A *scribe* is a person skilled in ....

8. .... are trained in *nautical* matters.

9. *Aquatic* sports are practiced in ....

10. A *regal* palace is the home of a ....

11. The group called itself a *fraternity* because its members acted like ....

12. By stepping on the *accelerator* he made the car go ....

13. The *debit* side of a ledger shows how much money one ....

14. By traveling *incognito* his identity was ....

15. A *demonstrative* adjective is so called because it ....

16. During the .... months, some animals go into *hibernation*.

17. His tale was so *incredible* that no one _____ him.

18. With their *liberation* the slaves finally became _____.

19. An *incipient* case of pneumonia, being in its _____ stage, can more easily be cured.

20. The manuscript was so *illegible* that no one could _____ it.

21. An *equilateral* triangle has sides which are _____.

22. His *nocturnal* stroll lasted late into the _____.

23. She displayed such *fortitude* that people admired her for her _____.

24. *Manual* labor requires the use of one's _____.

25. His *pugnacity* gave him many opportunities to _____.

H. Each of the following English words is composed of a Latin root, a prefix, and a suffix. In the appropriate columns fill in the various elements with their meanings.

	ROOT	PREFIX	SUFFIX
1. insuperable	_____	_____	_____
2. premonition	_____	_____	_____
3. quadrilateral	_____	_____	_____
4. inundation	_____	_____	_____
5. benefactor	_____	_____	_____
6. intramural	_____	_____	_____
7. sublunary	_____	_____	_____
8. pellucid	_____	_____	_____
9. impecunious	_____	_____	_____
10. concupiscence	_____	_____	_____

I. For each of the following sentences, (*a*) write a Latin word with which the italicized word is associated by derivation, and (*b*) underline the word or expression in the accompanying list that best expresses the meaning of the italicized word.

1. The *conservation* of natural resources is important. _____
   (*a*) increase   (*b*) limitation   (*c*) protection   (*d*) loss

2. The government *initiated* a public works program. _____
   (*a*) began   (*b*) vetoed   (*c*) protested   (*d*) voted

3. The firm *interrogated* the applicant. _____
   (*a*) hired   (*b*) questioned   (*c*) investigated   (*d*) trained

4. The United States made a *unilateral* decision. _____
   (*a*) far-reaching   (*b*) limited   (*c*) sound   (*d*) one-sided

5. She had a *doleful* experience. _____
   (*a*) happy   (*b*) sad   (*c*) thrilling   (*d*) rewarding

6. We questioned the *legality* of the award. _____
   (*a*) handling   (*b*) lawfulness   (*c*) purpose   (*d*) value

7. He lived a *solitary* existence. _____
   (*a*) lonely   (*b*) miserly   (*c*) comfortable   (*d*) depressed

8. Alice displayed *sororal* hatred. _____
   (*a*) deep-seated   (*b*) rare   (*c*) cruel   (*d*) sisterly

9. In one *quinquennial* period the birth rate fell sharply. _____
   (*a*) 4-year   (*b*) 3-year   (*c*) 5-year   (*d*) 9-year

10. The senior *immured* himself for study. _____
    (*a*) braced   (*b*) confined   (*c*) prepared   (*d*) withdrew

11. They sought *refuge* in the attic. _____
    (*a*) comfort   (*b*) lost articles   (*c*) help   (*d*) shelter

12. Some people believe in *corporal* punishment. _____
    (*a*) bodily   (*b*) military   (*c*) total   (*d*) positive

13. By his methods the politician *alienated* the people. _____
    (*a*) won over   (*b*) controlled   (*c*) defended   (*d*) estranged

14. The *gravity* of the situation impressed all. _____
    (*a*) humor   (*b*) complexity   (*c*) seriousness   (*d*) delicateness

15. He found a way to *augment* his income. _____
    (*a*) increase   (*b*) distribute   (*c*) share   (*d*) invest

16. The character in the novel had an *aversion* to labor. _____
    (*a*) fancy   (*b*) dislike   (*c*) disregard   (*d*) aptitude

17. As the lecturer spoke, some students took *copious* notes. _____
    (*a*) few   (*b*) important   (*c*) selective   (*d*) many

18. His *irate* manner betrayed his feelings. _____
    (*a*) calm   (*b*) outward   (*c*) angry   (*d*) deliberate

19. The many details lent *credibility* to the story. _____
    (*a*) proof   (*b*) believability   (*c*) color   (*d*) background

20. His manner of speaking was *grandiloquent*. _____
    (*a*) high-sounding   (*b*) soft   (*c*) careful   (*d*) studious

21. Why does he *minimize* the danger? _____
    (*a*) exaggerate   (*b*) emphasize   (*c*) underestimate   (*d*) reveal

22. They were determined to *invalidate* his claim. _____
    (*a*) weaken   (*b*) yield to   (*c*) support   (*d*) publish

23. The investor knew ways of *circumventing* the law. _____
    (*a*) changing   (*b*) interpreting   (*c*) getting around   (*d*) obeying

24. The speaker made a *perspicacious* remark. _____
    (*a*) stupid   (*b*) clever   (*c*) informative   (*d*) dull

25. He acted in an *imperious* manner. _____
    (*a*) rude   (*b*) persuasive   (*c*) peculiar   (*d*) commanding

26. The island was a *terrestrial* paradise. _____
    (*a*) restful   (*b*) underground   (*c*) earthly   (*d*) frightening

27. They noticed the *aperture* in the ceiling. _____
    (*a*) opening   (*b*) bump   (*c*) design   (*d*) spot

28. The entrance to the cave is *inaccessible*. _____
    (*a*) closed   (*b*) distant   (*c*) tremendous   (*d*) hard to reach

29. They *relinquished* their right to the money. _____
    (*a*) gave up   (*b*) claimed   (*c*) demanded   (*d*) enjoyed

30. He is so *verbose* that he bores me. ------------------------
(*a*) envious   (*b*) vain   (*c*) wordy   (*d*) grammatical

31. Throughout the attack he kept his *equanimity*. ---------------------
(*a*) horse near   (*b*) cheerfulness   (*c*) calm temper   (*d*) fearfulness

32. The parent *admonished* the naughty child. ----------------------
(*a*) scolded   (*b*) beat   (*c*) took the allowance from   (*d*) was ashamed of

33. Please *elucidate* your comments. ----------------------
(*a*) translate   (*b*) summarize   (*c*) crystallize   (*d*) clarify

34. He handles all his dealings with *equity*. ----------------------
(*a*) ease   (*b*) fairness   (*c*) thought   (*d*) skill

35. Exercise in moderation is *salutary*. -----------------------
(*a*) sensible   (*b*) wise   (*c*) healthful   (*d*) advisable

36. The Federal government *subsidizes* farm crops. ---------------------
(*a*) encourages   (*b*) aids with money   (*c*) plants   (*d*) harvests

37. The *magnitude* of the undertaking was overwhelming. -----------------------
(*a*) dullness   (*b*) great size   (*c*) fascination   (*d*) attraction

38. Of which *genus* is that plant? -----------------------
(*a*) kind   (*b*) coloring   (*c*) owner   (*d*) price range

39. The cost of the item is *prohibitive*. ----------------------
(*a*) very little   (*b*) of no importance   (*c*) too high   (*d*) listed

40. The government declared a *moratorium* on debts. ----------------------
(*a*) period of delay   (*b*) additional charge for interest   (*c*) penalty for nonpayment   (*d*) revaluation of losses

41. Joseph is an *impetuous* youth. ----------------------
(*a*) impish   (*b*) athletic   (*c*) affectionate   (*d*) headstrong

42. Don't speak in *circumlocutions*. ----------------------
(*a*) short sentences   (*b*) gesturing fashion   (*c*) roundabout expressions   (*d*) partial sentences

43. She was *vociferous* in her arguments. ----------------------
(*a*) ironic   (*b*) noisy   (*c*) convincing   (*d*) gentle

44. His words were rather *audacious*. ----------------------
(*a*) amusing   (*b*) daring   (*c*) long   (*d*) vulgar

45. Some old *murals* were destroyed by the explosion. ----------------------
(*a*) entrenchments   (*b*) mosaics   (*c*) sculptured works   (*d*) wall paintings

46. The boy's *timidity* was unusual. ----------------------
(*a*) dependability   (*b*) fearfulness   (*c*) generosity   (*d*) loyalty

47. "Shall," "will," and "may" are *auxiliary* verbs. -----------------------
(*a*) compound   (*b*) deponent   (*c*) helping   (*d*) transitive

48. The project required much *collaboration*. ----------------------
(*a*) checking   (*b*) efficiency   (*c*) library research   (*d*) working together

49. In our schools the study of English is *mandatory*. ------------------------
(*a*) neglected   (*b*) optional   (*c*) prolonged   (*d*) required

50. They had hopes of *reversing* the trend of modern German history. -------------------------
(*a*) hastening   (*b*) repeating   (*c*) slowing down   (*d*) turning back

J. Each word in column *A* has both a synonym and an antonym listed in column *B*. In the space before each word in column *A*, write first the letter of its synonym and then the letter of its antonym.

	Column A		Column B
---------	**1.** amīcus	*a.*	magnus
---------	**2.** cupiō	*b.*	interrogō
---------	**3.** amplus	*c.*	post
---------	**4.** quaerō	*d.*	paucī
---------	**5.** virtūs	*e.*	exitus
---------	**6.** ante	*f.*	inimīcus
---------	**7.** multī	*g.*	corpus
---------	**8.** aditus	*h.*	volō
---------	**9.** animus	*i.*	timidus
---------	**10.** fortis	*j.*	parvus
		k.	socius
		l.	mēns
		m.	respondeō
		n.	fortitūdō
		o.	complūrēs
		p.	fīrmus
		q.	adventus
		r.	timor
		s.	nōlō
		t.	prō

K. In each group, complete the second pair of words to make them bear the same relationship as the first pair.

1. *putō* is to *exīstimō* as *locō* is to   ---------------------------

2. *aestās* is to *hiems* as *pāx* is to   ---------------------------

3. *clāmō* is to *clāmor* as *pugnō* is to   ---------------------------

4. *ūllus* is to *nūllus* as *multī* is to   ---------------------------

5. *aequus* is to *pār* as *omnis* is to   ---------------------------

6. *sciō* is to *scientia* as *mūniō* is to   ---------------------------

7. *ante* is to *post* as *cum* is to   ---------------------------

8. *frūmentum* is to *frūmentārius* as *mare* is to   ---------------------------

9. *facilis* is to *difficilis* as *levis* is to   ---------------------------

10. *imperō* is to *iubeō* as *cupiō* is to   ---------------------------

Unit XV—Roman Civilization and Culture

Lesson 86—THE LIFE OF JULIUS CAESAR

SIGNIFICANT EVENTS

BIRTH

Gaius Julius Caesar was born on July 12, 100 B.C., the only son of a distinguished patrician family in Rome. Caesar traced his ancestry back to Iulus, son of the Trojan hero Aeneas, who in turn was reputed to have been the son of the goddess Venus.

EDUCATION

Caesar's early education was similar to that of other young Roman aristocrats. He received instruction, both in school and privately at home, in grammar, rhetoric, oratory, philosophy, literature, music, and Greek. Later, as a young man, to perfect himself in oratory, he traveled to the island of Rhodes to study under the celebrated teacher, Apollonius Molo. He was then prepared for the only career suitable for a young patrician, namely, service to the Republic, either through public office or the military.

PRIVATE LIFE

In 83 B.C. Caesar married Cornelia, the daughter of Cinna, who was one of the leaders of the popular, or democratic, party. They had one daughter, Julia, who later became the wife of Pompey. In 67 B.C. Cornelia died, and Caesar married Pompeia, a cousin of Pompey. This marriage ended in divorce a few years later, and in 59 B.C. Caesar entered into his final marriage, with Calpurnia, daughter of Lucius Piso.

POLITICAL CAREER

The two dominant political parties in Rome in Caesar's time were the **Optimātēs** (the aristocratic party) and the **Populārēs** (the popular, or democratic, party). The Optimātēs, under the leadership of Sulla, wanted power kept in the hands of the Senate. The Populārēs, led by Marius, championed the rights of the common people. Though aristocratic by birth, Caesar nevertheless joined the Populārēs and thus incurred the anger of Sulla.

In 68 B.C., by being elected **quaestor,** Caesar started on the **cursus honōrum,** a series of political offices leading to the consulship. In 62 B.C. he became **praetor,** and in 59 B.C. was elected **consul.** As quaestor he was sent to Spain, where he attended to the financial duties of that office. As praetor he presided as judge over a Roman court.

Between the time that he was quaestor and the time that he was consul, Caesar held several other important positions. In 65 B.C., as **aedile,** he was in charge of public games and amusements. Although not a requirement in the cursus honōrum, the aedileship nevertheless gave Caesar an opportunity to bestow favors on the people and thus win them over to his political side. His lavish personal spending on festivals and games brought him heavily into debt, and forced him to borrow money from Crassus, then the wealthiest man in Rome.

In 63 B.C. Caesar was appointed to the lifetime post of **pontifex maximus,** the head of the Roman state religion. This was chiefly an honorary position. Finally, in 61 B.C., he held the office of **propraetor** (governor) in Spain, where he demonstrated his administrative and military ability.

On his return from Spain in 60 B.C., Caesar, together with Pompey and Crassus, entered into a political alliance known as the **First Triumvirate,** or three-man rule. The aim was to gain control of the government. Caesar furnished political experience, Pompey military prestige, and Crassus his wealth. Through the influence of the Triumvirate, Caesar became **proconsul** (governor) of Gaul in 58 B.C., a position that he held for ten years.

ITALIA, c. 200 B.C.

100 MILES

MILITARY CAREER

Caesar began his military career in 81 B.C. as a soldier in the war against Mithridates, King of Pontus, in Asia Minor. It was during this campaign that he won the **corōna cīvica** (civic crown) for saving the life of a fellow citizen in battle. In 74 B.C., as **military tribune,** he assisted in overthrowing Sulla's constitution.

It was while governor of Gaul that Caesar made military history destined to rank him among the greatest generals of all time. As proconsul of Cisalpine Gaul, Transalpine Gaul, and Illyricum, Caesar had no legal right to exercise his power outside the boundaries of these provinces. However, on the ground that the Gallic migrations—that started when he arrived in Gaul—would eventually become a threat to the provinces and to Rome itself, Caesar acted swiftly and decisively, and fought the Gauls with consummate generalship. In seven years of the **Gallic War,** he completed the conquest of Gaul, Romanized the region, and invaded Germany and Britain.

The **Civil War** was the next important episode in Caesar's exploits as a general. With the death of Crassus in 53 B.C., and a cooling of relations between Caesar and Pompey, the Triumvirate had come to a virtual end. Pompey began to view Caesar's successes in the field with distrust and alarm. In 49 B.C. war broke out between these two mighty leaders, and once again Caesar displayed his military genius, this time fighting against Roman generals. Pompey was defeated at **Pharsalus** in Greece in 48 B.C., and fled to Egypt where he was murdered.

The next war that occupied Caesar's time was called the **Alexandrine War,** in which Caesar supported the claims of Cleopatra to rule in common with her brother Ptolemy. This war ended victoriously for Caesar in 47 B.C.

Other famous military successes of Caesar were:

1. The **Battle of Zela** in 47 B.C. in Pontus, an area in Asia Minor, where Caesar easily defeated King Pharnaces.

2. The **Battle of Thapsus** in north Africa, 46 B.C., where Caesar won a complete victory over the remnants of the Pompeian forces.

3. The **Battle of Munda** in Spain, 45 B.C., where Caesar annihilated the army commanded by the sons of Pompey.

LAST DAYS AND DEATH

By 45 B.C. Caesar was undisputed master of the Roman world, and the Senate, whose members were now mainly of his own choosing, conferred many honors upon him. He became **Dictator** for life (a title heretofore bestowed in times of emergency for a six-month period) and **Imperātor** (the origin of the word *emperor*).

With so much authority centered in one man, it was inevitable that some influential Romans, moved by envy and fear, would form an opposition. On the Ides of March (March 15), 44 B.C., while presiding over a meeting of the Senate, Caesar was assassinated by a group of Roman citizens headed by Cassius and Brutus.

ANECDOTES ABOUT CAESAR

CAESAR AND SULLA

When Caesar married Cornelia (whose father was a leader of the Populārēs) in 83 B.C., he was threatened with death by the dictator Sulla unless he divorced her. Caesar refused and fled from Rome, but was later pardoned. However, Sulla, suspicious of Caesar whose uncle was Sulla's archfoe Marius, said of Caesar, "I see in him many a Marius."

CAESAR AND THE PIRATES

On his way to Rhodes in 76 B.C., Caesar was captured by pirates and held for ransom. While a prisoner he vowed that he would return some day and crucify them. The pirates laughed at what they considered a huge joke. Shortly after his release, Caesar manned some vessels, overpowered the pirates, and, true to his word, had them crucified.

CAESAR AND BIBULUS

When Caesar was consul in 59 B.C., his colleague in office was Marcus Bibulus. Bibulus was a very weak executive, compared to the towering Caesar, and made vain attempts to oppose him. Bibulus was content to shut himself up in his house and was so rarely seen in public that the term of office came to be jokingly known as the consulship of Julius and Caesar.

ĀLEA IACTA EST

After the successful conclusion of the Gallic War in 49 B.C., Caesar was ready to return to Rome as a victorious general. The Senate, however, first ordered him to give up command of his army. Realizing that he had many enemies back home, and that without an army he was defenseless, Caesar defied the Senate, crossed the **Rubicon,** a small stream separating his province from Italy, and began his march to Rome. The famous words he uttered at the time, **"Ālea iacta est"** (The die is cast), signified that he had made his decision and that there was no turning back.

VĒNĪ, VĪDĪ, VĪCĪ

On his way home from the East in 47 B.C., Caesar attacked Pharnaces, King of Pontus, and defeated him in the Battle of Zela with such ease that he informed the Roman Senate of his victory with the words, **"Vēnī, vīdī, vīcī"** (I came, I saw, I conquered).

ET TŪ, BRŪTE!

On the Ides of March (March 15), 44 B.C., Caesar was stabbed to death by a group of conspirators. Among them was Marcus Brutus, who had lived with him on terms of the most intimate friendship. When Caesar saw his close friend with dagger in hand, he is said to have exclaimed, **"Et tū, Brūte!"** (Even you, Brutus!)

PERSONAL CHARACTERISTICS

Physically, Caesar was tall and of commanding presence. He was bald in his later years and was so sensitive to this condition that he usually wore a laurel crown to conceal his baldness. He displayed astonishing powers of endurance and, by example, inspired his men to feats of heroism. He was a strict, though fair, disciplinarian and won the loyalty of his soldiers.

Brilliant in mind, swift in action, cool and resourceful in times of crisis—these were some of the qualities that made Caesar invincible. To balance the picture, he was considered overambitious, cruel in war, and unscrupulous in politics.

ACCOMPLISHMENTS AND INFLUENCE

Caesar is considered by many the greatest Roman of them all, by some "the most complete man." History ranks him as one of the most outstanding men because of the far-reaching influence of his achievements. These achievements were:

MILITARY AFFAIRS

Caesar was a military genius, on a par with Alexander the Great, Scipio, Hannibal, and Napoleon. A master strategist, he was expert at moving large forces rapidly. He believed in taking the offensive and in using the surprise attack. He extended the Roman Empire by his conquest of Gaul, invasions of Britain and Germany, and successes in the East. His military achievements freed Rome from the fear of aggression for centuries.

STATESMANSHIP

As a statesman Caesar's name looms large in the history of Rome. After peace had been established, Caesar set himself the task of completely reorganizing the Roman state and its administration. He aimed at an efficient and stabilized central government, ruling over Italy and the provinces. He improved the legal system and began codification of the laws. He revised the method of taxation, established a program of public works, initiated a building campaign to beautify Rome, and planned an extensive highway system. Unfortunately, death prevented the completion of all these projects.

As pontifex maximus Caesar undertook the long overdue reform of the calendar, introducing a solar year of 365 days (the Julian calendar). He was subsequently honored when the month of his birth, Quīnctīlis, was changed to July, after Julius. (Later the Emperor Augustus was given a similar honor when the month Sextīlis was changed to August.) The name *Caesar* also survives in the titles of recent monarchs, *Kaiser* in Germany and *Czar* in Russia.

LITERATURE

Caesar's writings, most of which have been lost, covered a wide range of subjects. These included works on grammar, astronomy, philosophy, and poetry. It is in the field of history, however, that Caesar is best known. His *Commentaries on the Gallic War* furnish important information not only on the wars themselves, but on the geography of western Europe, and the economy, government, religion, and customs of the people living there. Caesar also wrote *Commentaries on the Civil War*. Both accounts were written in a simple, clear, vivid style and have served as models of military histories.

ORATORY

As an orator Caesar ranked next to Cicero, the most eloquent of all Romans. Unfortunately, Caesar's orations have disappeared, but Cicero himself described them as remarkably logical, lucid, and persuasive.

CHRONOLOGY OF IMPORTANT EVENTS IN CAESAR'S LIFE

B.C.

100   Born July 12, in Rome.

83   Married Cornelia, daughter of Cinna, one of the leaders of the popular party **(Populārēs).**

82   Incurred the enmity of Sulla, leader of the senatorial party **(Optimātēs),** for refusing to divorce Cornelia.

81   Fled to Asia Minor, where he served in the war against Mithridates.

80   Awarded the civic crown **(corōna cīvica)** for saving the life of a fellow citizen in battle.

76   Studied oratory at Rhodes under Apollonius Molo. On the way he was captured by pirates, and later released.

74   Military tribune.

68   Quaestor in Spain.

67   Death of Cornelia; Caesar married Pompeia.

65   Aedile.

63   Pontifex maximus.

62   Praetor; divorced Pompeia.

61   Propraetor (governor) in Spain.

60   First Triumvirate (Caesar, Pompey, and Crassus).

59   Consul with Bibulus; married Calpurnia; Caesar gave his daughter Julia in marriage to Pompey.

58–49   Proconsul (governor) of Cisalpine and Transalpine Gaul and Illyricum.

58   Defeated the Helevetians and Ariovistus, German leader.

57   Conquered the Belgians.

56   Conquered the Veneti in a naval campaign.

55   First invasions of Germany and Britain.

54   Second invasion of Britain; death of Julia.

53   Second invasion of Germany; end of the Triumvirate.

52   Surrender of the Gauls under Vercingetorix; fall of Alesia.

49   Caesar crossed the Rubicon; **"Ālea iacta est"** (The die is cast); civil war between Caesar and Pompey.

48   Consul second time; Pompey defeated at Pharsalus, Greece.

47   Defeated Ptolemy, King of Egypt; conquered the country of Pontus in Asia Minor and reported the victory with the words **"Vēnī, vīdī, vīcī."**

46   Consul third time.

45   Dictator for life.

44   Assassinated on the Ides of March (March 15).

EXERCISES

A. In the space before each item in column *A*, write the letter of the matching item in column *B*.

	Column A	Column B
------	**1.** Civil War	*a.* Caesar's teacher
------	**2.** Marius	*b.* leader of the Optimātēs
------	**3.** Apollonius Molo	*c.* Spain, 45 B.C.
------	**4.** Cornelia	*d.* Caesar and Bibulus
------	**5.** Battle of Thapsus	*e.* Caesar's uncle
------	**6.** consulship	*f.* Caesar's final marriage
------	**7.** Sulla	*g.* wealthy Roman
------	**8.** Calpurnia	*h.* Caesar and Pompey
------	**9.** Battle of Munda	*i.* Africa, 46 B.C.
------	**10.** Crassus	*j.* Caesar's first marriage

B. If the italicized term in each of the following statements is correct, write *true*. If the italicized term is incorrect, write the correct term.

1. Caesar's final marriage was with *Calpurnia*.   _____

2. Caesar was assassinated on the Ides of March, *44* B.C.   _____

3. *Mithridates* was defeated by Caesar at Pharsalus, Greece.   _____

4. Cicero attested to Caesar's achievements in *philosophy*.   _____

5. Caesar traced his ancestry back to the goddess *Venus*.   _____

6. By allying himself with the *Optimātēs*, Caesar angered Sulla.   _____

7. Caesar held the position of *propraetor* of Gaul for ten years.   _____

8. Caesar won the *corōna cīvica* for saving a fellow citizen in battle. _____

9. In Egypt Caesar *supported* the claims of Cleopatra.   _____

10. In reforming the calendar, Caesar introduced a *lunar* year of   _____
365 days.

C. Complete the following statements:

1. The First Triumvirate consisted of Caesar, Pompey, and _____.

2. By _____ B.C. Caesar was master of the Roman world.

3. Caesar was once captured and held for ransom by _____.

4. Caesar's name is commemorated by the month of _____.

5. Caesar's daughter _____ became the wife of Pompey.

6. The cursus honōrum consisted of quaestor, _____, and consul.

7. As head of the Roman state religion, Caesar held the office of _____.

8. Caesar was governor of Cisalpine Gaul, _____, and Illyricum.

9. Caesar was assassinated by a group of Roman citizens headed by Cassius and _____.

10. Caesar usually wore a laurel crown to conceal his _____.

D. Indicate the proper chronological sequence of the following events connected with Caesar, by numbering them from 1 to 10:

_____ praetorship   _____ defeat of Pompey

_____ fall of Alesia   _____ consulship with Bibulus

_____ First Triumvirate   _____ invasion of Britain

_____ aedileship   _____ war with the Helvetians

_____ fought against Mithridates   _____ quaestorship in Spain

E. Underline the word or expression in parentheses that will complete the statement correctly.

1. The saying "Ālea iacta est" is associated with the (Battle of Thapsus, crossing of the Rubicon, Alexandrine War, invasion of Germany).

2. As aedile Caesar was concerned with (public games, the courts, the treasury, religion).

3. In the First Triumvirate Pompey furnished (money, political experience, oratorical ability, military prestige).

4. Caesar completed the conquest of Gaul in (3, 5, 7, 10) years.

5. Civil war between Caesar and Pompey broke out in (51, 49, 47, 45) B.C.

6. The sons of Pompey were decisively beaten in the Battle of (Munda, Thapsus, Zela, Pharsalus).

7. Caesar's victory over Pharnaces, King of Pontus, was proclaimed with the words ("Excelsior"; "Vēnī, vīdī, vīcī"; "Ē plūribus ūnum"; "Et tū, Brūte!").

8. The term of office known as "the consulship of Julius and Caesar" was so called in derision of (Crassus, Brutus, Cassius, Bibulus).

9. Caesar served in Spain in the capacities of quaestor and (praetor, propraetor, consul, proconsul).

10. Caesar studied oratory in (Spain, Gaul, Rhodes, Asia Minor).

Diana, identified by the Romans with the Greek Artemis, was the goddess of the chase and the moon. As a huntress, she carries a bow, quiver, and arrows. As the goddess of the moon, she wears a long robe reaching down to her feet. A veil covers her head, and above her forehead rises the crescent of the moon.

Lesson 87—THE ROMAN ART OF WAR

ARMY UNITS

A. ROMAN LEGIONARY SOLDIERS

These were the **peditēs** (infantry) who formed the backbone of the Roman army. This group consisted of Roman citizens between the ages of seventeen and forty-six, most of whom volunteered to serve for twenty years as professional soldiers. Infantry units were organized as follows:

1. **legiō** (legion), the largest unit, often compared to a division or brigade in the United States Army. Originally consisting of 6000 men, the legion in Caesar's army averaged 3600 men, divided into ten cohorts. In the Gallic War Caesar had as many as ten legions. His favorite one was the Tenth (Decima), commanded by Labienus.

2. **cohors** (cohort), a tenth of a legion, or 360 men, divided into three maniples. A cohort is roughly the equivalent of a battalion in the United States Army.

3. **manipulus** (maniple), a third of a cohort, or 120 men, divided into two centuries.

4. **centuria** (century), the smallest unit. It consisted of 60 men, or one-half of a maniple. As the name implies, it originally had 100 men.

B. AUXILIA (AUXILIARY TROOPS)

Peditēs (infantry troops). These were soldiers drawn from allied and subject peoples, or hired as mercenaries from independent nations. They included:

1. **levis armātūrae peditēs** (light-armed foot soldiers), mostly from Gaul and Germany.

2. **funditōrēs** (slingers), from the Balearic Islands.

3. **sagittāriī** (bowmen or archers), from Crete and Numidia.

Equitēs (cavalry). A contingent of cavalry generally accompanied each legion. These horsemen were noncitizens from Gaul, Spain, and Germany who served for pay. Caesar used about four or five thousand cavalry in the Gallic War for purposes of scouting, starting battle, and pursuing the enemy, as well as for surprise attacks. The cavalry was organized as follows:

1. **āla**, a squad of about 300 men.

2. **turma**, a squad of about 30 men, or one tenth of an āla.

3. **decuria**, a squad of 10 men, or one-third of a turma.

C. NONCOMBATANTS

1. **cālōnēs**, slaves who performed menial tasks for the camp and the officers.

2. **mercātōrēs**, traders who conducted canteens outside the camp, selling the soldiers extra provisions and buying booty from them.

3. **mūliōnēs**, muleteers who took care of the pack animals and the heavy baggage.

4. **fabrī**, engineers or mechanics who were employed to construct bridges, ships, engines of war, etc.

5. **explōrātōrēs** (scouts) and **speculātōrēs** (spies) who were sent ahead of an army on the march to reconnoiter and secure information about the enemy and the terrain. They were usually mounted.

ARMY OFFICERS

1. **Dux** (commanding officer or general). After his first important victory he had a right to the title **imperātor** (commander-in-chief). Caesar used the title imperātor from the time he defeated the Helvetians in 58 B.C. until his death.

2. **Lēgātī** (staff officers). The lēgātus was next in rank to the dux, equivalent to the lieutenant-general in the United States Army. Lēgātī were men of senatorial rank appointed by the Roman Senate. Their duties were to command one or more legions, to advise the general, to serve as envoys or ambassadors on special missions, and to be in charge of **hīberna** (winter quarters).

3. **Quaestōrēs** (quartermasters). They were also of senatorial rank, elected for one year by the Roman people. The quaestors handled pay, military equipment, and the food supply. Sometimes a quaestor commanded a legion in battle.

4. **Tribūnī mīlitum** (military tribunes). They were the lowest-ranking commissioned officers, and numbered six to a legion. They were men of good families, without previous military experience, who gained appointment for political or personal reasons. Their duties included: command of a legion in camp or on the march, supervision of drill exercises, and muster and discharge of soldiers.

5. **Centuriōnēs** (centurions or captains). They were noncommissioned officers of plebeian origin, equivalent in rank to sergeants in the United States Army. Unlike military tribunes, centurions were experienced soldiers who rose from the ranks by virtue of courage and ability on the battlefield. There was one centurion in each century, and sixty in a legion.

6. **Praefectī** (prefects). They were in command of the auxiliaries of cavalry.

7. **Decuriōnēs** (decurions). They were in command of the decuriae.

EQUIPMENT OF THE LEGIONARY

CLOTHING

1. **tunica** (tunic), a short-sleeved woolen undergarment, reaching almost to the knees.

2. **sagum,** a woolen cloak for severe weather, which could also serve as a blanket.

3. **caligae,** leather shoes with heavy hobnailed soles, fastened on by straps.

DEFENSIVE ARMOR

1. **lōrīca,** a cuirass, or breastplate, made of leather and strengthened with metal bands.

2. **galea,** a helmet, made of leather or metal, often ornamented with a crest.

3. **scūtum,** a curved, rectangular shield, made of wood. It was strengthened with leather on the outside and with a rim of metal at the edges. It was about 4 feet long and 2½ feet wide, and weighed about 20 pounds.

OFFENSIVE WEAPONS

1. **pīlum,** a javelin, or pike, about 6 feet long, weighing approximately 10 pounds. It consisted of two parts, a wooden shaft about 4 feet long, into which was fitted a 2-foot iron shaft with pointed head. A pīlum could be hurled a distance of about 75 feet with deadly effect.

2. **gladius,** a heavy, pointed, two-edged sword, about 2 feet long. It was used in close combat and was very effective for stabbing.

PROVISIONS AND PAY

Frūmentum (grain) was the main food ration of the legionary. It consisted mostly of wheat, which the soldier ground in a hand mill for making bread or cereal. About thirty pounds of frūmentum were portioned out every fifteen days. Thus, a soldier consumed about two pounds a day. This diet was supplemented with meat and vegetables.

Army pay was very small, equivalent to about $45 a year. However, a soldier could increase his income by receiving bonuses, gifts of money, and a share of the booty **(praeda).**

MILITARY STANDARDS

1. **aquila** (eagle), the standard of the legion. It was made of silver or bronze, mounted on a pole, and carried by the eagle-bearer, the **aquilifer.** The loss of the eagle was considered a catastrophe.

2. **signum,** the standard of the cohort or maniple, also mounted on a pole. Its bearer was called the **signifer.**

3. **vexillum,** a rectangular banner or flag, attached to a staff. Vexilla served as standards for the auxiliaries. A red vexillum over the commander's tent was the signal to prepare for battle.

BATTLE FORMATION

The usual battle formation of a Roman legion (10 cohorts) was the **aciēs triplex** (triple line), arranged as follows:

1. **prīma aciēs** (first line), consisting of 4 cohorts of experienced soldiers. These were the first to engage in battle.

2. **secunda aciēs** (second line), consisting of 3 cohorts stationed about 150 feet behind the first line. Their duty was to relieve the wounded or fallen soldiers of the first line.

3. **tertia aciēs** (third line), consisting of the remaining 3 cohorts stationed farther back. They were used as a reserve and as a defense against an attack from the rear.

To give signals in battle, the Romans used the following:

1. **tuba** (trumpet), a straight instrument, about three feet long, made of metal.

2. **cornū** (horn), a large curved instrument, also made of metal.

MARCHING FORMATION

The army on the march comprised three sections:

1. **prīmum agmen,** the vanguard, consisting of scouts, cavalry squads, and light-armed infantrymen.

2. **agmen,** the main column of legionary troops.

3. **novissimum agmen,** the rear guard, consisting of the least experienced legionaries.

The **impedīmenta** (heavy baggage) usually followed each legion. It was carried on pack animals (horses and mules) or in wagons, and consisted of extra weapons, food, clothing, artillery, tools, tents, etc.

The **sarcina** (personal pack of a soldier) was carried over the left shoulder in a bundle tied to a forked pole. It contained clothing, cooking utensils, rations, tools, rampart stakes, and other personal equipment. When carrying his sarcina, the soldier was referred to as **impedītus** (encumbered); without his pack, he was **expedītus** (unencumbered).

An average day's march **(iter),** from sunrise to noon, covered about 15 miles. An **iter magnum** (forced march) covered approximately 25 miles.

THE ROMAN CAMP

The **castra** (camp) was built after a day's march as a protection and place of retreat. The location, selected by an advance party, was preferably on the slope of a hill, near an ample supply of wood and water. The camp, usually in the shape of a rectangle, had two **viae prīncipālēs** (main streets) at right angles to each other. At opposite ends of each street were **portae** (gates), four in all.

In the fortification of a castra, the following terms were used:

1. **fossa,** a ditch or trench dug around the camp, from 7 to 10 feet deep and from 12 to 18 feet wide.

2. **agger,** an embankment constructed from the earth of the fossa, about 10 feet high and 10 feet wide, surrounding the entire camp.

3. **vāllum** (rampart), the entire defensive wall, composed of the agger and a row of strong wooden stakes or palisades firmly driven in at the outer edge of the agger.

4. **praetōrium,** the general's tent or quarters, situated near the middle of the camp.

5. **tabernācula,** the tents of the soldiers, made of leather. Each tabernāculum was occupied by ten men.

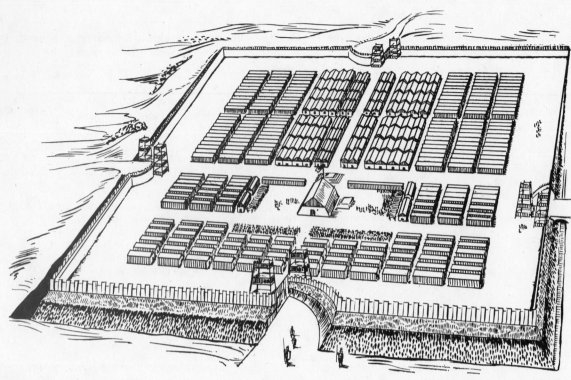

Castra

The camp was carefully guarded by sentries day and night. For patrols the night was divided into four **vigiliae** (watches), from sunset to sunrise. Watches lasted three hours each, and were distributed as follows:

1. **prīma vigilia** (first watch): from 6 p.m. to 9 p.m.

2. **secunda vigilia** (second watch): from 9 p.m. to 12 midnight.

3. **tertia vigilia** (third watch): from 12 midnight to 3 a.m.

4. **quarta vigilia** (fourth watch): from 3 a.m. to 6 a.m.

Many a Roman camp often became the center around which a permanent settlement sprang up. Thus, the word **castra** survives today, in one form or another, in names of English cities. Examples are Chester, Manchester, Lancaster, Worcester, etc.

MILITARY OPERATIONS

An attack (**oppugnātiō**) upon a fortified place, such as a walled town, and a siege (**obsidiō**) involved the following devices and tactics:

1. **agger** (same term used in the construction of a camp), a sloping plane made of earth, stones, and logs, begun at a distance from the enemy's wall, and gradually lengthened and raised until the top was on a level with the top of the wall. The agger was used as a means of approach and for moving up siege machines.

2. **ariēs,** a battering ram made of a heavy log with a metal head, used for battering down the enemy's wall or making a breach in it. The ariēs (literally *ram*) derived its name from the metal head that was usually in the form of a ram's head.

3. **pluteus,** a small, movable, wooden screen, used as a protection for a group of soldiers advancing under attack.

4. **scāla,** a ladder for scaling walls.

5. **testūdō,** a protective screen formed by the overlapping of shields held above the heads of soldiers as they moved forward in close formation. The term was also applied to a wooden shed with a slanting roof, used to cover soldiers near the enemy wall. The testūdō (literally *tortoise*) derived its name from its resemblance to the shell of a tortoise.

6. **turris ambulātōria,** a huge, movable, wooden tower, several stories high, with a platform for the besiegers to reach the top of the enemy wall. The turris, the height of which varied from 50 to 180 feet high, was moved forward on rollers.

7. **vīnea,** a heavy, movable shed, mounted on rollers. Several were often placed together along the agger to protect the men fighting close to the walls of the enemy. The vīnea (literally *vineyard*) derived its name from its resemblance to a grape arbor.

In storming a town the Romans made use of **tormenta** (artillery), of which there were three common types:

1. **ballista,** a machine for hurling heavy stones and blocks of wood.

2. **catapulta** (catapult), a machine for hurling large arrows and javelins.

3. **scorpiō,** a light catapult for hurling stones and darts.

ROMAN SHIPS

In his naval campaigns, Caesar used the following types of ships:

1. **nāvis longa,** a battleship or war galley, propelled by oars and sails. It had a sharp metal beak (**rōstrum**) at the prow, which was used to ram enemy ships. The most common type of battleship was the **trireme,** a vessel with three banks of oars.

2. **nāvis onerāria,** a transport, broader and slower than the battleship. It was used to carry soldiers, horses, and provisions, and was propelled chiefly by sails.

EXERCISES

A. In the space before each number, connected with Roman warfare, in column *A*, write the letter of the matching item in column *B*.

Column A	Column B
_____ **1.** 2	*a.* men in a cohort
_____ **2.** 3	*b.* men in Caesar's legion
_____ **3.** 4	*c.* main streets of a camp
_____ **4.** 10	*d.* watches in a night
_____ **5.** 15	*e.* cohorts in a legion
_____ **6.** 25	*f.* original strength of a legion
_____ **7.** 120	*g.* miles covered on a forced march
_____ **8.** 360	*h.* hours in a watch
_____ **9.** 3600	*i.* men in a maniple
_____ **10.** 6000	*j.* miles covered on an average day's march

B. Each item below is followed by four words or expressions. In each group draw a line through the word or expression that does *not* belong.

1. Roman siege terms: agger, vigilia, catapulta, ariēs

2. noncombatants: auxilia, mercātōrēs, explōrātōrēs, fabrī

3. unit of a Roman legion: cohors, manipulus, centuria, equitēs

4. defensive armor: lōrīca, pīlum, scūtum, galea

5. articles of clothing of the legionary: toga, tunica, sagum, caligae

6. auxiliary infantry troops: sagittāriī, funditōrēs, speculātōrēs, levis armātūrae peditēs

7. Roman artillery: ballista, vīnea, scorpiō, catapulta

8. military standards: aciēs, signum, aquila, vexillum

9. divisions of the cavalry: turma, āla, decuria, tuba

10. parts of a camp: vāllum, fossa, pluteus, tabernācula

C. Complete the following statements:

1. The vanguard in a marching formation was called ....

2. The general term for a Roman battleship was ....

3. After his first important victory, a *dux* had a right to the title ....

4. Two important offensive weapons were the *gladius* and the ....

5. A protective trench built around a camp was called a ....

6. There was one centurion in each century, but each legion had .... centurions.

7. The main food ration of the legionary soldier was called in Latin ....

8. Army pay was very small, amounting to about .... dollars a year.

9. A red *vexillum* over the general's tent was the signal to ....

10. To give signals in battle, the Romans made use of musical instruments, such as the *tuba* and the

....

D. If the italicized term in each of the following statements is correct, write *true*. If the italicized term is incorrect, write the correct term.

1. The Latin name for a line of battle was *aciēs*.   ....

2. Slingers and bowmen were part of the *auxilia*.   ....

3. Traders who sold provisions to the soldiers were called *cālōnēs*.   ....

4. Military tribunes were the lowest-ranking *noncommissioned* officers.   ....

5. *Caligae* were heavy leather shoes worn by Roman soldiers.   ....

6. A soldier burdened with his sarcina was referred to as *expedītus*.   ....

7. A castra was generally built with *two* portae.   ....

8. The tertia vigilia lasted from *12 midnight to 3 a.m.*   ....

9. A battering ram used in an assault was called a *pluteus*.   ....

10. The metal beak on the prow of a Roman battleship was called a *scorpiō*.   ....

E. Each incomplete statement below is followed by four words or expressions in parentheses. Underline the word or expression that will complete the statement correctly.

1. The officer who was often sent as envoy on a special mission was the (quaestor, lēgātus, praefectus, centuriō).

2. *Tormenta* were used to (punish deserters, guard the artillery, hurl missiles, signal a battle).

3. A *nāvis onerāria* was a Roman (transport, war galley, cavalry squad, standard).

4. The branch of the armed forces on which Caesar chiefly relied was the (auxilia, equitēs, sagittāriī, peditēs).

5. The smallest division of the Roman army was the (maniple, legion, century, cohort).

6. Caesar's favorite legion, commanded by Labienus, was the (5th, 7th, 10th, 12th).

7. *Explōrātōrēs* were used chiefly to (perform camp services, conduct drills, care for the baggage, reconnoiter the terrain).

8. The name given to the heavy, movable shed, mounted on rollers, and used in a siege was (agger, vīnea, testūdō, scāla).

9. The officer in charge of pay, supplies, and equipment in the Roman army was the (tribūnus, lēgātus, quaestor, praefectus).

10. The winter camp used by the Roman army was known as (lōrīca, hīberna, pīla, praeda).

F. In the following passage, ten words or expressions are italicized and repeated in the questions below. Underline the alternative that best explains each of these ten words or expressions as it is used in the passage.

Upon reaching the *required age*, Lucius, the son of a prominent Roman *lēgātus*, enlisted in the army. Through political connections he received an appointment as a *commissioned officer*, even though he lacked military experience. His legion, headed by Caesar's *most trusted lieutenant*, was preparing for a *forced march* into enemy territory. The soldiers were adjusting their *personal packs* prior to setting out. They had each been given their *proper allotment* of frūmentum distributed every 15 days. The bearer of the *eagle* was assigned a safe position near the *baggage*. The signal was given at the *beginning of the second watch*, and the march was on.

1. *required age*
   1 17   2 21   3 25   4 30

2. *lēgātus*
   1 quartermaster   2 captain   3 lieutenant-general   4 commander-in-chief

3. *commissioned officer*
   1 centuriō   2 quaestor   3 praefectus   4 tribūnus mīlitum

4. *most trusted lieutenant*
   1 Cicero   2 Pompey   3 Labienus   4 Sabinus

5. *forced march*
   1 10 miles   2 15 miles   3 25 miles   4 40 miles

6. *personal packs*
   1 sarcinae   2 ālae   3 galeae   4 turmae

7. *proper allotment*
   1 10 pounds   2 20 pounds   3 30 pounds   4 40 pounds

8. *eagle*
   1 lōrīca   2 vexillum   3 aquila   4 caliga

9. *baggage*
   1 expedīta   2 impedīmenta   3 agmina   4 itinera

10. *beginning of the second watch*
   1 9 p.m.   2 12 midnight   3 3 a.m.   4 6 p.m.

Lesson 88—HIGHLIGHTS OF THE GALLIC WAR

CAESAR'S *COMMENTARIES ON THE GALLIC WAR*

Caesar wrote the *Commentaries on the Gallic War* for two main reasons:

1. to put in writing an authoritative account of a very important period in Roman history;
2. to justify to the Roman people his military actions in Gaul, Germany, and Britain.

In order to give *The Gallic War* an appearance of detached objectivity, Caesar refers to himself in the third person. As far as the factual content is concerned, few historians question the substantial accuracy of the account.

The Gallic War is divided into seven books, each book narrating the campaigns of one year. An eighth book, containing the events of 51 and 50 B.C. in Gaul, was later added by Aulus Hirtius, one of Caesar's generals. The following summary relates the main incidents:

BOOK I—58 B.C.

The Geography of Gaul. Three divisions: the Belgians, the Aquitanians, and the Celts or Gauls. Caesar considers the Belgians the bravest: "Hōrum omnium fortissimī sunt Belgae." He cites these reasons for their bravery: their distance from the refinements of the Roman province, little contact with traders who bring luxuries to weaken men's courage, constant wars with the neighboring Germans.

War With the Helvetians. The Helvetians (a warlike tribe living in what is now Switzerland) feel restricted in their small territory. Aroused by a powerful chief, Orgetorix, they decide to migrate into western Gaul. Caesar, on learning of the proposed migration and of the conspiracy of Orgetorix to gain control of all Gaul, hastens to Geneva. Finally defeated by Caesar, the Helvetians are forced to abandon their migration and return home.

War With the Germans. Gallic tribes, especially the Aeduans, are worried by the invasion of Germans and ask Caesar's help in driving them from Gaul. Caesar wages a campaign against the Germans, who are led by their haughty and powerful chief, Ariovistus. The Germans are routed and flee across the Rhine River.

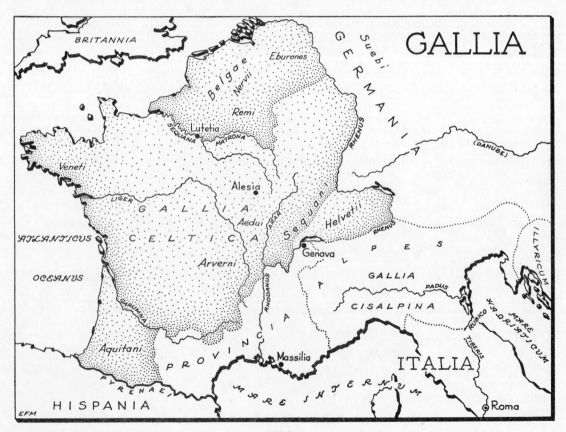

BOOK II—57 B.C.

War With the Belgians. When the Belgian tribes form a confederacy as a defensive alliance against the Romans, Caesar attacks them and forces them to disperse. He breaks the resistance of the tribes, completing a successful campaign with the defeat of the Nervii.

BOOK III—56 B.C.

Naval War With the Venetī. The seafaring Venetī lead a group of coastal tribes in northwestern Gaul in revolt. Caesar has a fleet built and defeats the Venetī in a naval campaign.

BOOK IV—55 B.C.

First Invasion of Germany. After routing the German tribes that had crossed into northern Gaul, Caesar bridges the Rhine, leads his army across the river, and devastates the land of the Germans in order to terrorize them. After only eighteen days in Germany, he returns to Gaul.

First Expedition to Britain. Similarly, to impress the Britons, who have given protection to rebellious Gauls, Caesar invades Britain with a fleet. He stays there about three weeks, successfully meets the Britons in battle, is impressed by their fighting from war chariots, and gets firsthand information about the people and their island.

BOOK V—54 B.C.

Second Expedition to Britain. Caesar invades Britain for the second time with a larger force. He meets more resistance than on the first expedition, and his legions are halted by the war chariots of the Britons, led by Cassivellaunus. After about ten weeks, he succeeds in imposing peace terms upon the enemy, and then embarks for Gaul without making any permanent conquests.

Massacre of Sabinus and Cotta. The Gauls, under the leadership of Ambiorix, revolt and attack the camp of Caesar's lieutenants, Sabinus and Cotta. The lieutenants are treacherously ambushed and slain, together with a large number of their troops.

Defense of Quintus Cicero's Camp. Another attack is made by the Gauls on the camp of the lieutenant Quintus Cicero, who valiantly defends the besieged camp until Caesar arrives and turns the tide of battle to victory.

BOOK VI—53 B.C.

Second Invasion of Germany. After reinforcing his army and checking revolts in northern Gaul, Caesar invades Germany for the second time.

The Customs of the Gauls and the Germans. Caesar gives an interesting and informative description of the customs and life of the Gauls and Germans.

He finds many opposing factions among the Gauls. The people are ruled by Druids (or priests) and by Knights (or warriors). The Druids are very influential, learned men who control not only the religious but also many other aspects of the life of the Gauls. They are teachers and also act as judges. Human sacrifice is part of their rites.

The Germans are a warlike people with little interest in agriculture. Their land is owned in common, under government supervision. Caesar describes the Hercynian forest and the extraordinary animals found there.

Pursuit of Ambiorix. On his return to Gaul, Caesar quells revolts and tries to capture his enemy, Ambiorix, who succeeds in escaping.

BOOK VII—52 B.C.

Revolt and Defeat of the United Gauls. All the Gauls, united under the leadership of the brilliant chief of the Arvernians, Vercingetorix, rebel against Roman rule. Caesar suffers severe losses in this fierce campaign.

Vercingetorix finally retreats to the town of Alesia. After a desperate siege of the town by Caesar, the Gauls are forced to surrender.

RESULTS OF THE GALLIC WAR

The battle of Alesia is the last decisive battle of the Gallic War. The gallant Vercingetorix, who is often considered the first national hero of France, was taken to Rome in Caesar's triumphal procession and, after several years of imprisonment, was executed.

The Greek writer Plutarch sums up the results of the Gallic War as follows: "Caesar was engaged in the Gallic War for less than ten years. In that time he captured more than eight hundred towns, subdued three hundred tribes, fought against three million foes, killed a million, and took a million prisoners."

With the final defeat of the Gauls, Rome colonized western Europe. Her culture and language spread throughout the area. From Latin there gradually developed the modern Romance languages, including French, Spanish, Italian, Portuguese, and Rumanian.

PROMINENT PERSONALITIES OF THE GALLIC WAR

Ambiorix. A chief of the Eburones. He started a revolt and led the ambush of the troops of Sabinus and Cotta. Ambiorix succeeded in escaping Caesar.

Ariovistus. An arrogant German chief whom Caesar defeated and drove from Gaul back into Germany.

Cassivellaunus. Leader of the Britons. He finally surrendered to Caesar.

Casticus. A chief of the Sequanians. He joined with Orgetorix and Dumnorix in the conspiracy to gain control of Gaul.

Cicero, Quintus Tullius. Brother of the famous orator. One of Caesar's best lieutenants, Quintus won renown by resisting a siege of his winter quarters by the rebellious Gauls.

Commius. King of the Atrebates, a Belgian tribe friendly to Caesar. He was sent by Caesar as an envoy to Britain in 55 B.C., where he was thrown into chains, but later released.

Diviciacus. A prominent pro-Roman Aeduan. Unlike his brother, Dumnorix, he was loyal to Caesar.

Dumnorix. An influential and ambitious anti-Roman Aeduan who continually opposed Caesar. Dumnorix was finally killed in an attempt to escape from Caesar's camp.

Eporedorix. An Aeduan noble, loyal to Caesar at first. Eporedorix later joined Vercingetorix as one of the leaders of the Gallic army that went to relieve the siege of Alesia.

Labienus, Titus. Caesar's right-hand man and most trusted lieutenant in the Gallic War. During the Civil War, however, he fought against Caesar and was killed at Munda.

Orgetorix. Wealthiest of the Helvetian chiefs. He planned the migration into western Gaul. Orgetorix attempted to seize control of Helvetia and plotted with Casticus and Dumnorix to conquer all Gaul. When arrested by the Helvetians, he is said to have taken his life.

Pullo, Titus and **Vorenus, Lucius.** Rival centurions who acted heroically at the siege of Quintus Cicero's camp.

Sabinus, Quintus and **Cotta, Lucius.** Lieutenants of Caesar who were killed in ambush during the revolt of the Gauls under Ambiorix.

Vercingetorix. Chief of the Arvernians. He united all the Gauls against Caesar in the last campaign of the Gallic War. He was finally defeated and captured at Alesia. Vercingetorix is regarded as the first national hero of France.

Volusenus, Gaius. A tribune in Caesar's army. He was sent by Caesar to Britain on a scouting expedition in 55 B.C.

GEOGRAPHICAL TERMS

COUNTRIES

Aquītānia. The southwestern part of Gaul, separated from Spain by the Pyrenees Mountains. Aquitania was one of the three main divisions of Gaul.

Belgium. Land of the Belgae, another of the three main divisions of Gaul. It was located in the northern part of Gaul.

Britannia. The island of Britain, described by Caesar as "triangular in shape."

Gallia. A general term comprising modern France and parts of Switzerland, Belgium, and Holland; all the territory between the Pyrenees Mountains and the Rhine River. When referring to Gallia, Caesar usually means the central or Celtic part of Gaul, the third main division of Gaul.

Gallia Cisalpīna (Citerior). Cisalpine Gaul, extending north from Italy proper to the Alps.

Gallia Trānsalpīna (Ulterior). Transalpine Gaul; also called **Prōvincia.** It is now known as Provence, a region of southeastern France.

Germānia. Germany, a country of indefinite extent, east of the Rhine River.

Helvētia. The homeland of the Helvētiī, divided into four cantons; modern Switzerland.

Hispānia. Ancient Spain, which included modern Spain and Portugal.

Illyricum. A narrow province that bordered Cisalpine Gaul at the head of the Adriatic Sea; modern Yugoslavia and Albania.

CITIES

Alesia. Chief city of the Mandubiī, a Gallic tribe. It was here that Vercingetorix, uniting all the Gauls against Caesar, made his last stand.

Genava. Geneva, located on Lake Geneva in Switzerland.

Lutetia. Modern Paris; a city of the tribe named Parisiī on an island in the Seine River.

RIVERS AND LAKES

Arar. The modern Saône River, a tributary of the Rhone.

Axona. The modern Aisne, a river in the southern part of Belgic Gaul.

Garumna. The modern Garonne, a river of southwestern France.

Lemannus. Lake Geneva in Switzerland.

Liger. The modern Loire, the largest river in Gaul.

Matrona. The modern Marne River, a tributary of the Seine.

Rhēnus. The Rhine River, separating Gaul and Germany.

Rhodanus. The Rhone River, which flows through Lake Geneva and empties into the Mediterranean.

Sēquana. The modern Seine, the principal river of northern France.

MOUNTAINS

Alpēs. The Alps, separating Cisalpine Gaul from Transalpine Gaul and Germany.

Iūra. The Jura, a range of mountains extending from the Rhine to the Rhone.

Pȳrēnaeī. The Pyrenees, separating Gaul from Spain.

EXERCISES

A. Identify each place-name by putting a check in the proper column.

	COUNTRY	CITY	RIVER	MOUNTAIN
1. Liger	-------	-------	-------	-------
2. Helvētia	-------	-------	-------	-------

3. Iūra   -------   -------   -------   -------

4. Sēquana   -------   -------   -------   -------

5. Lutetia   -------   -------   -------   -------

6. Aquītānia   -------   -------   -------   -------

7. Axona   -------   -------   -------   -------

8. Alesia   -------   -------   -------   -------

9. Pȳrēnaeī   -------   -------   -------   -------

10. Illyricum   -------   -------   -------   -------

B. Each item below is followed by four words or expressions. In each group draw a line through the word or expression that does *not* belong.

1. leaders of a conspiracy to seize control of Gaul: Dumnorix, Diviciacus, Casticus, Orgetorix

2. contents of Book I of *The Gallic War:* war with the Belgians, war with the Germans, war with the Helvetians, geography of Gaul

3. lieutenant-generals in Caesar's army: Labienus, Sabinus, Quintus Cicero, Commius

4. Romance languages: Spanish, French, Greek, Rumanian

5. in his second invasion of Britain, Caesar: was impressed by British war chariots, met greater resistance than previously, made a permanent conquest, imposed peace terms on the enemy

6. Gallic leaders: Volusenus, Eporedorix, Ambiorix, Vercingetorix

7. reasons for the bravery of the Belgians: little contact with merchants, superior weapons, distance from the Roman province, constant wars with the Germans

8. customs of the Gauls: rule by Druids and Knights, human sacrifice, no religious life, existence of many opposing factions

9. rivers in Gaul: Rhodanus, Garumna, Arar, Lemannus

10. in his first invasion of Germany, Caesar: fought many naval battles, bridged the Rhine, stayed only eighteen days, devastated German territory

C. In the space before each Latin place-name in column *A*, write the letter of its English equivalent in column *B*.

Column A	Column B
------ **1.** Matrona	*a.* Lake Geneva
------ **2.** Hispānia	*b.* Rhine River
------ **3.** Lemannus	*c.* Garonne River
------ **4.** Rhodanus	*d.* Switzerland
------ **5.** Alpēs	*e.* Saône River
------ **6.** Garumna	*f.* Marne River
------ **7.** Helvētia	*g.* Paris
------ **8.** Rhēnus	*h.* Alps Mountains
------ **9.** Lutetia	*i.* Rhone River
------ **10.** Arar	*j.* Spain

D. If the italicized term in each of the following statements is correct, write *true*. If the italicized term is incorrect, write the correct term.

1. Historians generally agree that the content of Caesar's GALLIC WAR is substantially *accurate*.

2. Volusenus, a Roman tribune, was sent by Caesar to *Germany* on a scouting expedition in 55 B.C.

3. Britannia was described by Caesar as *rectangular* in shape.

4. Gallia Cisalpīna was also called Gallia *Citerior*.

5. Lutetia was located on the flumen *Sēquana*.

6. The Pyrenees Mountains separated Gaul from *Germany*.

7. THE GALLIC WAR is divided into seven books, each narrating Caesar's campaign *with one tribe*.

8. It was at Alesia that *Orgetorix* united all the Gauls against Caesar.

9. By the end of the Gallic War, Caesar had captured over *eight hundred towns*.

10. Caesar defeated the tribe called *Venetī* in a naval campaign in 56 B.C.

E. Underline the word or expression in parentheses that will complete the statement correctly.

1. The Druids were (merchants and tradesmen, priests and teachers, soldiers and farmers, politicians and lawyers).

2. During the siege of Quintus Cicero's camp in Book V of *The Gallic War*, Caesar tells of the rivalry between (Pullo and Vorenus, Sabinus and Cotta, Labienus and Commius, Volusenus and Casticus).

3. Caesar's lieutenant who fought against him in the Civil War was (Pompey, Brutus, Cicero, Labienus).

4. In describing the customs of the Germans in Book VI of *The Gallic War*, Caesar says that they (believed in private ownership of land, had little interest in agriculture, were a peace-loving people, engaged in wars only when attacked).

5. The leader of the Britons was (Orgetorix, Dumnorix, Cassivellaunus, Ariovistus).

6. In *The Gallic War* Caesar refers to himself in the third person in order to (glorify the name Caesar, simplify the Latin, remove any charge of egoism, appear objective).

7. Caesar's three divisions of Gaul were inhabited by the Belgae, the Celtae, and the (Etruscī, Aquitānī, Helvētiī, Sēquanī).

8. Stamps and coins with the imprint *Helvetia* are issued by (France, Switzerland, Holland, Belgium).

9. In Book VII of *The Gallic War*, Caesar tells of (the siege of Alesia, his second expedition to Britain, the defense of Cicero's camp, his campaign against Ariovistus).

10. Caesar wrote "Hōrum omnium fortissimī sunt" to describe the (Aeduī, Celtae, Belgae, Aquitānī).

11. Caesar's first expedition to Britain took place in (58, 55, 53, 51) B.C.

12. A Belgian king who was sent by Caesar as an envoy to Britain was (Eporedorix, Ambiorix, Casticus, Commius).

13. In Book II of *The Gallic War*, Caesar says that he attacked the Belgians because they (sent spies to his camps, formed an alliance against him, crossed the Channel into Britain, invaded Celtic Gaul).

14. Orgetorix was a leader of the (Britons, Helvetians, Aeduans, Germans).

15. The Gallic leader who is considered the first national hero of France was (Vercingetorix, Volusenus, Ariovistus, Diviciacus).

Lesson 89—ROMAN HISTORY, GOVERNMENT, AND SOCIETY

IMPORTANT EVENTS BEFORE JULIUS CAESAR

FOUNDING OF ROME

April 21, 753 B.C., is the traditional date for the founding of Rome by Romulus, a descendant of Aeneas, the Trojan hero. As an infant, Romulus, with his twin brother Remus, was said to have been cared for by a she-wolf.

THE MONARCHY (FROM 753 B.C. TO 509 B.C.)

According to legend, there were seven kings, beginning with Romulus and ending with Tarquinius Superbus (Tarquin the Proud). Supreme authority of the king was symbolized by a bundle of rods with an ax, called **fascēs,** which is the origin of the modern term *fascism*. The fascēs were carried by the king's **lictors,** or attendants. The cruel despotism of Tarquin drove the Romans to overthrow the monarchy and establish a republic.

THE REPUBLIC (FROM 509 B.C. TO 27 B.C.)

During the period of the Republic, which lasted almost 500 years, Rome made most of her great conquests and expanded her territory until she became the dominant world power. During this period Rome's chief executives were called consuls.

The first period of the Republic, extending to 265 B.C., was the period of conquest in the Italian peninsula itself. It ended with the defeat of Pyrrhus, the Greek king of Epirus, who was aiding the resistance in southern Italy.

Rome then engaged in wars of conquest outside Italy. In the course of the three Punic Wars of the third century B.C., the Romans under Scipio defeated the brilliant Carthaginian general, Hannibal, thus establishing Rome as the only power in the western Mediterranean. Macedonia was subjugated in 168 B.C., and in quick succession Greece, Africa, and Spain became provinces of Rome. With victories in Asia Minor, Roman territory now encircled the Mediterranean, and that sea became known as **Mare Nostrum** (Our Sea).

The final phase of the Republic was marked by civil strife. The social reformers, Tiberius and Gaius Gracchus, were murdered. Civil war between Marius and Sulla shook the Roman state, ending in the dictatorship of Sulla and the establishment of the aristocracy as the ruling class in 82 B.C.

IMPORTANT EVENTS AFTER JULIUS CAESAR

THE EMPIRE (FROM 27 B.C. TO 476 A.D.)

The assassination of Julius Caesar in 44 B.C. found Rome in a state of utter confusion. Soon new actors appeared upon the scene, men struggling to fill the void as leader. Among them were Gaius Octavius, Caesar's adopted son and heir, and Marcus Antonius and Marcus Lepidus, friends of Caesar. These three formed the Second Triumvirate in 43 B.C., an alliance that lasted twelve years. Lepidus was eventually deposed from his position as triumvir, and relations between the remaining two soon came to a breaking point. In 31 B.C., in the Battle of Actium in Greece, Octavius gained a decisive victory over Antony. Later he returned triumphant to Rome, master of the world. In 27 B.C. the Roman Senate bestowed upon him the name of Augustus, and the Empire was born.

Augustus reigned from 27 B.C. until 14 A.D., a period marked by the flowering of Roman genius in art and literature. It has truly been said that Augustus "found Rome a city of brick and left it a city of marble." Rome had more than twenty-five emperors before its fall in 476 A.D. The last of the emperors was Romulus Augustulus.

THE FALL OF ROME

Many reasons have been advanced for the fall of Rome and, with it, the collapse of civilization and social order. Among them are: (1) the system of slavery and serfdom that demoralized a large segment of the population, (2) the decay and corruption of the ruling class and the imperial court, (3) heavy taxation, and (4) the incursions into Italy made by the enemies of Rome, such as the Visigoths and the Vandals.

ROMAN GOVERNMENT

The Senate. The most powerful body in ancient Rome was the Senate. It consisted of about 600 members, mostly former officials, who held office for life. It managed foreign affairs, declared war, and controlled taxation. The power of the Senate was symbolized by the abbreviation **S.P.Q.R. (Senātus Populusque Rōmānus),** found on buildings, coins, and standards. The senators usually held their meetings in the **cūria** (senate house).

Popular Assemblies. Two assemblies administered the elective and legislative business of the Roman state. One assembly, called the **Comitia Centūriāta,** elected the higher magistrates—consuls, praetors, and censors. The other assembly, called the **Comitia Tribūta,** elected the tribunes, quaestors, aediles, and minor officials.

Cursus Honōrum. This was the order in which the various important offices might be held according to law. The highest official was the consul. Before one could become consul, he had to serve as praetor. Before being praetor, he had to serve as quaestor.

Consul. Two consuls, elected annually, held office for one year only. They were the chief executives during the Republic, and each served as a check upon the other.

Praetor. Eight praetors were elected annually for one year. Their chief duty was to serve as judges in court.

Quaestor. Twenty quaestors were elected annually for one year. They served as public treasurers.

Aedile. Although not in the cursus honōrum, the aedile used his position to gain popularity for election to higher office. He was in charge of public games and amusements, public works, markets, streets, etc. There were four aediles in Rome, elected annually for one year.

Tribune of the People. Ten tribunes were elected annually for one year. They had the extraordinary right to veto any decree or law passed by the Senate or the assemblies.

Censor. There were two censors elected every five years for a term of eighteen months. Their duties were to assess property, determine the order of society to which each citizen belonged, fix the eligibility of senators, raise revenue for public works, and maintain high standards of morality.

Dictator. In times of extreme public danger, a dictator was appointed with supreme power for a period of six months.

CLASSES OF SOCIETY

The Senatorial Order, also called the **Patricians** or **Optimātēs,** consisted of officeholders (magistrates) and their descendants.

The Equestrian Order, or **Equitēs,** was the wealthy class, consisting of those whose possessions were equivalent to at least $20,000.

The Plebeian Order, the working class embracing the vast majority of the population, consisted of those freeborn citizens who possessed less than $20,000.

Below these three orders of society were the **slaves,** who had no rights whatsoever; and the **freedmen** (former slaves), who had the right to vote and own property, but not to hold office.

EXERCISES

A. If the italicized term in each of the following statements is correct, write *true*. If the italicized term is incorrect, write the correct term.

1. Supreme authority of the kings of Rome was symbolized by a bundle of rods with an ax, called *lictors*.   _____

2. In times of emergency in Rome, a dictator was appointed for a period of *two years*.   _____

3. Caesar's adopted son and heir was *Gaius Octavius*.   _____

4. *Antonius* found Rome "a city of brick and left it a city of marble."   _____

5. *Quaestors* in ancient Rome served as public treasurers.   _____

6. The Roman senate house was called the *comitia*.   _____

7. The traditional date given for the founding of Rome is *753* B.C.   _____

8. Tiberius and Gaius *Gracchus* were social reformers in ancient Rome.   _____

9. The Battle of *Pharsalus* in Greece in 31 B.C. made Octavius virtual master of the world.   _____

10. The *Equestrian* Order represented the wealthy class of ancient Rome.   _____

B. Complete the following statements:

1. The Roman Republic lasted from 509 B.C. until _____.

2. With the Roman conquest of all the territory encircling the Mediterranean, the sea became known as _____.

3. Octavius in later life received the title of Emperor _____.

4. Rome had over twenty-five emperors before its fall in the year _____ A.D.

5. The abbreviation S.P.Q.R. stood for Senātus _____ _____.

6. The two popular assemblies were called Comitia Centūriāta and Comitia _____.

7. The Equestrian Order consisted of citizens whose possessions were equivalent to at least _____ _____ dollars.

8. The tribunes of the people had the right to _____ any decree or law passed by the Roman legislature.

9. The civil war between Sulla and _____ ended in victory for the former.

10. The Second Triumvirate, formed in 43 B.C., lasted _____ years.

C. In the space before each proper name in column *A*, write the letter of the matching item in column *B*.

	Column A		*Column B*
_____	**1.** Gaius Gracchus	*a.*	Trojan hero
_____	**2.** Romulus Augustulus	*b.*	brother of Romulus
_____	**3.** Marcus Lepidus	*c.*	hero in the Punic Wars
_____	**4.** Remus	*d.*	Roman dictator
_____	**5.** Pyrrhus	*e.*	last of the emperors
_____	**6.** Aeneas	*f.*	last of the kings
_____	**7.** Hannibal	*g.*	social reformer
_____	**8.** Sulla	*h.*	Carthaginian general
_____	**9.** Tarquinius	*i.*	king of Epirus
_____	**10.** Scipio	*j.*	triumvir

D. Underline the word or expression in parentheses that will complete the sentence correctly.

1. An important factor contributing to Rome's fall, besides slavery, corruption, and taxation, was (poor roads, barbaric invasions, lack of generals).

2. The Senatorial Order was the order of the Patricians or (Optimātēs, Equitēs, Quaestōrēs).

3. The higher magistrates in Rome were elected by the (Senātus, pontifex maximus, Comitia Centūriāta).

4. The members of the Second Triumvirate included Octavius, Lepidus, and (Augustus, Antonius, Caesar).

5. The office not included in the cursus honōrum was the (aedileship, praetorship, quaestorship).

6. Augustus reigned until the year (31 A.D., 27 A.D., 14 A.D.).

7. The Roman Senate managed foreign affairs, declared war, and (elected minor officials, assessed property, controlled taxation).

8. Freedmen were not permitted to (vote, hold office, own property).

9. Roman censors were elected every (year, three years, five years).

10. The chief duty of a praetor was to (manage finances, serve as judge, supervise public works).

E. Indicate the proper chronological sequence of the following events by numbering them from 1 to 10:

_____	assassination of Caesar	_____	dictatorship of Sulla
_____	Punic Wars	_____	war with Pyrrhus
_____	founding of Rome	_____	rule of Tarquinius Superbus
_____	Battle of Actium	_____	conquest of Macedonia
_____	reign of Augustus	_____	formation of Second Triumvirate

Lesson 90—ROMAN LIFE

Much of our knowledge of Roman life has come from the excavations at Pompeii, a city near Naples that was a favorite resort of wealthy Romans. In 79 A.D. an eruption of Mount Vesuvius buried the city, at the same time preserving it with volcanic ash. Most of Pompeii has already been excavated.

THE CITY OF ROME

LOCATION

Situated on the Tiber River near the west central coast of Italy, Rome encompassed seven hills, of which the two most celebrated were the **Capitoline** and the **Palatine.** The area in which Rome was situated was called **Latium,** the origin of the word *Latin.* Rome's outlet to the sea was at **Ostia,** a seaport about sixteen miles away. The marketplace and the center of civic life in Rome was the **Forum.** Here were located shops **(tabernae),** temples **(templa),** law courts **(basilicae),** other public buildings, and the speaker's platform **(rōstra).**

STREETS AND ROADS

Streets were narrow and crooked, often unpaved. At corners, stepping-stones were placed at intervals to assist in crossing to the other side. Streets were unlighted, and **vigilēs** (policemen-firemen) carrying small lanterns walked the dark alleys to afford protection.

The Romans constructed an extensive system of highways connecting the principal cities of Italy with Rome. Hence the expression, "All roads lead to Rome." The most famous road was the **Via Appia** (the Appian Way), also called **Rēgīna Viārum,** connecting Rome with Brundisium on the southeastern coast of Italy. Other roads were the **Via Flāminia,** leading northeast toward Umbria; and the **Via Aurēlia,** a military road running along the west coast toward Gaul.

FAMILY LIFE

THE FAMILY

The basic unit of Roman society was the **familia** (household). It consisted of the **paterfamiliās** (father), mother, unmarried daughters, sons with their wives and children, and slaves. The father was supreme in his own home. He had unlimited power over his children and could command absolute obedience.

The mother, who was held in high esteem, was mistress of the home. She managed the household affairs and advised her husband in business and politics.

Families descended from a common ancestor often formed a clan, called **gēns.** Like the family, the gēns was united by common religious rites and was governed by a common ruler.

NAMES

A Roman citizen generally had three names: a **praenōmen,** a **nōmen,** and a **cognōmen.**

praenōmen—corresponded to our given name. The Romans had very few given names and often abbreviated them in writing. Some common abbreviations were:

A. Aulus	**D.** Decimus	**M.** Mārcus	**Q.** Quīntus	**T.** Titus
C. Gāius	**L.** Lūcius	**P.** Pūblius	**S.** Sextus	**Ti.** Tiberius

nōmen—the family name, indicated the clan (gēns).

cognōmen—indicated the particular branch of the gēns.

Thus, in the name Gāius Iūlius Caesar, Gāius is the praenōmen, Iūlius is the nōmen, and Caesar is the cognōmen.

An honorary cognōmen was sometimes given a person for some noteworthy accomplishment. Thus, Pompey received the title *Magnus* for his military exploits. Scipio, after destroying Carthage, was surnamed *Africānus,* and the cognōmen *Augustus* was bestowed upon Octavian by the Roman Senate.

ROMA ANTIQUA

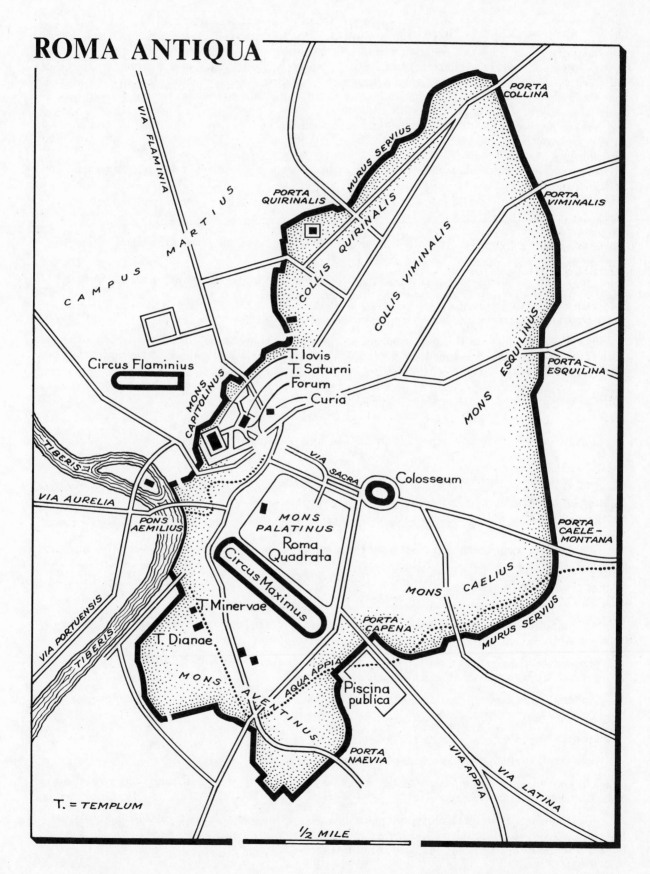

PORTA COLLINA

PORTA QUIRINALIS

VIA FLAMINIA

MURUS SERVIUS

PORTA VIMINALIS

CAMPUS MARTIUS

COLLIS QUIRINALIS

COLLIS VIMINALIS

MONS ESQUILINUS

PORTA ESQUILINA

Circus Flaminius

MONS CAPITOLINUS

T. Iovis
T. Saturni
Forum
Curia

MONS

VIA SACRA

Colosseum

TIBERIS

VIA AURELIA

PONS AEMILIUS

MONS PALATINUS
Roma Quadrata

Circus Maximus

PORTA CAELE-MONTANA

MONS CAELIUS

VIA PORTUENSIS

TIBERIS

T. Minervae

T. Dianae

MONS AVENTINUS

PORTA CAPENA

MURUS SERVIUS

AQUA APPIA

Piscina publica

PORTA NAEVIA

VIA APPIA

VIA LATINA

T. = TEMPLUM

1/2 MILE

EDUCATION

There was no compulsory public education. Up to the age of seven, children received training in the home. After that, a boy whose parents could afford the cost was sent to a private elementary school (**lūdus**), where the teacher (**litterātor**) taught him reading, writing, and simple arithmetic. He often had an educated slave, called a **paedagōgus,** who served as tutor and accompanied him to school. Upon completing elementary school, the Roman boy attended a grammar school, where the teacher (**grammaticus**) taught him Latin and Greek literature.

Next came the school of rhetoric, or college, where the boy received training in oratory and politics. Finally, as a youth, he could travel abroad to Greece, Rhodes, or Asia Minor to take specialized courses in philosophy, law, and oratory.

As a rule, Roman girls did not attend school. Instead they learned domestic arts from their mothers.

DRESS

MALE

tunica (tunic), a short-sleeved, woolen shirt reaching to the knees. It was the usual garment for indoor wear.

toga, a large, white, woolen cloth extending to the feet and draped gracefully around the body. It was worn over the tunic. The toga was the formal garment of Roman citizens.

toga candida, a pure white toga worn by a man seeking public office (hence our word "candidate").

toga praetexta, a toga with a purple border, worn by a boy of aristocratic family until about the age of 16. The adolescent then assumed the **toga virīlis,** or toga of the adult male. Priests and magistrates also wore the toga praetexta.

FEMALE

Over a tunic, women wore the

stola, a long, full garment extending to the feet and fastened by a belt at the waist. It was worn indoors.

palla, a woolen, shawl-like wrap for use outdoors.

THE HOUSE

ātrium, the spacious front hall used as a reception room.

compluvium, the opening in the ceiling of the atrium to admit light and air, since the Roman house usually had no windows.

impluvium, the marble basin built directly beneath the compluvium, to catch the rainwater that came through the opening.

tablīnum, the study or office of the master of the house, located opposite the entrance in full view of the atrium.

peristȳlium, the open courtyard, usually with garden and columns, entered by a passageway from the atrium. The peristyle was the center of family living.

triclīnium, the dining room adjoining the peristyle, containing a dining table flanked by three couches.

culīna, the kitchen.

Bedrooms, kitchen, and bath were built around the peristyle.

The above is a description of a city house belonging to a wealthy Roman, many of whom also had elaborate country homes called **vīllae.**

Most Romans, however, lived in tenement or apartment houses called **īnsulae** (islands), a name originally applied to city blocks, detached from one another. Tenements were usually five or six stories high and were unsafe, especially in the event of fire.

OTHER ASPECTS OF ROMAN LIFE

RELIGION

The Romans lived constantly in the presence of the gods, and their numerous festivals, offerings, and prayers testified to their eagerness to please their deities and obtain favors. From earliest times, the imagination of the Romans saw gods everywhere in nature, and *polytheism*, or the belief in many gods, was universally practiced. There were gods who protected the crops and herds, gods of the weather and seasons, gods of the earth and sky. Gods had to be appeased, and when a disaster struck, it proved that some god was offended.

Festivals were held all the year round, the most famous being the **Saturnalia,** dedicated to the god Saturn. This holiday took place at about the time we celebrate Christmas. It was a period of riotous merrymaking when even slaves were allowed their freedom.

Since religion was the function of the state, all temples, statues, and altars to the gods were built by the government. A very important temple was the **Temple of Vesta,** where six Vestal Virgins kept the sacred fire continuously burning. The priests, including the **pontifex maximus** (chief priest), were government officials, not necessarily trained for the priesthood.

After the conquest of Greece, the Romans identified their own gods with those of Greece. Below is a list of Roman deities, their Greek equivalents, their functions, and their principal attributes.

ROMAN DEITY	GREEK EQUIVALENT	FUNCTION	ATTRIBUTE
Apollo	Apollo	god of the sun, song, and prophecy	the lyre
Bacchus	Dionysus	god of wine	the vine
Ceres	Demeter	goddess of agriculture	a garland of ears of corn
Cupid	Eros	god of love	bow and arrow
Diana	Artemis	goddess of the chase and moon	bow and arrow, spear, and stags
Faunus	Pan	god of flocks and shepherds	horns and goat's feet
Janus	(none)	god of beginnings and doorways	two faces
Juno	Hera	queen of the gods, wife of Jupiter	crown, veil, scepter, and peacock
Jupiter	Zeus	king of the gods	scepter, eagle, and thunderbolt
Lares and Penates	(none)	household gods	perpetual fire on the hearth
Mars	Ares	god of war	shield, helmet, and coat of mail
Mercury	Hermes	messenger of the gods	winged sandals and hat, and staff (caduceus)
Minerva	Athena	goddess of wisdom	owl, helmet, and spear

ROMAN DEITY	GREEK EQUIVALENT	FUNCTION	ATTRIBUTE
Neptune	Poseidon	god of the sea	trident and dolphin
Pluto	Hades	god of the lower world	the dog Cerberus and a two-pronged fork
Saturn	Cronus	god of the harvest	sickle
Venus	Aphrodite	goddess of love and beauty	myrtle tree
Vesta	Hestia	goddess of the hearth	perpetual fire on the hearth
Vulcan	Hephaestus	god of fire	hammer and anvil

AMUSEMENTS

Entertainment and amusements were provided by the government and formed an important part of the daily life of the Romans. The most popular amusements were the public spectacles, such as chariot races and gladiatorial combats. The expression **"pānem et circēnsēs"** (bread and circus games) was a familiar cry of the mob. Theatrical performances, mainly drama, dance, and pantomime, were presented in open-air theaters. A visit to the baths was also a favorite social pastime of the Romans.

The **Colosseum,** the greatest amphitheater in Rome, was used chiefly for combats between gladiators, or between gladiators and wild beasts. Schools for training gladiators were established in various parts of Italy. The greeting **"Nōs moritūrī tē salūtāmus"** (We who are about to die salute you) was uttered by the gladiators before the contest. Perhaps the most famous gladiator in Roman history was a Thracian slave named **Spartacus,** who led a formidable uprising of slaves against the Roman state.

The **Circus Maximus,** the most famous arena in Rome, was used chiefly for chariot races. Other contests, such as wrestling and racing, were also held there.

The **Campus Martius** was a large field set aside for athletic exercises and military training. Here the young men of Rome engaged in track and field events, such as running, jumping, wrestling, boxing, archery, and discus throwing.

Thermae, or **balneae,** were elaborate baths corresponding to our country clubs. In addition to all varieties of bathing facilities, the buildings contained gymnasiums, lounging rooms, libraries, and gardens. Perhaps the most famous were the **Baths of Caracalla,** where today operatic performances are staged.

ROMAN CONTRIBUTIONS TO CIVILIZATION

Modern civilization is indebted to ancient Rome for many significant contributions. These include:

LANGUAGE

The Roman alphabet, derived originally from that of the Phoenicians, is in use today throughout most of the world. Latin is the basis of the Romance languages, the chief ones being Italian, Spanish, French, Portuguese, and Rumanian. English, though not a Romance language, has been profoundly influenced by Latin. Roman numerals are still in limited use as chapter headings in books, as hours on the faces of clocks, as dates on the cornerstones of buildings, etc.

LAW

Considered by many to be Rome's most valuable gift to the modern world, Roman law forms the basis of many legal systems today. The **Laws of the Twelve Tables,** engraved on bronze tablets and displayed in the Forum, were the foundation of Roman law.

Rome's greatest jurists recognized the equality of man before the law and the need for equal protection of the rights of person and property. Our own Declaration of Independence has embodied these ideas of justice. The Emperor Justinian codified the great mass of laws and thus facilitated the transmission of Roman law to the modern world.

LITERATURE

In prose and poetry, Roman writers have left us a rich legacy, outstanding in the field of world literature. We need but mention Caesar and Livy in the field of history; Cicero in the field of oratory, philosophy, and letters; and Vergil and Horace in the field of poetry. These authors are still read and enjoyed today in schools throughout the world and have exercised a profound influence upon modern writers.

GOVERNMENT

In the organization and administration of the Republic, the Romans have left their imprint on modern political systems. With the expansion of her territory and the formation and administration of her provinces, Rome showed a genius for organization that became a model for many modern governments.

ENGINEERING AND ARCHITECTURE

The Romans were famous for their construction of roads, aqueducts, and bridges. They also perfected the rounded arch and the dome.

In imperial times Rome became an imposing city of magnificent public buildings, temples, aqueducts, basilicas, theaters, columns, triumphal arches, and tombs. Today's tourist can still see the ancient Roman Forum with its ruins, the Colosseum, the Pantheon, the mausoleum of Hadrian, the arches of Titus, Severus, and Constantine, and other monuments to Roman genius.

THE CALENDAR

The calendar in use today is based essentially on the calendar revised by Julius Caesar. It was thus known as the *Julian calendar*. In the sixteenth century, Pope Gregory XIII made some further minor corrections, whence the term *Gregorian calendar*.

EXERCISES

A. In the space before each deity in column *A*, write the letter of the matching item in column *B*.

	Column A		Column B
------	**1.** Vulcan	*a.*	goddess of wisdom
------	**2.** Ceres	*b.*	god of love
------	**3.** Neptune	*c.*	goddess of the hearth
------	**4.** Minerva	*d.*	god of the sea
------	**5.** Bacchus	*e.*	queen of the gods
------	**6.** Vesta	*f.*	god of fire
------	**7.** Saturn	*g.*	messenger of the gods
------	**8.** Cupid	*h.*	god of the harvest
------	**9.** Mercury	*i.*	goddess of agriculture
------	**10.** Juno	*j.*	god of wine

B. Each item below is followed by four words or expressions. In each group draw a line through the word or expression that does *not* belong.

1. articles of clothing: palla, balnea, tunica, stola

2. inheritance from Rome: pointed arch, basic law, calendar, alphabet

3. Roman house: tablīnum, ātrium, impluvium, impedīmentum

4. religion: Vestal Virgins, pontifex maximus, thermae, Larēs

5. education: lūdus, litterātor, grammaticus, vigilēs

6. buildings in the Forum: basilicae, vīllae, tabernae, templa

7. Roman amusements: chariot races, gladiatorial combats, opera, drama

8. Campus Martius: large field, chariot races, athletic exercises, military training

9. location of Rome: Tiber, Mount Vesuvius, Capitoline Hill, Latium

10. toga praetexta: reached to the knees, had a purple border, worn by boys to the age of 16, worn by priests and magistrates

C. If the italicized term in each of the following statements is correct, write *true*. If the italicized term is incorrect, write the correct term.

1. The *compluvium* was used to catch rain-water.   ------------------------------

2. The *paedagōgus* served as tutor to a Roman boy and accompanied him to school.   ------------------------------

3. The laws engraved on bronze tablets were known as *Justinian's Code*.   ------------------------------

4. The *māter familiās* had absolute power over the children of the household.   ------------------------------

5. The Greek equivalent of Mars was *Ares*.   ------------------------------

6. The name Mārcus was a *praenōmen*.   ------------------------------

7. Rome's outlet to the sea, sixteen miles away, was at *Pompeii*.   ------------------------------

8. The speaker's platform in the Forum was called the *rōstra*.   ------------------------------

9. Families with a common ancestor often formed a clan, called *gēns*.   ------------------------------

10. The *Circus Maximus* was used chiefly for gladiatorial combats.   ------------------------------

D. In the following passage, ten words or expressions are italicized and repeated in the questions below. Underline the alternative that best explains each of these ten words or expressions as it is used in the passage.

At the age of seven Marcus Furius *Crassus*, son of a patrician, began attending *school*, where the *teacher* taught him reading, writing, and arithmetic. Then came the grammar school. At the age of sixteen Marcus assumed the *garb of the adult male*. A trip *abroad* to complete his education made him proficient in philosophy and oratory. At home he often used to declaim in the open *courtyard*.

Marcus loved to walk along the *Rēgīna Viārum* and dream of the day when he would march in a triumphal procession. He was also fond of the *amphitheater* where he admired the courage of the gladiators uttering their *farewell message* before the contest. He had once read about the famous *Thracian gladiator* who had led a revolt against Rome, and wondered what would have happened had the uprising succeeded.

1. *Crassus*

| 1 praenōmen | 2 nōmen | 3 cognōmen | 4 gēns |

2. *school*

| 1 lūdus | 2 grammaticus | 3 paedagōgus | 4 campus |

3. *teacher*

| 1 dictātor | 2 litterātor | 3 pontifex | 4 cēnsor |

4. *garb of the adult male*

| 1 toga candida | 2 toga praetexta | 3 tunica | 4 toga virīlis |

5. *abroad*

| 1 Gaul | 2 Spain | 3 Britain | 4 Greece |

6. *courtyard*

| 1 peristȳlium | 2 trīclīnium | 3 tablīnum | 4 ātrium |

7. *Rēgīna Viārum*

| 1 Via Flāminia | 2 Via Aurēlia | 3 Via Appia | 4 Via Latīna |

8. *amphitheater*

| 1 Circus Maximus | 2 Colosseum | 3 Campus Martius | 4 balneae |

9. *farewell message*

| 1 Pānem et circēnsēs | 2 In hōc signō vincēs | 3 Nōs moritūrī tē salūtāmus | 4 Valēte |

10. *Thracian gladiator*

| 1 Caracalla | 2 Janus | 3 Justinian | 4 Spartacus |

E. In the space before each item in column *A*, write the letter of the matching item in column *B*.

	Column A		*Column B*
------	**1.** vigilēs	*a.*	apartment houses
------	**2.** Roman Diana	*b.*	woman's outdoor wrap
------	**3.** trīclīnium	*c.*	Greek Aphrodite
------	**4.** basilicae	*d.*	master's study
------	**5.** stola	*e.*	policemen-firemen
------	**6.** vīllae	*f.*	Greek Artemis
------	**7.** palla	*g.*	woman's long indoor garment
------	**8.** Roman Venus	*h.*	dining room
------	**9.** tablīnum	*i.*	country homes
------	**10.** īnsulae	*j.*	law courts

F. Complete the following statements:

1. The praenōmen *S.* stood for ----------------------.

2. The two best-known hills of Rome were the Capitoline and the ------------------------------.

3. The front hall used as a reception room in a Roman house was called the ----------------------.

4. The tabernae in the Roman Forum were the --------------------.

5. The distance of Ostia from Rome was about ----------------------- miles.

6. The expression *pānem et circēnsēs* meant --.

7. The famous bathing establishment in ancient Rome that is used today for opera was called the Baths of ------------------------------.

8. The speaker's platform in the Forum was called the ----------------------.

9. Rome is situated on the ------------------- River.

10. The Roman god Jupiter corresponded to the Greek ------------------.

G. In the space before the name of each deity in column *A*, write the letter of the matching attribute in column *B*.

Column A	*Column B*
------ **1.** Neptune	*a.* thunderbolt
------ **2.** Vulcan	*b.* lyre
------ **3.** Jupiter	*c.* vine
------ **4.** Minerva	*d.* trident
------ **5.** Apollo	*e.* ears of corn
------ **6.** Pan	*f.* owl
------ **7.** Janus	*g.* sickle
------ **8.** Bacchus	*h.* hammer
------ **9.** Saturn	*i.* two faces
------ **10.** Ceres	*j.* goat's feet

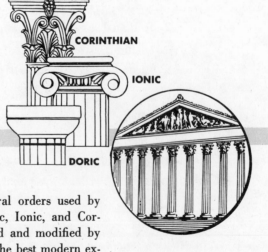

Columns

The three architectural orders used by the Greeks—the Doric, Ionic, and Corinthian—were adopted and modified by the Romans. One of the best modern examples of the Corinthian style, which the Romans favored, appears in the National Archives Building in Washington, D.C.

Lesson 91—ADDITIONAL CULTURAL MATERIAL

NAMES IN FACT AND FICTION

Aeëtes. King of Colchis. He was the father of Medea.

Aeneas. Trojan leader and hero. His wanderings are described in Vergil's *Aeneid*. The Romans believed that Aeneas was their ancestor.

Atalanta. Greek girl; said to have been the most swift-footed of mortals.

Camillus. General and hero of the Republic. He saved Rome by defeating the Gauls.

Castor and **Pollux.** Twin brothers of Helen of Troy. Castor was expert in training horses; Pollux was skilled in boxing. The constellation *Gemini* is named in their honor.

Cato. A severe censor of morals. Cato hated Carthage so much that he ended all his speeches by saying: "Dēlenda est Carthāgō" (Carthage must be destroyed).

Cincinnatus. Patriot of the Roman Republic. He was persuaded to leave his farm to become dictator in an emergency. After leading his army to victory, Cincinnatus returned to his plow.

Circe. Enchantress skilled in magic. She changed Ulysses' men into swine.

Cornelia. Mother of the Gracchi brothers. Known as a model mother, she called her sons her "jewels."

Curtius, Mettius. Symbol of Roman gallantry. He sacrificed himself for Rome by jumping into an abyss.

Daedalus. Mythical craftsman who built the Labyrinth to confine the Minotaur. Daedalus was the first man to fly; he flew safely over the Aegean Sea by means of wings fastened with wax. His son, Icarus, who flew too near the sun, was drowned in the sea when the wax melted.

Fabricius. Honorable Roman consul who refused to be bribed by Pyrrhus.

Hercules. Greek hero admired for his strength. He performed the famous "Twelve Labors."

Horatius. Valiant Roman patriot who defended a bridge to delay the Etruscan army of Porsena.

Jason. Legendary leader of the Argonauts. He succeeded in obtaining the Golden Fleece.

Medea. Sorceress skilled in magic, who assisted Jason in gaining the Golden Fleece. Medea slew her brother to escape her father, Aeëtes.

Medusa. One of the Gorgons (female monsters), who had wings and claws. Any person who looked at her was turned to stone. Perseus cut off her head, which was covered with serpents.

Midas. Mythical king of Asia Minor, known for his riches. Whatever he touched turned to gold.

Olympus. Celebrated mountain in Greece. In ancient mythology, Olympus was considered the abode of the gods.

Orpheus. Celebrated Greek poet, musician, and singer. When his wife Eurydice died, he was able, with the charm of his music, to enter Hades and bring her back, only to lose her again when he gazed back.

Perseus and **Andromeda.** Perseus, a Greek hero, slew a sea monster which threatened the life of Andromeda, chained to a rock as a sacrifice. Perseus later married the girl he had saved.

Pluto. God of the underworld.

Porsena, Lars. Etruscan king who led an army against Rome in an attempt to return Tarquin the Proud to the throne. Porsena later made peace with Rome.

Proserpina. Queen of the underworld. With Pluto, her husband, she ruled over the souls of the dead. Her mother was Ceres, goddess of agriculture.

Pyrrhus. Greek king of Epirus. He invaded Italy but was repulsed. Although Pyrrhus won battles, his losses were so great that he was unable to continue. A *pyrrhic* victory is a success gained at too great a cost.

Regulus. Outstanding patriot, consul, and general. Captured in the first Punic War, he kept his word to return to his Carthaginian captors although he knew death awaited him.

Scaevola, Mucius. Roman patriot and hero. Nicknamed "left-handed" because he lost the use of his right hand when he plunged it into the fire to show the Etruscans his courage.

Theseus. A Greek hero who slew the Minotaur, a monster half-man and half-bull. Theseus was aided by Ariadne, daughter of King Minos.

Ulysses. Greek hero and king of Ithaca. He took part in the Trojan War. Ulysses' ten years of adventures before returning home to his wife, Penelope, are described in *The Odyssey* of Homer.

LATIN PHRASES AND MOTTOES USED IN ENGLISH

Ad astra per aspera, To the stars through difficulties (motto of Kansas)

ad hoc, for this particular purpose

ad infinitum, indefinitely, without limit

ad nauseam, to the degree of disgust

alma mater, foster mother (applied to one's college or school)

alter ego, a second self; a very close friend

Annuit coeptis, He (God) has favored our undertakings (found on the Great Seal of the United States)

ars artis gratia, art for art's sake

ars longa, vita brevis, art is long, life short

bona fide, in good faith; genuine

carpe diem, make the most of today (literally: "seize the day")

caveat emptor, let the buyer beware (for he buys at his own risk)

corpus delicti, the body of the crime

cum grano salis, with a grain of salt

de facto, in fact; actual

de gustibus non est disputandum, there is no accounting for tastes; everyone to his own taste

de iure (*jure*), by right; legally

de mortuis nil nisi bonum, of the dead say nothing but good

divide et impera, divide and rule (Roman policy of conquest best exemplified by Caesar)

Dum spiro, spero, While I breathe, I hope (motto of South Carolina)

E pluribus unum, Out of many, one (motto found on the Great Seal of the United States)

errare humanum est, to err is human

ex libris, from the book collection of

ex officio, by virtue of office

ex post facto, retroactive

ex tempore, on the spur of the moment

Excelsior, Higher (motto of New York State)

festina lente, make haste slowly

habeas corpus, a writ to bring before a judge a person who is detained (literally: "you must produce the body") in **absentia,** in one's absence

in **hoc signo vinces,** by this sign you will conquer

in **loco parentis,** in the place of a parent

in **medias res,** into the midst of things

in **memoriam,** to the memory (of)

in **re,** in the matter of; concerning

in **toto,** entirely

ipso facto, by the very nature of the case; by the fact itself

Labor omnia vincit, Work conquers everything (motto of Oklahoma)

lapsus linguae, a slip of the tongue

mens sana in corpore sano, a sound mind in a sound body

modus operandi, a method of working

modus vivendi, a method of living or getting along together

multum in parvo, much in a small space

ne plus ultra, nothing more beyond; perfection

non compos mentis, not of sound mind

non sequitur, an inference that does not follow from the original statement

novus ordo seclorum, a new world order

pax vobiscum, peace be with you

per annum, by the year; each year

per capita, for each individual (by heads)

per diem, by the day

per se, by itself; essentially

persona non grata, a person who is not acceptable

post mortem, occurring after death

post proelium, praemium, after the battle comes the reward

prima facie, on first sight or appearance

pro and con(tra), for and against

pro bono publico, for the public welfare

quid pro quo, something for something

Semper fidelis, Ever faithful (motto of the United States Marines)

Semper paratus, Always prepared (motto of the United States Coast Guard)

Sic semper tyrannis, Thus always to tyrants (motto of Virginia)

sic transit gloria mundi, thus passes away the glory of the world

sine die, without appointing a day for meeting again

sine qua non, something indispensable; a necessity

status quo, the existing state

stet, let it remain (printing term)

tempus fugit, time flies

terra firma, solid ground

vade mecum, something carried by a person at all times (literally: "go with me")

verbatim, word for word

via, by way of

vice versa, the other way around; conversely

vigilantia pretium libertatis, vigilance is the price of liberty

viva voce, by word of mouth; orally

vox populi, vox Dei, the voice of the people is the voice of God

LATIN ABBREVIATIONS USED IN ENGLISH

A.D. *annō Dominī,* in the year of (our) Lord (used for dates in the Christian era as opposed to B.C.)

ad lib. *ad libitum,* at pleasure

a.m. *ante merīdiem,* before noon

A.U.C. *ab urbe conditā; annō urbis conditae,* from the founding of the city (of Rome) (used as a reference point by the Romans for establishing dates, as we use A.D. today)

cf. *cōnfer,* compare

e.g. *exemplī grātiā,* for example

et al. *et aliī,* and others; *et alibī,* and elsewhere

etc. *et cētera,* and so forth

ibid. *ibīdem,* in the same place

id. *īdem,* the same (author)

i.e. *id est,* that is

m. *merīdiē,* at midday; noon

N.B. *notā bene,* note well; take notice

op. cit. *opere citātō,* in the volume quoted

p.m. *post merīdiem,* afternoon

pro tem. *prō tempore,* for the time being

P.S. *post scriptum,* written afterwards; postscript

Q.E.D. *quod erat dēmōnstrandum,* that which was to be proved (sometimes found at the end of the solutions of geometry problems)

q.v. *quod vidē,* which see

℞ *recipe,* take as prescribed (medical term)

viz. *vidēlicet (vidēre licet),* namely

vs. *versus,* against

EXERCISES

A. Name the person referred to in each of the following:

1. He succeeded in obtaining the Golden Fleece. -------------------------------

2. He was god of the underworld. -------------------------------

3. Enchantress who changed Ulysses' men into swine. -------------------------------

4. Greek hero who slew the Minotaur. -------------------------------

5. Whatever he touched turned to gold. -------------------------------

6. He defended a bridge to delay the Etruscans. -------------------------------

7. Portrayed in mythology as the first man to fly. -------------------------------

8. Mother of the Gracchi brothers, her "jewels." -------------------------------

9. Noted musician, husband of Eurydice. -------------------------------

10. Queen of the underworld and daughter of Ceres. -------------------------------

B. Underline the word or expression in parentheses that will complete the statement correctly.

1. An inference that does not follow from the original statement is called (a quid pro quo, a status quo, a non sequitur, an ipso facto).

2. Favored to win in an Olympic running contest would be (Atalanta, Icarus, Regulus, Olympus).

3. In reckoning time, the Romans used the abbreviation A.U.C. as we use (P.M., N.B., A.D., A.M.).

4. The hero who performed the famous "Twelve Labors" was (Orpheus, Ulysses, Perseus, Hercules).

5. The motto of New York State is (Excelsior, E Pluribus Unum, Novus Ordo Seclorum, Annuit Coeptis).

6. The Latin abbreviation *cf.* means in English (careful, compare, conform, compose).

7. Penelope waited faithfully many years for the return of (Theseus, Orpheus, Ulysses, Cato).

8. A government recognized legally is called (de facto, ex officio, ex post facto, de jure).

9. The goddess of agriculture was (Ceres, Proserpina, Medea, Medusa).

10. The saying "each to his own taste" may be expressed by the Latin proverb beginning with the words (ars artis, in loco, de gustibus, mens sana).

C. In the space before each item in column *A*, write the letter of the matching item in column *B*.

Column A	*Column B*
_____ **1.** Jason	*a.* female monster
_____ **2.** Andromeda	*b.* in the same place
_____ **3.** Aeëtes	*c.* a legal writ
_____ **4.** Medusa	*d.* rescued by Perseus
_____ **5.** habeas corpus	*e.* refused to be bribed
_____ **6.** ad lib.	*f.* leader of the Argonauts
_____ **7.** Fabricius	*g.* defeated the Gauls
_____ **8.** corpus delicti	*h.* father of Medea
_____ **9.** ibid.	*i.* at pleasure
_____ **10.** Camillus	*j.* the body of the crime

D. In each of the following sentences, supply the missing Latin words:

1. No one is perfect, for **errare** _____.

2. After Pearl Harbor, the Japanese ambassador to the United States was ordered to leave, since he was **persona** _____.

3. The motto of the United States Marines is _____ **fidelis.**

4. The orator kept on talking without end or, as they say in Latin, _____.

5. For survival in a hostile world, some people believe in a _____ **vivendi.**

6. The need for both mental and physical well-being is indicated in the expression **mens sana in**

_____.

7. The coat-of-arms of astronaut John H. Glenn contained the motto _____ **per aspera.**

8. Caesar conquered his enemies by the policy of **divide et** ....

9. The Latin equivalent of "haste makes waste" is **festina** ....

10. By blurting out a wrong reply, the candidate committed a **lapsus** ....

E. In the proper columns write the Latin words and the English meaning for each of the following abbreviations:

	LATIN WORDS	ENGLISH MEANING
1. e.g.		
2. ibid.		
3. N.B.		
4. q.v.		
5. pro tem.		
6. i.e.		
7. p.m.		
8. vs.		
9. op. cit.		
10. viz.		

Chariot Racing

Chariot racing was as popular among the ancient Romans as baseball is in the United States. Chariots drawn by a team of from two to six horses raced around the Circus Maximus, which could accommodate more than 200,000 spectators. Harness racing is the modern sport most closely paralleling chariot racing.

Lesson 92—REVIEW OF ROMAN CIVILIZATION AND CULTURE

A. Underline the word or expression in parentheses that will complete the statement correctly.

1. According to tradition, Rome was founded in (509 B.C., 753 B.C., 23 B.C., 476 B.C.).

2. The opening in the ceiling of the *ātrium*, which admitted light and air, was called the (compluvium, trīclīnium, tablīnum, impluvium).

3. Julius Caesar's *praenōmen* was (Mārcus, Gāius, Lūcius, Augustus).

4. The dictator who threatened Caesar was (Marius, Pompey, Brutus, Sulla).

5. The expression *ālea iacta est* means (bread and circus games, we who are about to die salute you, the die is cast, thus ever to tyrants).

6. A sacred flame was kept burning perpetually in the Temple of (Vesta, Janus, Venus, Vulcan).

7. The word *cālōnēs* refers to (cavalry squads, slaves in camp, auxiliaries, infantrymen).

8. Much of our knowledge of Roman life comes from the excavations at (Naples, Vesuvius, Pompeii, Athens).

9. The gods of the household were (the Vestal Virgins, Juno and Hera, the Larēs and Penātēs, the Saturnalia).

10. The section in France known as Provence was called in Caesar's time (Gallia Citerior, Helvētia, Illyricum, Gallia Ulterior).

11. According to legend, Rome had (3, 5, 7, 9) kings.

12. Caesar's daughter Julia became the wife of (Antony, Pompey, Crassus, Lepidus).

13. The words *āla*, *turma*, and *decuria* refer to the (noncombatants, peditēs, legiō, equitēs).

14. The *Axona flūmen* is known today as the (Arar, Saône, Aisne, Seine).

15. The general who posed the gravest threat to Rome was (Pyrrhus, Hannibal, Orgetorix, Vercingetorix).

16. The Roman Senate usually held its meetings in the (cūria, Campus Martius, Circus Maximus, Colosseum).

17. The Roman *Saturnalia* was celebrated at about the time we celebrate (Thanksgiving, Easter, Christmas, Hallowe'en).

18. Caesar held the office of aedile after he was (praetor, quaestor, consul, propraetor).

19. *The Gallic War* deals with the war with the Belgians in Book (I, II, III, IV).

20. Officials held their position for a term that generally lasted (6 months, 1 year, 2 years, 4 years).

B. If the italicized term in each of the following statements is correct, write *true*. If the italicized term is incorrect, write the correct term.

1. In order to appear objective in writing THE GALLIC WAR, Caesar referred to himself in the *first* person.   _____

2. The *quarta vigilia* lasted from 3 a.m. to 6 a.m.   _____

3. Britannia was described by Caesar as *triangular* in shape.   _____

4. Mt. Vesuvius erupted in *79* B.C., burying the city of Pompeii.   _____

5. An eighth book of THE GALLIC WAR was added by Caesar's general *Hirtius*.   _____

321

6. The abbreviation T. stood for the praenōmen *Tiberius*. `----------------------------`

7. The Greek god Poseidon was called *Saturn* by the Romans. `----------------------------`

8. The stola and palla were garments worn by *women*. `----------------------------`

9. Apartment houses in ancient Rome were called *vīllae*. `----------------------------`

10. Cassivellaunus, who finally surrendered to Caesar, was a leader of the *Britons*. `----------------------------`

11. The god *Mercury* is represented with two faces. `----------------------------`

12. The calendar revised by Caesar was the *Julian* calendar. `----------------------------`

13. The dining room containing a table flanked by three couches was called the *tablīnum*. `----------------------------`

14. The Pyrenees Mountains separated Gaul from *Germany*. `----------------------------`

15. Caesar studied in Rhodes under the famous *Apollonius Molo*. `----------------------------`

C. In the space before each item in column *A*, write the letter of the matching item in column *B*.

Column A	Column B
_____ 1. Comitia Tribūta	*a.* beginning of the Civil War
_____ 2. toga candida	*b.* old name for July
_____ 3. 49 B.C.	*c.* Caesar's last wife
_____ 4. Bibulus	*d.* elected the higher magistrates
_____ 5. Quīnctīlis	*e.* offensive weapon
_____ 6. Cornelia	*f.* worn by an adolescent
_____ 7. scūtum	*g.* conqueror of Hannibal
_____ 8. Scipio	*h.* elected minor officials
_____ 9. praetōrium	*i.* old name for August
_____ 10. Comitia Centūriāta	*j.* worn by an office seeker
_____ 11. pīlum	*k.* beginning of the Gallic War
_____ 12. Calpurnia	*l.* defensive armor
_____ 13. toga virīlis	*m.* general's tent
_____ 14. Sextīlis	*n.* Caesar's wife and mother of Julia
_____ 15. 58 B.C.	*o.* colleague of Caesar

D. In the following passage, ten words or expressions are italicized and repeated in the questions below. Underline the alternative that best explains each of these ten words or expressions as it is used in the passage.

The Saturnalia, dedicated to the *god of the harvest*, was marked, on this festive day, by tumultuous mobs paying homage to yet another god, *Bacchus*. In the Forum near a *basilica*, a person, not completely sober, had ascended the *speaker's platform* and was haranguing the crowd in mock imitation of *Rome's greatest orator*. He wore a *magistrate's garment* and looked ludicrous in his inebriated condition. Suddenly he threw up his hands in a gesture, and, with an *exclamation*, imitated Caesar on being assassinated. The crowd yelled its approval, but soon its attention was diverted to a group of *attendants* that came by carrying the *fascēs*. In front of them walked a *praetor*, and the jovial mob calmed down as a note of solemnity intruded upon the Saturnalia.

1. *god of the harvest*

    1 Apollo   2 Neptune   3 Saturn   4 Vulcan

2. *Bacchus*

    1 god of beginnings   2 god of wine   3 god of fire   4 chief priest

3. *basilica*

    1 law court   2 senate house   3 temple   4 statue

4. *speaker's platform*

    1 vigil   2 palla   3 cursus   4 rōstra

5. *Rome's greatest orator*

    1 Demosthenes   2 Caesar   3 Augustus   4 Cicero

6. *magistrate's garment*

    1 toga candida   2 toga praetexta   3 toga virīlis   4 tunica

7. *exclamation*

    1 Pānem et circēnsēs   2 Vēnī, vīdī, vīcī   3 Et tū, Brūte!   4 Ālea iacta est

8. *attendants*

    1 līctōrēs   2 vigilēs   3 tribūnī   4 equitēs

9. *fascēs*

    1 symbol of supreme power 2 bundle of swords   3 flags   4 tablets

10. *praetor*

    1 treasurer   2 public works administrator   3 judge   4 chief executive

E. Replace each of the following English expressions in italics by a Latin equivalent:

1. The student related the story *word for word.* --

2. In making purchases, one must bear in mind the old saying, *"Let the buyer beware."* --

3. Everyone agreed that the offer was *in good faith.* --

4. Henry realized that, if he earned only $5000 *a year,* he could not afford a new car. --

5. The stranger was confused by a sign in the train marked, *"By way of* Tunnel." --

6. Conservative people dislike any change; they prefer the *existing state of things.* --

7. The tourist told his friends how he yearned for *solid ground* while seasick aboard ship. --

8. The father taught his children not to be gullible, but to accept statements *with a grain of salt.* --

9. Congress adjourned *without setting a day for the next meeting.* --

10. *"Time flies"* is a favorite theme of the Roman poet Horace. --

Unit XVI—Vocabularies

Lesson 93—LATIN MASTERY LIST

NOUNS

aciēs, -ēī (*f.*), line of battle

adventus, -ūs (*m.*), arrival, approach

aestās, -ātis (*f.*), summer

ager, agrī (*m.*), field, land

agricola, -ae (*m.*), farmer

amīcitia, -ae (*f.*), friendship

amīcus, -ī (*m.*), friend

animus, -ī (*m.*), mind, spirit

annus, -ī (*m.*), year

aqua, -ae (*f.*), water

arma, -ōrum (*n. pl.*), arms

auxilium, -ī (*n.*), aid, help

bellum, -ī (*n.*), war

caput, -itis (*n.*), head

castra, -ōrum (*n. pl.*), camp

causa, -ae (*f.*), cause, reason

celeritās, -ātis (*f.*), speed, swiftness

cīvis, -is (*m.*), citizen

cīvitās, -ātis (*f.*), state

cohors, -tis (*f.*), cohort

cōnsilium, -ī (*n.*), plan, advice

cōpia, -ae (*f.*), supply, abundance; (*pl.*), troops

corpus, -oris (*n.*), body

diēs, -ēī (*m.*), day

domus, -ūs (*f.*), house, home

dux, ducis (*m.*), leader, general

eques, -itis (*m.*), horseman

exercitus, -ūs (*m.*), army

fēmina, -ae (*f.*), woman

fidēs, -eī (*f.*), faith, trust

fīlia, -ae (*f.*), daughter

fīlius, -ī (*m.*), son

fīnis, -is (*m.*), end, boundary; (*pl.*), territory

flūmen, -inis (*n.*), river

frāter, -tris (*m.*), brother

frūmentum, -ī (*n.*), grain

fuga, -ae (*f.*), flight

gladius, -ī (*m.*), sword

glōria, -ae (*f.*), glory, fame

hiems, -emis (*f.*), winter

homō, -inis (*m.*), man, person

hōra, -ae (*f.*), hour

hostis, -is (*m.*), enemy

impedīmentum, -ī (*n.*), hindrance; (*pl.*), baggage

imperātor, -ōris (*m.*), general

imperium, -ī (*n.*), command, rule

impetus, -ūs (*m.*), attack

īnsula, -ae (*f.*), island

iter, itineris (*n.*), march, journey, route

lēgātus, -ī (*m.*), lieutenant, envoy

legiō, -ōnis (*f.*), legion

lēx, lēgis (*f.*), law

liber, -brī (*m.*), book

littera, -ae (*f.*), letter (of the alphabet); (*pl.*), communication

locus, -ī (*m.*); (*pl.*), loca, -ōrum (*n.*), place

lūx, lūcis (*f.*), light

manus, -ūs (*f.*), hand, band

mare, -is (*n.*), sea

māter, -tris (*f.*), mother

memoria, -ae (*f.*), memory

mīles, -itis (*m.*), soldier

modus, -ī (*m.*), manner, way

mōns, montis (*m.*), mountain

mors, mortis (*f.*), death

multitūdō, -inis (*f.*), multitude, crowd

mūrus, -ī (*m.*), wall

nātiō, -ōnis (*f.*), nation, tribe

nātūra, -ae (*f.*), nature

nauta, -ae (*m.*), sailor

nāvis, -is (*f.*), ship

nōmen, -inis (*n.*), name

nox, noctis (*f.*), night

numerus, -ī (*m.*), number

nūntius, -ī (*m.*), messenger, message

oppidum, -ī (*n.*), town

pars, partis (*f.*), part

passus, -ūs (*m.*), pace, step

pater, -tris (*m.*), father

patria, -ae (*f.*), country, native land

pāx, pācis (*f.*), peace

pecūnia, -ae (*f.*), money

perīculum, -ī (*n.*), danger

pēs, pedis (*m.*), foot

poena, -ae (*f.*), punishment

pōns, pontis (*m.*), bridge

populus, -ī (*m.*), people

porta, -ae (*f.*), gate

praemium, -ī (*n.*), reward, prize

praesidium, -ī (*n.*), protection, guard

prīnceps, -ipis (*m.*), chief, leader

proelium, -ī (*n.*), battle

prōvincia, -ae (*f.*), province

puella, -ae (*f.*), girl

puer, puerī (*m.*), boy

regiō, -ōnis (*f.*), region, district

rēgnum, -ī (*n.*), kingdom, rule

rēs, reī (*f.*), thing, matter

rēx, rēgis (*m.*), king

salūs, -ūtis (*f.*), safety, welfare

senātor, -ōris (*m.*), senator

senātus, -ūs (*m.*), senate

servus, -ī (*m.*), slave

signum, -ī (*n.*), signal, standard

silva, -ae (*f.*), forest

socius, -ī (*m.*), ally, comrade

soror, -ōris (*f.*), sister

spēs, speī (*f.*), hope

studium, -ī (*n.*), eagerness, enthusiasm

tēlum, -ī (*n.*), weapon

tempus, -oris (*n.*), time

terra, -ae (*f.*), land

timor, -ōris (*m.*), fear

urbs, urbis (*f.*), city

verbum, -ī (*n.*), word

via, -ae (*f.*), way, road, street

victōria, -ae (*f.*), victory

vīcus, -ī (*m.*), village

vigilia, -ae (*f.*), watch, guard

vīlla, -ae (*f.*), country house, farm

vir, virī (*m.*), man

virtūs, -ūtis (*f.*), courage

vīta, -ae (*f.*), life

vulnus, -eris (*n.*), wound

ADJECTIVES AND PRONOUNS

ācer, ācris, ācre, sharp, fierce
altus, -a, -um, high, deep
amīcus, -a, -um, friendly
bonus, -a, -um, good
brevis, -e, short
celer, -eris, -ere, swift
certus, -a, -um, certain, sure
clārus, -a, -um, clear, famous
ego, I
facilis, -e, easy
fīnitimus, -a, -um, neighboring
fortis, -e, brave, strong
hic, haec, hoc, this, he, she, it
īdem, eadem, idem, the same
ille, illa, illud, that, he, she, it
ipse, ipsa, ipsum, -self, very

is, ea, id, this, that, he, she, it
līber, -era, -erum, free
longus, -a, -um, long
magnus, -a, -um, great, large
malus, -a, -um, bad, evil
medius, -a, -um, middle (of)
meus, -a, -um, my, mine
miser, -era, -erum, wretched, poor
multus, -a, -um, much, many
noster, -tra, -trum, our, ours
nōtus, -a, -um, known, famous
novus, -a, -um, new, strange
nūllus, -a, -um, no, none
omnis, -e, all, every

parvus, -a, -um, small, little
paucī, -ae, -a, few
potēns, powerful
quantus, -a, -um, how great
quī, quae, quod, who, which, that
quis, quid, who, what
suī, of himself, herself, itself, themselves
suus, -a, -um, his (her, its, their) own
tantus, -a, -um, so great, so much
tōtus, -a, -um, whole, entire
tū, you
tuus, -a, -um, your, yours
vester, -tra, -trum, your, yours

VERBS

accipiō, -ere, -cēpī, -ceptus, receive
agō, -ere, ēgī, āctus, drive, do
amō, -āre, -āvī, -ātus, love, like
appellō, -āre, -āvī, -ātus, name
arbitror, -ārī, -ātus sum, think
audiō, -īre, -īvī, -ītus, hear
capiō, -ere, cēpī, captus, take, seize
cognōscō, -ere, -nōvī, -nitus, find out, learn
cōnficiō, -ere, -fēcī, -fectus, finish
cōnstituō, -ere, -stituī, -stitūtus, decide, station
contendō, -ere, -tendī, -tentus, hasten, fight
conveniō, -īre, -vēnī, -ventus, come together, assemble
convocō, -āre, -āvī, -ātus, call together, summon
cupiō, -ere, -īvī, -ītus, wish, desire
dēbeō, -ēre, -uī, -itus, owe, ought
dēfendō, -ere, -fendī, -fēnsus, defend
dēligō, -ere, -lēgī, -lēctus, choose
dīcō, -ere, dīxī, dictus, say, speak, tell
discēdō, -ere, -cessī, -cessūrus, leave, depart
dō, dare, dedī, datus, give
dūcō, -ere, dūxī, ductus, lead
eō, īre, īvī (iī), itūrus, go

exīstimō, -āre, -āvī, -ātus, think
faciō, -ere, fēcī, factus, make, do
ferō, ferre, tulī, lātus, bear, carry, bring
fugiō, -ere, fūgī, fugitūrus, flee
gerō, -ere, gessī, gestus, carry on, wage
habeō, -ēre, -uī, -itus, have
iaciō, -ere, iēcī, iactus, throw
imperō, -āre, -āvī, -ātus, command, order
incipiō, -ere, -cēpī, -ceptus, begin
īnferō, -ferre, -tulī, illātus, bring in, wage
intellegō, -ere, -lēxī, -lēctus, understand, realize
interficiō, -ere, -fēcī, -fectus, kill
iubeō, -ēre, iussī, iussus, order
labōrō, -āre, -āvī, -ātus, work
laudō, -āre, -āvī, -ātus, praise
līberō, -āre, -āvī, -ātus, free
locō, -āre, -āvī, -ātus, place
maneō, -ēre, mānsī, mānsūrus, remain, stay
mittō, -ere, mīsī, missus, send
moneō, -ēre, -uī, -itus, advise, warn
moveō, -ēre, mōvī, mōtus, move
mūniō, -īre, -īvī, -ītus, fortify, build
nāvigō, -āre, -āvī, -ātus, sail
nūntiō, -āre, -āvī, -ātus, announce
occupō, -āre, -āvī, -ātus, seize
oppugnō, -āre, -āvī, -ātus, attack

parō, -āre, -āvī, -ātus, prepare
persuādeō, -ēre, -suāsī, -suāsūrus, persuade
perveniō, -īre, -vēnī, -ventus, arrive
petō, -ere, -īvī, -ītus, seek, ask
pōnō, -ere, posuī, positus, put, place
portō, -āre, -āvī, -ātus, carry
possum, posse, potuī, be able, can
proficīscor, -ficīscī, -fectus sum, set out
prōgredior, -gredī, -gressus sum, advance
prohibeō, -ēre, -uī, -itus, hold back, prevent
properō, -āre, -āvī, -ātus, hurry
pugnō, -āre, -āvī, -ātus, fight
putō, -āre, -āvī, -ātus, think
recipiō, -ere, -cēpī, -ceptus, take back, receive
redeō, -īre, -iī, -itūrus, go back, return
regō, -ere, rēxī, rēctus, rule, guide
relinquō, -ere, -līquī, -lictus, leave, abandon
respondeō, -ēre, -spondī, -spōnsus, reply, answer
retineō, -ēre, -tinuī, -tentus, hold back, keep
rogō, -āre, -āvī, -ātus, ask, beg
sciō, -īre, -īvī, -ītus, know
scrībō, -ere, scrīpsī, scrīptus, write

sequor, sequī, secūtus sum, follow

servō, -āre, -āvī, -ātus, save, keep

spectō, -āre, -āvī, -ātus, look at

spērō, -āre, -āvī, -ātus, hope

sum, esse, fuī, futūrus, be

superō, -āre, -āvī, -ātus, defeat, surpass

temptō, -āre, -āvī, -ātus, try

teneō, -ēre, -uī, hold, keep

timeō, -ēre, -uī, fear

trādō, -ere, -didī, -ditus, surrender, hand over

ūtor, ūtī, ūsus sum, use

veniō, -īre, vēnī, ventus, come

videō, -ēre, vīdī, vīsus, see

vincō, -ere, vīcī, victus, conquer

vocō, -āre, -āvī, -ātus, call

volō, velle, voluī, want, wish

vulnerō, -āre, -āvī, -ātus, wound

ADVERBS, CONJUNCTIONS, PREPOSITIONS, ENCLITICS

ā, ab (*with abl.*), from, by

ad (*with acc.*), to, toward, near

ante (*with acc.*), before, in front of

circum (*with acc.*), around

contrā (*with acc.*), against, opposite

cum (*with abl.*), with

cum, when, since, although

cūr, why

dē (*with abl.*), down from, concerning, about

diū, for a long time

ē, ex (*with abl.*), out of, from

et, and; et . . . et, both . . . and

ibi, there

in (*with abl.*), in, on; (*with acc.*), into

inter (*with acc.*), between, among

ita, so, thus

itaque, and so, therefore

nē, in order not

-ne, sign of a question

nōn, not

nunc, now

ob (*with acc.*), on account of

per (*with acc.*), through

post (*with acc.*), after, behind

postquam, after

prō (*with abl.*), before, for

prope, near

propter (*with acc.*), because of

-que, and

quod, because

saepe, often

sed, but

semper, always

sine (*with abl.*), without

sub (*with acc. and abl.*), under

tam, so

trāns (*with acc.*), across

tum, then

ubi, where, when

ut, in order to, that

NUMERALS

CARDINAL	ORDINAL
ūnus, -a, -um, one	prīmus, -a, -um, first
duo, duae, duo, two	secundus, -a, -um, second
trēs, tria, three	tertius, -a, -um, third
quattuor, four	quārtus, -a, -um, fourth
quīnque, five	quīntus, -a, -um, fifth
sex, six	sextus, -a, -um, sixth
septem, seven	septimus, -a, -um, seventh
octō, eight	octāvus, -a, -um, eighth
novem, nine	nōnus, -a, -um, ninth
decem, ten	decimus, -a, -um, tenth
vīgintī, twenty	
centum, one hundred	
mīlle, one thousand	

ROMAN NUMERALS

I	1	XIV	14
II	2	XV	15
III	3	XVI	16
IIII or IV	4	XX	20
V	5	XXX	30
VI	6	XL	40
VII	7	L	50
VIII	8	LX	60
VIIII or IX	9	C	100
X	10	D	500
XI	11	M	1000

EXERCISES

A. In the space before each word in column *A*, write the letter of its English equivalent in column *B*.

	Column A	*Column B*
------	**1.** amīcitia	*a.* so
------	**2.** dēligō	*b.* often
------	**3.** īdem	*c.* night
------	**4.** sciō	*d.* finish
------	**5.** saepe	*e.* neighboring
------	**6.** vīgintī	*f.* light
------	**7.** tam	*g.* friendship
------	**8.** paucī	*h.* begin
------	**9.** cōnficiō	*i.* the same
------	**10.** prōgredior	*j.* twenty
------	**11.** lūx	*k.* choose
------	**12.** nox	*l.* because of
------	**13.** fīnitimus	*m.* few
------	**14.** propter	*n.* advance
------	**15.** incipiō	*o.* know

B. Translate the following numerical expressions into English:

1. XXV pedēs --
2. legiō decima --
3. MD hominēs --
4. IX oppida --
5. CXL rēs --
6. octāvus numerus --
7. DC verba --
8. septimus rēx --
9. MCXIV servī --
10. nōnus annus --

C. Underline the correct translation of the Latin word.

1. *ibi:*   where, when, there, here
2. *temptō:*   try, hold, fear, surrender
3. *tantus:*   so, such, whole, so great
4. *praesidium:*   reward, protection, punishment, danger
5. *redeō:*   return, take back, hold back, leave
6. *potēns:*   small, few, powerful, poor
7. *vester:*   our, your, his, their
8. *sine:*   with, under, but, without

9. *spērō:*   look at, see, hope, fear
10. *brevis:*   brave, short, long, light
11. *fīnis:*   end, territory, faith, ship
12. *regiō:*   kingdom, king, district, legion
13. *novus:*   famous, new, none, ninth
14. *cōnstituō:*   hasten, finish, decide, assemble
15. *rogō:*   rule, think, place, ask
16. *cūr:*   with, why, when, although
17. *cīvitās:*   citizen, horseman, state, speed
18. *itaque:*   thus, and, therefore, after
19. *cupiō:*   take, wage, wish, flee
20. *salūs:*   safety, alone, hope, eagerness

D. Draw a line through the word that does *not* belong with the others in each group. Explain why it does not belong.

1. prīmus, centum, novus, octō

----

2. quis, cūr, quantus, sed

----

3. hōra, īnsula, diēs, tempus

----

4. rēgnum, rēx, prīnceps, imperātor

----

5. oppidum, patria, vīcus, pars

----

6. proficīscor, maneō, prōgredior, redeō

----

7. altus, fortis, tuus, celer

----

8. ab, ex, per, ita

----

9. tēlum, nāvis, gladius, arma

----

10. relinquō, dīcō, nūntiō, respondeō

----

11. mīlle, vīgintī, quīntus, septem

----

12. ibi, semper, dē, tum

----

13. ego, tuus, vōs, tū

----

14. caput, manus, cōnsilium, pēs

----

15. virtūs, salūs, celeritās, vulnus

E. In the space before each verb in column *A*, write the letter of its synonym in column *B*.

Column A	Column B
_____ **1.** cupiō	*a.* portō
_____ **2.** pōnō	*b.* arbitror
_____ **3.** putō	*c.* agō
_____ **4.** imperō	*d.* superō
_____ **5.** properō	*e.* volō
_____ **6.** ferō	*f.* petō
_____ **7.** vincō	*g.* occupō
_____ **8.** rogō	*h.* contendō
_____ **9.** capiō	*i.* locō
_____ **10.** faciō	*j.* iubeō

F. Underline the correct translation of the English word.

1. *peace:*   pāx, pēs, nox, lēx
2. *fortify:*   maneō, moneō, mūniō, moveō
3. *seventh:*   sex, sextus, septem, septimus
4. *then:*   cum, tum, cūr, ita
5. *fierce:*   celer, certus, ācer, potēns
6. *danger:*   perīculum, praemium, praesidium, proelium
7. *mind:*   annus, nātiō, poena, animus
8. *so great:*   quantus, tōtus, tantus, clārus
9. *ought:*   discēdō, dēbeō, dēligō, dō
10. *understand:* īnferō, interficiō, ūtor, intellegō

G. Underline the word in parentheses that you would use to translate the italicized English word.

1. He received a severe *wound*.   (vulnus, vulnerō)
2. This was her *fifth* prize.   (quīnque, quīntus)
3. Lincoln was determined to *free* the slaves.   (līber, līberō)
4. He will *command* the soldiers to flee.   (imperium, imperō)
5. *Because* of the danger, we stayed at home.   (Quod, Propter)
6. The king defended his *rule*.   (rēgnum, regō)
7. *After* the war, the soldiers returned home.   (Post, Postquam)
8. They will *name* him Marcus.   (nōmen, appellō)
9. The Romans withstood the *attack*.   (impetus, oppugnō)
10. Her *swiftness* surprised everyone.   (celer, celeritās)

ā, ab (*with abl.*), from, by

abeō, -īre, -iī, -itūrus, go away

absum, -esse, āfuī, āfutūrus, be away, be absent

accēdō, -ere, -cessī, -cessūrus, go to, approach

accidō, -ere, -cidī, befall, happen

accipiō, -ere, -cēpī, -ceptus, receive

ācer, ācris, ācre, sharp, fierce

aciēs, -ēī (*f.*), line of battle

ācriter, sharply, fiercely

ad (*with acc.*), to, toward, near

addūcō, -ere, -dūxī, -ductus, lead to, influence

adeō, -īre, -iī, -itūrus, go to, approach

adhortor, -ārī, -ātus sum, encourage

aditus, -ūs (*m.*), approach

admīror, -ārī, -ātus sum, wonder at, admire

adsum, -esse, -fuī, -futūrus, be near, be present

adulēscēns, -entis (*m.*), young man

adulēscentia, -ae (*f.*), youth

adventus, -ūs (*m.*), arrival, approach

aedificium, -ī (*n.*), building

aedificō, -āre, -āvī, -ātus, build

aeger, -gra, -grum, sick

aequus, -a, -um, equal, level, fair

aestās, -ātis (*f.*), summer

aetās, -ātis (*f.*), age

ager, agrī (*m.*), field, land

aggredior, -gredī, -gressus sum, attack

agmen, -inis (*n.*), marching column

agō, -ere, ēgī, āctus, drive, do

agricola, -ae (*m.*), farmer

aliquis, -quid, someone, something

alius, -a, -ud, other, another

alter, -era, -erum, the other (of two)

altitūdō, -inis (*f.*), height, depth

altus, -a, -um, high, deep

ambulō, -āre, -āvī, -ātus, walk

amīcitia, -ae (*f.*), friendship

amīcus, -a, -um, friendly

amīcus, -ī (*m.*), friend

āmittō, -ere, -mīsī, -missus, send away, lose

amō, -āre, -āvī, -ātus, love, like

amor, -ōris (*m.*), love

amplus, -a, -um, large, spacious

ancora, -ae (*f.*), anchor

angustus, -a, -um, narrow

animadvertō, -ere, -tī, -sus, notice

animal, -ālis (*n.*), animal

animus, -ī (*m.*), mind, spirit

annus, -ī (*m.*), year

ante (*with acc.*), before, in front of

anteā, previously, formerly

antequam, before

apertus, -a, -um, open, exposed

appellō, -āre, -āvī, -ātus, name

appropinquō, -āre, -āvī, -ātus, approach

apud (*with acc.*), among, in the presence of, near

aqua, -ae (*f.*), water

aquila, -ae (*f.*), eagle

arbitror, -ārī, -ātus sum, think

arbor, -oris (*f.*), tree

arēna, -ae (*f.*), sand, arena

arma, -ōrum (*n. pl.*), arms

armō, -āre, -āvī, -ātus, arm, equip

at, but

atque (ac), and, and especially

ātrium, -ī (*n.*), atrium

auctōritās, -ātis (*f.*), influence, authority

audācia, -ae (*f.*), boldness

audācter, boldly

audāx, bold, daring

audeō, -ēre, ausus sum, dare

audiō, -īre, -īvī, -ītus, hear

augeō, -ēre, auxī, auctus, increase

aut, or; **aut . . . aut,** either . . . or

autem, however, but, moreover

auxilium, -ī (*n.*), aid, help

barbarus, -a, -um, foreign, uncivilized, savage

barbarus, -ī (*m.*), barbarian, native

bellum, -ī (*n.*), war

bene, well

beneficium, -ī (*n.*), benefit, favor, kindness

bis, twice

bonus, -a, -um, good

brevis, -e, short

cadō, -ere, cecidī, cāsurus, fall

caedēs, -is (*f.*), murder

caedō, -ere, cecīdī, caesus, cut, kill

caelum, -ī (*n.*), sky

calamitās, -ātis (*f.*), disaster

campus, -ī (*m.*), plain, field

capiō, -ere, cēpī, captus, take, seize

captīvus, -ī (*m.*), prisoner

caput, -itis (*n.*), head

carrus, -ī (*m.*), wagon, cart

casa, -ae (*f.*), hut

castra, -ōrum (*n. pl.*), camp

cāsus, -ūs (*m.*), chance, accident

causa, -ae (*f.*), cause, reason

causā, for the sake of

caveō, -ēre, cāvī, cautūrus, beware of

cēdō, -ere, cessī, cessūrus, move, yield

celer, -eris, -ere, swift

celeritās, -ātis (*f.*), speed, swiftness

cēna, -ae (*f.*), dinner

cēnō, -āre, -āvī, -ātus, dine, eat

centum, one hundred

centuriō, -ōnis (*m.*), centurion

certus, -a, -um, certain, sure

cēterī, -ae, -a, the others, the rest

cibus, -ī (*m.*), food

circiter, about

circum (*with acc.*), around

circumdō, -dare, -dedī, -datus, place around, surround

circumveniō, -īre, -vēnī, -ventus, surround

circus, -ī (*m.*), circus

citerior, -ius, nearer

citō, -āre, -āvī, -ātus, excite, rouse

cīvīlis, -e, civil

cīvis, -is (*m.*), citizen

cīvitās, -ātis (*f.*), state

clam, secretly

clāmō, -āre, -āvī, -ātus, shout

clāmor, -ōris (*m.*), shout, noise

clārus, -a, -um, clear, famous

classis, -is (*f.*), fleet

claudō, -ere, clausī, clausus, close

coepī, coepisse, coeptus, began

cognōscō, -ere, -nōvī, -nitus, find out, learn

cōgō, -ere, coēgī, coāctus, compel, collect

cohors, -tis (f.), cohort

cohortor, -ārī, -ātus sum, encourage

collis, -is (m.), hill

collocō, -āre, -āvī, -ātus, put together, station

colloquium, -ī (n.), conference

colloquor, -quī, -cūtus sum, converse with

colōnia, -ae (f.), colony

committō, -ere, -mīsī, -missus, join, entrust

commodus, -a, -um, convenient, suitable

commoveō, -ēre, -mōvī, -mōtus, move deeply, alarm

commūnis, -e, common

comparō, -āre, -āvī, -ātus, get together, prepare

compleō, -ēre, -ēvī, -ētus, fill

complūrēs, -a, several, many

comportō, -āre, -āvī, -ātus, bring together

concēdō, -ere, -cessī, -cessūrus, yield, withdraw

concilium, -ī (n.), meeting

condiciō, -ōnis (f.), terms, agreement

cōnferō, -ferre, -tulī, collātus, bring together, collect

cōnficiō, -ere, -fēcī, -fectus, finish

cōnfirmō, -āre, -āvī, -ātus, encourage, strengthen

coniciō, -ere, -iēcī, -iectus, hurl

coniungō, -ere, -iūnxī, -iūnctus, join, unite

cōnor, -ārī, -ātus sum, try, attempt

cōnscrībō, -ere, -scrīpsī, -scrīptus, enlist, enroll

cōnsequor, -ī, -secūtus sum, pursue, overtake

cōnservō, -āre, -āvī, -ātus, preserve, keep

cōnsīdō, -ere, -sēdī, -sessūrus, sit down, encamp

cōnsilium, -ī (n.), plan, advice

cōnsistō, -ere, -stitī, -stitūrus, take one's stand, halt

cōnspectus, -ūs (m.), sight

cōnspiciō, -ere, -spexī, -spectus, notice

cōnstituō, -ere, -stituī, -stitūtus, decide, station

cōnsuētūdō, -inis (f.), custom, habit

cōnsul, -is (m.), consul

cōnsulāris, -e, consular

cōnsulātus, -ūs (m.), consulship

cōnsūmō, -ere, -sūmpsī, -sūmptus, use up, spend

contendō, -ere, -tendī, -tentus, hasten, fight

contineō, -ēre, -tinuī, -tentus, hold together, hem in

continuus, -a, -um, continuous, successive

contrā (with acc.), against, opposite

contrōversia, -ae (f.), argument

conveniō, -īre, -vēnī, -ventus, come together, assemble

convocō, -āre, -āvī, -ātus, call together, summon

cōpia, -ae (f.), supply, abundance; (pl.), troops

cornū, -ūs (n.), horn, wing (of an army)

corpus, -oris (n.), body

crās, tomorrow

crēdō, -ere, -idī, -itus, believe

cum (with abl.), with

cum, when, since, although

cupiditās, -ātis (f.), desire

cupidus, -a, -um, desirous, eager

cupiō, -ere, -īvī, -ītus, wish, desire

cūr, why

cūra, -ae (f.), care, anxiety

cūrō, -āre, -āvī, -ātus, care for, attend to

currō, -ere, cucurrī, cursūrus, run

currus, -ūs (m.), chariot

cursus, -ūs (m.), running, course

dē (with abl.), down from, concerning, about

dea, -ae (f.), goddess

dēbeō, -ēre, -uī, -itus, owe, ought

decem, ten

decimus, -a, -um, tenth

dēditiō, -ōnis (f.), surrender

dēdō, -ere, dēdidī, dēditus, surrender, devote

dēdūcō, -ere, -dūxī, -ductus, bring or lead down, launch

dēfendō, -ere, -fendī, -fēnsus, defend

dēfēnsor, -ōris (m.), defender

dēficiō, -ere, -fēcī, -fectus, fail, revolt

dēiciō, -ere, -iēcī, -iectus, throw down, dislodge

dēligō, -ere, -lēgī, -lēctus, choose

dēmōnstrō, -āre, -āvī, -ātus, point out, show

dēns, dentis (m.), tooth

dēspērō, -āre, -āvī, -ātus, despair, lose hope

dēsum, -esse, -fuī, -futūrus, be wanting, fail

deus, -ī (m.), god

dexter, -tra, -trum, right

dīcō, -ere, dīxī, dictus, say, speak, tell .

diēs, -ēī (m.), day

difficilis, -e, hard, difficult

difficultās, -ātis (f.), difficulty

digitus, -ī (m.), finger

dīligēns, careful

dīligentia, -ae (f.), carefulness, diligence

dīmittō, -ere, -mīsī, -missus, send away, let go

discēdō, -ere, -cessī, -cessūrus, leave, depart

disciplīna, -ae (f.), training

discipulus, -ī (m.), pupil

dissimilis, -e, unlike

diū, for a long time

dīvidō, -ere, -vīsī, -vīsus, divide

dō, dare, dedī, datus, give

doceō, -ēre, -uī, -tus, teach, explain

dolor, -ōris (m.), pain, grief, suffering

domicilium, -ī (n.), home

domina, -ae (f.), mistress

dominor, -ārī, -ātus sum, domineer, rule

dominus, -ī (m.), master

domus, -ūs (f.), house, home

dōnō, -āre, -āvī, -ātus, give

dōnum, -ī (n.), gift

dormiō, -īre, -īvī, -ītus, sleep

dubitō, -āre, -āvī, -ātus, doubt, hesitate

dūcō, -ere, dūxī, ductus, lead

dum, while, until

duo, duae, duo, two

dux, ducis (m.), leader, general

ē, ex (with abl.), out of, from

ēdūcō, -ere, -dūxī, -ductus, lead out

efficiō, -ere, -fēcī, -fectus, bring about, accomplish

ego, meī, I; (pl.), nōs, nostrum, we

ēgredior, -gredī, -gressus sum, go out, leave

ēgregius, -a, -um, outstanding, remarkable

ēiciō, -ere, -iēcī, -iectus, throw out

enim, for

ēnūntiō, -āre, -āvī, -ātus, declare, announce

eō, īre, īvī (iī), itūrus, go

eō, there, to that place

eōdem, to the same place

epistula, -ae (f.), letter

eques, -itis (m.), horseman

equitātus, -ūs (m.), cavalry

equus, -ī (m.), horse

et, and; et ... et, both ... and

etiam, even, also

etsī, although

excēdō, -ere, -cessī, -cessūrus, go out, depart

excipiō, -ere, -cēpī, -ceptus, receive

exeō, -īre, -iī, -itūrus, go out

exerceō, -ēre, -ercuī, -ercitus, train

exercitus, -ūs (m.), army

exīstimō, -āre, -āvī, -ātus, think

exitus, -ūs (m.), outcome, departure

expellō, -ere, -pulī, -pulsus, drive out

experior, -īrī, -pertus sum, test, try

explōrātor, -ōris (m.), scout

explōrō, -āre, -āvī, -ātus, search out, reconnoiter

expōnō, -ere, -posuī, -positus, put out, set forth

expugnō, -āre, -āvī, -ātus, capture

exsequor, -quī, -cūtus sum, pursue

exspectō, -āre, -āvī, -ātus, wait (for)

exterior, -ius, outer, exterior

extrā (with acc.), outside of, beyond

extrēmus, -a, -um, farthest

fābula, -ae (f.), story

facile, easily

facilis, -e, easy

faciō, -ere, fēcī, factus, make, do

factum, -ī (n.), deed, act

facultās, -ātis (f.), ability, opportunity

falsus, -a, -um, false

fāma, -ae (f.), report, rumor, reputation

familia, -ae (f.), household

fēlīx, happy, fortunate

fēmina, -ae (f.), woman

ferō, ferre, tulī, lātus, bear, carry, bring

fidēlis, -e, faithful

fidēs, -eī (f.), faith, trust

fīlia, -ae (f.), daughter

fīlius, -ī (m.), son

fīniō, -īre, -īvī, -ītus, limit

fīnis, -is (m.), end, boundary; (pl.), territory

fīnitimus, -a, -um, neighboring

fīō, fierī, factus sum, become, be made, happen

fīrmō, -āre, -āvī, -ātus, strengthen

fīrmus, -a, -um, strong

flūmen, -inis (n.), river

fōrma, -ae (f.), shape, beauty

fortis, -e, brave, strong

fortiter, bravely

fortitūdō, -inis (f.), courage, strength

fortūna, -ae (f.), fortune, luck

forum, -ī (n.), forum, marketplace

fossa, -ae (f.), trench

frāter, -tris (m.), brother

frīgidus, -a, -um, cold

frūmentārius, -a, -um, abounding in grain, fertile

frūmentum, -ī (n.), grain

frūstrā, in vain

fuga, -ae (f.), flight

fugiō, -ere, fūgī, fugitūrus, flee

fugitīvus, -ī (m.), fugitive

gēns, gentis (f.), family, nation, tribe

genus, -eris (n.), race, birth, kind

gerō, -ere, gessī, gestus, carry on, wage

gladiātor, -ōris (m.), gladiator

gladius, -ī (m.), sword

glōria, -ae (f.), glory, fame

gradior, gradī, gressus sum, step, walk

grātia, -ae (f.), gratitude, favor, influence

grātus, -a, -um, pleasing, grateful

gravis, -e, heavy, severe, serious

habeō, -ēre, -uī, -itus, have

habitō, -āre, -āvī, -ātus, live, dwell

hīberna, -ōrum (n. pl.), winter quarters

hīc, here

hic, haec, hoc, this, he, she, it

hiemō, -āre, -āvī, -ātūrus, spend the winter

hiems, -emis (f.), winter

hodiē, today

homō, -inis (m.), man, person

honor, -ōris (m.), honor, office

hōra, -ae (f.), hour

hortor, -ārī, -ātus sum, urge

hostis, -is (m.), enemy

hūmānus, -a, -um, human

iaciō, -ere, iēcī, iactus, throw

iam, already, soon, now

iānua, -ae (f.), door

ibi, there

īdem, eadem, idem, the same

idōneus, -a, -um, suitable

igitur, therefore

ignis, -is (m.), fire

ignōtus, -a, -um, unknown

ille, illa, illud, that, he, she, it

immortālis, -e, immortal

impedīmentum, -ī (n.), hindrance; (pl.), baggage

impediō, -īre, -īvī, -ītus, hinder

impellō, -ere, -pulī, -pulsus, drive on, influence

imperātor, -ōris (m.), general

imperium, -ī (n.), command, rule

imperō, -āre, -āvī, -ātus, command, order

impetus, -ūs (m.), attack

importō, -āre, -āvī, -ātus, bring in, import

in (with abl.), in, on; (with acc.), into

incendō, -ere, -cendī, -cēnsus, set fire to, burn

incertus, -a, -um, uncertain

incipiō, -ere, -cēpī, -ceptus, begin

incitō, -āre, -āvī, -ātus, urge on, arouse

incola, -ae (m.), inhabitant

incolumis, -e, unharmed, safe

ineō, -īre, -iī, -itūrus, enter upon

īnfēlīx, unhappy, unfortunate

īnferior, -ius, lower

īnferō, -ferre, -tulī, illātus, bring in, wage

inimīcus, -a, -um, unfriendly

inīquus, -a, -um, unequal, uneven, unfavorable

initium, -ī (n.), beginning

iniūria, -ae (f.), injury, wrong, injustice

inopia, -ae (*f.*), lack, scarcity

īnsequor, -sequī, -secūtus sum, follow after, pursue

īnsidiae, -ārum (*f. pl.*), ambush, treachery

īnstituō, -ere, -stituī, -stitūtus, establish, decide

īnstruō, -ere, -strūxī, -strūctus, draw up, arrange

īnsula, -ae (*f.*), island

integer, -gra, -grum, whole, untouched, unharmed

intellegō, -ere, -lēxī, -lēctus, realize, understand

inter (*with acc.*), between, among

intereā, meanwhile

interficiō, -ere, -fēcī, -fectus, kill

interim, meanwhile

intermittō, -ere, -mīsī, -missus, stop, discontinue

interrogō, -āre, -āvī, -ātus, ask, question

intervāllum, -ī (*n.*), space between, distance

intrā (*with acc.*), within

inveniō, -īre, -vēnī, -ventus, find, come upon

ipse, ipsa, ipsum, -self, very

īra, -ae (*f.*), anger

is, ea, id, this, that, he, she, it

ita, so, thus

itaque, and so, therefore

item, likewise

iter, itineris (*n.*), march, journey, route

iubeō, -ēre, iussī, iussus, order

iūdicium, -ī (*n.*), judgment, trial

iūdicō, -āre, -āvī, -ātus, judge, decide

iugum, -ī (*n.*), yoke, ridge

iungō, -ere, iūnxī, iūnctus, join

iūrō, -āre, -āvī, -ātus, swear

iūs, iūris (*n.*), right, law

labor, -ōris (*m.*), work, task

labōrō, -āre, -āvī, -ātus, work

lātitūdō, -inis (*f.*), width

latus, -eris (*n.*), side

lātus, -a, -um, wide

laudō, -āre, -āvī, -ātus, praise

laus, laudis (*f.*), praise

lēgātus, -ī (*m.*), lieutenant, envoy

legiō, -ōnis (*f.*), legion

legō, -ere, lēgī, lēctus, choose, read

levis, -e, light, mild

lēx, lēgis (*f.*), law

liber, -brī (*m.*), book

līber, -era, -erum, free

līberī, -ōrum (*m. pl.*), children

līberō, -āre, -āvī, -ātus, free

lībertās, -ātis (*f.*), liberty, freedom

licet, licēre, licuit, it is permitted, one may

lingua, -ae (*f.*), tongue, language

littera, -ae (*f.*), letter (of the alphabet); (*pl.*), communication

lītus, -oris (*n.*), shore

locō, -āre, -āvī, -ātus, place

locus, -ī (*m.*); (*pl.*), loca, -ōrum (*n.*), place

longus, -a, -um, long

loquor, -quī, -cūtus sum, speak, say

lūdō, -ere, lūsī, lūsus, play

lūdus, -ī (*m.*), game, school

lūna, -ae (*f.*), moon

lūx, lūcis (*f.*), light

magis, more

magister, -trī (*m.*), teacher

magistrātus, -ūs (*m.*), magistrate, office

magnitūdō, -inis (*f.*), greatness, size

magnopere, greatly

magnus, -a, -um, great, large

maiōrēs, -um (*m. pl.*), ancestors

malus, -a, -um, bad, evil

mandō, -āre, -āvī, -ātus, entrust, order

maneō, -ēre, mānsī, mānsūrus, remain, stay

manus, -ūs (*f.*), hand, band

mare, -is (*n.*), sea

maritimus, -a, -um, maritime

māter, -tris (*f.*), mother

māteria, -ae (*f.*), timber

mātrōna, -ae (*f.*), wife, lady

maximē, most of all, especially

medius, -a, -um, middle (of)

memoria, -ae (*f.*), memory

mēns, mentis (*f.*), mind

mēnsa, -ae (*f.*), table

mēnsis, -is (*m.*), month

mercātor, -ōris (*m.*), trader

merīdiēs, -ēī (*m.*), noon

meus, -a, -um, my, mine

mīles, -itis (*m.*), soldier

mīlitāris, -e, military

mīlle, one thousand

mīror, -ārī, -ātus sum, wonder at

miser, -era, -erum, wretched, poor

mittō, -ere, mīsī, missus, send

modo, only

modus, -ī (*m.*), manner, way

moneō, -ēre, -uī, -itus, advise, warn

mōns, montis (*m.*), mountain

mōnstrō, -āre, -āvī, -ātus, show

mora, -ae (*f.*), delay

morior, morī, mortuus sum, die

moror, -ārī, -ātus sum, delay, stay

mors, mortis (*f.*), death

mōs, mōris (*m.*), custom

moveō, -ēre, mōvī, mōtus, move

mox, soon

multitūdō, -inis (*f.*), multitude, crowd

multus, -a, -um, much, many

mūniō, -īre, -īvī, -ītus, fortify, build

mūnītiō, -ōnis (*f.*), fortification

mūrus, -ī (*m.*), wall

nam, for

nancīscor, -cīscī, nactus sum, find, obtain

nārrō, -āre, -āvī, -ātus, tell, relate

nāscor, nāscī, nātus sum, be born

nātiō, -ōnis (*f.*), nation, tribe

nātūra, -ae (*f.*), nature

nauta, -ae (*m.*), sailor

nāvigium, -ī (*n.*), boat

nāvigō, -āre, -āvī, -ātus, sail

nāvis, -is (*f.*), ship

-ne (sign of a question)

nē, in order not

nē . . . quidem, not even

necessārius, -a, -um, necessary

necesse, necessary

negōtium, -ī (*n.*), business, task

nēmō, no one

neque (nec), and not, nor; neque . . . neque, neither . . . nor

nesciō, -īre, -īvī, not know

neuter, -tra, -trum, neither (of two)

nihil, nothing

nisi, if not, unless

nōbilis, -e, noble, famous

nōbilitās, -ātis (*f.*), nobility, fame

noceō, -ēre, -uī, -itūrus, harm

nōlō, nōlle, nōluī, not want

nōmen, -inis (*n.*), name

nōn, not

nōndum, not yet

nōnne, not?

nōnus, -a, -um, ninth
noster, -tra, -trum, our, ours
nōtus, -a, -um, known, famous
novem, nine
novus, -a, -um, new, strange
nox, noctis (f.), night
nūllus, -a, -um, no, none
numerus, -ī (m.), number
numquam, never
nunc, now
nūntiō, -āre, -āvī, -ātus, announce
nūntius, -ī (m.), messenger, message

ob (with acc.), on account of
obses, obsidis (m.), hostage
obsideō, -ēre, -sēdī, -sessus, besiege
obtineō, -ēre, -tinuī, -tentus, hold, possess
occāsus, -ūs (m.), setting
occīdō, -ere, -cīdī, -cīsus, kill
occupō, -āre, -āvī, -ātus, seize
ōceanus, -ī (m.), ocean
octāvus, -a, -um, eighth
octō, eight
oculus, -ī (m.), eye
officium, -ī (n.), duty
ōlim, once, formerly
omnis, -e, all, every
opera, -ae (f.), effort, work
oportet, -ēre, -uit, it is necessary
oppidum, -ī (n.), town
opportūnus, -a, -um, suitable, appropriate
opprimō, -ere, -pressī, -pressus, crush, subdue
oppugnō, -āre, -āvī, -ātus, attack
opus, operis (n.), work
ōrātiō, -ōnis (f.), speech
ōrdō, -inis (m.), order, rank
orior, orīrī, ortus sum, rise
ōrō, -āre, -āvī, -ātus, beg, plead
ostendō, -ere, -dī, -tus, show, display

pācō, -āre, -āvī, -ātus, subdue
paene, almost
pār, equal, like
parātus, -a, -um, prepared, ready
pāreō, -ēre, -uī, -itūrus, obey
parō, -āre, -āvī, -ātus, prepare
pars, partis (f.), part
parvus, -a, -um, small, little
passus, -ūs (m.), pace, step
pateō, -ēre, -uī, lie open, extend
pater, -tris (m.), father

patior, patī, passus sum, suffer, allow
patria, -ae (f.), country, native land
paucī, -ae, -a, few
paulō, a little
paulum, a little
pāx, pācis (f.), peace
pecūnia, -ae (f.), money
pedes, -itis (m.), infantryman
pellō, -ere, pepulī, pulsus, drive, rout
per (with acc.), through
perficiō, -ere, -fēcī, -fectus, finish
perīculum, -ī (n.), danger
permittō, -ere, -mīsī, -missus, allow, entrust
permoveō, -ēre, -mōvī, mōtus, move deeply, arouse
persequor, -sequī, -secūtus sum, pursue
perspiciō, -ere, -spexī, -spectus, notice, perceive
persuādeō, -ēre, -suāsī, -suāsūrus, persuade
perterreō, -ēre, -uī, -itus, terrify
pertineō, -ēre, -tinuī, reach, extend, pertain
perturbō, -āre, -āvī, -ātus, throw into confusion
perveniō, -īre, -vēnī, -ventus, arrive
pēs, pedis (m.), foot
petō, -ere, -īvī, -ītus, seek, ask
pīlum, -ī (n.), javelin
plēbs, plēbis (f.), common people
poena, -ae (f.), punishment
poēta, -ae (m.), poet
polliceor, -ērī, -icitus sum, promise
pōnō, -ere, posuī, positus, put, place
pōns, pontis (m.), bridge
populus, -ī (m.), people
porta, -ae (f.), gate
portō, -āre, -āvī, -ātus, carry
portus, -ūs (m.), harbor
possum, posse, potuī, be able, can
post (with acc.), after, behind
posteā, afterwards
posterus, -a, -um, following, next
postquam, after
postrīdiē, the next day
postulō, -āre, -āvī, -ātus, demand
potēns, powerful
potestās, -ātis (f.), power

praeda, -ae (f.), booty
praeficiō, -ere, -fēcī, -fectus, put in charge of
praemittō, -ere, -mīsī, -missus, send ahead
praemium, -ī (n.), reward, prize
praesidium, -ī (n.), protection, guard
praestō, -āre, -stitī, -stitūrus, excel
praesum, -esse, -fuī, -futūrus, be in command
praeter (with acc.), beyond, except, besides
praetereā, besides
praetor, -ōris (m.), praetor, judge
premō, -ere, pressī, pressus, press, oppress
pretium, -ī (n.), price
prīdiē, the day before
prīmō, at first
prīmum, first
prīmus, -a, -um, first
prīnceps, -ipis (m.), chief, leader
prīncipātus, -ūs (m.), leadership
prior, prius, former, previous
priusquam, before
prō (with abl.), before, for
prōcēdō, -ere, -cessī, -cessūrus, advance
prōcurrō, -ere, -currī, -cursūrus, run forward
prōdūcō, -ere, -dūxī, -ductus, lead forth
proelium, -ī (n.), battle
proficīscor, -ficīscī, -fectus sum, set out
prōgredior, -gredī, -gressus sum, proceed, advance
prohibeō, -ēre, -uī, -itus, hold back, prevent
prope, near
properō, -āre, -āvī, -ātus, hurry
propinquō, -āre, -āvī, -ātus, approach
propinquus, -a, -um, near, neighboring
prōpōnō, -ere, -posuī, -positus, set forth, offer
propter (with acc.), because of
proptereā, for this reason
prōsequor, -sequī, -secūtus sum, pursue
prōvincia, -ae (f.), province
proximus, -a, -um, nearest, next
prūdēns, foreseeing, wise
pūblicus, -a, -um, public
puella, -ae (f.), girl

puer, puerī (*m.*), boy
pugna, -ae (*f.*), fight, battle
pugnō, -āre, -āvī, -ātus, fight
pulcher, -chra, -chrum, beautiful
putō, -āre, -āvī, -ātus, think

quaerō, quaerere, -sīvī, -sītus, seek, ask
quaestor, -ōris (*m.*), quaestor
quam, how, as, than
quantus, -a, -um, how great
quārtus, -a, -um, fourth
quattuor, four
-que, and
quī, quae, quod, who, which, that
quīdam, quaedam, quoddam, a certain
quidem, indeed, in fact
quīnque, five
quīntus, -a, -um, fifth
quis, quid, who, what
quisque, quidque, each one, each thing
quō, where
quod, because
quot, how many, as many as

ratiō, -ōnis (*f.*), method, plan, reason
recēns, recent, fresh
recipiō, -ere, -cēpī, -ceptus, take back, receive
rēctus, -a, -um, straight
reddō, -ere, -didī, -ditus, give back, return
redeō, -īre, -iī, -itūrus, go back, return
reditus, -ūs (*m.*), return
redūcō, -ere, -dūxī, -ductus, lead back
referō, -ferre, rettulī, relātus, bring back
rēgīna, -ae (*f.*), queen
regiō, -ōnis (*f.*), region, district
rēgnum, -ī (*n.*), kingdom, rule
regō, -ere, rēxī, rēctus, rule, guide
relinquō, -ere, -līquī, -lictus, leave, abandon
reliquus, -a, -um, remaining, rest of
remaneō, -ēre, -mānsī, -mānsūrus, remain
remittō, -ere, -mīsī, -missus, send back
removeō, -ēre, -mōvī, -mōtus, move back, withdraw

renūntiō, -āre, -āvī, -ātus, bring back word, report
repellō, -ere, reppulī, repulsus, drive back
rēs, reī (*f.*), thing, matter
rēs pūblica, reī pūblicae (*f.*), republic, government
resistō, -ere, -stitī, resist
respondeō, -ēre, -spondī, -spōnsus, reply, answer
respōnsum, -ī (*n.*), reply
retineō, -ēre, -tinuī, -tentus, hold back, keep
revertō, -ere, -tī, -sus, turn back, return
rēx, rēgis (*m.*), king
rīpa, -ae (*f.*), bank of a river
rogō, -āre, -āvī, -ātus, ask, beg
rosa, -ae (*f.*), rose
rūrsus, again

saepe, often
sagitta, -ae (*f.*), arrow
salūs, -ūtis (*f.*), safety, welfare, health
salvus, -a, -um, safe
satis, enough
schola, -ae (*f.*), school
scientia, -ae (*f.*), knowledge
sciō, -īre, -īvī, -ītus, know
scrībō, -ere, scrīpsī, scrīptus, write
scūtum, -ī (*n.*), shield
secundus, -a, -um, second
sed, but
sedeō, -ēre, sēdī, sessūrus, sit
semper, always
senātor, -ōris (*m.*), senator
senātus, -ūs (*m.*), senate
sententia, -ae (*f.*), feeling, opinion
sentiō, -īre, sēnsī, sēnsus, feel, perceive
septem, seven
septimus, -a, -um, seventh
sequor, sequī, secūtus sum, follow
servō, -āre, -āvī, -ātus, save, keep
servus, -ī (*m.*), slave
sex, six
sextus, -a, -um, sixth
sī, if
sīc, thus, so
signum, -ī (*n.*), signal, standard
silentium, -ī (*n.*), silence
silva, -ae (*f.*), forest
similis, -e, similar, like

simul, at the same time; simul atque (ac), as soon as
sine (*with abl.*), without
singulī, -ae, -a, one at a time
sinister, -tra, -trum, left
socius, -ī (*m.*), ally, comrade
sōl, sōlis (*m.*), sun
sōlum, only
sōlus, -a, -um, alone, only
solvō, -ere, solvī, solūtus, loosen, set sail
somnus, -ī (*m.*), sleep
soror, -ōris (*f.*), sister
spatium, -ī (*n.*), space, distance
speciēs, -ēī (*f.*), appearance, sight
speciō, -ere, spexī, spectus, see
spectō, -āre, -āvī, -ātus, look at
spērō, -āre, -āvī, -ātus, hope
spēs, speī (*f.*), hope
statim, immediately
statua, -ae (*f.*), statue
statuō, -ere, statuī, statūtus, station, decide
stō, -āre, stetī, statūrus, stand
studeō, -ēre, studuī, be eager for, desire
studium, -ī (*n.*), eagerness, enthusiasm
sub (*with acc. and abl.*), under
subitō, suddenly
subsequor, -sequī, -secūtus sum, follow closely
subsidium, -ī (*n.*), aid
suī, of himself, herself, itself, themselves
sum, esse, fuī, futūrus, be
summus, -a, -um, highest, top of
sūmō, -ere, sūmpsī, sūmptus, take
super (*with acc.*), above
superior, -ius, higher, upper
superō, -āre, -āvī, -ātus, defeat, surpass
superus, -a, -um, upper
suprā, above
suscipiō, -ere, -cēpī, -ceptus, undertake
suspīciō, -ōnis (*f.*), suspicion
sustineō, -ēre, -tinuī, -tentus, hold up, withstand
suus, -a, -um, his (her, its, their) own

taberna, -ae (*f.*), shop
tālis, -e, such
tam, so
tamen, however, still, yet
tantus, -a, -um, so great, so much

tardō, -āre, -āvī, -ātus, slow up, stop

tardus, -a, -um, slow, late

tēlum, -ī (n.), weapon

tempestās, -ātis (f.), weather, storm

templum, -ī (n.), temple

temptō, -āre, -āvī, -ātus, try

tempus, -oris (n.), time

teneō, -ēre, -uī, hold, keep

tergum, -ī (n.), back

terra, -ae (f.), land

terreō, -ēre, -uī, -itus, frighten

terror, -ōris (m.), fright

tertius, -a, -um, third

theātrum, -ī (n.), theater

timeō, -ēre, -uī, fear

timidus, -a, -um, fearful

timor, -ōris (m.), fear

toga, -ae (f.), toga

tollō, -ere, sustulī, sublātus, raise

tot, so many

tōtus, -a, -um, whole, entire

trādō, -ere, -didī, -ditus, surrender, hand over

trādūcō, -ere, -dūxī, -ductus, lead across

trahō, -ere, trāxī, trāctus, draw, drag

trāns (with acc.), across

trānseō, -īre, -iī, -itūrus, go across

trānsportō, -āre, -āvī, -ātus, carry across

trēs, tria, three

tribūnus, -ī (m.), tribune

tū, you; (pl.), vōs, you

tuba, -ae (f.), trumpet

tum, then

tunica, -ae (f.), tunic

turbō, -āre, -āvī, -ātus, throw into confusion

turris, -is (f.), tower

tuus, -a, -um, your, yours

ubi, where, when

ūllus, -a, -um, any

ulterior, -ius, farther

ūnā, together

unda, -ae (f.), wave

undique, from everywhere

ūnus, -a, -um, one

urbs, urbis (f.), city

ūsus, -ūs (m.), use, experience

ut, utī, in order to, that

uter, utra, utrum, which (of two)

uterque, utraque, utrumque, each (of two), both

ūtilis, -e, useful

ūtor, ūtī, ūsus sum, use

vacuus, -a, -um, empty, free

valeō, -ēre, -uī, -itūrus, be well, be strong

validus, -a, -um, strong

vallēs, -is (f.), valley

vāllum, -ī (n.), wall, rampart

vāstō, -āre, -āvī, -ātus, destroy

vel, or

veniō, -īre, vēnī, ventus, come

ventus, -ī (m.), wind

verbum, -ī (n.), word

vereor, -ērī, -itus sum, fear, respect

vērō, in truth, indeed

vertō, -ere, -tī, -sus, turn

vērum, but

vērus, -a, -um, true

vesper, -erī (m.), evening

vester, -tra, -trum, your, yours

via, -ae (f.), way, road, street

victor, -ōris (m.), conqueror, victor

victōria, -ae (f.), victory

vīcus, -ī (m.), village

videō, -ēre, vīdī, vīsus, see

vigilia, -ae (f.), watch, guard

vigilō, -āre, -āvī, -ātus, keep awake, watch

vigintī, twenty

vīlla, -ae (f.), country house, farm

vincō, -ere, vīcī, victus, conquer

vir, virī (m.), man

virtūs, -ūtis (f.), courage

vīs, vīs (f.), force, violence, strength

vīta, -ae (f.), life

vīvus, -a, -um, alive, living

vocō, -āre, -āvī, -ātus, call

volō, velle, voluī, want, wish

voluntās, -ātis (f.), will, wish

vōx, vōcis (f.), voice, word

vulnerō, -āre, -āvī, -ātus, wound

vulnus, -eris (n.), wound

EXERCISES

A. Underline the correct translation of the Latin word.

1. *fīrmus:* neighboring, strong, faith, happy

2. *enim:* also, although, for, there

3. *pāreō:* obey, prepare, extend, suffer

4. *nōnus:* known, new, our, ninth

5. *aditus:* building, young man, age, approach

6. *redeō:* give back, take back, go back, lead back

7. *inopia:* lack, supply, inhabitant, attack

8. *obses:* hostage, setting, besiege, work

9. *quidem:* a certain, fifth, indeed, who

10. *subsidium:* eagerness, under, highest, aid

11. *vertō:* fear, turn, be well, destroy

12. *statim:* immediately, often, but, so

13. *inīquus:* unfriendly, unhappy, unequal, uncertain

14. *iūrō:* order, swear, judge, join

15. *lītus:* letter, tribe, shore, school

B. In each of the following sentences, there appears one Latin word. Show that you understand its meaning by underlining the word in parentheses that correctly completes the sentence.

1. When one experiences *dolor*, it is (illegal, pleasant, unpleasant, indecent).

2. We would use the word *altitūdō* in describing a (mountain, legion, camp, battle).

3. When Henry decided to *ēgredī*, his direction was (in, out, up, down).

4. One is most concerned with *pretium* while (eating, singing, talking, buying).

5. Mention would be made of a *rīpa* in connection with a (hill, river, tunnel, house).

6. The soldiers lost all *spēs*, since they were (desperate, lucky, excited, winning).

7. Since John was very *aeger*, he decided to (swim, study, rest, travel).

8. You would expect to find *arborēs* in a (hotel, lake, forest, cave).

9. If something is *ūtilis*, it means it can be (eaten, read, cooked, used).

10. *Obsidēs* are given in times of (prosperity, war, peace, celebration).

C. In the space before each word in column *A*, write the letter of its English equivalent in column *B*.

	Column A	Column B
_____	**1.** adsum	*a.* plan
_____	**2.** nox	*b.* tribe
_____	**3.** ratiō	*c.* halt
_____	**4.** oportet	*d.* be away
_____	**5.** cōnsilium	*e.* it is permitted
_____	**6.** aequus	*f.* method
_____	**7.** absum	*g.* notice
_____	**8.** mox	*h.* night
_____	**9.** apertus	*i.* meeting
_____	**10.** licet	*j.* soon
_____	**11.** cōnsistō	*k.* decide
_____	**12.** cōnspiciō	*l.* be present
_____	**13.** nātiō	*m.* open
_____	**14.** cōnstituō	*n.* equal
_____	**15.** concilium	*o.* it is necessary

D. Draw a line through the word that does *not* belong with the others in each group. Explain why it does not belong.

1. pater, soror, fīlia, socius _____

2. spectō, superō, videō, cōnspiciō _____

3. certus, nōbilis, clārus, nōtus _____

4. appropinquō, ēgredior, cūrō, eō _____

5. numquam, nihil, neuter, ūllus _____

6. manus, pedes, digitus, caput _____

7. aestās, hiems, merīdiēs, numerus _____

8. templum, aedificium, aquila, domus _____

9. cibus, campus, collis, ager _____

10. vāstō, interficiō, īnsequor, caedō _____

E. Next to each Latin verb write a Latin noun related to it. Then give the meaning of the Latin noun.

	LATIN NOUN	MEANING
EXAMPLE: armāre	arma	arms
1. timēre		
2. terrēre		
3. amāre		
4. clāmāre		
5. cēnāre		
6. dōnāre		
7. fugere		
8. facere		
9. vulnerāre		
10. laudāre		
11. mūnīre		
12. līberāre		
13. imperāre		
14. nāvigāre		
15. respondēre		
16. cupere		
17. iūdicāre		
18. dēdere		
19. aedificāre		
20. redīre		
21. hiemāre		
22. studēre		
23. morī		
24. morārī		
25. velle		

F. Each of the following items consists of a pair of related Latin words followed by the first word of a second pair *related in the same way*. Complete each of the second pairs by supplying the proper Latin word.

EXAMPLE: PUER : PUELLA :: pater : *māter*

1. RĒX : RĒGĪNA :: vir : ....

2. AMĪCUS : INIMĪCUS :: socius : ....

3. BREVIS : BREVITER :: fortis : ....

4. CELER : CELERITĀS :: difficilis : ....

5. SCIŌ : NESCIŌ :: volō : ....

6. LIBER : LEGŌ :: tēlum : ....

7. PRŌ : CONTRĀ :: ante : ....

8. NAUTA : NĀVIS :: eques : ....

9. TIMEŌ : VEREOR :: temptō : ....

10. MARE : MARITIMUS :: fīnis : ....

G. Below is a list of 50 Latin nouns that fall into five categories. Indicate in which category each noun belongs by putting a check in the appropriate column.

	PARTS OF THE BODY	MILITARY TERMS	ABSTRACT NOUNS	TIME	PLACE
1. dēns	-------	-------	-------	-------	-------
2. mēnsis	-------	-------	-------	-------	-------
3. amīcitia	-------	-------	-------	-------	-------
4. pīlum	-------	-------	-------	-------	-------
5. vallēs	-------	-------	-------	-------	-------
6. cohors	-------	-------	-------	-------	-------
7. fidēs	-------	-------	-------	-------	-------
8. regiō	-------	-------	-------	-------	-------
9. nox	-------	-------	-------	-------	-------
10. aciēs	-------	-------	-------	-------	-------
11. spēs	-------	-------	-------	-------	-------
12. collis	-------	-------	-------	-------	-------
13. fīnēs	-------	-------	-------	-------	-------
14. castra	-------	-------	-------	-------	-------
15. potestās	-------	-------	-------	-------	-------
16. forum	-------	-------	-------	-------	-------
17. oculus	-------	-------	-------	-------	-------
18. vīcus	-------	-------	-------	-------	-------
19. digitus	-------	-------	-------	-------	-------
20. virtūs	-------	-------	-------	-------	-------

21. centuriō ----- ----- ----- ----- -----
22. aetās ----- ----- ----- ----- -----
23. campus ----- ----- ----- ----- -----
24. ōceanus ----- ----- ----- ----- -----
25. fortitūdō ----- ----- ----- ----- -----
26. prōvincia ----- ----- ----- ----- -----
27. lingua ----- ----- ----- ----- -----
28. merīdiēs ----- ----- ----- ----- -----
29. impetus ----- ----- ----- ----- -----
30. aestās ----- ----- ----- ----- -----
31. rīpa ----- ----- ----- ----- -----
32. nōbilitās ----- ----- ----- ----- -----
33. manus ----- ----- ----- ----- -----
34. equitātus ----- ----- ----- ----- -----
35. annus ----- ----- ----- ----- -----
36. caput ----- ----- ----- ----- -----
37. facultās ----- ----- ----- ----- -----
38. agmen ----- ----- ----- ----- -----
39. pēs ----- ----- ----- ----- -----
40. lītus ----- ----- ----- ----- -----
41. legiō ----- ----- ----- ----- -----
42. portus ----- ----- ----- ----- -----
43. audācia ----- ----- ----- ----- -----
44. vesper ----- ----- ----- ----- -----
45. hōra ----- ----- ----- ----- -----
46. amor ----- ----- ----- ----- -----
47. tergum ----- ----- ----- ----- -----
48. diēs ----- ----- ----- ----- -----
49. schola ----- ----- ----- ----- -----
50. domicilium ----- ----- ----- ----- -----

abandon, relinquō, -ere, -līquī, -lictus

able (be), possum, posse, potuī

about, dē (*with abl.*)

absent (be), absum, -esse, āfuī, āfutūrus

abundance, cōpia, -ae (*f.*)

across, trāns (*with acc.*)

advice, cōnsilium, -ī (*n.*)

advise, moneō, -ēre, -uī, -itus

after, post (*with acc.*)

after, postquam

afterwards, posteā

against, contrā (*with acc.*)

aid, auxilium, -ī (*n.*)

alarm, commoveō, -ēre, -mōvī, -mōtus

all, omnis, -e

allow, permittō, -ere, -mīsī, -missus

ally, socius, -ī (*m.*)

already, iam

also, etiam

although, cum

always, semper

among, apud (*with acc.*)

and, et

and not, neque

and so, itaque

announce, nūntiō, -āre, -āvī, -ātus

answer, respondeō, -ēre, -spondī, -spōnsus

approach, appropinquō, -āre, -āvī, -ātus

arms, arma, -ōrum (*n. pl.*)

army, exercitus, -ūs (*m.*)

around, circum (*with acc.*)

arouse, permoveō, -ēre, -mōvī, -mōtus

arrival, adventus, -ūs (*m.*)

arrive, perveniō, -īre, -vēnī, -ventus

arrow, sagitta, -ae (*f.*)

ask, rogō, -āre, -āvī, -ātus

assemble, conveniō, -īre, -vēnī, -ventus

attack, impetus, -ūs (*m.*)

attack, oppugnō, -āre, -āvī, -ātus

authority, auctōritās, -ātis (*f.*)

away (be), absum, -esse, āfuī, āfutūrus

bad, malus, -a, -um

baggage, impedīmenta, -ōrum (*n. pl.*)

bank, rīpa, -ae (*f.*)

barbarian, barbarus, -ī (*m.*)

battle, proelium, -ī (*n.*)

be, sum, esse, fuī, futūrus

be able, possum, posse, potuī

be distant, absum, -esse, āfuī, āfutūrus

be in command, praesum, -esse, -fuī, -futūrus

be near, adsum, -esse, -fuī, -futūrus

be present (see **be near**)

bear, ferō, ferre, tulī, lātus

because, quod

because of, propter (*with acc.*)

before, ante (*with acc.*)

begin, incipiō, -ere, -cēpī, -ceptus

behind, post (*with acc.*)

benefit, beneficium, -ī (*n.*)

between, inter (*with acc.*)

body, corpus, -oris (*n.*)

book, liber, -brī (*m.*)

both . . . and, et . . . et

boundary, fīnis, -is (*m.*)

boy, puer, puerī (*m.*)

brave, fortis, -e

bravely, fortiter

bridge, pōns, pontis (*m.*)

bring, ferō, ferre, tulī, lātus

bring in, īnferō, -ferre, -tulī, illātus

brother, frāter, -tris (*m.*)

build, mūniō, -īre, -īvī, -ītus

business, negōtium, -ī (*n.*)

but, sed

by, ā, ab (*with abl.*)

call, vocō, -āre, -āvī, -ātus

call together, convocō, -āre, -āvī, -ātus

camp, castra, -ōrum (*n. pl.*)

can, possum, posse, potuī

carry, portō, -āre, -āvī, -ātus

carry on, gerō, -ere, gessī, gestus

cause, causa, -ae (*f.*)

cavalry, equitātus, -ūs (*m.*)

certain, certus, -a, -um

chief, prīnceps, -ipis (*m.*)

children, līberī, -ōrum (*m. pl.*)

choose, dēligō, -ere, -lēgī, -lēctus

citizen, cīvis, -is (*m.*)

city, urbs, urbis (*f.*)

clear, clārus, -a, -um

cohort, cohors, -tis (*f.*)

collect, cōgō, -ere, coēgī, coāctus

come, veniō, -īre, vēnī, ventus

come together, conveniō, -īre, -vēnī, -ventus

command, imperium, -ī (*n.*)

command, imperō, -āre, -āvī, -ātus

common, commūnis, -e

compel, cōgō, -ere, coēgī, coāctus

comrade, socius, -ī (*m.*)

concerning, dē (*with abl.*)

conquer, vincō, -ere, vīcī, victus

conqueror, victor, -ōris (*m.*)

consul, cōnsul, -is (*m.*)

country, patria, -ae (*f.*)

country house, vīlla, -ae (*f.*)

courage, virtūs, -ūtis (*f.*)

crowd, multitūdō, -inis (*f.*)

custom, cōnsuētūdō, -inis (*f.*)

danger, perīculum, -ī (*n.*)

daughter, fīlia, -ae (*f.*)

day, diēs, -ēī (*m.*)

death, mors, mortis (*f.*)

decide, cōnstituō, -ere, -stituī, -stitūtus

deep, altus, -a, -um

defeat, superō, -āre, -āvī, -ātus

defend, dēfendō, -ere, -fendī, -fēnsus

depart, discēdō, -ere, -cessī, -cessūrus

depth, altitūdō, -inis (*f.*)

desire, cupiditās, -ātis (*f.*)

desire, cupiō, -ere, -īvī, -ītus

desirous, cupidus, -a, -um

difficult, difficilis, -e

difficulty, difficultās, -ātis (*f.*)

display, ostendō, -ere, -dī, -tus

distance, spatium, -ī (*n.*)

distant (be), absum, -esse, āfuī, āfutūrus

do, faciō, -ere, fēcī, factus

doubt, dubitō, -āre, -āvī, -ātus

down from, dē (*with abl.*)

draw up, īnstruō, -ere, -strūxī, -strūctus

drive, agō, -ere, ēgī, āctus

eagerness, studium, -ī (n.)
easily, facile
easy, facilis, -e
eight, octō
eighth, octāvus, -a, -um
either . . . or, aut . . . aut
encourage, cōnfīrmō, -āre, -āvī,
  -ātus
end, fīnis, -is (m.)
enemy, hostis, -is (m.)
enlist, cōnscrībō, -ere, -scrīpsī,
  -scrīptus
enough, satis
enroll (see enlist)
enthusiasm, studium, -ī (n.)
entrust, permittō, -ere, -mīsī,
  -missus
envoy, lēgātus, -ī (m.)
equal, aequus, -a, -um
especially, maximē
even, etiam; not even, nē . . .
  quidem
every, omnis, -e
evil, malus, -a, -um
extend, pertineō, -ēre, -tinuī

fair, aequus, -a, -um
faith, fidēs, -eī (f.)
fame, glōria, -ae (f.)
famous, nōbilis, -e
farm, vīlla, -ae (f.)
farmer, agricola, -ae (m.)
father, pater, -tris (m.)
favor, beneficium, -ī (n.)
fear, timor, -ōris (m.)
fear, timeō, -ēre, -uī
feel, sentiō, -īre, sēnsī, sēnsus
few, paucī, -ae, -a
field, ager, agrī (m.)
fierce, ācer, ācris, ācre
fiercely, ācriter
fifth, quīntus, -a, -um
fight, pugna, -ae (f.)
fight, pugnō, -āre, -āvī, -ātus
find, inveniō, -īre, -vēnī, -ventus
find out, cognōscō, -ere, -nōvī,
  -nitus
finish, cōnficiō, -ere, -fēcī, -fectus
first, prīmus, -a, -um
five, quīnque
flee, fugiō, -ere, fūgī, fugitūrus
flight, fuga, -ae (f.)
follow, sequor, sequī, secūtus
  sum
foot, pēs, pedis (m.)
for, enim

for, prō (with abl.)
for a long time, diū
force, vīs, vīs (f.)
forest, silva, -ae (f.)
formerly, anteā
fortify, mūniō, -īre, -īvī, -ītus
fortune, fortūna, -ae (f.)
forum, forum, -ī (n.)
four, quattuor
fourth, quārtus, -a, -um
free, līber, -era, -erum
free, līberō, -āre, -āvī, -ātus
freedom, lībertās, -ātis (f.)
friend, amīcus, -ī (m.)
friendly, amīcus, -a, -um
friendship, amīcitia, -ae (f.)
from, ā, ab (with abl.)

gate, porta, -ae (f.)
general, imperātor, -ōris (m.)
get together, comparō, -āre, -āvī,
  -ātus
girl, puella, -ae (f.)
give, dō, dare, dedī, datus
give back, reddō, -ere, -didī,
  -ditus
glory, glōria, -ae (f.)
go, eō, īre, īvī (iī), itūrus
go back redeō, -īre, -iī, -itūrus
go out, excēdō, -ere, -cessī,
  -cessūrus
god, deus, -ī (m.)
good, bonus, -a, -um
government, rēs pūblica, reī
  pūblicae (f.)
grain, frūmentum, -ī (n.)
great, magnus, -a, -um
greatly, magnopere
greatness, magnitūdō, -inis (f.)
guard, praesidium, -ī (n.)

hand, manus, -ūs (f.)
hand over, trādō, -ere, -didī,
  -ditus
hard, difficilis, -e
hasten, contendō, -ere, -tendī,
  -tentus
have, habeō, -ēre, -uī, -itus
he, is, ea, id
head, caput, -itis (n.)
health, salūs, -ūtis (f.)
hear, audiō, -īre, -īvī, -ītus
heavy, gravis, -e
height, altitūdō, -inis (f.)
help, auxilium, -ī (n.)
hem in, contineō, -ēre, -tinuī,
  -tentus
hesitate, dubitō, -āre, -āvī, -ātus

high, altus, -a, -um
hill, collis, -is (m.)
hindrance, impedīmentum, -ī (n.)
his (her, its, their) own, suus,
  -a, -um
hold, teneō, -ēre, -uī
hold back, prohibeō, -ēre, -uī,
  -itus
hold together, contineō, -ēre,
  -tinuī, -tentus
hold up, sustineō, -ēre, -tinuī,
  -tentus
home, domus, -ūs (f.)
hope, spēs, speī (f.)
hope, spērō, -āre, -āvī, -ātus
horn, cornū, -ūs (n.)
horse, equus, -ī (m.)
horseman, eques, -itis (m.)
hour, hōra, -ae (f.)
house, domus, -ūs (f.)
however, tamen
how great, quantus, -a, -um
how many, quot
hundred, centum
hurl, iaciō, -ere, iēcī, iactus
hurry, properō, -āre, -āvī, -ātus

I, ego, meī
if, sī
in, in (with abl.)
indeed, vērō
in fact, quidem
inflict, īnferō, -ferre, -tulī, illātus
influence, auctōritās, -ātis (f.)
influence, addūcō, -ere, -dūxī,
  -ductus
in front of, ante (with acc.)
injury, iniūria, -ae (f.)
injustice, iniūria, -ae (f.)
in order not to, nē
in order to, ut
in the presence of, apud (with
  acc.)
into, in (with acc.)
in truth, vērō
island, īnsula, -ae (f.)

join, committō, -ere, -mīsī, -missus
journey, iter, itineris (n.)

keep, teneō, -ēre, -uī
kill, interficiō, -ere, -fēcī, -fectus
kind, genus, -eris (n.)
kindness, beneficium, -ī (n.)
king, rēx, rēgis (m.)
kingdom, rēgnum, -ī (n.)
know, sciō, -īre, -īvī, -ītus
known, nōtus, -a, -um

lack, inopia, -ae (*f.*)
land, terra, -ae (*f.*)
language, lingua, -ae (*f.*)
large, magnus, -a, -um
law, lēx, lēgis (*f.*)
lead, dūcō, -ere, dūxī, ductus
lead forth, prōdūcō, -ere, -dūxī, -ductus
lead to, addūcō, -ere, -dūxī, -ductus
leader, dux, ducis (*m.*)
learn, cognōscō, -ere, -nōvī, -nitus
leave, discēdō, -ere, -cessī, -cessūrus
leave behind, relinquō, -ere, -līquī, -lictus
left, sinister, -tra, -trum
legion, legiō, -ōnis (*f.*)
let go, dīmittō, -ere, -mīsī, -missus
letter (*of alphabet*), littera, -ae (*f.*); (*communication*), litterae, -ārum (*f. pl.*)
level, aequus, -a, -um
liberty, lībertās, -ātis (*f.*)
lieutenant, lēgātus, -ī (*m.*)
life, vīta, -ae (*f.*)
light, levis, -e
light, lūx, lūcis (*f.*)
like, similis, -e
like, amō, -āre, -āvī, -ātus
line of battle, aciēs, -ēī (*f.*)
little, parvus, -a, -um
long, longus, -a, -um
long time, diū
look at, spectō, -āre, -āvī, -ātus
lose, āmittō, -ere, -mīsī, -missus
love, amō, -āre, -āvī, -ātus
luck, fortūna, -ae (*f.*)

make, faciō, -ere, fēcī, factus
man, vir, virī (*m.*)
manner, modus, -ī (*m.*)
many, multī, -ae, -a
march, iter, itineris (*n.*)
march, iter facere
maritime, maritimus, -a, -um
master, dominus, -ī (*m.*)
matter, rēs, reī (*f.*)
meanwhile, interim
memory, memoria, -ae (*f.*)
message, nūntius, -ī (*m.*)
messenger, nūntius, -ī (*m.*)
method, ratiō, -ōnis (*f.*)
middle (of), medius, -a, -um
mind, animus, -ī (*m.*)
mine, meus, -a, -um

money, pecūnia, -ae (*f.*)
month, mēnsis, -is (*m.*)
moon, lūna, -ae (*f.*)
more, magis
moreover, autem
most of all, maximē
mother, māter, -tris (*f.*)
mountain, mōns, montis (*m.*)
move, moveō, -ēre, mōvī, mōtus
move back, removeō, -ēre, -mōvī, -mōtus
move deeply, permoveō, -ēre, -mōvī, -mōtus
much, multus, -a, -um
multitude, multitūdō, -inis (*f.*)
my, meus, -a, -um

name, nōmen, -inis (*n.*)
name, appellō, -āre, -āvī, -ātus
nation, nātiō, -ōnis (*f.*)
native land, patria, -ae (*f.*)
nature, nātūra, -ae (*f.*)
near, prope
near, propinquus, -a, -um
necessary, necessārius, -a, -um
neighboring, fīnitimus, -a, -um
neither . . . nor, neque . . . neque
new, novus, -a, -um
night, nox, noctis (*f.*)
nine, novem
ninth, nōnus, -a, -um
no, none, nūllus, -a, -um
noble, nōbilis, -e
noon, merīdiēs, -ēī (*m.*)
nor, neque
not, nōn
not even, nē . . . quidem
now, nunc
number, numerus, -ī (*m.*)

offer, prōpōnō, -ere, -posuī, -positus
often, saepe
on, in (*with abl.*)
on account of, propter (*with acc.*)
once, ōlim
one, ūnus, -a, -um
opportunity, facultās, -ātis (*f.*)
oppress, premō, -ere, pressī, pressus
or, aut
order, ōrdō, -inis (*m.*)
order, iubeō, -ēre, iussī, iussus
ought, dēbeō, -ēre, -uī, -itus
our, ours, noster, -tra, -trum
out of, ē, ex (*with abl.*)
outstanding, ēgregius, -a, -um
owe, dēbeō, -ēre, -uī, -itus

pace, passus, -ūs (*m.*)
part, pars, partis (*f.*)
peace, pāx, pācis (*f.*)
people, populus, -ī (*m.*)
perceive, sentiō, -īre, sēnsī, sēnsus
persuade, persuādeō, -ēre, -suāsī, -suāsūrus
pertain, pertineō, -ēre, -tinuī
place, locus, -ī (*m.*); (*pl.*), loca, -ōrum (*n.*)
place, pōnō, -ere, posuī, positus
plain, campus, -ī (*m.*)
plan, cōnsilium, -ī (*n.*)
play, lūdō, -ere, lūsī, lūsus
poet, poēta, -ae (*m.*)
point out, dēmōnstrō, -āre, -āvī, -ātus
poor, miser, -era, -erum
possess, obtineō, -ēre, -tinuī, -tentus
power, potestās, -ātis (*f.*)
powerful, potēns
praise, laudō, -āre, -āvī, -ātus
prepare, parō, -āre, -āvī, -ātus
prepared, parātus, -a, -um
preserve, cōnservō, -āre, -āvī, -ātus
press, premō, -ere, pressī, pressus
prevent, prohibeō, -ēre, -uī, -itus
previously, anteā
prize, praemium, -ī (*n.*)
proceed, prōgredior, -gredī, -gressus sum
protection, praesidium, -ī (*n.*)
province, prōvincia, -ae (*f.*)
public, pūblicus, -a, -um
punishment, poena, -ae (*f.*)
put, pōnō, -ere, posuī, positus
put out, expōnō, -ere, -posuī, -positus

queen, rēgīna, -ae (*f.*)

race, genus, -eris (*n.*)
rank, ōrdō, -inis (*m.*)
reach, pertineō, -ēre, -tinuī
read, legō, -ere, lēgī, lēctus
ready, parātus, -a, -um
realize, intellegō, -ere, -lēxī, -lēctus
reason, causa, -ae (*f.*)
receive, accipiō, -ere, -cēpī, -ceptus
recent, recēns
region, regiō, -ōnis (*f.*)
remain, maneō, -ēre, mānsī, mānsūrus
remaining, reliquus, -a, -um

remarkable, ēgregius, -a, -um
reply, respondeō, -ēre, -spondī, -spōnsus
report, renūntiō, -āre, -āvī, -ātus
republic, rēs pūblica, reī pūblicae (f.)
rest (of), reliquus, -a, -um
return, reddō, -ere, -didī, -ditus
revolt, dēficiō, -ere, -fēcī, -fectus
reward, praemium, -ī (n.)
right, dexter, -tra, -trum
right, iūs, iūris (n.)
river, flūmen, -inis (n.)
road, via, -ae (f.)
route, iter, itineris (n.)
rule, rēgnum, -ī (n.)
rule, regō, -ere, rēxī, rēctus

safety, salūs, -ūtis (f.)
sail, nāvigō, -āre, -āvī, -ātus
sailor, nauta, -ae (m.)
same, īdem, eadem, idem
savage, barbarus, -a, -um
save, servō, -āre, -āvī, -ātus
say, dīcō, -ere, dīxī, dictus
scarcity, inopia, -ae (f.)
sea, mare, -is (n.)
second, secundus, -a, -um
see, videō, -ēre, vīdī, vīsus
seek, petō, -ere, -īvī, -ītus
seize, occupō, -āre, -āvī, -ātus
-self, ipse, -a, -um
self (reflexive), sē
senate, senātus, -ūs (m.)
senator, senātor, -ōris (m.)
send, mittō, -ere, mīsī, missus
send ahead, praemittō, -ere, -mīsī, -missus
send away, dīmittō, -ere, -mīsī, -missus
send back, remittō, -ere, -mīsī, -missus
serious, gravis, -e
set forth, prōpōnō, -ere, -posuī, -positus
set out, proficīscor, -ficīscī, -fectus sum
seven, septem
seventh, septimus, -a, -um
severe, gravis, -e
sharp, ācer, ācris, ācre
sharply, ācriter
she, ea
ship, nāvis, -is (f.)
short, brevis, -e
show, dēmōnstrō, -āre, -āvī, -ātus
signal, signum, -ī (n.)

similar, similis, -e
since, cum
sister, soror, -ōris (f.)
six, sex
sixth, sextus, -a, -um
size, magnitūdō, -inis (f.)
slave, servus, -ī (m.)
small, parvus, -a, -um
so, ita, tam
so great, so much, tantus, -a, -um
soldier, mīles, -itis (m.)
son, fīlius, -ī (m.)
soon, iam
space, spatium, -ī (n.)
speak, dīcō, -ere, dīxī, dictus
speech, ōrātiō, -ōnis (f.)
speed, celeritās, -ātis (f.)
spirit, animus, -ī (m.)
standard, signum, -ī (n.)
state, cīvitās, -ātis (f.)
station, cōnstituō, -ere, -stituī, -stitūtus
stay, maneō, -ēre, mānsī, mānsūrus
step, passus, -ūs (m.)
still, tamen
stop, intermittō, -ere, -mīsī, -missus
strange, novus, -a, -um
street, via, -ae (f.)
strength, vīs, vīs (f.)
strengthen, cōnfīrmō, -āre, -āvī, -ātus
strong, fortis, -e
suitable, idōneus, -a, -um
summer, aestās, -ātis (f.)
summon, convocō, -āre, -āvī, -ātus
sun, sōl, sōlis (m.)
supply, cōpia, -ae (f.)
sure, certus, -a, -um
surpass, superō, -āre, -āvī, -ātus
surrender, trādō, -ere, -didī, -ditus
surround, circumveniō, -īre, -vēnī, -ventus
swift, celer, -eris, -e
swiftness, celeritās, -ātis (f.)
sword, gladius, -ī (m.)

take, capiō, -ere, cēpī, captus
task, negōtium, -ī (n.)
teach, doceō, -ēre, -uī, -tus
teacher, magister, -trī (m.)
tell, dīcō, -ere, dīxī, dictus
ten, decem
tenth, decimus, -a, -um

terms, condiciō, -ōnis (f.)
terrify, perterreō, -ēre, -uī, -itus
territory, fīnēs, -ium (m. pl.)
than, quam
that, ille, illa, illud
that, quī, quae, quod
that, ut
then, tum
there, ibi
therefore, itaque
thing, rēs, reī (f.)
think, putō, -āre, -āvī, -ātus
third, tertius, -a, -um
this, hic, haec, hoc
thousand, mīlle
three, trēs, tria
through, per (with acc.)
throw, iaciō, -ere, iēcī, iactus
thus, ita
time, tempus, -oris (n.)
to, toward, ad (with acc.)
today, hodiē
toga, toga, -ae (f.)
tongue, lingua, -ae (f.)
town, oppidum, -ī (n.)
tree, arbor, -oris (f.)
tribe, nātiō, -ōnis (f.)
troops, cōpiae, -ārum (f. pl.)
true, vērus, -a, -um
trumpet, tuba, -ae (f.)
trust, fidēs, -eī (f.)
try, temptō, -āre, -āvī, -ātus
twenty, vīgintī
two, duo, duae, duo

under, sub (with acc. and abl.)
understand, intellegō, -ere, -lēxī, -lēctus
unequal, inīquus, -a, -um
uneven, inīquus, -a, -um
unfavorable, inīquus, -a, -um
unfriendly, inimīcus, -a, -um
use, ūtor, ūtī, ūsus sum

very, ipse, ipsa, ipsum
victor, victor, -ōris (m.)
victory, victōria, -ae (f.)
village, vīcus, -ī (m.)
violence, vīs, vīs (f.)
voice, vōx, vōcis (f.)

wage, gerō, -ere, gessī, gestus
wait (for), exspectō, -āre, -āvī, -ātus
wall, mūrus, -ī (m.)
want, volō, velle, voluī
war, bellum, -ī (n.)
warn, moneō, -ēre, -uī, -itus

watch, vigilia, -ae (f.)
water, aqua, -ae (f.)
way, modus, -ī (m.)
we, nōs
weapon, tēlum, -ī (n.)
welfare, salūs, -ūtis (f.)
well, bene
what, quid
when, cum
where, ubi
which, quī, quae, quod
who, quī, quae, quod
who, quis
whole, tōtus, -a, -um

why, cūr
wide, lātus, -a, -um
width, lātitūdō, -inis (f.)
wing, cornū, -ūs (n.)
winter, hiems, -emis (f.)
wise, prūdēns
wish, cupiō, -ere, -īvī, -ītus
with, cum (with abl.)
withdraw, removeō, -ēre, -mōvī, -mōtus
without, sine (with abl.)
withstand, sustineō, -ēre, -tinuī, -tentus
woman, fēmina, -ae (f.)
word, verbum, -ī (n.)

work, labōrō, -āre, -āvī, -ātus
wound, vulnus, -eris (n.)
wound, vulnerō, -āre, -āvī, -ātus
wretched, miser, -era, -erum
write, scrībō, -ere, scrīpsī, scrīptus
wrong, iniūria, -ae (f.)

year, annus, -ī (m.)
yet, tamen
yield, cēdō, -ere, cessī, cessūrus
you, tū; (pl.), vōs
your, tuus, -a, -um; vester, -tra, -trum

EXERCISES

A. In the space before each word in column *A*, write the letter of its Latin equivalent in column *B*.

Column A	Column B
------ **1.** hand	*a.* moneō
------ **2.** eight	*b.* domus
------ **3.** arrival	*c.* paucī
------ **4.** attack	*d.* sequor
------ **5.** advise	*e.* manus
------ **6.** home	*f.* cōnficiō
------ **7.** few	*g.* octāvus
------ **8.** flee	*h.* magnitūdō
------ **9.** advice	*i.* impetus
------ **10.** eighth	*j.* incipiō
------ **11.** follow	*k.* octō
------ **12.** size	*l.* multitūdō
------ **13.** begin	*m.* cōnsilium
------ **14.** finish	*n.* fugiō
------ **15.** crowd	*o.* adventus

B. Underline the correct translation of the English word.

1. *short:* longus, brevis, fortis, altus

2. *supply:* cōpia, inopia, superus, spatium

3. *remain:* moneō, mūniō, cōnstituō, maneō

4. *true:* vērō, vertō, vērus, verbum

5. *so great:* tot, tantus, quot, quantus

6. *although:* cum, tum, etiam, dum

7. *kindness:* auxilium, concilium, beneficium, subsidium

8. *hold up:* teneō, sustineō, contineō, habeō

9. *collect:* agō, collocō, cōnor, cōgō

10. *fierce:* ācriter, aciēs, ācer, aeger

11. *spirit:* animus, corpus, modus, ventus

12. *remaining:* relinquō, recēns, summus, reliquus

13. *because:* causa, nisi, nē, quod

14. *especially:* facile, maximē, nam, ōlim

15. *oppress:* oportet, prīmō, premō, praestō

C. Underline the word in parentheses that you would use to translate the italicized English word.

1. They all *hope* the war will end soon.   (spēs, spērō)

2. She looks *like* her mother.   (amō, similis)

3. He *left* without eating.   (sinister, discēdō)

4. The *fear* of attack united the Romans.   (timor, timeō)

5. We *desire* nothing for our trouble.   (cupiō, cupiditās)

6. They fought *for* their country.   (enim, prō)

7. My shield is heavy; yours is *light*.   (levis, lūx)

8. The enemy took the *right* road.   (iūs, dexter)

9. They will *order* him to leave.   (ōrdō, iubeō)

10. She was so tired *that* she slept.   (ut, ille)

D. Underline the word in parentheses that best completes each sentence.

1. Imperātor exercitum in castra (interfēcit, dūxit, mūnīvit).

2. Post multōs (annōs, animōs, mūrōs) mortuus est.

3. (Domum, Rīpam, Vim) hostium prohibēre nōn potuit.

4. Caput est pars (corporis, generis, temporis).

5. (Ex, Cum, Propter) castrīs profectī sunt.

6. Caesar (spatium, salūtem, aciem) īnstrūxit.

7. Mīlitēs (altē, fortiter, breviter) contendērunt.

8. Dē tertiā (celeritāte, vulnere, vigiliā) pugnātum est.

9. Dum haec geruntur signum (datum, ductum, gestum) est.

10. Nūntiōs in omnēs partēs (timuit, scrīpsit, mīsit).

E. Write the opposite of each English word and then translate your answer into Latin.

	OPPOSITE	TRANSLATION
EXAMPLE: boy	girl	puella
1. winter		
2. with		
3. equal		
4. begin		
5. into		
6. easy		
7. find		
8. day		
9. life		
10. ask		

LATIN TWO YEARS

Part 1

Translate passage *a* into English. Write your translation in the space provided in the separate answer booklet. [20]

[The inhabitants of Zama, who have outlawed their king, fear reprisal, and seek help from Caesar.]

a. Incolae Zamae interim lēgātōs dē hīs rēbus ad Caesarem Uticam mittunt petuntque ab eō ut sibi auxilium mittat antequam rēx manum cōgat et oppugnet. Dīcunt sē parātōs esse oppidum armaque eī trādere. Caesar lēgātōs laudat; tum eōs domum redīre iubet ac suum adventum nūntiāre. Ipse posterō diē Uticā ēgressus cum equitātū, in rēgnum īre contendit. In itinere ducēs complūrēs ex cōpiīs rēgis ad Caesarem veniunt petuntque ut sibi *veniam* det. Veniā datā, ad oppidum pervenit. Fāmā interim dē eius *clēmentiā* narrātā, paene omnēs equitēs rēgis Zamam perveniunt; ā Caesare timōre perīculōque līberātī sunt.

—Caesar, *Dē Bellō Africō*, 92 (adapted)

veniam—from *venia*, pardon
clēmentiā—from *clēmentia*, mercy

Directions (1-20): Do *not* write a translation of passage *b*; read it through carefully several times to ascertain the meaning. Then in the spaces provided in your separate answer booklet, write the *number* of the alternative that best translates *each* of the underlined expressions *as it is used in the passage.* [20]

b. Hōc proeliō factō, Caesar neque sibi lēgātōs audiendōs esse neque condiciōnēs accipiendās esse arbitrābātur ab eīs quī, per īnsidiās petītā pāce, suā voluntāte bellum intulissent. Putābat sē exspectāre nōn dēbēre dum cōpiae hostium augērentur et equitātus reverterētur. Et cognōscēbat īnfīrmitātem Gallōrum et sentiēbat ūnō proeliō iam quantam auctōritātem hostēs apud eōs cōnsecūtī essent. Eīs nihil temporis dandum esse ut cōnsilia caperent existimābat. Hīs rēbus cōnstitūtīs et cōnsiliō lēgātīs et quaestōrī nūntiātō, nē diem pugnae āmitteret, rēs opportūnissima accidit. Postrīdiē eius diēī Germānī eīsdem īnsidiīs ūsī sunt et complūrēs ad eum in castra vēnērunt. Cum vērō dīcerent sē contrā condiciōnēs pācis prīdiē proelium commīsisse, tamen spērāvērunt aliquid dē indūtiīs cōnsequī. At Caesar eōs ad sē lātōs esse gāvīsus est et illōs retinērī iussit. Ipse omnēs cōpiās castrīs ēdūxit equitātumque quī recentī proeliō perterritus erat agmen subsequī iussit.

Aciē triplicī īnstrūctā et itinere octō mīlium passuum cōnfectō, ad castra hostium pervēnit priusquam Germānī quid agerētur sentīre possent.

—Caesar, *Dē Bellō Gallicō*, IV, 13-14 (adapted)

indūtiīs—from *indūtiae*, truce
gāvīsus est—rejoiced

1. Hōc proeliō factō
   (1) After this battle had been fought
   (2) This battle a fact
   (3) This prize having been gained
   (4) With this battle begun

2. neque sibi lēgātōs audiendōs esse
   (1) he ought not to listen to the ambassadors
   (2) not hearing the laws himself
   (3) the legates ought not to see him
   (4) the ambassadors themselves must not attack him

3. per īnsidiās petītā pāce
   (1) through the plots of petitioned peace
   (2) through petitions sought by deceit
   (3) while peace had been requested through envoys
   (4) having sought peace through trickery

4. suā voluntāte bellum intulissent
   (1) would have terminated the war voluntarily
   (2) had waged war voluntarily
   (3) declared war voluntarily
   (4) ended the war voluntarily

5. dum cōpiae hostium augērentur
   (1) while the abundance of the enemy was being increased
   (2) while the enemies' grain was growing
   (3) until the wealth of the enemy had grown
   (4) until the forces of the enemy were enlarged

6. cognōscēbat īnfīrmitātem Gallōrum
   (1) he learned the strength of the Gauls
   (2) he became acquainted with the Gauls' bravery
   (3) he knew the weakness of the Gauls
   (4) he recognized the fear of the Gauls

347

7. quantam auctōritātem hostēs apud eōs cōnsecūtī essent
    (1) how much influence the enemy had gained over them
    (2) how much authority the enemy had lost
    (3) the amount of authority the visitors had among them
    (4) with how much influence they had followed the enemy

8. Eīs nihil temporis dandum esse
    (1) Nothing temporal ought to be given them
    (2) No good weather had been given them
    (3) No time should be given them
    (4) No presents should be given them

9. ut cōnsilia caperent
    (1) that they might attend the meetings
    (2) to form plans
    (3) to seize the consuls
    (4) that they might form their lines

10. rēs opportūnissima accidit
    (1) the thing happened opportunely
    (2) the race was a fortunate accident
    (3) a very fortunate event occurred
    (4) the opportunity was lost

11. Postrīdiē eius diēī
    (1) The next day
    (2) Within a week
    (3) The morning before
    (4) The day before

12. Germānī eīsdem īnsidiīs ūsī sunt
    (1) the Germans took advantage of the enemy's treachery
    (2) the Germans were accustomed to the same treachery
    (3) the Germans are useful in their treachery
    (4) the Germans used the same treachery

13. complūrēs ad eum in castra vēnērunt
    (1) several came to him in camp
    (2) frequently they came to camp for him
    (3) they went toward his camp all the time
    (4) they went from him into camp in crowds

14. Cum vērō dīcerent sē contrā condiciōnēs pācis prīdiē proelium commīsisse
    (1) Although they admitted that they committed a crime the day before contrary to the terms of peace
    (2) Although they admitted that they had begun battle the day before contrary to the terms of peace
    (3) When they confessed that they themselves had sent conditions for the battle's end
    (4) On the other hand they admitted that they were commissioned by them to make peace

15. spērāvērunt aliquid dē indūtiīs cōnsequī
    (1) they hoped to gain something with respect to a truce
    (2) they despaired of a truce being undertaken
    (3) they gave commands concerning a truce
    (4) they hoped to end the truce

16. eōs ad sē lātōs esse
    (1) they were carried from him
    (2) they belonged to him
    (3) they were known to him
    (4) they had been brought to him

17. illōs retinērī iussit
    (1) he helped them to stay
    (2) he helped them to be detained
    (3) he ordered them to be detained
    (4) he ordered them to leave

18. Ipse omnēs cōpiās castrīs ēdūxit
    (1) He himself had all the supplies of the camp
    (2) He even produced all the forces in the camp
    (3) All the forces were led into the same camp
    (4) He himself led all the forces from camp

19. quī recentī proeliō perterritus erat
    (1) who recently had left the battle
    (2) which had been thoroughly frightened by the recent conflict
    (3) which had been brought into battle recently
    (4) who had given battle because of the recent attack

20. Aciē triplicī īnstrūctā
    (1) The three armies having been drawn up
    (2) The forces having been instructed three times
    (3) After a triple battle line had been drawn up
    (4) After a triple battle line was disbanded

Part 2

Directions (21-30): In the space provided in the separate answer booklet, rewrite *completely each* of the following sentences, substituting for the italicized Latin term the grammatical form called for or the proper form of the expression in parentheses. *Make any other changes in each sentence that are required by the substitution,* but, unless the meaning is changed by the parenthetical instructions, be sure to retain the general idea of the original sentence. [10]

21. Nauta est sīc perterritus ut *loquī* nōn possit.   (moveō)
22. Dīcit, "Virī veniunt."   (indirect statement)
23. Hannibal *dē* montibus altīs cōpiās dūxit.   (trāns)
24. *Spectā, amīce,* domōs pulchrās!   (plural)
25. *Illō tempore* glōria Ītaliae erat maxima.   (Hic annus)
26. *Postquam hostēs repulsī erant,* dux virōs suōs laudāvit.   (ablative absolute)
27. *Oppidum* ab hostibus trāditum est.   (plural)
28. Pater multa dōna frātribus *dedit.*   (portō)
29. Hannibal erat *socius* patris.   (grātus)
30. Imperātor tēlum *parāvit.*   (ūtor)

Part 3

Directions (31-40) : Read the following passages carefully, but do *not* write a translation. Below *each* passage you will find five questions or incomplete statements. Each statement or question is followed by four suggested answers numbered 1 through 4. Select the answer that best completes *each on the basis of the information given in the passages* and write its *number* in the space provided in the separate answer booklet.   [20]

a. Apion scrīpsit sē neque audīvisse neque lēgisse haec sed sē ipsum vīdisse in urbe Rōmā oculīs suīs. Dīxit, "In Circō Maximō pugna bēstiārum populō dabātur. Cum Rōmae essem, spectātor hōrum lūdōrum fuī. Ibi multa animālia incrēdibilī magnitūdine erant. Sed praeter omnia alia, magnitūdō *leōnum* fuit admīrātiōnī et ūnus maximē omnēs cēterōs superāvit. Is ūnus leō impetū corporis et terrificō *fremitū* animōs oculōsque in sē verterat.

Servus, cui Androclus nōmen fuit, intrōductus erat inter complūrēs cēterōs. Ille leō ubi servum vīdit subitō stetit et tum placidē ad hominem accēdit. Tum *caudam* mōre amantium animālium movet et tangit linguā suā manūs hominis quī magnopere perterrētur.

—Aulus Gellius, *Noctēs Atticae*, V, 14 (adapted)

> *leōnum*—from *leō*, lion
> *fremitū*—from *fremitus*, roar
> *caudam*—from *cauda*, tail

31. Quō modō Apion cognōvit dē fābulā quae suprā nārrātur?
    (1) Apion dē hāc fābulā audīverat.
    (2) Vir Apiōnī dē hāc fābulā scrīpserat.
    (3) Apion hanc fābulam lēgerat.
    (4) Apion ipse hās rēs spectāverat.

32. Quid in Circō Maximō accidit?
    (1) Populus ōrātiōnem audiēbat.
    (2) Lūdī mōnstrābantur.
    (3) Apion vulnerātus est.
    (4) Spectātōrēs interfectī sunt.

33. Ubi Apion Rōmam vēnit, quid fēcit?
    (1) Magna animālia cōnspēxit.
    (2) In lūdīs pugnāvit.
    (3) Animālia līberāvit.
    (4) Leōnem interfēcit.

34. Omnēs ūnum leōnem spectāvērunt quod
    (1) albus erat
    (2) minimus erat
    (3) nūllam caudam habēbat
    (4) fortior erat quam cēterī

35. Cum leō Androclum spectāret, coepit
    (1) virum oppugnāre
    (2) ad virum amīcō modō venīre
    (3) ā virō terrērī
    (4) ā Circō currere

b. Cūriō cum omnibus cōpiīs quartā vigiliā exierat; cohortēs quīnque castrīs praesidiō relīquit. Prōgressus mīlia passuum VI equitēs convēnit et ab eīs rēs gestās cognōvit. Cum Cūriō ē captīvīs quaesīvisset quis castrīs ad *Bagradam* praeesset, respondērunt *Saburram*. Tum Cūriō, studēns iter cōnficere, dīxit sē atque suōs mīlitēs facile superāre posse multitūdinem *Numidārum*, cum rēx abesset et cōpiae hostium parvae essent. Equitēs sequī iussit. Ipse in itinere contendit ut in hostēs perterritōs impetum facere posset. Sed illī, itinere tōtīus noctis cōnfectī, sequī nōn potuērunt, atque cōnsistere statuērunt.

—Caesar, *Dē Bellō Cīvīlī*, II, 39 (adapted)

> *Bagradam*—from *Bagrada*, a river near Carthage
> *Saburram*—from *Saburra*, an African general
> *Numidārum*—from *Numidae*, people of Numidia

36. Cūriō quīnque cohortēs relīquit ut
    (1) exīrent quartā vigiliā
    (2) castra dēfenderent
    (3) omnibus cōpiīs praeessent
    (4) castra pōnerent

37. Captīvī Cūriōnī dīxērunt
    (1) Saburram esse imperātōrem castrōrum prope flūmen
    (2) sē convocāre equitēs
    (3) sē mīlia passuum VI prōgressōs esse
    (4) rēs gestās hostium esse maximās

38. Cūr Cūriō dīxit sē vincere posse Numidās?
    (1) quod in eō locō cōnsistere cupīvit
    (2) quod rēx aderat
    (3) quod hostēs paucōs mīlitēs habuērunt
    (4) quod iter erat parvum

39. Hōc dictō, quid Cūriō fēcit?
    (1) Fūgit ab hostibus.
    (2) In itinere cōnstitit.
    (3) Multitūdinem Numidārum coēgit.
    (4) Imperāvit equitātuī ut sequerētur.

40. Cūriō quam celerrimē prōgressus est ut
    (1) equōs perterrēret
    (2) multitūdinem Numidārum fugeret
    (3) hostēs oppugnāret
    (4) cum Saburrā loquerētur

Part 4

Directions (41-50) : In the space provided in the separate answer booklet, write the *number* of the word or expression which, when inserted in the blank, makes each sentence grammatically correct.   [10]

41. Decem . . . Graecī Trōiam oppugnābant.
(1) annī (2) annōs (3) annōrum (4) annīs
42. Explōrātōrēs aquam . . . poterant.
(1) inventam esse (2) invenīre (3) invēnisse (4) invenīrī
43. Amīcus meus librōs . . . ā Rōmānīs clārīs legit.
(1) scrīptīs (2) scrīptus (3) scrīptōs (4) scrīptī
44. Magister . . . librum novum dēmōnstrāvit.
(1) mihi (2) ad mē (3) ab mē (4) mē
45. Exercitus . . . discessit.
(1) urbem (2) ex urbe (3) urbe (4) urbs
46. Rogāvit quid . . . .
(1) faciunt (2) facere (3) faciēbant (4) fēcissent
47. Rēgēs . . . mānsērunt.
(1) Asiā (2) Asiam (3) Asia (4) in Asiā
48. . . . proelium dux mīlitēs laudāvit.
(1) Post (2) Posteā (3) Posterus (4) Postquam
49. Homō . . . appellātus est.
(1) Scīpiōnem (2) Scīpiōnis (3) Scīpiō (4) Scīpiōnī
50. Vir . . . vīdistī est frater meus.
(1) quod (2) cui (3) quis (4) quem

Part 5

Directions (51-60): For *each* sentence below, write in column I in the separate answer booklet a Latin word with which the italicized word is associated by derivation. Then in column II in the answer booklet write the *number* preceding the word or expression that best expresses the meaning of the italicized word. [10]

[Illustration: The explanation was made in a very *amicable* manner.

    (1) angry   (2) belligerent   (3) friendly   (4) verbose

Column I — amīcus   Column II — 3]

51. The law was enacted through the *concurrence* of all senators.
(1) oratory (2) interest (3) agreement (4) lobbying
52. The President's arrival caused much *commotion*.
(1) interest (2) conversation (3) concern (4) confusion
53. The eldest boy received his father's *benediction*.
(1) sympathy (2) inheritance (3) kindness (4) blessing
54. *Tenacity* is a quality of successful businessmen.
(1) Persistence (2) Diplomacy (3) Charm (4) Shrewdness
55. The child learned how to *comport* himself.
(1) behave (2) satisfy (3) rest (4) comfort
56. The spies whose assignment it was to *subvert* the government were arrested.
(1) alarm (2) undermine (3) support (4) deceive
57. The secretary found the job *confining*.
(1) stimulating (2) rewarding (3) uninteresting (4) limiting
58. The principal *supervises* the school program.
(1) interprets (2) overrules (3) oversees (4) criticizes
59. The *edifices* of today are so unlike those of yesterday.
(1) achievements (2) buildings (3) armaments (4) customs
60. His state of *dejection* was temporary.
(1) wrath (2) rebellion (3) discouragement (4) indecision

Part 6

Directions (61-75): Select *ten* of the following statements. In the space provided in the separate answer booklet, write the *number* of the word or expression which best completes the statement. [10]

61. Which expression warns a person of the presence of a dog?
(1) *Bonā fidē* (2) *Tempus fugit* (3) *Cavē canem* (4) *Caveat emptor*
62. The rear guard of the Roman army was called
(1) *aciēs* (2) *cornū* (3) *primum agmen* (4) *novissimum agmen*
63. Of which state is *Excelsior* the motto?
(1) Massachusetts (2) Virginia (3) New York (4) New Jersey
64. The funeral oration over Caesar was delivered by
(1) Antony (2) Brutus (3) Cato (4) Lepidus
65. Daedalus and his son Icarus might be considered the equivalent in ancient times of the
(1) Wright brothers (2) Eisenhower brothers (3) Barrymore brothers (4) Kennedy brothers
66. A Roman running for public office would wear the *toga*
(1) *virīlis* (2) *candida* (3) *pīcta* (4) *praetexta*

67. In its early period of expansion, Rome had to defeat the mighty naval power of
    (1) Carthage   (2) Syria   (3) Spain   (4) Britain
68. Which river is associated with Caesar's campaign in Gaul?
    (1) Tiber   (2) Rhone   (3) Danube   (4) Vistula
69. A great general whom Caesar, as a boy, admired was
    (1) *Vercingetorīx*   (2) *Ambiorīx*   (3) *Labiēnus*   (4) *Marius*
70. The officer in charge of the Roman army's supplies was the
    (1) *lēgātus*   (2) *centuriō*   (3) *quaestor*   (4) *praefectus*
71. The formal reception room where a Roman met his friends and clients was the
    (1) *peristylium*   (2) *vestibulum*   (3) *tablīnum*   (4) *atrium*
72. In the expression *"de facto* segregation*" de facto* means
    (1) actual   (2) comparative   (3) legal   (4) temporary
73. The Gracchi were
    (1) historians   (2) poets   (3) reformers   (4) consuls
74. *Lemannus* was the Latin name for
    (1) the Loire River   (2) Lake Geneva   (3) Paris   (4) Lucerne
75. Which architectural feature used today is copied from the ancient Romans?
    (1) minaret   (2) rounded arch   (3) flying buttress   (4) church spire

LATIN, LEVEL 2

Part 1

Translate passage *a* into English. Write your translation in the space provided in the separate answer booklet.   [20]

[The horse that brought bad luck]

a. Dīcitur Gnaeum Sēium habuisse equum nātum in terrā Graeciā. Dīcunt illum equum fuisse magnum et omnēs aliōs equōs superāvisse, sed fortūnam equī fuisse *tālem* ut vir quī eum habēret cum omnī familiā ē vītā exīret. Itaque prīmum Gnaeus Sēius ā M. Antōniō, quī posteā ūnus ex triumvirīs fuit, interfectus est. Tum C. Dolabella, cōnsul, fāmā illius equī adductus, eum magnā pecūniā obtinuit; sed bellō cīvīlī hic vir etiam necātus est. Mox eundum equum C. Cassius abdūxit; Cassium ipsum, victō exercitū suō, modō horribilī occīsum esse nārrant. Tum post mortem Cassī, Antōnius, equō acceptō, etiam ē vītā excessit. Nunc cum homō multās calamitātēs habeat dīcimus, "Ille homō habet equum Sēī."

—Aulus Gellius, *Noctēs Atticae*, III, 9 (adapted)

tālem—from *tālis*, such

Directions (1-20): Do *not* write a translation of passage *b*; read it through carefully several times to ascertain the meaning. Then in the spaces provided in your separate answer booklet, write the *number* of the alternative that best translates *each* of the underlined expressions *as it is used in the passage*.   [20]

b. Tīmoleōn, cum vetus iam esset, lūcem oculōrum āmīsit. Hanc calamitātem ita bene tulit ut nēmō
<u>(1)</u> <u>(2)</u> <u>(3)</u>
audīret eum dīcere malum. Veniēbat autem in theātrum cum ibi concilium populī habērētur; et dē vehiculō
<u>(4)</u> <u>(5)</u>
sententiam suam dīcēbat. Neque aliquis putābat eum esse inimīcum. Hic quidem cum suās laudēs audīret
<u>(6)</u> <u>(7)</u> <u>(8)</u>
dīcī, maximē deīs ēgit grātiās. Habuit grātiam quod, cum cīvēs Siciliam reficere cōnstituissent, sē ducem
<u>(9)</u> <u>(10)</u> <u>(11)</u>
esse voluerant. Nihil enim rērum hūmānārum sine auxiliō deōrum gerī putābat; itaque suae domī templum
<u>(12)</u> <u>(13)</u>
Fortūnae cōnstituerat.
<u>(14)</u>

Erant multa exempla suae fortūnae bonae; nam proelia maxima *nātālī diē* suō fēcit ut tōta Sicilia eius
<u>(15)</u>
nātālem diem *festum* habēret. Cum quīdam Dēmaenetus in conciliō populī dē rēbus gestīs Tīmoleontis male
<u>(16)</u> <u>(17)</u>
dīceret, Tīmoleōn fēlix erat; namque crēdidit iūs darī dēbēre Syrācūsānīs ut quisque līberē dīcere posset.
<u>(18)</u> <u>(19)</u>
Cum mortuus esset, pūblicē ā Syrācūsānīs in gymnasiō quod Tīmoleontēum appellātur *sepultus est*.
<u>(20)</u>

—Nepos, XX *Tīmoleōn* 4-5

nātālī diē—from *nātālis diēs*, birthday
festum—holiday
sepultus est—from *sepeliō*, bury

1. cum vetus iam esset
   (1) although he was an old man
   (2) since he no longer was old
   (3) when he was already old
   (4) he was with an old man

2. lūcem oculōrum āmīsit
   (1) the light shone in his eyes
   (2) the light blinded his eyes
   (3) regained his eyesight
   (4) lost the sight of his eyes

3. Hanc calamitātem ita bene tulit
   (1) This burden overwhelmed him so much
   (2) This accident happened in this manner
   (3) He endured this misfortune so patiently
   (4) He bore this calamity with such difficulty

4. ut nēmō audīret eum dīcere malum
   (1) that no one heard him complain
   (2) as no one spoke evil
   (3) that no one will hear him speak badly
   (4) that no one dared him to speak evil

5. cum ibi concilium populī habērētur
   (1) when an assembly of people was being held there
   (2) when the people formed a plan there
   (3) although there the people asked for counsel
   (4) since the plan of the people was being considered there

6. dē vehiculō sententiam suam dīcēbat
   (1) he gave his opinion about the performance
   (2) he denied his statement about chariot races
   (3) running from the chariot he spoke his mind
   (4) he gave his opinion from his carriage

7. Neque aliquis putābat eum esse inimīcum.
   (1) He thought that no one was friendly.
   (2) Nor did a certain man think they were hostile.
   (3) Neither did he think that anyone could be friendly.
   (4) And no one thought that he was unfriendly.

352

8. Hic quidem cum suās laudēs audīret dīcī
   (1) In fact when he heard his praises sung
   (2) Here a certain man when he dared to sing his praises
   (3) Although this man heard certain ones sing his praises
   (4) Indeed this man agreed with the praises given
9. maximē deīs ēgit grātiās
   (1) he especially thanked the gods
   (2) he asked the gods for favors
   (3) the gods thanked him profusely
   (4) they were grateful to the greatest gods
10. Habuit grātiam
    (1) He had favors
    (2) He had prestige
    (3) He felt resentment
    (4) He was grateful
11. cum cīvēs Siciliam reficere cōnstituissent
    (1) although the citizens determined to rebuild Sicily
    (2) when the citizens had decided to restore Sicily
    (3) because the citizens will decide to rehabilitate the Sicilians
    (4) when the states had ceased to rebuild Sicily
12. sē ducem esse voluerant
    (1) they had wished him to be their leader
    (2) he had wished to be their leader
    (3) they had wished to be leaders
    (4) they had flown to their leader
13. Nihil enim rērum hūmānārum sine auxiliō deōrum gerī putābat
    (1) He thought that human affairs could go on without the help of the gods
    (2) For he believed that nothing in human affairs came to pass without the aid of the gods
    (3) For he thought that no human things occurred with the help of the gods
    (4) No one thought that humanity could advance without the gods
14. suae domī templum Fortūnae cōnstituerat
    (1) Fortune had set up a shrine for his home
    (2) from his home he had taken the shrine for Fortune
    (3) at his home he had set up a shrine in honor of Fortune
    (4) he worshipped the shrine of money in his home
15. nam proelia maxima nātalī dīe suō fēcit
    (1) for he did many things on his birthday
    (2) for he fought his greatest battles on his birthday
    (3) for everything important he received on his birthday
    (4) for his birthday he caused many battles
16. ut tōta Sicilia eius nātālem diem festum habēret
    (1) that all Sicily might celebrate his birthday as a holiday
    (2) that the birthday of Sicily was a holiday
    (3) that he held all Sicily during his birthday festival
    (4) that he celebrated the birthday of all Sicilians
17. Cum quīdam Dēmaenetus in conciliō populī dē rēbus gestīs Tīmoleontis male dīceret
    (1) When a certain Demaenetus according to the plan of the people spoke badly about the achievements of Timoleon
    (2) Since the same Demaenetus in the meeting of the people preferred to speak about the evil deeds of Timoleon
    (3) When a certain Demaenetus in an assembly of the people spoke in an uncomplimentary fashion about the exploits of Timoleon
    (4) When a certain Demaenetus in a gathering of the people praised the gestures of Timoleon
18. namque crēdidit iūs darī dēbēre Syrācūsānīs
    (1) now he believed that freedom ought to be protected by the Syracusans
    (2) for he realized that Syracuse ought to refuse independence
    (3) now he believed that he ought to trade Syracuse for freedom
    (4) for he believed that the right ought to be given to the Syracusans
19. ut quisque līberē dīcere posset
    (1) that all may speak rashly
    (2) so that each one could speak freely
    (3) so that certain ones could speak freely
    (4) that each had to speak about liberty
20. Cum mortuus esset
    (1) Although he had delayed
    (2) Before he died
    (3) When he had died
    (4) Since there was a delay

Part 2

Directions (21-30): In the space provided in the separate answer booklet, rewrite *completely each* of the following sentences, substituting for the italicized Latin term the grammatical form called for or the proper form of the expression in parentheses. *Make any other changes in each sentence that are required by the substitution,* but, unless the meaning is changed by the parenthetical instructions, be sure to retain the general idea of the original sentence.   [10]

21. Lūcius dominō suō *pārēbit*.   (videō)
22. Lēgātus legiōnem *dūcit*.   (praesum)
23. *Nautae* nāvigant.   (Precede sentence by putat.)

24. Sulla obsidēs *vulnerāverat.* (passive voice)
25. Caesar in oppidō *erat.* (properō)
26. Nostrī *pervēnērunt* ut victōriam nūntiārent. (present tense)
27. Ad urbem ambulāvit *ad amīcōs videndōs.* (ut clause)
28. Hic *gladius* est ācer. (plural)
29. Epistulam ad sorōrem *scrībit.* (dō)
30. Caesar *hodiē* proficīscētur. (idem tempus)

Part 3

Directions (31-40): Read the following passages carefully, but do *not* write a translation. Below each passage you will find five questions or incomplete statements. Each statement or question is followed by four suggested answers numbered 1 through 4. Select the answer that best completes *each on the basis of the information given in the passage* and write its *number* in the space provided in the separate answer booklet. [20]

a. Boiī erant *stīpendiāriī* Haeduōrum et amīcī Caesaris. Caesar cognōvit Vercingetorīgem oppidum Boiōrum oppugnāre. Haec rēs Caesarī magnam difficultātem ad consilium capiendum adferēbat. Legiōnēs suās ūnō locō reliquam partem hiemis continēre voluit ad rem frūmentāriam obtinendam.

Tandem amīcīs suīs autem auxilium dare cōnstituit et omnēs difficultātēs sustinēre. Itaque cohortātus est Haeduōs dē rē frūmentāriā supportandā. Lēgātōs igitur praemittit ad Boiōs quī dē suō adventū doceant hortenturque ut in fidē maneant atque hostium impetum magnō animō sustineant. Duābus legiōnibus atque impedīmentīs tōtīus exercitūs relictīs, ad fīnēs Boiōrum proficīscitur.

— Caesar, *De Bellō Gallicō*, VII, 10 (adapted)

stīpendiāriī—tributaries

31. Cum Vercingetorīx impetum in oppidum Boiōrum faceret, effēcit ut
    (1) Caesarem caperet
    (2) magnam cōpiam tēlōrum invenīret
    (3) Caesar difficultātem habēret
    (4) incolae oppidī magnā vōce clāmārent

32. Caesar in hibernīs manēre cupīvit ut
    (1) cōnsilia ad sē recipiendum caperet
    (2) cōpiam frūmentī parāret
    (3) Haeduī fīnēs Boiōrum expugnārent
    (4) Vercingetorīx legiōnēs movēret

33. Caesar Haeduōs hortātus est ut
    (1) pontem servārent
    (2) cohortēs convocārent
    (3) iter ad Boiōs facerent
    (4) frūmentum sibi ferrent

34. Lēgātī Caesaris Boiīs nūntiāvērunt
    (1) Caesarem ventūrum esse
    (2) Caesarem castra Haeduōrum oppugnātūrum esse
    (3) hostēs sēsē receptūrōs esse
    (4) Caesarem Rōmam reditūrum esse

35. Cum ad Boiōs īret, Caesar relīquit
    (1) cōpiam aquae
    (2) tōtum exercitum
    (3) omnia impedīmenta et legiōnēs duās
    (4) nūlla impedīmenta et legiōnēs duās

b. Dum Rōmānī lēgātiōnēs Carthāginem mittunt, Hannibal, quod mīlitēs esse *dēfessōs* proeliīs operibusque cognōscēbat, eīs *quiētem* paucōrum diērum dedit, praesidiīs positīs ad servanda mīlitāria opera. Interim animōs mīlitum suōrum nunc īrā in hostēs, nunc spē praemiōrum incitāvit; suīs mīlitibus dīxit eōs praedam captae urbis receptūrōs esse. Omnēs mīlitēs ita commōtī sunt ut vidērētur nūllam vim posse resistere eīs. Cum Saguntīnī, contrā quōs Carthāginiēnsēs bellum gerēbant, ā proeliīs *quiētem* habērent, tamen nocte et diē labōrāvērunt ut novum mūrum reficerent.

— Līvius, *Ab Urbe Conditā*, XXI, 11 (adapted)

dēfessōs—from *dēfessus,* tired
quiētem—from *quiēs,* rest

36. In prīmā parte fābulae, quid fēcērunt Rōmānī?
    (1) Carthāginiēnsēs vīcērunt.
    (2) Rōmam rediērunt.
    (3) Ad hostēs lēgātōs mīsērunt.
    (4) Legiōnēs cōnscrīpsērunt.

37. Cūr Hannibal suīs mīlitibus diēs quiētis dedit?
    (1) Mīlitēs suās familiās vidēre voluērunt.
    (2) Carthāginiēnsēs victōriam celebrāvērunt.
    (3) Mīlitēs omnem spem āmiserant.
    (4) Mīlitēs magnopere labōrāverant.

38. Hannibal mīlitēs movēbat
    (1) audāciā cōnsilī
    (2) amōre vītae
    (3) praemiīs futūrīs
    (4) spē multī cibī

39. Mīlitēs Hannibalis ita excitātī sunt ut
    (1) signum dare vellent
    (2) nihil eōs prohibēre posse vidērētur
    (3) ad oppidum statim currerent
    (4) essent perterritī

40. Dum Saguntīnī brevem pācem habent, quid accidēbat?
    (1) Nihil faciēbant.
    (2) Lēgātōs Rōmam mittēbant.
    (3) Suās mūnītiōnēs rūrsus aedificābant.
    (4) Ab oppidō discēdēbant.

Part 4

Directions (41-50): In the space provided in the separate answer booklet, write the *number* of the word or expression which, when inserted in the blank, makes *each* sentence grammatically correct. [10]

41. Caesar audīvit . . . hostium appropinquāre.
    (1) cōpiīs (2) cōpiās (3) cōpiārum (4) cōpiae
42. Pīlum trāns . . . iacit.
    (1) campō (2) campum (3) campīs (4) campōrum
43. Dā nōbīs pecūniam tuam, . . . !
    (1) Mārcus (2) Mārce (3) Mārco (4) Mārcum
44. Caesar praemia ad partem . . . mīsit.
    (1) prōvinciā (2) prōvincia (3) prōvinciae (4) prōvinciam
45. Caesar . . . celeriter pervēnit.
    (1) cum exercitū (2) exercitum (3) exercitus (4) exercitū
46. Belgae . . . reliquōs Gallōs superābant.
    (1) virtūte (2) virtūtis (3) ā virtūte (4) virtūtī
47. Mīlitēs . . . ūtēbantur.
    (1) magnōs gladiōs (2) magnōrum gladiōrum (3) magnīs gladiīs (4) magnī gladiī
48. Ducēs bonī . . . possunt.
    (1) laudant (2) laudārī (3) laudāns (4) laudātus esse
49. Puer . . . vidēbātur.
    (1) potentī (2) potentis (3) potentem (4) potēns
50. Nūntius rogat cūr tardī . . . .
    (1) sint (2) fuērunt (3) erant (4) sunt

Part 5

Directions (51-60): For *each* sentence below, write in column I in the separate answer booklet a Latin word with which the italicized word is associated by derivation. Then in column II in the answer booklet write the *number* preceding the word or expression that best expresses the meaning of the italicized word. [10]

	Column I	Column II
[Illustration: The explanation was made in a very *amicable* manner.	amīcus	3
(1) angry (2) belligerent (3) friendly (4) verbose	....	................]

51. The mute person indicated his *affirmation* with a gesture.
    (1) understanding (2) approval (3) rejection (4) recollection
52. War may sometimes cause citizens to be *expatriated*.
    (1) fearful (2) resourceful (3) extravagant (4) exiled
53. It is sometimes possible to *circumvent* regulations.
    (1) avoid (2) ridicule (3) improve (4) reduce
54. The judge granted a *moratorium* to the debtor.
    (1) delay (2) pardon (3) bankruptcy writ (4) hearing
55. The man uttered a *malediction*.
    (1) reply (2) curse (3) challenge (4) denial
56. The actor's *soliloquy* revealed the background for the drama.
    (1) greeting to the rest of the cast (3) proclamation to the audience
    (2) prayer to the heavenly spirits (4) talk to himself
57. The prisoner searched for a means of *egress*.
    (1) communication (2) defense (3) escape (4) diversion
58. The *defection* of the soldiers undermined the morale of the army.
    (1) desertion (2) misery (3) poor discipline (4) cowardice
59. There is a time and place for *levity*.
    (1) constancy (2) severity (3) frivolity (4) inquisitiveness
60. The president's words *expedited* my release.
    (1) facilitated (2) prevented (3) cancelled (4) delayed

Part 6

Directions (61-75): Select *ten* of the following statements or questions. In the space provided in the separate answer booklet, write the *number* of the word or expression which best completes the statement or answers the question. [10]

61. The Roman numeral MCMXL is equivalent to (1) 1570 (2) 1910 (3) 1940 (4) 2050
62. The large island at the "toe of Italy" is called (1) *Crēta* (2) *Corsica* (3) *Sardinia* (4) *Sicilia*
63. "To cross the Rubicon" is to (1) cast aside all plans (2) cross one bridge at a time (3) make an irrevocable decision (4) make the most of an opportunity

64. Who helped Jason obtain the Golden Fleece? (1) Absyrtus (2) Aeetes (3) Glauce (4) Medea

65. Caesar's chief opponent during the Civil War was (1) *Octāviānus* (2) *Pompeius* (3) *Cinna* (4) *Cassius*

66. The usual battle formation of the Roman army was the (1) *triplex aciēs* (2) *phalanx* (3) *prīmum agmen* (4) *novissimum agmen*

67. A modern fortuneteller may be compared to a Roman (1) *līctor* (2) *pater familiās* (3) *pontifex maximus* (4) *augur*

68. The Punic Wars refer to the wars between Rome and (1) Gaul (2) Greece (3) Britain (4) Carthage

69. The mountains which Hannibal crossed with his elephants on his way to attack the Romans were the (1) Pyrenees (2) Apennines (3) Alps (4) Atlas

70. Roman students who wished advanced study in oratory would often go to (1) *Athēnae* (2) *Lūtētia* (3) *Brundisium* (4) *Syrācūsae*

71. The Latin abbreviation which means "take notice" is (1) *i.e.* (2) *P.S.* (3) *N.B.* (4) *et al.*

72. Which group contains three men *all* of whom gained fame in the area indicated? (1) Roman generals—Sulla, Marius, Hannibal (2) Latin authors—Vergil, Cicero, Caesar (3) Caesar's lieutenants —Labienus, Augustus, Sabinus (4) Gallic leaders—Horatius, Orgetorix, Ariovistus

73. The name of the Roman two-faced deity survives in the name of our month of (1) January (2) March (3) May (4) June

74. The greatest significance of Caesar's conquest of Gaul is that it (1) added Belgium to the Roman Empire (2) gave Rome a market for its products (3) relieved unemployment (4) made possible the spread of Graeco-Roman civilization

75. The town *Chester* has its origin in the Latin word (1) *castra* (2) *caedēs* (3) *cīvitās* (4) *circiter*

LATIN, LEVEL 2

Part 1

Translate passage *a* into English. Write your translation in the space provided in the separate answer booklet. [20]

[Some Romans sacrifice their lives to save their army.]

a. Imperātor Carthāginiēnsis in terrā Siciliā, bellō Pūnicō prīmō, contrā Rōmānōs prōgreditur; collēs locōsque idōneōs occupat. Mīlitēs Rōmānī igitur in locō perīculōsō erant. Tribūnus cōnsulem monuit ut CCCC mīlitēs ad terram altam occupandam mitteret. "Hostēs enim," dīcit, "hōs mīlitēs sequentur eōsque interficere cōnābuntur. Tum intereā, dum hostēs hoc faciunt, tempus habēbis et exercitum reliquum ex hōc locō ēducere poteris." Hoc cōnsilium cōnsulī bonum vidēbātur, sed rogāvit quis dux hōrum mīlitum esse vellet. Tribūnus respondit, "Ego tibi et reī pūblicae vītam meam dō." Cōnsul tribūnō grātiās agit eumque laudat. Tribūnus et CCCC mīlitēs ad moriendum profectī sunt.

—Aulus Gellius, *Noctēs Atticae*, III, 7 (adapted)

Directions (1-20): Do *not* write a translation of passage *b*; read it through carefully several times to ascertain the meaning. Then in the spaces provided in your separate answer booklet, write the *number* of the alternative that best translates *each* of the underlined expressions *as it is used in the passage.* [20]

b. (I) Titus Mānlius appellātus est Torquātus quod semper gerēbat torquem ex aurō dētrāctam ex hoste quem occīderat. ōlim cum exercitus Rōmānus cum Gallīs ācerrimē contenderet, quīdam Gallus prōcessit quī
$\overline{(1)}$ $\overline{(2)}$
vīribus et magnitūdine et virtūte omnibus cēterīs praestābat. Silentiō factō, vōce maximā postulāvit ut ūnus
$\overline{(3)}$ $\overline{(4)}$
ex Rōmānīs prōcēderet ad sēcum pugnandum. Cum nēmō id facere audēret propter magnitūdinem et ferōci-
$\overline{(5)}$ $\overline{(6)}$
tātem, Gallus rīdēre coepit. Tum Titus Mānlius, intellegēns nēminem ē tantō exercitū prōgressūrum esse,
$\overline{(7)}$
prōcessit: nōluit virtūtem Rōmānam ab Gallō contāminārī. Scūtō gladiōque armātus, contrā ingentem Gallum
$\overline{(8)}$ $\overline{(9)}$
cōnstitit. Cōnfīsus virtūte magis quam arte, Gallum petīvit ēvertitque. Magnā victōriā factā, duōbus exerci-
$\overline{(10)}$ $\overline{(11)}$
tibus spectantibus, Mānlius torquem Gallī dētrāxit et eam sibi imposuit.
$\overline{(12)}$

—Aulus Gellius, *Noctēs Atticae*, IX, 13 (adapted)

> *torquem*—from *torquis*, necklace
> *rīdēre*—from *rīdeō*, laugh

1. gerēbat torquem ex aurō dētrāctam ex hoste quem occīderat
   (1) he wore a golden necklace torn from an enemy who had attacked him
   (2) he had killed an enemy wearing a necklace made of gold
   (3) he wore a golden necklace torn from an enemy whom he had killed
   (4) he had killed an enemy who had torn a golden necklace from him

2. cum exercitus Rōmānus cum Gallīs ācerrimē contenderet
   (1) when a Roman army had beaten the Gauls in a very bitter battle
   (2) when the Roman army was fighting very hard with the Gauls
   (3) wherever the Gauls were struggling in a very bitter contest
   (4) since the Roman army was hurrying to fight the Gauls

3. quī vīribus et magnitūdine et virtūte omnibus cēterīs praestābat
   (1) who surpassed all the others in strength, size, and courage
   (2) who presented all the rest with strength, men, and courage
   (3) who was pushed forward by all the others because of his strength, stature, and courage
   (4) who towered above all the others because of his strength, generosity, and prestige

4. Silentiō factō
   (1) With sudden silence   (3) By a silent deed
   (2) Silently   (4) When silence fell

5. ut ūnus ex Rōmānīs prōcēderet ad sēcum pugnandum
   (1) with the result that one of the Romans came forward to fight him
   (2) when one of the Romans advanced by fighting hard with him
   (3) that one of the Romans should come forward to fight him
   (4) so that one of the Romans was pushed forward to challenge him

6. Cum nēmō id facere audēret propter magnitūdinem et ferōcitātem
   (1) Since no one dared to do so because of his huge size and fierce manner
   (2) Although no one dared to make a sound because of his greatness and fierceness
   (3) Since no one was able to hear him because of the great fierceness of the fighting
   (4) When his great size and fierceness made him bold enough to do this

357

7. intellegēns nēminem ē tantō exercitū prōgressūrum esse
   (1) understanding why no one from so great an army had advanced
   (2) no one from that army was intelligent enough to advance
   (3) realizing that no one from so great an army would come forward
   (4) requesting no one from the great army to come forward

8. nōluit virtūtem Rōmānam ab Gallō contāminārī
   (1) he was unwilling that a Gaul be corrupted for the sake of Roman valor
   (2) he did not think that Roman courage could be tested by the Gauls
   (3) he did not know why Roman valor was being degraded by Gauls
   (4) he did not want Roman valor to be tarnished by a Gaul

9. Scūtō gladiōque armātus, contrā ingentem Gallum cōnstitit.
   (1) He stood opposite the huge Gaul whose armor consisted of a shield and sword.
   (2) He halted across from the great Gaul who was carrying a shield and sword as weapons.
   (3) Armed with shield and sword, he confronted the mighty Gaul.
   (4) The huge Gaul, equipped with shield and sword, stood opposite him.

10. Confīsus virtūte magis quam arte, Gallum petīvit ēvertitque.
    (1) The Gaul, trusting his strength more than his skill, struck and overcame him.
    (2) Relying on courage more than on skill, he attacked and overthrew the Gaul.
    (3) Confident of his strength as well as his artfulness, the Gaul attacked and killed him.
    (4) He struck and overcame the Gaul, who trusted in his strength and skill.

11. Magnā victōriā factā, duōbus exercitibus spectantibus
    (1) After he had achieved a great victory while the two armies watched
    (2) Watching the two armies win a great victory
    (3) With a great victory won by two alert armies
    (4) The great victory having made the two armies watchful

12. Mānlius torquem Gallī dētrāxit et eam sibi imposuit
    (1) Manlius dragged the Gaul away by his necklace and took it away from him
    (2) Manlius snatched the Gaul's necklace and broke it in pieces
    (3) Manlius tore off his necklace and put it on the Gaul
    (4) Manlius tore off the Gaul's necklace and put it on himself

(II) Eōdem tempore C. Fabius lēgātus complūrēs cīvitātēs in fidem recipit, litterīsque Gaī Canīnī Rebilī fit
      (13)   (14)
certior quae apud Pictonēs gerantur. Quibus rēbus cognitīs proficīscitur ad auxilium Duratiō ferendum.
         (15)   (16)
Subitō ex eō locō cum cōpiīs recēdit nec sē satis salūtis habitūrum esse arbitrātur, nisi flūmen Ligerem, quod
        (17)   (18)
erat trānseundum ponte propter magnitūdinem, cōpiās trādūxisset. Fabius crēdidit hostēs perterritōs petī-
                                                                                    (19)
tūrōs esse eum locum quem petēbant. Itaque cum cōpiīs ad eundem pontem contendit equitātumque ante agmen
                                                                                 (20)
legiōnum prōcēdere iussit.

—Caesar, *Dē Bellō Gallicō*, VIII, 27 (adapted)

13. complūrēs cīvitātēs in fidem recipit
    (1) recovered rights in several states   (3) took several states under his protection
    (2) asked for the loyalty of many states   (4) demanded payment from several states

14. litterīsque Gaī Canīnī Rebilī fit certior
    (1) and informed Gaius Caninius Rebilus of the message
    (2) and was informed by the message of Gaius Caninius Rebilus
    (3) and made a proposal through a message to Gaius Caninius Rebilus
    (4) and was disappointed by the message of Gaius Caninius Rebilus

15. quae apud Pictonēs gerantur
    (1) what was driving the Pictones   (3) why the Pictones were waging war
    (2) whom the Pictones were attacking   (4) what was going on among the Pictones

16. ad auxilium Duratiō ferendum
    (1) to report to Duratius about help   (3) to show gratitude for the help of Duratius
    (2) to secure help from Duratius   (4) to bring help for Duratius

17. Subitō ex eō locō cum cōpiīs recēdit
    (1) Therefore, he carried the supplies with him from the place
    (2) He withdrew suddenly from that place with his troops
    (3) He immediately procured supplies from that place
    (4) He yielded with his forces because of a sudden attack

18. nec sē satis salūtis habitūrum esse arbitrātur
    (1) and he did not think he would be safe enough
    (2) and he did not think his home was secure for the time
    (3) and it was not thought to be safe
    (4) and he did not think that he had lived satisfactorily

19. hostēs perterritōs petītūrōs esse eum locum
    (1) that the enemy would attack the terrified in that place
    (2) that the terrified enemy would seek that place
    (3) that he would seize the terrified enemy in that place
    (4) that he, thrown into confusion by the enemy, would withdraw from that place

20. equitātumque ante agmen legiōnum prōcēdere iussit
    (1) and he commanded the infantry to take the field before the cavalry
    (2) and he ordered the cavalry to advance in front of the marching column of the legions
    (3) and he instructed the cavalry to form a line of battle behind the legions
    (4) and previously he had ordered the cavalry to proceed on foot with the infantry

Part 2

Directions (21-30) : In the space provided in the separate answer booklet, rewrite *completely each* of the following sentences, substituting for the italicized Latin term the grammatical form called for or the proper form of the expression in parentheses. *Make any other changes in each sentence that are required by the substitution*, but, unless the meaning is changed by the parenthetical instructions, be sure to retain the general idea of the original sentence. [10]

21. Hostēs magnam urbem *cēpērunt*.   (occupō)
22. Equitēs hostēs *sequī* nōn poterant.   (inveniō)
23. Dux Rōmānus cum *multīs nautīs* trāns mare nāvigāvit.   (trēs legiōnēs)
24. Impedīmenta *in* castrīs posita sunt.   (circum)
25. Rēx virīs *magnum et clārum* praemium pollicitus est.   (superlative)
26. Mīlitēs fugiēbant *quod equitēs superātī sunt*.   (ablative absolute)
27. *Prīnceps* quī in triumphō portātur est barbarus.   (Rēgīna)
28. Māter ā puellā amātur.   (active)
29. Dux mīlitēs *rogāvit* ut oppidum dēfenderent.   (imperō)
30. Tribūnus *ad incolās videndōs* vēnerat.   (ut clause)

Part 3

Directions (31-40) : Read the following passage carefully, but do *not* write a translation. Below the passage you will find ten questions or incomplete statements. Each statement or question is followed by four suggested answers numbered 1 through 4. Select the answer that best completes *each on the basis of the information given in the passage* and write its *number* in the space provided in the separate answer booklet.   [20]

Cum Vercingetorīx ad suās cōpiās redisset, mīlitēs eī dīxērunt, "Nostram causam *prōdidistī* quod nostra castra propius Rōmānōs mōvistī, quod cum omnī equitātū discessistī et quod sine imperātōre tantās cōpiās relīquistī. Tuō discessū Rōmānī ad nōs cum celeritāte vēnērunt. Haec omnia nōn sine cōnsiliō nōn accidērunt. Rēgnum Galliae auctōritāte Caesaris habēre cupis."

Accūsātus hōc modō, Vercingetorix ad haec respondit, "Inopiā frūmentāriae reī castra mōvī. Persuāsus nātūrā locī quem sine mūnītiōne dēfendere possum, propius Rōmānōs mōvī. Omnēs equitēs discessērunt quod hīc eīs ūtī nōn potuī et sunt ūtilēs in locō in quem iērunt. Cum abessem, summum imperium nūllī virō dedī nē is proelium committere studiō vestrō impellerētur. Ex complūribus captīvīs cognōvī inopiā frūmentī exercitum Rōmānum nōn diūtius labōrāre posse. Itaque Caesar statuit tribus diēbus exercitum abdūcere. Meō opere sine proeliō exercitum Caesaris paene superārī vidētis. Victōria iam Gallīs est certa."

—Caesar, *Dē Bellō Gallicō*, VII, 20 (adapted)

Prōdidistī—from *prōdō*, betray

31. Cum Vercingetorīx ad suum exercitum revertisset, quid mīlitēs ēgērunt?
    (1) Eum laudāvērunt.   (3) Eum captīvum fēcērunt.
    (2) Statim discessērunt.   (4) Eum accūsāvērunt.

32. Quod Vercingetorīx discesserat, quid fēcit exercitus Rōmānus?
    (1) Ad castra hostium appropinquāvit.   (3) In flūmen rediit.
    (2) Ē castrīs fūgit.   (4) Proelium intermisīt.

33. Mīlitēs dīxērunt Vercingetorīgem cupere
    (1) mortem Caesaris   (3) salūtem Caesaris
    (2) laudem Rōmānōrum   (4) imperium Galliae

34. Vercingetorīx dīxit castra Gallica in aliō locō posita esse quod
    (1) inopia aquae fuerat   (3) satis cibī nōn fuerat
    (2) Gallī potestātem Caesaris timuerant   (4) equitēs superātī erant

35. Cūr locus est idōneus castrīs?
    (1) Magnus est.   (3) Aqua adest.
    (2) Facile dēfendī potest.   (4) In colle est.

36. Equitēs dīmissī sunt cum
    (1) in hōc locō nōn essent ūtilēs   (3) Rōmānī discēderent
    (2) sōlum paucī essent   (4) equīs cibus nōn relictus esset

359

37. Cōpiae Gallicae sine duce relictae erant quod Vercingetorīx
    (1) in montibus manēre cōnstituit
    (2) fugere volēbat
    (3) vulnerātus erat
    (4) pugnam prohibēre volēbat

38. Vercingetorīx intellēxit Rōmānōs
    (1) impetum parāre
    (2) multum frūmentum habēre
    (3) parvam cōpiam cibī habēre
    (4) cupidōs pugnandī esse

39. Cum mīlitēs Rōmānī labōrāre nōn possint, Caesar in animō habet
    (1) statim proelium committere
    (2) nūntiōs ad Vercingetorīgem mittere
    (3) cum suō exercitū discēdere
    (4) concilium habēre

40. Victōria Gallica est facilis propter
    (1) tēla mīlitum
    (2) labōrem Vercingetorīgis
    (3) fortitūdinem mīlitum
    (4) tempus annī

Part 4

Directions (41-50): In the space provided in the separate answer booklet, write the *number* of the word or expression which, when inserted in the blank, makes each sentence grammatically correct.   [10]

41. Nautae in īnsulā . . . exspectābant.
    (1) in multīs annīs   (2) multōs annōs   (3) multī annī   (4) multōrum annōrum

42. Explōrātor dīxit . . . discessisse.
    (1) equitēs   (2) equitum   (3) equitī   (4) equitibus

43. Exercitum mittit ut regiōnem . . .
    (1) vāstat   (2) vāstābit   (3) vāstāre   (4) vāstet

44. Dā . . . lībertātem!
    (1) mē   (2) ad mē   (3) nōs   (4) mihi

45. Peditēs tam fortiter pugnāvērunt ut nōn . . .
    (1) captī sunt   (2) capiēbantur   (3) capiuntur   (4) caperentur

46. Rōmānī . . . pugnāvērunt.
    (1) in montem   (2) monte   (3) in monte   (4) montēs

47. Ego sum . . .
    (1) Americānus   (2) Americānō   (3) Americānum   (4) Americānī

48. Omnēs . . . permōtī sunt.
    (1) cum tempestāte   (2) tempestātī   (3) tempestāte   (4) ā tempestāte

49. . . . erat dux Rōmānōrum?
    (1) Quae   (2) Quis   (3) Quid   (4) Cui

50. Eum monēbō . . . in viā ambulet.
    (1) nōn   (2) neque   (3) nē   (4) nisi

Part 5

Directions (51-60): For *each* sentence below, write in column I in the separate answer booklet a Latin word with which the italicized word is associated by derivation. Then in column II in the answer booklet write the *number* preceding the word or expression that best expresses the meaning of the italicized word.   [10]

	Column I	Column II
[Illustration: The explanation was made in a very *amicable* manner.	amīcus	3
(1) angry (2) belligerent (3) friendly (4) verbose	....	...............]

51. This drug has a *curative* effect.
    (1) depressing   (2) damaging   (3) toxic   (4) healing

52. His decision was *irrevocable*.
    (1) inopportune   (2) unalterable   (3) insincere   (4) wrong

53. He showed *malevolence* in his dealings with others.
    (1) ill will   (2) will power   (3) cleverness   (4) forcefulness

54. The convention ended with *animated* discussions.
    (1) ridiculous   (2) angry   (3) searching   (4) lively

55. The experience so *devitalized* the youth that he did not return to the game.
    (1) weakened   (2) antagonized   (3) frustrated   (4) disappointed

56. The tribe was *decimated* by the epidemic.
    (1) struck   (2) nearly wiped out   (3) greatly worried   (4) sickened

57. You arrived at a *felicitous* time.
    (1) dull   (2) critical   (3) fortunate   (4) depressing

58. The discussions between employer and employees were *protracted* in order to reach an agreement.
    (1) lengthened   (2) arranged   (3) improvised   (4) postponed

59. During World War II, the *ubiquitous* GI became a legend.
    (1) very personable   (2) everywhere present   (3) unconquerable   (4) heroic

60. The author was a *precursor* of the realistic movement in literature.
    (1) forerunner   (2) foe   (3) follower   (4) critic

Part 6

Directions (61-75): Select *ten* of the following statements. In the space provided in the separate answer booklet, write the *number* of the word or expression which best completes the statement.   [10]

61. What are the Quirinal, Esquiline, Aventine, and Capitoline?
    (1) hills   (2) roads   (3) buildings   (4) aqueducts

62. The Roman numeral DCC is equivalent to
    (1) 250   (2) 700   (3) 900   (4) 1200

63. In ancient times, Southern Italy was colonized by settlers from
    (1) *Hispānia*   (2) *Graecia*   (3) *Numidia*   (4) *Persia*

64. Which was a symbol of a conquered army?
    (1) building an arch   (2) passing under the yoke   (3) marching under a bridge   (4) falling on the sword

65. The alliance between Pompey and Caesar in 59 B.C. was strengthened by
    (1) an interchange of hostages   (2) the payment of tribute   (3) a marriage between the two families
    (4) a signed contract

66. The goddess of the rainbow was
    (1) *Īris*   (2) *Cerēs*   (3) *Iūnō*   (4) *Diāna*

67. A chairman *pro tem* holds authority for
    (1) a one-year term   (2) a ten-year term   (3) the time being   (4) life

68. The Gauls were separated from the Germans by the river
    (1) *Matrona*   (2) *Sēquana*   (3) *Rhēnus*   (4) *Liger*

69. The sacred flame of Rome was kept burning in the Temple of
    (1) Vesta   (2) Saturn   (3) Vulcan   (4) Venus

70. A Roman official in charge of finances was called
    (1) *aedīlis*   (2) *cōnsul*   (3) *praetor*   (4) *quaestor*

71. Roman soldiers used a *turris ambulātōria* to
    (1) store army rations   (2) store a legion's equipment   (3) storm a besieged city   (4) strengthen a battle line

72. As governor of Gaul, Caesar had the official title of
    (1) *dux*   (2) *imperātor*   (3) *prōpraetor*   (4) *prōcōnsul*

73. Caesar was first confronted with the use of war chariots in his invasion of
    (1) *Britannia*   (2) *Lūsitānia*   (3) *Germānia*   (4) *Helvētia*

74. Delphi in Greece was noted for its
    (1) Amazons   (2) volcano   (3) oracle   (4) gladiators

75. The lictors who accompanied Roman consuls carried as emblems of authority
    (1) *animālia*   (2) *tubae*   (3) *scūta*   (4) *fascēs*

361

LATIN, LEVEL 2

Part 1

Translate passage *a* into English. Write your translation in the space provided in the separate answer booklet. [20]

(The author tells of incidents and accomplishments of two early Roman kings. He also describes a combat between two pairs of triplet brothers, the Horatians and the Curiatians.)

a. Tertius rēx Rōmānōrum fuit Tullus Hostīlius, cui propter virtūtem rēgnum datum est. Secūtus est Numam Pompilium quī pācem iūstitiamque amābat. Tullus omnem mīlitārem disciplīnam artemque bellī cōnfīrmāvit. Mīlitibus Rōmānīs parātīs, prōvocāre audēbat potentēs Albānōs.

Cum exercitūs Rōmānōrum et Albānōrum longum bellum cōnficere vellent, fortūna bellī commissa est *trigeminīs* frātribus in utrōque exercitū, Horātiīs et Curiātiīs. Pugna inter eōs erat ācerrima. Tribus frātribus vulnerātīs *illinc, hinc* duōbus occīsīs, Horātius sōlus fugam *simulāvit.* Cum Curiātiī eum sequerentur, trēs omnēs Curiātiōs superāvit. Sīc victōria Rōmāna fuit unīus mīlitis manū.

—Flōrus, Epitomae I, 3 (adapted)

trigeminīs—from *trigeminī,* triplet
illinc ... hinc—on one side ... on the other side
simulāvit—from *simulō,* pretend

Directions (1-20): Do *not* write a translation of passage *b;* read it through carefully several times to ascertain the meaning. Then in the spaces provided in your separate answer booklet, write the *number* of the alternative that best translates *each* of the underlined expressions *as it is used in the passage.* [20]

b. Statim Sabīnī Rōmānōs terruērunt; tumultus enim fuit, nōn bellum. Nocte in urbe nūntiātum est exer-
(1)
citum Sabīnum pervēnisse ad flūmen Aniēnem praedae capiendae causā et ibi undique vīllās incendī. A. Pos-
(2)   (3)
tumius, quī ōlim bellō Latīnō dictātor fuerat, cum omnibus cōpiīs equitum eō celeriter missus est, et Servilius
(4)   (5)
cōnsul cum dēlēctā manū peditum secūtus est. Equitēs multōs virōs relictōs circumvēnērunt sed Sabīna legiō
(6)   (7)
agminī peditum advenientī nōn restitit. Dēfessī nōn sōlum itinere sed etiam populātiōne nocturnā, multī in
(8)   (9)
vīllīs cibō et vīnō complētī sunt, et vix satis vīrium ad fugiendum habuērunt.
(10)   (11)
Nocte ūnā audītō perfectōque bellō Sabīnō, posterō diē magna spēs pācis erat. Lēgātī Auruncī ad senā-
(12)   (13)   (14)
tum vēnērunt. Dīxērunt sī Rōmānī ex fīnibus Volscōrum nōn discēderent, sē proelium commissūrōs esse. Ex-
(15)
ercitus Auruncōrum cum lēgātīs simul domō profectus erat et nūntiātum est hunc exercitum iam vīsum esse
(16)   (17)
nōn longē ab Arīciā. Haec fāma tantō tumultū Rōmānōs perturbāvit ut rēs referrī ad senātum nōn posset.
(18)   (19)
Neque Rōmānī pācātum respōnsum populīs īnferentibus arma dare potuērunt. Arīciam iter fēcērunt et eō
cum Auruncīs signa cōnlāta sunt et proeliō ūnō bellum cōnfēcērunt.
(20)

—Līvius, Ab Urbe Conditā, II, 26 (adapted)

Dēfessī—from *dēfessus,* exhausted, tired out
populātiōne—from *populātiō,* plundering
vīnō—from *vīnum,* wine

1. Statim Sabīnī Rōmānōs terruērunt.
   (1) Unexpectedly the Sabines attacked the Romans
   (2) At once the Romans ambushed the Sabines
   (3) Suddenly the Sabines held back the Romans
   (4) Immediately the Sabines terrified the Romans

2. nūntiātum est exercitum Sabīnum pervēnisse ad flūmen Aniēnem
   (1) the Sabines announced that their army would come to the river Anio
   (2) it was announced that the Sabine army had arrived at the river Anio
   (3) the army told the Sabines to come to the river Anio
   (4) a messenger came through to the Sabine army from the river Anio

3. ibi undique vīllās incendī
   (1) that here and everywhere he attacked the villas
   (2) that there the farmhouses on all sides were being burned
   (3) that havoc and conflagration were rampant
   (4) that the people in the villages were incensed

4. quī ōlim bellō Latīnō dictātor fuerat
   (1) who had formerly been dictator in the Latin war
   (2) who had once been chosen for the Latin war
   (3) who once upon a time had been about to describe the Latin war
   (4) who long ago had been trained for the Latin war

362

5. cum omnibus cōpiīs equitum eō celeriter missus est
    (1) quickly sent all the cavalry troops to a distant place
    (2) all the supplies for the cavalry were sent to that place quickly
    (3) when the horsemen sent their supplies there quickly
    (4) was sent there quickly with all the cavalry forces

6. Servilius cōnsul cum dēlēctā manū peditum secūtus est
    (1) Servilius the consul followed with a picked band of footsoldiers
    (2) the consul Servilius was followed by the chosen infantry
    (3) with outstretched hands Servilius the consul pursued the infantry
    (4) when Servilius the consul followed the selected band of footsoldiers

7. Equitēs multōs virōs relictōs circumvēnērunt
    (1) Many of those abandoned cut off the cavalry
    (2) Many abandoned the encircling horsemen
    (3) The horsemen surrounded many men who had been left behind
    (4) Many horsemen came around to abandon the men

8. Sabīna legiō agminī peditum advenientī nōn restitit
    (1) the Sabine legion did not resist the approaching column of infantry
    (2) the marching column of footsoldiers will not resist the Sabine legion
    (3) as the infantry came near, they did not resist the advance of the Sabine troops
    (4) the Sabine legion resisted, not approaching the column of infantry

9. Dēfessī nōn sōlum itinere sed etiam populātiōne nocturnā
    (1) Exhausted not by the march but by the people's plundering
    (2) Exhausted not only by their march but also by their night plundering
    (3) Tired out not by the march but by the widespread plundering
    (4) Tired out not by the road but by the night mob

10. multī in vīllīs cibō et vīnō complētī sunt
    (1) many farmhouses were out of food and wine
    (2) many completed their trip to the farmhouses for food and wine
    (3) in the farmhouses many gorged themselves with food and wine
    (4) much food and wine were stolen from the farmhouses

11. vix satis vīrium ad fugiendum habuērunt
    (1) they had too few men to flee
    (2) they had more than enough strength for pursuit
    (3) they considered the number of men scarcely enough for flight
    (4) they had scarcely enough strength to run away

12. Nocte ūnā audītō perfectōque bellō Sabīnō
    (1) In one night the Sabine heard that the war had started
    (2) For one night the Sabines heard and saw preparation for war
    (3) Since the Sabine war had been heard about and finished in one night
    (4) After the war had been ended in one night and the Sabines heard that it would begin again

13. posterō diē magna spēs pācis erat
    (1) on the previous day men's hopes ran high for peace
    (2) on the following day there was great hope of peace
    (3) yesterday there was a great hope of peace
    (4) however there were great expectations for peace

14. Lēgātī Auruncī ad senātum vēnērunt
    (1) The Auruncian senators came to the ambassadors
    (2) The ambassadors came to the Auruncian senate
    (3) The Auruncian lieutenants came from the senate
    (4) The Auruncian legates came to the senate

15. sē proelium commissūrōs esse
    (1) that he would be sent into battle   (3) that he was continuing the battle
    (2) that they would begin battle   (4) that they would be commissioned for the battle

16. Exercitus Auruncōrum cum lēgātīs simul domō profectus erat
    (1) The Auruncian army had run home at the same time with the lieutenants
    (2) Simultaneously the Auruncian army and the legates came home
    (3) The Auruncian army had set out from home at the same time with the legates
    (4) The lieutenants and the Auruncian army will leave home at different times

17. nūntiātum est hunc exercitum iam vīsum esse
    (1) it was reported that this army had already been seen
    (2) he announced that that army had not seen
    (3) they announced that they had no longer seen the army
    (4) the army reported that they had seen no one

18. Haec fāma tantō tumultū Rōmānōs perturbāvit
    (1) This rumor threw the Romans into such confusion
    (2) The fame of such a revolt stimulated the Romans
    (3) This famine created so much confusion among the Romans
    (4) Such great a glory quickly spread through Rome

19. ut rēs referrī ad senātum nōn posset
    (1) that the matter could not be referred to the senate
    (2) that they vetoed the motion which was before the senate
    (3) that the senate could not vote on the bill
    (4) that it was impossible for the senate to approve the proposal

20. proeliō ūnō bellum cōnfēcērunt
    (1) they began the war with one defeat
    (2) they fought desperately in one battle
    (3) in one battle they finished the war
    (4) war cannot be determined by a single battle

Part 2

Directions (21-30): In the space provided in the separate answer booklet, rewrite *completely each* of the following sentences, substituting for the italicized Latin term the grammatical form called for or the proper form of the expression in parentheses. *Make any other changes in each sentence that are required by the substitution,* but, unless the meaning is changed by the parenthetical instructions, be sure to retain the general idea of the original sentence. [10]

21. *Ager* lātus est.   (precede sentence by putō)

22. *Postquam nūntius acceptus est*, cōnsul urbem relīquit.   (ablative absolute)

23. *Sociī* victōriam nūntiātūrī sunt.   (singular)

24. Puellae in viā *ambulābunt*.   (present tense)

25. Lēgātus ab imperātōre *vocātus est*.   (active voice)

26. *Statim* sē trādidērunt.   (Prīma lūx)

27. *Dominus* servum *laudat*.   (direct address and imperative)

28. *Oppidum* quod occupāvimus bene mūnītum est.   (plural)

29. Agricolae ad urbem *ībunt* ut aedificia videant.   (change to imperfect)

30. Lūcius est *miser*.   (change to superlative)

Part 3

Directions (31-40): Read the following passages carefully, but do *not* write a translation. Below each passage you will find five questions or incomplete statements. Each statement or question is followed by four suggested answers numbered 1 through 4. Select the answer that best completes *each on the basis of the information given in the passage* and write its *number* in the space provided in the separate answer booklet. [20]

a. Rōmā ab Horātiō servātā, tamen obsidiō erat et frūmentī inopia. Porsena, rēx Etrūscōrum, spem habēbat sē expugnātūrum esse urbem.

C. Mūcius, adulēscēns nōbilis sōlus in hostium castra penetrāre cōnstituit. Itaque senātum adiit.

"Transīre Tiberim," inquit, "patrēs, et intrāre, sī possim, castra hostium volō. Neque glōriam neque praemia petō."

Approbant patrēs.

Ubi eō vēnit, multitūdō mīlitum prope rēgis tabernāculum cōnstitit. Mūcius timēbat quaerere quis Porsena esset et per errōrem scrībam prō rēge interfēcit.

Dum per multitūdinem viam facit, ā mīlitibus captus ad rēgem tractus est.

Sine timōre clāmāvit, "Sum cīvis Rōmānus. Hostem occīdere voluī, et neque mors neque caedēs mē terret. Morī prō patriā bonum est."

Tum Mūcius in ignem dextram manum iniēcit. Rēx, tantam virtūtem admirātus, movērī ab altāribus virum iussit et līberum invulnerātumque dīmīsit.

Cum Rōmam redīsset, cognōmen *Scaevolae* Mūciō ā casū dextrae manūs datum est.

—Līvius, *Ab Urbe Conditā*, II, 12 (adapted)

Scaevolae—from *Scaevola*, "Lefty"

31. Quod Rōma rem frūmentāriam nōn habēbat, Porsena cupiēbat
    (1) urbem capere
    (2) Horātium servāre
    (3) cibum incendere
    (4) obsidēs cōnferre

32. Ubi erant castra Porsenae?
    (1) trāns flūmen
    (2) in urbe rēgis
    (3) in fīnibus Gallōrum
    (4) in lītore maris

33. Captus Mūcius dīxit sē
    (1) esse fortem Etrūscum
    (2) tīmidum esse
    (3) quid suscēpisset cōnfēcisse
    (4) neque mortem neque caedem timēre

34. Porsena adulēscentem līberāvit quod
    (1) alium impetum timēbat
    (2) īrā commōtus est
    (3) animō et audāciā Mūcī mōtus est
    (4) Mūcius erat perīculōsissimus

35. Mūcius Scaevola appellābātur quod
    (1) Horātium servāverat
    (2) Scaevola erat nōmen gentis eius
    (3) adulēscēns erat
    (4) dextram manum āmīserat

b. Caesar, postquam exercitum Cn. Pompeī proeliō superāvit, cōpiās hostium capere cupiēbat ut fīnem bellī faceret. Itaque, castrīs Pompeī occupātīs, montem in quō castra erant circumvenīre coepit. Pompeius ipse, ubi exercitum suum pulsum esse vīdit, ad mare fūgit nāvemque cōnscendit.

Sociī Pompeī, quod is mōns erat sine aquā, monte relictō, ad oppidum Lārīsam sē recipere coepērunt. Caesar secūtus est mīlitēs quī in proximum montem sē contulērunt. Sub hōc monte flūmen erat. Caesar, etsī mīlitēs erant labōre totīus diēī cōnfectī, tamen eōs mūnītiōnem circum montem facere iussit nē Pompeiānī noctū aquam obtinēre possent.

—Caesar, *Dē Bellō Cīvīlī*, III, 97 (adapted)

36. Exercitū Pompeī pulsō, quid Caesar facere voluit?
    (1) ad mare properāre
    (2) virōs Pompeī captīvōs facere
    (3) statim aquam obtinēre
    (4) proelium cum mīlitibus Pompeī committere

37. Caesar, postquam castra hostium cēpit,
    (1) mīlitēs suōs circum montem collocāvit
    (2) castra sua celeriter in monte posuit
    (3) Pompeium in castrīs capere cōnātus est
    (4) montem descendere coepit

38. Quid Pompeius fēcit?
    (1) Suōs in proelium dūxit.
    (2) Omnēs mīlitēs domum dīmīsit.
    (3) Ad lītus cucurrit.
    (4) Suōs hortātus est ut nāvēs incenderent.

39. Cōpiae Pompeī, timentēs inopiam aquae, coepērunt
    (1) ūniversī ad Caesarem sē cōnferre
    (2) pedem referre
    (3) oppidum Lārīsam mūnīre
    (4) montem explōrāre

40. Quid mīlitēs Caesaris fēcērunt?
    (1) Quam celerrimē ad hostēs in monte aquam portāvērunt.
    (2) Aquaeductum ad aquam obtinendam aedificāvērunt.
    (3) Hostēs ab aquā prohibuērunt.
    (4) Sōlum nocte labōrāvērunt.

Part 4

Directions (41-50): In the space provided in the separate answer booklet, write the *number* of the word or expression which, when inserted in the blank, makes *each* sentence grammatically correct. [10]

41. Cum perīculum . . . , amīcōs monuit.
    (1) vīdisset   (2) vidēbit   (3) videt   (4) vidēre
42. Ariovistō imperāvit ut . . . .
    (1) excesserat   (2) excēderet   (3) excessit   (4) excēdēbat
43. Nūntius . . . properat.
    (1) urbem   (2) urbs   (3) ad urbem   (4) urbī
44. Puer librum . . . dedit.
    (1) magister   (2) magistrō   (3) magistrum   (4) magistrōs
45. Rogāvit cūr discipulī . . . .
    (1) absunt   (2) aberant   (3) abesse   (4) abessent
46. Equitēs . . . peditibus veniunt.
    (1) auxiliō   (2) auxilium   (3) auxilī   (4) auxilia
47. Tam celeriter oppidum oppugnāmus ut fugere nōn . . . .
    (1) possunt   (2) potuerant   (3) potuērunt   (4) possint
48. "Cūr, . . . , nōn labōrās?"
    (1) Lūcius   (2) Lūcium   (3) Lūcī   (4) Lūciō
49. Lēgātus omnēs centuriōnēs . . . superāvit.
    (1) virtūtī   (2) virtūtem   (3) virtūs   (4) virtūte
50. Vēnērunt ut ōrātōrem . . . .
    (1) audient   (2) audīvērunt   (3) audiēbant   (4) audīrent

Part 5

Directions (51-60): For *each* sentence below, write in column I in the separate answer booklet a Latin word with which the italicized word is associated by derivation. Then in column II in the answer booklet write the *number* preceding the word or expression that best expresses the meaning of the italicized word. [10]

	Column I	Column II
[Illustration: The explanation was made in a very *amicable* manner.	amīcus	3
(1) angry (2) belligerent (3) friendly (4) verbose	....	................]

51. The newspaper account recalled his former *imperious* manner.
    (1) domineering   (2) unfriendly   (3) irritating   (4) impartial
52. He was *gratified* by his teacher's comments.
    (1) promoted   (2) pleased   (3) embittered   (4) dissatisfied
53. Pitching was the player's *forte*.
    (1) final test   (2) obsession   (3) strong point   (4) defense
54. His remarks were extremely *defamatory*.
    (1) slanderous   (2) helpful   (3) well-received   (4) humorous
55. The symptoms indicated the *inception* of a rare disease.
    (1) decline   (2) beginning   (3) complete cure   (4) development

56. The psychiatrist was aware of his *homicidal* tendencies.
    (1) hermit-like   (2) murderous   (3) hostile   (4) gregarious
57. The speaker's views were meant to be *incendiary*.
    (1) eccentric   (2) quieting   (3) elevating   (4) inflammatory
58. Many small boys seem to have a strong *affinity* for mud.
    (1) aversion   (2) abhorrence   (3) liking   (4) outlet
59. She tried to *affiliate* with the conservative group.
    (1) compete   (2) associate   (3) argue   (4) travel
60. I am unable to *elucidate* at this time.
    (1) make a decision   (2) withdraw   (3) donate   (4) clarify

Part 6

Directions (61-75): Select *ten* of the following statements. In the space provided in the separate answer booklet, write the *number* of the word or expression which best completes the statement. [10]

61. The abbreviation *et seq.* stands for   (1) and compare   (2) and the following   (3) pay special attention   (4) it does not follow

62. In many areas of Roman life, Julius Caesar initiated reforms, the most lasting of which has been   (1) the development of accurate clocks and sundials   (2) the abolition of slavery   (3) the calendar   (4) freedom of enterprise

63. Which Latin term means "in the existing condition"?   (1) *habeās corpus*   (2) *sine diē*   (3) *status quō*   (4) *per capita*

64. Which musical instruments were used by the Romans for signaling in battle?   (1) whistles   (2) trumpets   (3) drums   (4) oboes

65. The country home of a Roman was called   (1) *vīlla*   (2) *īnsula*   (3) *taberna*   (4) *tabernāculum*

66. When Caesar uttered the words, "Vēnī, vīdī, vīcī," he was   (1) about to pacify the Gauls   (2) rejoicing over the capture of pirates   (3) disappointed in a friend   (4) reporting a victory in Pontus

67. Almost a decade of Caesar's life was spent in   (1) Spain   (2) Egypt   (3) Gaul   (4) Asia Minor

68. The face of Helen of Troy has come down to us in legend as the face that   (1) made men fear   (2) turned men into swine   (3) turned men into stone   (4) launched a thousand ships

69. The three parts of Gaul described by Caesar were inhabited by the *Gallī Celticī*, the *Belgae*, and the   (1) *Aquītānī*   (2) *Gallī Cisalpīnī*   (3) *Germānī*   (4) *Hispānī*

70. Bordering the territory of the Helvetians on one side was   (1) Lake Geneva   (2) the Marne River   (3) the Mediterranean Sea   (4) the Vosges Mountain Range

71. Before going hunting, Romans made sacrifices to   (1) *Iūnō*   (2) *Iuppiter*   (3) *Diāna*   (4) *Venus*

72. Caesar went to Rhodes to study   (1) military tactics   (2) medicine   (3) rhetoric   (4) commerce

73. Which expression is frequently used by high school students in writing footnotes for term papers?   (1) *ibid.*   (2) *pro tem*   (3) *ad lib.*   (4) *quid pro quo*

74. Which Roman military unit is comparable to the division in the United States Army?   (1) cohort   (2) maniple   (3) century   (4) legion

75. The god called *Hermes* in Greece was called by the Romans   (1) *Faunus*   (2) *Cupīdo*   (3) *Iuppiter*   (4) *Mercurius*

366

Part 1

Translate passage *a* into English. Write your translation in the space provided in the separate answer booklet. [20]

[Although outnumbered in a surprise attack, Caesar routs the enemy and continues his march.]

a. Itaque cum Caesar castra movēre vellet, subitō ex oppidō *ērūpit* multitūdō. Equitātus quī missus erat ā Iubā ad *stīpendium* accipiendum, subsidiō eīs concurrit. Occupant castra quae Caesar relīquerat et eius novissimum agmen īnsequī coepērunt. Cum haec rēs animadversa esset, subitō mīlitēs Rōmānī cōnsistunt et equitēs, quamquam erant paucī, tamen contrā tantam multitūdinem audācissimē concurrunt. Accidit rēs incrēdibilis. Circiter **XXX** equitēs pellunt duo mīlia *Maurōrum* equitum ex locō in oppidum. Postquam repulsī et coniectī erant intrā mūnītiōnēs, Caesar iter facere rūrsus contendit. Interim in itinere ex oppidīs lēgātī pervēnērunt. Dīxērunt sē datūrōs esse frūmentum Caesarī et parātōs esse facere omnia quae imperāvisset. Itaque eō diē ad oppidum Ruspinam Caesar castra posuit.

—Caesar, *Dē Bellō Africō*, 6 (adapted)

ērūpit—from *ērumpō*, burst forth
stīpendium—pay
Maurōrum—from *Maurus*, Moorish

Directions (1-20): Do *not* write a translation of passage *b*; read it through carefully several times to ascertain the meaning. Then in the spaces in your separate answer booklet, write the *number* of the alternative that best translates *each* of the underlined expressions *as it is used in the passage.* [20]

b. (I) <u>Fuit in terrā Graeciā actor excellentissimus</u> quī fāmam obtinuerat. <u>Praestābat omnibus cēterīs clārā</u>
(1)
<u>suā vōce.</u> Dīcunt nōmen esse Polum. <u>Ad omnēs urbēs nōtās Graeciae iter fēcit.</u> Is actor Polus <u>maximē amātum</u>
(2)
<u>fīlium morte āmīsit,</u> et magnō cum dolōre afficiēbātur. <u>Dolōre sublātō,</u> post breve tempus ad scaenam rediit.
(4)   (5)
Agēbat in scaenā tālī modō <u>ut nēmō scīret illum miseriam ferre.</u>
(6)
Eō tempore Athēnīs in fabulā nōmine "Electrā" actūrus erat. In fabulā, <u>Polus trāns scaenam urnam cum</u>
(7)   (8)
<u>ossibus Orestis portāre dēbēbat.</u> Igitur, <u>Polus ē sepulchrō fīlī ossa atque urnam tulit,</u> atque, <u>ut fābula postulāvit,</u>
(9)   (10)
<u>dēmōnstrābat magnum dolōrem,</u> sed vērum dolōrem, nōn imitātiōnem.
(11)

—Aulus Gellius, *Noctēs Atticae*, VI, 5 (adapted)

scaenam—from *scaena*, stage
ossibus—from *os*, bone

1. Fuit in terrā Graeciā actor excellentissimus
   (1) There was a superb Greek actor in the land
   (2) There was an actor in the land who spoke excellent Greek
   (3) In the land of Greece, there was a superb actor
   (4) A very distinguished actor came into the land of Greece

2. Praestābat omnibus cēterīs clārā suā vōce.
   (1) His voice was clear to all others.
   (2) All others surpassed him in speaking ability.
   (3) All others praised his voice for its distinctness.
   (4) He surpassed all others with the clarity of his voice.

3. Ad omnēs urbēs nōtās Graeciae iter fēcit.
   (1) He built highways to all the noted cities of Greece.
   (2) He journeyed to all the famous cities of Greece.
   (3) He made forced marches to all the celebrated cities of Greece.
   (4) Well-known roads led to all the cities of Greece.

4. maximē amātum fīlium morte āmīsit
   (1) he lost his most beloved son in death
   (2) he sent his son away on an important mission
   (3) his oldest son died of a broken heart
   (4) his favorite son suffered greatly before death

5. Dolōre sublātō
   (1) Outwitted by trickery
   (2) When the plot was revealed
   (3) When his grief was diminished
   (4) Dramatizing his grief

6. ut nēmō scīret illum miseriam ferre
   (1) so that no one realized that he was a miser
   (2) so that he knew that no one was miserable
   (3) so that no one knew how to express that grief
   (4) so that no one realized that he was suffering grief

367

7. Eō tempore Athēnīs in fābulā nōmine "Electrā" actūrus erat
   (1) At that time he was to act in the play "Electra" at Athens
   (2) At that time an Athenian actress named "Electra" wrote the play
   (3) In time the play "Electra" came to Athens
   (4) Athens was called "Electra" in the play given at that time

8. Polus trāns scaenam urnam cum ossibus Orestis portāre dēbēbat
   (1) Orestes had to carry Polus across the stage in a large urn
   (2) Polus had to carry an urn with the bones of Orestes across the stage
   (3) the urn, which was on the stage, was carried to Polus
   (4) Orestes had to carry the urn full of bones to Polus

9. Polus ē sepulchrō fīlī ossa atque urnam tulit
   (1) Polus took the bones and the urn from his son's tomb
   (2) Polus left the bones and the urn of his son in the tomb
   (3) Polus carried his son's bones in an urn to the tomb
   (4) Polus left an urn at the tomb of his son

10. ut fābula postulāvit
    (1) in order that he would demand a play
    (2) as the story required
    (3) so that the play was read
    (4) as he demanded a story

11. dēmōnstrābat magnum dolōrem, sed vērum dolōrem, nōn imitātiōnem
    (1) he showed great sorrow, but real sorrow, not pretense
    (2) he demonstrated that his grief was not real but artificial
    (3) he showed that real sorrow cannot be acted
    (4) he displayed grief, but it was fictitious, not real

(II) Pompēius longius bellum dūxit quod loca sunt ad castrōrum mūnītiōnēs idōnea. Nam tōtīus ulteriōris
(12)
Hispāniae regiō cōpiam aquae habet sed difficilis oppugnātiō est. Propter multōs impetūs barbarōrum omnia
(13)   (14)
loca quae sunt ab oppidīs remōta, turribus et mūnītiōnibus retinentur. Ob altitūdinem lātē longēque spectāre
(15)   (16)   (17)
possunt. Item magna pars oppidōrum montibus mūnīta est et nātūrā excellentibus locīs sīc est cōnstitūta ut
(18)
aditūs ascēnsūsque difficilēs sint. Ita ab oppugnātiōnibus nātūra locī distinentur ut cīvitātēs Hispāniae nōn
(19)
facile ab hostibus capiantur. Pompēius habuit castra facta in cōnspectū duōrum oppidōrum et terra ab suīs
(20)
castrīs circiter mīlia passuum IV est excellēns nātūrā.
                                                  —Caesar, Dē Bellō Hispāniensī, 8 (adapted)

12. quod loca sunt ad castrōrum mūnītiōnēs idōnea
    (1) because the places are far from the camp's fortifications
    (2) which places are near the camp's fortifications
    (3) because the places are suitable for the fortifications of a camp
    (4) which are places unsuitable to camp fortification

13. Nam tōtīus ulteriōris Hispāniae regiō cōpiam aquae habet
    (1) For the region of all outer Spain has a supply of water
    (2) Now all the region of outer Spain has a shortage of water
    (3) Thus all Spain has a shortage of water in certain regions
    (4) For the region which has water carries it to outer Spain

14. Propter multōs impetūs barbarōrum
    (1) Near many of the barbarian attacks
    (2) Because of the savage attacks of many barbarians
    (3) On account of the frequent attacks of the barbarians
    (4) Because many barbarians' attacks were nearby

15. quae sunt ab oppidīs remōta
    (1) whatever has been removed from the towns
    (2) which are distant from the towns
    (3) what is removed from the towns
    (4) who are carried away from the towns

16. turribus et mūnītiōnibus retinentur
    (1) the towers and fortifications are held
    (2) are holding the towers and fortifications
    (3) are destroying their towers and fortifications
    (4) are protected with towers and fortifications

17. Ob altitūdinem lātē longēque spectāre possunt
    (1) on account of the height they can see far and wide
    (2) far and wide they can see a great height
    (3) they could see mountains far and wide
    (4) they were able to see because of the far distant altitude

18. magna pars oppidōrum mōntibus mūnīta est
    (1) a large part of the town was set on a mountain
    (2) a great section of the town was guarded by fortifications

(3) the greatest towns were partially fortified by mountains
(4) a large number of towns was fortified by mountains

19. ut aditūs ascēnsūsque difficilēs sint
    (1) so that entrances and exits caused difficulty
    (2) so that approach and ascent are difficult
    (3) as climbing-up presented difficulty
    (4) in order to make approach and ascent difficult

20. Pompēius habuit castra facta in cōnspectū duōrum castrōrum
    (1) Pompey had a camp constructed in sight of two other camps
    (2) Pompey intended to have camp made in a circle around two other camps
    (3) Pompey's camp had been made far distant from two other camps
    (4) Pompey pitched camp away from two other camps

Part 2

Directions (21-30): In the space provided in the separate answer booklet, rewrite *completely each* of the following sentences, substituting for the italicized Latin term the grammatical form called for or the proper form of the expression in parentheses. *Make any other changes in each sentence that are required by the substitution,* but, unless the meaning is changed by the parenthetical instructions, be sure to retain the general idea of the original sentence.   [10]

21. Puerī *ex* agrīs cucurrērunt.   (per)
22. Fēminae pulchrae *Rōmam* vēnērunt.   (Italia)
23. Pugnāte, *virī*, prō patriā!   (sing.)
24. Agricola *mīlle* passūs ambulābat.   (duo mīlia)
25. *Postquam Gallī superātī* erant, Caesar discessit.   (ablative absolute)
26. *Bellum* erat breve.   (plural)
27. Mea *puella* est fīlia quae est alta.   (puer)
28. Cīvēs cōnsulī *pārēre* dēbent.   (vocō)
29. Rēgīna lēgātō *imperāvit* ut oppidum caperet.   (iubeō)
30. Cicero *ad urbem servandam* labōrābat.   (ut clause)

Part 3

Directions (31-40): Read the following passages carefully, but do *not* write a translation. Below the passages you will find questions or incomplete statements. Each statement or question is followed by four suggested answers numbered 1 through 4. Select the answer that best completes *each on the basis of the information given in the passage* and write its *number* in the space provided in the separate answer booklet. [20]

a. Caesar ad exercitum prīmā aestāte proficīscitur. Eō cum vēnisset, cognōvit legātiōnēs ab nōn nūllīs cīvitātibus Gallicīs ad Germānōs missās esse. Hae cīvitātēs rogāvērunt ut Germānī ab Rhēnō discēderent et in fīnēs Gallicōs trānsīrent. Lēgātī dīxērunt praetereā Germānōs omnia quae vellent acceptūrōs esse. Hāc spē adductī, Germānī longiōra itinera faciēbant et in fīnēs Gallōrum trāns Rhēnum pervēnērunt. Prīncipibus Galliae convocātīs, Caesar ea quae cognōverat nōn nūntianda esse putāvit. Eōs cohortātus, bellum cum Germānīs gerere cōnstituit.

Caesar, *Dē Bellō Gallicō*, IV, 6 (adapted)

31. Caesar ad exercitum vēnit cum
    (1) annus terminābat
    (2) hiems appropinquābat
    (3) aestās cōnfecta est
    (4) aestās incipiēbat

32. Adventū suō Caesar invēnit
    (1) Germānōs ad gentēs Galliae frūmentum mīsisse
    (2) Germānōs rogāvisse lēgātōs
    (3) Gallōs vīdisse lēgātōs Germānōrum
    (4) lēgātōs Gallōrum ad Germānōs vēnisse

33. Germānī invītātī sunt ut
    (1) in Britanniam trānsīrent
    (2) in Galliam iter facerent
    (3) pontem in flūmine aedificārent
    (4) ex Galliā discēderent

34. Spē incitātī, quid Germānī fēcērunt?
    (1) Belgās convocāvērunt.
    (2) Impetum fēcērunt.
    (3) Lātius frūmentum coēgērunt.
    (4) Ex suīs fīnibus discessērunt.

35. Caesar in animō habuit bellum gerere postquam
    (1) equitātum in hīberna dīmīsit
    (2) obsidēs postulāvit
    (3) prīncipēs cohortātus est
    (4) satis cōpiārum habuit

b. Philippus erat rēx terrae Macedoniae. Propter virtūtem et industriam Philippī, populī Macedoniae imperium auxerant et gentēs nātiōnēsque multās vincere coeperant. Dēmosthenēs in suīs ōrātiōnibus dīxit tōtam Graeciam timēre dēbēre et vim et arma Philippī. Is Philippus cum in omnī paene tempore negōtiīs bellī victōriīsque studēret, tamen ā studiīs *hūmānitātis* numquam āfuit. Epistulae eius *prūdentiam* dēmōnstrant. Sunt illae litterae quibus Aristotelī nūntiāvit nātum esse sibi Alexandrum. Haec epistula

cūram et dīligentiam in disciplīnā līberōrum hortātur. Philippus scrīpsit: "Fīlius mihi nātus est. Deīs habeō grātiam quod nātus est temporibus vītae tuae. Sperō enim tē futūrum esse magistrum eius."
—Aulus Gellius, *Noctēs Atticae*, IX, 3 (adapted)

hūmānitātis—from *hūmānitās*, culture
prūdentiam—from *prūdentia*, wisdom

36. Macedonia multās terrās superāverat quod
    (1) Macedonia multōs mīlitēs habuit
    (2) Macedonia potentēs nāvēs habuit
    (3) multae gentēs ad Macedoniam auxilium mīsērunt
    (4) Philippus fortis et dīligens dux erat

37. Dēmosthenēs dīxit oportēre
    (1) Graecōs Macedoniam statim oppugnāre
    (2) Philippum ad Graeciam īre
    (3) Graecōs potestātem Philippī timēre
    (4) Graeciam auxilium ex Macedoniā petere

38. Quamquam Philippus erat magnus imperātor, tamen amābat
    (1) hūmānitātem
    (2) poenam
    (3) pācem
    (4) pecūniam

39. Philippus Aristotelī scrīpsit
    (1) omnēs gentēs timēre Macedoniam
    (2) pulchrum esse morī prō patriā
    (3) Alexandrum rēctūrum esse omnēs terrās
    (4) sē novum fīlium habēre

40. In hāc epistulā Philippus spērāvit
    (1) Aristotelem doctūrum esse Alexandrum
    (2) Alexandrum futūrum esse magistrum
    (3) sē futūrum esse inimīcum Aristotelī
    (4) sē habitūrum esse multōs fīliōs

Part 4

Directions (41-50): In the space provided in the separate answer booklet, write the *number* of the word or expression which, when inserted in the blank, makes each sentence grammatically correct.   [10]

41. Caesar . . . cum cohortibus duābus proficīscētur.
    (1) prīmam lūcem   (2) prīmārum lūcum   (3) prīmae lūcis   (4) prīmā lūce

42. Mīlitēs, cum dēfessī . . . , tamen fortiter pugnāvērunt.
    (1) fuērunt   (2) fuerant   (3) essent   (4) erant

43. Adulescens . . . habitat.
    (1) in Britanniā   (2) ē Britanniā   (3) ā Britanniā   (4) in Britanniam

44. Puella librum . . . dat.
    (1) puerō   (2) ad puerum   (3) puer   (4) puerum

45. Agricola . . . in silvās fugere audīvit.
    (1) virōs   (2) virōrum   (3) virīs   (4) virī

46. Eius dolor erat tantus ut nōn dormīre . . .
    (1) poterat   (2) potest   (3) posset   (4) potuit

47. Dōnum . . . grātum est.
    (1) hominī   (2) hominem   (3) hominēs   (4) homō

48. Legiō ad flūmen progreditur ut proelium
    (1) committit   (2) committat   (3) commīsisse   (4) committere

49. Captīvī rogāvērunt ubi hostēs . . .
    (1) fuisse   (2) esse   (3) fuērunt   (4) essent

50. Castra sub . . . sunt.
    (1) mōns   (2) monte   (3) montī   (4) montis

Part 5

Directions (51-60): For *each* sentence below, write in column I in the separate answer booklet a Latin word with which the italicized word is associated by derivation. Then in column II in the answer booklet write the *number* preceding the word or expression that best expresses the meaning of the italicized word.   [10]

[Illustration: The explanation was made in a very *amicable* manner.   *Column I*   *Column II*
                                                                                         amīcus   3
    (1) angry   (2) belligerent   (3) friendly   (4) verbose   ....]

51. The prime minister delivered a very *provocative* message to the assembly.
    (1) inclusive   (2) significant   (3) stimulating   (4) elegant

52. The man *inadvertently* left his umbrella on the subway.
    (1) unintentionally   (2) presumably   (3) unfortunately   (4) willingly

53. When an underdeveloped nation begins to assert itself, it may do so in a *belligerent* manner.
    (1) nationalistic   (2) hostile   (3) powerful   (4) poor

54. The *acrid* fumes filled the room.
    (1) pleasant   (2) thick   (3) hot   (4) sharp

55. A battalion was *annihilated* in the ambush.
    (1) hidden   (2) frightened   (3) completely destroyed   (4) successfully defended

56. According to Cicero each individual ought to try to *ameliorate* the society in which he lives.
    (1) recognize   (2) accept   (3) improve   (4) preserve

57. A *loquacious* person is not necessarily intelligent.
    (1) silent   (2) thoughtful   (3) talkative   (4) studious

58. The *efficacy* of his methods was the deciding factor.
    (1) speed   (2) novelty   (3) influence   (4) success

59. *Procrastinating* frequently becomes habitual.
    (1) Postponing   (2) Hurrying   (3) Abstaining   (4) Worrying

60. The speaker expressed his thoughts in a very *lucid* manner.
    (1) disorganized   (2) forceful   (3) detailed   (4) clear

Part 6

Directions (61-75): Select *ten* of the following statements or questions. In the space provided in the separate answer booklet, write the *number* of the word or expression which best completes the statement or answers the question. [10]

61. Caesar's official title as head of the Roman religion was   (1) *Sacerdōs*   (2) *Flāmen*   (3) *Pontifex Maximus*   (4) *Augur*

62. Mt. Olympus is located in   (1) Greece   (2) Sicily   (3) Italy   (4) Asia Minor

63. The *stilus* was a   (1) sword   (2) dagger   (3) writing instrument   (4) spear

64. A *magnum iter* consisted of approximately   (1) 35 miles   (2) 25 miles   (3) 15 miles   (4) 10 miles

65. In ancient Rome the men who performed the services of modern policemen were known as   (1) *peditēs*   (2) *vigilēs*   (3) *aquiliferī*   (4) *nūntiī*

66. Who led a slave revolt against the Romans in the first century B.C.?   (1) *Torquātus*   (2) *Rēgulus*   (3) *Horātius*   (4) *Spartacus*

67. Caesar's favorite legion was the   (1) first   (2) third   (3) seventh   (4) tenth

68. The man who accompanied the Roman child to school was called the   (1) *paedagōgus*   (2) *magister*   (3) *litterātor*   (4) *grammaticus*

69. Julius Caesar's daughter became the wife of   (1) *Pompēius*   (2) *Antōnius*   (3) *Lepidus*   (4) *Augustus*

70. Caesar's Gallic campaigns began in   (1) 63 B.C.   (2) 50 B.C.   (3) 58 B.C.   (4) 100 B.C.

71. The short-sleeved, knee-length woolen undergarment worn by Roman soldiers was the   (1) *toga*   (2) *tunica*   (3) *sagum*   (4) *stola*

72. Which leader defeated the Romans in a battle at such a great cost to himself and his armies that he was unable to take advantage of his victory?   (1) *Hannibal*   (2) *Themistoclēs*   (3) *Xenophōn*   (4) *Pyrrhus*

73. In mythology, Daphne escaped Apollo by being transformed into a   (1) bird   (2) dog   (3) rock   (4) tree

74. During her stay in the underworld, Proserpina ate a part of a   (1) pomegranate   (2) pear   (3) golden apple   (4) green plum

75. "Caesar conquered Gaul with a spade." This quotation refers to Caesar's practice of   (1) crumbling walls   (2) planting trees   (3) pitching camps   (4) playing cards

LATIN, LEVEL 2

Part 1

Translate passage *a* into English. Write your translation in the space provided in the separate answer booklet. [20]

[The inhabitants of Alexandria, concerned about their freedom, plan to drive Caesar out of their city.]

a. Urbs Alexandrīa māximam cōpiam omnium generum *apparātūs* habēbat. Hominēs eius urbis erant *ingeniōsī* atque poterant facere ea quae ā Rōmānīs fierī vīderant. Multās aliās rēs *suā sponte* cōnficiēbant. Eōdem tempore nostrās mūnītiōnēs oppugnābant et sua loca dēfendēbant. In conciliīs, prīncipēs eōrum dīxērunt populum Rōmānum ad suum rēgnum occupandum vēnisse. Cōnfīrmāvērunt Aulum Gabīnium cum exercitū in Aegyptō anteā fuisse et Pompeium in eundem locum ex fugā sē recēpisse. Nunc crēdēbant Caesarem cum cōpiīs vēnisse et post mortem Pompeī mānsūrum esse.

Itaque volēbant statim expellere Caesarem nē ā Rōmānīs regerentur. Sine morā id agere parābant quod Caesar propter tempestātēs huius temporis annī auxilium obtinēre nōn poterat.

—Caesar, *Dē Bellō Alexandrīnō*, 3 (adapted)

apparātūs—from *apparātus*, equipment
ingeniōsī—from *ingeniōsus*, inventive
suā sponte—on their own

Directions (1–20): Do *not* write a translation of passage *b*; read it through carefully several times to ascertain the meaning. Then in the spaces provided in your separate answer booklet, write the *number* of the alternative that best translates *each* of the underlined expressions *as it is used in the passage.* [20]

b. Paene trēs hōrās pugnātum est undique ācriter; circum cōnsulem tamen ācrior pugna. Fortissimī mīlitēs eum sequēbantur et
                  (1)   (2)

ipse, in illam partem quā suōs premī et labōrāre scīverat, auxilium ferēbat. Hostēs eum summā vī oppugnābant et cīvēs eum dē-
                    (3)   (4)   (5)

fendēbant. Tum eques, Dūcārius nōmine, quī cōnsulem cognōvit, dīxit, "Hic est vir quī legiōnēs nostrās interfēcit agrōsque nos-
                              (6)

trōs et urbem vāstāvit. Iam ego eum propter caedem nostrōrum cīvium interficiam." Per mediōs hostēs impetum fēcit et cōn-
(7)   (8)   (9)

sulem pīlō interfēcit. Mīlitēs cōnsulis, Dūcārium cupientem praedam capere prohibuērunt. Māgna pars Rōmānōrum fugere coepit.
(10)   (11)

Multī quod nūllus locus fugae erat, in aquam prōgressī sunt, sed ab equitibus hostium interfectī sunt.
            (12)   (13)   (14)

Sex mīlia, proeliō commissō, effūgērunt. Cum in colle quōdam cōnstitissent, clāmōrem audientēs nōn scīre poterant quae for-
           (15)   (16)   (17)

tūna pugnae esset. Posterō diē clāra lūx in monte Rōmānum exercitum vincī dēmōnstrāvit. Tum quam celerrimē discessērunt.
                                     (18)

Cum inopiā cibī premerentur, Maharbal quī cum omnibus equitibus nocte cōnsecūtus erat dīxit si arma tradidissent, sē passūrum
                                                                           (19)

esse eōs abīre et sē dēdidērunt. Ab Hannibale omnēs in vincula coniectī sunt. Haec est nōbilis pugna ad Trasumēnum.
(19)   (20)

—Līvius, *Ab Urbe Conditā*, XXII, 6 (adapted)

1. pugnātum est undique ācriter
   (1) they will fight everywhere ferociously
   (2) each side was tired of battle
   (3) they fought fiercely on all sides
   (4) the battle took place under serious conditions
2. Fortissimī mīlitēs eum sequēbantur
   (1) The veteran soldiers persecuted him
   (2) The bravest soldiers followed him
   (3) The most valiant soldiers defeated them
   (4) The bravest soldiers encouraged him
3. suōs premī et labōrāre scīverat
   (1) he had realized that his own men were hard pressed and struggling
   (2) he had sensed that the enemy were laboring and pressing hard
   (3) he realized his own men had excelled and won
   (4) he noticed that their soldiers were no longer weary and tired
4. auxilium ferēbat
   (1) he refused help
   (2) he dismissed the auxiliary troops
   (3) he had asked for assistance
   (4) he was bringing help
5. summā vī
   (1) with the greatest force
   (2) by the best route
   (3) with the highest praise
   (4) with the least effort
6. quī cōnsulem cognōvit
   (1) who elected him consul
   (2) whom the consul saw
   (3) who recognized the consul
   (4) who blamed the consul
7. agrōsque nostrōs et urbem vāstāvit
   (1) honored our fields and our city
   (2) plundered your territory and villages
   (3) devastated their farms and towns
   (4) laid waste our fields and our city
8. propter caedem nostrōrum cīvium
   (1) on account of the slaughter of our citizens
   (2) in behalf of the honor of our countrymen
   (3) near the grave of your fellowmen
   (4) because of the defeat of their citizens

9. impetum fēcit
   (1) he made a treaty   (2) he made an attack   (3) they turned and fled   (4) they surrendered
10. cōnsulem pīlō interfēcit
   (1) he killed the consul with a javelin
   (2) he will slay the general with a sword
   (3) the consul killed the lieutenant
   (4) the consul wounded him with his spear
11. fugere coepit
   (1) forced him to escape   (2) stopped the flight   (3) began to flee   (4) put him to flight
12. quod nūllus focus fugae erat
   (1) because there was no place to flee
   (2) where no one tried to flee
   (3) when no order was broken
   (4) since no one wanted to flee
13. in aquam prōgressī sunt
   (1) made no progress in the water
   (2) waded out into the water
   (3) the river overflowed
   (4) came out of the water
14. ab equitibus hostium interfectī sunt
   (1) the enemy will kill the horsemen
   (2) the cavalrymen were slain by the enemy
   (3) they were killed by the horsemen of the enemy
   (4) they were intercepted by the hostile horsemen
15. proeliō commissō
   (1) after the battle was begun
   (2) after the battle was avoided
   (3) since no reward was offered
   (4) when the outcome was uncertain
16. Cum in colle quōdam cōnstitissent
   (1) When they had stopped on a certain hill
   (2) Although indeed they had set up quarters on a mound
   (3) Since they climbed up some hill
   (4) Because they stood on the same hill
17. nōn scīre poterant
   (1) they could not surrender
   (2) they will not be able to see
   (3) they could not know
   (4) they did not place any hope
18. Rōmānum exercitum vincī
   (1) that the army conquered Rome
   (2) that the Roman army was defeated
   (3) that the Romans were invincible
   (4) that the Romans were about to win
19. sē passūrum esse eōs abīre
   (1) they would suffer him to abduct
   (2) he would allow them to depart
   (3) he did not permit them to surrender
   (4) they would depart through the pass
20. omnēs in vincula coniectī sunt
   (1) everyone was hurled into exile
   (2) they threw away all their weapons
   (3) all were thrown into chains
   (4) all threw themselves into victory

Part 2

Directions (21-30): In the space provided in the separate answer booklet, rewrite *completely each* of the following sentences, substituting for the italicized Latin term the grammatical form called for or the proper form of the expression in parentheses. *Make any other changes in each sentence that are required by the substitution*, but, unless the meaning is changed by the parenthetical instructions, be sure to retain the general idea of the original sentence. [10]

21. Amīcīs ut īrent *imperāvit*. (iubeō)
22. Castra *ā legiōne* mūnīta sunt. (vāllum)
23. Hostēs, *mīles*, oppugnā. (lēgātus)
24. Tribūnus virum *vulnerāvit*. (passive voice)
25. *Mox* hostēs vincēmus. (paucī annī)
26. *Oppida* in Italia erant magna. (Via)
27. *Quod* erat bonus discipulus, māter eum laudābat. (Cum)
28. Populus rēgem *servat*. (persuādeō)
29. *Postquam cibus parātus est*, servī in culīnam vēnērunt. (ablative absolute)
30. Caesar ex urbe proficīscitur. (precede the sentence with putant)

Part 3

Directions (31-40): Read the following passages carefully, but do *not* write a translation. Below each passage you will find several questions or incomplete statements. Each statement or question is followed by four suggested answers numbered 1 through 4. Select the answer that best completes *each on the basis of the information given in the passage*, and write its *number* in the space provided in the separate answer booklet. [20]

a. Cum Caesar ad flūmen *Baetim* vēnisset, propter altitūdinem aquārum trānsīre nōn potuit. Itaque, ponte factō, cōpiās suās ad castra prope oppidum trādūxit. Pompeius quī ad eundem locum cum suīs cōpiīs vēnit, item castra posuit. Caesar, ut Pompeium ab oppidō frūmentōque exclūderet, mūnītiōnēs ad pontem facere coepit. Pompeius idem fēcit. Duo ducēs ad capiendum pontem contendēbant. Multīs proeliīs factīs et multīs mīlitibus interfectīs, neque Caesar neque Pompeius vīcit.

Itaque Caesar cōnstituit dēdūcere hostēs in locum idōneum pūgnandō. Cum vidēret hostēs id nōn facere, noctū flūmen trānsiit et Ateguam properāvit. Hoc erat praesidium Pompeī fīrmissimum. Cum Pompeius id ab fugitīvīs cognōvisset, eōdem diē carrōs et impedīmenta per angustās viās ad Caesarem dūxit. Caesar oppugnāre Ateguam incēpit.

Cum nūntiātum esset Pompeium ventūrum esse, Caesar omnia parābat. Multa castella occupāvit; ibi et equitēs et peditēs posuit ut castra dēfenderent. Mox Pompeius vēnit. Eō diē caelum tam obscūrum erat ut pars cōpiārum Caesaris circumvenīre et occīdere plūrimōs hostēs posset. Paucī effūgērunt.

—Caesar, *Dē Bellō Hispāniēnsī*, 5-6 (adapted)

Baetim—from *Baetis*, a river in Spain, presently called the Guadalquivir

31. Cūr Caesar pontem fēcit?
    (1) Flūmen erat lātum.
    (2) Flūmen erat altum.
    (3) Vulnerātōs portāre voluit.
    (4) Ab hostibus fugiēbat.
32. Caesar in animō habēbat
    (1) ē castrīs discēdere
    (2) castra ponere
    (3) Pompeium servāre
    (4) Pompeium ab cibō prohibēre
33. Quid ad pontem accidit?
    (1) Caesar suās cōpiās dīmīsit.
    (2) Ācriter pugnātum est.
    (3) Caesar Pompeium superāvit.
    (4) Pompeius pontem occupāvit.
34. Caesar cōpiās trāns flūmen dūxit quod
    (1) aqua nōn erat
    (2) Pompeius excesserat
    (3) hostēs in eōdem locō manēbant
    (4) paucās cōpiās habuit
35. Pompeius profectus est quod
    (1) Caesar Ateguam contendēbat
    (2) suī mīlitēs erant defessī
    (3) viae erant bonae
    (4) Caesar superātus est
36. Adventū Pompeī nūntiātō, Caesar cōnstituit
    (1) nūntium exspectāre
    (2) ad Pompēium properāre
    (3) castra praesidiīs mūnīre
    (4) equitēs praemittere

b. Dum Tarquinius ōrātōrem audit, duo virī eum vulnerāvērunt. Cum virī, quī prope eum erant, Tarquinium morientem tenērent, lictōrēs rēgis virōs fugientēs capiunt. Tum erat clāmor populī. Tanaquil uxor inter tumultum iubet rēgiam claudī et omnēs excedunt. Simul illa parat ea quae necessāria sunt cūrandō vulnerī rēgis. Celeriter Servium vocat et dīcit, "Servī, sī es vir, rēgnum est tuum. Surge et audī deōs quī dīxērunt tē futūrum esse clārum." Cum clāmor impetusque multitūdinis vix possent sustinērī, Tanaquil cum populō loquitur. Nūntiat rēgem vulnerātum esse et tēlum nōn dēscendisse altē in corpus.
—Līvius, *Ab Urbe Conditā*, I, 41 (adapted)

37. Cum Tarquinius morīrētur, quid prīmō Tanaquil fēcit?
    (1) Ē rēgiā fūgit.
    (2) Imperāvit ut portae rēgiae clauderentur.
    (3) Docuit quid accidisset.
    (4) Lictōrēs ad Galliam dīmīsit.
38. Tanaquil dīxit
    (1) Servium habitūrum esse rēgnum
    (2) sē interfectūram esse Servium
    (3) sē vastātūram esse rēgiam
    (4) multōs servōs esse in rēgiā
39. Deī nūntiāvērunt
    (1) Tanaquīlem occīsam esse
    (2) Servium poenam dare
    (3) sē laudātūrōs esse duōs virōs
    (4) Servium futūrum esse clārum
40. Tanaquil populō affīrmāvit rēgem
    (1) vulnus habēre
    (2) moritūrum esse
    (3) ē vītā discessisse
    (4) optimē valēre

Part 4

Directions (41–50): In the space provided in the separate answer booklet, write the *number* of the word or expression that, when inserted in the blank, makes *each* sentence grammatically correct. [10]

41. Virī discessērunt ut frūmentum . . .
    (1) inveniunt   (2) inveniēbant   (3) invēnērunt   (4) invenīrent
42. Gladiātōrēs ex Hispāniā . . . mittēbantur.
    (1) Graecia   (2) ad Graeciam   (3) Graeciae   (4) in Graeciā
43. Sine . . . senātus cōnsilium cēpit.
    (1) timōre   (2) timor   (3) timōris   (4) timōrem
44. Illōs equōs . . . celeriter spectat.
    (1) currentibus   (2) currentium   (3) currentēs   (4) currentem
45. Mārcus est . . . grātus.
    (1) patrī   (2) patrēs   (3) patrem   (4) patris
46. Puer bene . . . potest.
    (1) dīcere   (2) dīxit   (3) dīxī   (4) dictum est
47. Mīles in proeliō . . . accēpit.
    (1) vulnerī   (2) vulnere   (3) vulnus   (4) vulneris
48. Pulcher equus . . . est.
    (1) in agrō   (2) in agrum   (3) ager   (4) agrum
49. Magister rogat cūr puella librum . . .
    (1) amat   (2) amāvit   (3) amābit   (4) amet
50. Nūntius epistulam . . . dēmōnstrābat.
    (1) socius   (2) sociō   (3) socium   (4) sociōs

Part 5

Directions (51–60): For *each* sentence following, write in column I in the separate answer booklet a Latin word with which the italicized word is associated by derivation. Then in column II in the answer booklet, write the *number* preceding the word or expression that best expresses the meaning of the italicized word. [10]

[Illustration: The explanation was made in a very *amicable* manner.
    (1) angry   (2) belligerent   (3) friendly   (4) verbose

Column I   Column II
amīcus   . . . .3 . . .]

51. The *desperation* of the soldiers was obvious to their leader.
    (1) hopelessness   (2) courage   (3) hostility   (4) indifference
52. He could see his errors in *retrospect.*
    (1) advance   (2) proofreading   (3) judgment   (4) looking back
53. The civil rights marchers were a very *amiable* group.
    (1) emotional   (2) good-natured   (3) quarrelsome   (4) serious-minded
54. We were able to *circumvent* all obstacles.
    (1) meet   (2) oppose   (3) destroy   (4) avoid
55. His desire for knowledge was *insatiable.*
    (1) easily satisfied   (2) limited   (3) impossible to meet   (4) incomprehensible
56. The treaty was a *unilateral* agreement.
    (1) far-reaching   (2) forced   (3) one-sided   (4) well-defined
57. Some people are easily *pacified.*
    (1) appeased   (2) bribed   (3) flattered   (4) disturbed
58. Instead of a city, artists often prefer a *sylvan* setting.
    (1) wooded   (2) roomy   (3) mechanized   (4) comfortable
59. The student resorted to *subterfuge.*
    (1) copying   (2) violence   (3) sarcasm   (4) deception
60. He answered with a *non sequitur.*
    (1) sneer   (2) taunt   (3) false conclusion   (4) long speech

Part 6

Directions (61–75): Select *ten* of the following statements or questions. In the space provided in the separate answer booklet, write the *number* of the word or expression that best completes the statement or answers the question.   [10]

61. Caesar's wars in Gaul gave him a firm basis of prestige, party strength, military experience, and resources for the Civil War that was to result in his becoming   (1) *praetor*   (2) *dictātor*   (3) *aedīlis*   (4) *tribūnus*
62. Pluto ruled over the realm of the   (1) underworld   (2) sea   (3) heavens   (4) forests
63. The minotaur was a mythological creature, half man and half   (1) bird   (2) bull   (3) reptile   (4) lion
64. Which Latin expression refers to the policy of stirring up dissension and rivalries within the ranks of one's enemies, as Caesar did in Gaul and elsewhere?   (1) *Infrā dignitātem*   (2) *Dīvide et imperā*   (3) *Sīc trānsit gloria*   (4) *Novus Ōrdō Sēculōrum*
65. During a surprise attack by the Gauls against the citadel on the Capitoline Hill, the Roman guards were awakened by the
    (1) barking of dogs   (2) lowing of cattle   (3) cackling of geese   (4) wailing of women
66. Who is "the rosy-fingered child of the morning" who presided over the coming of dawn?   (1) *Aurōra*   (2) *Īris*   (3) *Latona*   (4) *Diāna*
67. In ancient Rome there were some 44,000 tenement blocks called   (1) *domūs*   (2) *īnsulae*   (3) *vīllae*   (4) *vīcī*
68. What hill was the original site of Rome and later the place where the wealthy resided?   (1) Esquiline   (2) Quirinal   (3) Palatine   (4) Viminal
69. The Roman who thrust his right hand into a fire to avoid betraying his friends to the enemy was   (1) *Appius Claudius*   (2) *Tiberius Gracchus*   (3) *Mūcius Scaevola*   (4) *Mārcus Brūtus*
70. The Twelve Tables were very significant as   (1) a manifestation of dictatorship   (2) a pattern of multiplication   (3) the beginning of Roman law   (4) a system of land reform
71. Along which road would ancient Romans have viewed a triumphal procession?   (1) *Via Aurēlia*   (2) *Via Sacra*   (3) *Via Flāminia*   (4) *Via Rōmāna*
72. In what year did the Romans adopt a republican form of government?   (1) 44 B.C.   (2) A.D. 479   (3) 509 B.C.   (4) 753 B.C.
73. A monument dedicated to a dead person might be likely to bear the abbreviation   (1) in mem.   (2) D.D.   (3) cf.   (4) e.g.
74. Which weapon of a Roman soldier parallels in importance the modern infantryman's rifle?   (1) *scūtum*   (2) *galea*   (3) *lōrīca*   (4) *gladius*
75. In the language of diplomacy, which individual is unwelcome to a foreign government?   (1) *homō sapiēns*   (2) *amicus cūriae*   (3) *vir bonus et perītus*   (4) *persōna nōn grāta*